Workers of the Empire, Unite

Radical and Popular Challenges to British Imperialism, 1910s–1960s

STUDIES IN LABOUR HISTORY 15

Studies in Labour History

'...a series which will undoubtedly become an important force in re-invigorating the study of Labour History.' *English Historical Review*

Studies in Labour History provides reassessments of broad themes along with more detailed studies arising from the latest research in the field of labour and working-class history, both in Britain and throughout the world. Most books are single-authored but there are also volumes of essays focussed on key themes and issues, usually emerging from major conferences organized by the British Society for the Study of Labour History. The series includes studies of labour organizations, including international ones, where there is a need for new research or modern reassessment. It is also its objective to extend the breadth of labour history's gaze beyond conventionally organized workers, sometimes to workplace experiences in general, sometimes to industrial relations, but also to working-class lives beyond the immediate realm of work in households and communities.

Workers of the Empire, Unite

Radical and Popular Challenges to British Imperialism, 1910s–1960s

edited by
Yann Béliard and Neville Kirk

LIVERPOOL UNIVERSITY PRESS

First published 2021 by
Liverpool University Press
4 Cambridge Street
Liverpool
L69 7ZU

This paperback edition published 2024

British Library Cataloguing-in-Publication data
A British Library CIP record is available

ISBN 978-1-800-85968-5 (hardback)
ISBN 978-1-80207-539-7 (paperback)

Typeset by Carnegie Book Production, Lancaster
Printed and bound by CPI Group (UK) Ltd, Croydon CR0 4YY

Contents

II Labour, Decolonisation and Independence (1940s–1960s)

Abbreviations

Geographical indications (in between brackets) have only been added where disambiguation is needed.

AACR	Association for the Advancement of Civil Rights
AESD	Association of Engineering and Shipbuilding Draughtsmen
AEU	Amalgamated Engineering Union
AFL	American Federation of Labor
AIRF	All-India Railwaymen's Federation
AITUC	All-India Trade Union Congress
AN	Archives nationales (Pierrefitte-sur-Seine, France)
ANC	African National Congress
ASIO	Australian Security Intelligence Organisation
AUCCTU	All Union Central Council of Trade Unions (USSR)
BCAI	British Centre Against Imperialism
BCIA	British Committee on India Affairs
BDLU	Beja Dock Labourers' Union (Sudan)
BIUSR	Bureau international d'unité socialiste révolutionnaire (or IBRSU in English)
BSP	British Socialist Party
CI	Communist International
CIO	Congress of Industrial Organizations
CLAC	Colonial Labour Advisory Committee
CLC	Caribbean Labour Congress
CMRI	Centre marxiste révolutionnaire international
CNT	Confederación Nacional del Trabajo
COPAI	Congress of Peoples Against Imperialism

CPA	Communist Party of Australia
CPA (M–L)	Communist Party of Australia (Marxist–Leninist)
CPB (M–L)	Communist Party of Britain (Marxist–Leninist)
CP–BSTI	Communist Party – British Section of the Third International
CPEAA	Congress of the Peoples of Europe, Asia and Africa
CPGB	Communist Party of Great Britain
CPI	Communist Party of India
CPI	Communist Party of Ireland
CPNZ	Communist Party of New Zealand
CPSA	Communist Party of South Africa
CP–SASTI	Communist Party – South African Section of the Third International
CPUSA	Communist Party of the United States of America
CS	*Correspondance Socialiste*
CSCA	Civil Service Clerical Association
CSI	*Correspondance Socialiste Internationale*
EAS	*East African Standard*
EATUC	East African Trade Union Congress
EATUF	East African Trade Union Federation
ECCI	Executive Committee of the Communist International
EHESS	École des hautes études en sciences sociales (Paris)
ELFS	East London Federation of Suffragettes
EPOU	Electrical Power Operators Union (Kenya)
FBU	Fire Brigades Union
FKE	Federation of Kenya Employers
FLN	Front de libération nationale (Algeria)
FO	Foreign Office
FOI	Front ouvrier international contre la guerre
FRELIMO	Frente de Libertação de Moçambique
GCL	Gibraltar Congress of Labour
GR	Gauche révolutionnaire
HO	Home Office
HRL	Home Rule League (India)
IASB	International African Service Bureau
IBRSU	International Bureau for Revolutionary Socialist Unity (or BIUSR in French)

ICA	Irish Citizens' Army
ICFTU	International Confederation of Free Trade Unions
ICU	Industrial and Commercial Union (South Africa)
IFPAW	International Federation of Plantation and Agricultural Workers
IFTU	International Federation of Trade Unions
IIIL	Indian–Irish Independence League
IISH	International Institute of Social History (Amsterdam)
ILO	International Labour Organisation
ILP	Independent Labour Party
INC	Indian National Congress
IO	India Office
IPI	Indian Political Intelligence
IRA	Irish Republican Army
ISU	Indian Seamen's Union
IT&GWU	Irish Transport and General Workers' Union
IWW	Industrial Workers of the World
KADU	Kenya African Democratic Union
KANU	Kenya African National Union
KAPD	Kommunistische Arbeiterpartei Deutschlands
KAU	Kenya African Union
KFL	Kenya Federation of Labour
KK	Khudai Khidmatgars (India)
KLGWU	Kenya Local Government Workers' Union
KPAWU	Kenya Plantation and Agricultural Workers Union
KTDA	Kenya Tea Development Authority
KTGA	Kenya Tea Growers Association
LAI	League Against Imperialism
LIG	London Indian Group
LSB	London School Board
MCF	Movement for Colonial Freedom
MCP	Malayan Communist Party
MDU	Malayan Democratic Union
MEUSE	Mouvement pour les Etats-Unis socialistes d'Europe (or MUSSE in English)
MJLOM	Mouvement justice et liberté outre-mer
MLU	Madras Labour Union

MNA	Mouvement national algérien
MRC	Modern Records Centre (Warwick)
MUSSE	Movement for the United Socialist States of Europe (or MEUSE in French)
NATO	North Atlantic Treaty Organization
NCCL	National Council of Civil Liberties
NLF	National Liberal Federation
NMLH	National Museum of Labour History (Manchester)
NSFU	National Seamen and Firemen's Union
NUDAW	National Union of Distributive and Allied Workers
NUP	National Unionist Party (Sudan)
NWFP	North West Frontier Province (India)
OCI	Organisation communiste internationaliste (France)
OIOC	Oriental and India Office Collection
PAP	People's Action Party (Singapore)
PCF	Parti communiste français
PCI	Parti communiste internationaliste (France)
PLP	Parliamentary Labour Party
POUM	Partido Obrero de Unificación Marxista
PPP	People's Progressive Party (Guyana)
PRIB	People's Russia Information Bureau
PSOP	Parti socialiste ouvrier et paysan
PS–SFIO	Parti socialiste – Section française de l'Internationale ouvrière (or SFIO)
REC	Rural Employers Committee (Kenya)
RGASPI	Russian State Archive of Socio-Political History (Moscow)
RILU	Red Trade Union International
SACP	South African Communist Party
SDF	Social-Democratic Federation
SDP	Social-Democratic Party (New Zealand)
SF	Sinn Féin
SFIO	Section française de l'Internationale ouvrière (or PS-SFIO)
SLP	Socialist Labour Party
SNP	Scottish National Party
SPS	Sudan Political Service
SRWU	Sudan Railway Workers' Union
SWL	Socialist Women's League (Australia)

SWTUF	Sudan Workers' Trade Union Federation
TAWU	Transport and Allied Workers Union (Kenya)
TGWU	Transport and General Workers' Union
TNA	The National Archives (London)
TPWU	Tea Plantation Workers' Union (Kenya)
TUC	Trades Union Congress
UGTT	Union générale des travailleurs tunisiens
WAA	Workers' Affairs Association (Sudan)
WCCL	World Council for Colonial Liberation
WD	*Workers' Dreadnought*
WFTU	World Federation of Trade Unions
WILPF	Women's International League of Peace and Freedom
WIPL	Workers' Industrial Propaganda League (New Zealand)
WPA	Women's Peace Army (Australia)
WPP	Workers and Peasants Party (Bengal)
WPPs	Workers and Peasants Parties
WSF	Workers' Suffrage Federation
WSPU	Women's Social and Political Union
YCL	Young Communist League

Notes on Contributors

Yann Béliard is Senior Lecturer in British studies at Sorbonne Nouvelle University. Since the completion of his PhD on class relations in Hull from 1894 to 1910 (2007), he has directed a special issue of the *Labour History Review* (April 2014) revisiting 'The Great Labour Unrest, 1911–1914' and co-edited *Labour United and Divided from the 1830s to the Present* (2018). His research focuses on British labour in the age of empire, with particular emphasis on workplace struggles and transnational activism.

Gareth Curless is a social historian of decolonisation at the University of Exeter. His work is principally concerned with histories of work, class and everyday life at the end of empire. He is currently finishing a monograph based on these research interests entitled *Labour, Decolonization and Class: Re-Making Colonial Workers at the End of Empire.*

Quentin Gasteuil is a PhD student in history at École normale supérieure (ENS) Paris-Saclay and Sorbonne University. His research deals with the attitudes of French socialists and British Labour Party members regarding colonial issues during the interwar years. He focuses on the intellectual and practical interactions of French and British working-class movements with colonialism and the colonial world. He investigates the perception of empires in Europe within a specific category of political activists defined by their socialist thought.

Dave Hyde was formerly Senior Lecturer in International Development at the University of East London. He has published work on African railwaymen, coffee and tea plantation workers and land reform during the period of late colonialism in Kenya. He is currently working on a monograph entitled *Labour, Decolonisation and Resistance in Kenya*, which examines the part played by organised labour in Kenya's anti-colonial struggle.

Neville Kirk is Emeritus Professor of Labour and Social History at Manchester Metropolitan University. He has published extensively in the fields of modern British history and comparative and transnational history. His most recent publication is *Transnational Radicalism and the Connected Lives of Tom Mann and Robert Samuel Ross* (2017). He is editor of the Studies in Labour History series edited by Liverpool University Press. He is currently writing a book entitled *Modern Britain in Crisis.*

Nicholas Owen teaches and researches politics at the University of Oxford. He is the author of *Other People's Struggles: Outsiders in Social Movements* (2019), *The British Left and India: Metropolitan Anti-Imperialism, 1885–1947* (2007) and articles in *Past & Present*, *Journal of Modern History*, *Historical Journal*, *Journal of Imperial and Commonwealth History*, *Twentieth Century British History* and many edited collections.

Matt Perry is Reader in Labour History at the University of Newcastle. He has published widely on British and French twentieth-century labour history. He has written on the protests of the unemployed, including *The Jarrow Crusade: Protest and Legend* (2005) and *Prisoners of Want: The Experience and Protests of the Unemployed in France, 1921–45* (2007). The chapter published in this volume was part of research that resulted in *'Red Ellen' Wilkinson: Her Ideas, Movements and World* (2014). He has recently scrutinised French mutineers in the wave of unrest of 1919 in a monograph entitled *Mutinous Memories: A Subjective History of French Military Protest in 1919* (2019).

Tom Sibley is a retired trade union official and Oxford University graduate. He was for many years head of the MSF (now part of Unite) Research Department. A former General Secretary of the International Centre for Trade Union Rights (ICTUR), during the firefighters' dispute he worked in the FBU's Research Department. On retirement he became General Secretary of the ICTUR while continuing work on his PhD dissertation, 'Anti-Communism: Studies of Its Impact on the UK Labour Movement in the Early Years of the Cold War' (Keele University, 2008). Tom has written widely on the labour movement and international questions. His recent publications include *A Political Biography of Bert Ramelson* (2013).

Evan Smith is Research Fellow in History in the College of Humanities, Arts and Social Sciences, Flinders University of South Australia. He has published widely on political extremism, social movements and national/border security in Britain, Australia and South Africa. His last monograph was *British Communism and the Politics of Race* (2018). He is currently part of the 'Managing Migrants and Border Control in Britain and Australia' project funded by the Australian Research Council.

Marie Terrier completed her PhD on Annie Besant's socialism in 2015 and studies the socialist revival of the 1880s at CREW, Sorbonne Nouvelle University. Among other publications on the radical and labour movements in the late nineteenth and early twentieth centuries, she contributed a chapter to Muriel Pécastaing-Boissière's *Annie Besant (1847–1933): Struggles and Quest* (2017). She currently teaches at the Maison d'Education de la Légion d'Honneur, in Saint-Denis, near Paris.

Foreword

Paul Pickering

This volume comprises chapters given originally as work-in-progress papers at a conference organised by Yann Béliard and Neville Kirk at the Sorbonne Nouvelle early in November 2013. The focus was capacious: 'Mouvement ouvrier et décolonisation. L'expérience britannique, 1919–1984'. It was the third of a series of conferences exploring an even broader canvas, both chronological and geographical, which, at the time, seemed like an attempt to engineer a shotgun wedding between historians of labour and historians of the British Empire.

My task then was to offer comments in summation, which is, of course, the exact opposite of my assignment here. Having dusted off my notes of the conference and the overview I offered at that time, however, it is clear that the two roles do work in reverse order.

The first point to make is that after seven years the papers have not gone stale. On the contrary, they have matured into important pieces in an ongoing conversation. They show, first, the value of the work-in-progress model in cross-fertilising and honing ideas and approaches. As Kirk notes in his perspicacious concluding essay, for all that the chapters are eclectic they cohere around key themes. Let me mention two in anticipation of what is to follow.

First, it struck me then that the idea of a hub-and-spokes model of empire, whereby political ideas, cultural practices and people flowed in one direction – from centre to periphery – was rusting into obsolescence. In fact, the chapters in this volume add substance to the idea that the imperial metropolis was no more or less than one node in a matrix operating across time and space. The forces that sustained this matrix were multidirectional, centripetal and centrifugal. Inevitably they were complex.

Second, it is clear that the agents of empire came not only from the ranks of officialdom, from Knights of the Realm to foot soldiers in the British army, but were also ordinary women and men in search of better Britains.

This was 'globalisation from below'. William Cobbett once quipped that 'any man, not actually tired of his life', who considers emigrating to New South Wales, 'is wholly unworthy of my attention'. He was wrong: those millions of ordinary Britons who populated the empire deserve study. Of course, the official empire was more often than not exclusionary, oppressive, ruthless and systematically violent but so were its everyday colonisers. They often abetted and, many times, surpassed their political masters in their enthusiasm for dispossession and violence. But these agents were equally often suffused with hope. We meet many of both in this volume.

In my overview at the end of the conference I warned of the dangers of eliding transnational and comparative enquiry; they are not one and the same and to collapse them is to diminish them. The chapters in this collection avoid this error and thus enrich comparative and transnational endeavour.

This is an important book that not only ties off significant work presented in embryo on a grey day in Paris six years ago but also provides an important stimulus to further research. There are many threads here to pull. For all that the terms 'labour history' and 'imperial history' have fallen out of fashion in some quarters, the editors and contributors are to be congratulated for helping to ensure that the conversations continue.

Introduction

Labour, Empire and Decolonisation: Historiographical Landmarks

Yann Béliard

As mentioned by Paul Pickering in his foreword, the origin of this book lies in a one-day conference held in Paris on 8 November 2013 at the Sorbonne Nouvelle. The primary aim of the conference was to help postgraduate students taking the 'agrégation d'anglais', a competitive examination in which the British civilisation question was that of 'British Decolonisation, 1919–1984'.[1] The event was a sequel to conferences organised at other French universities which had focused on subjects as varied as the decolonisation of India, the mutations of the Commonwealth and the Falklands War.[2] Our call for papers read:

> Specialists of the British Empire and researchers in British labour history can no longer afford to ignore each other, and historians such as Andrew Thompson and Catherine Hall, among others, have helped us take giant steps in the direction of a social history of the Empire. Yet a social history of decolonisation still needs to be written. In most studies attempting to explain the demise of the British Empire, the world of labour does

I am grateful to Fabrice Bensimon and Gareth Curless for their comments on previous drafts of this introduction.

[1] Many thanks to the students who followed my course on the topic between 2012 and 2014, in particular to those who collaborated to the organisation of the conference: this text owes a lot to our exchanges.

[2] This led to the publication of three textbooks on the topic on the French side of the English Channel: Mélanie Torrent, *British Decolonisation (1919–1984): The Politics of Power, Liberation and Influence* (Paris, 2012); Richard Davis, Trevor Harris and Philippe Vervaecke, *La Décolonisation britannique: perspectives sur la fin d'un empire, 1919–1984* (Paris, 2012); Michel Naumann, *La Décolonisation britannique, 1919–1984* (Paris, 2012). The Sorbonne Nouvelle conference prolonged the reflections initiated there on two previous occasions: a conference on 'The British World-System, 1815–1931' (12–13 Mar. 2010) and another on 'The Great Labour Unrest, 1911–1914' (15–16 Sept. 2011), with respectively Bernard Porter and Jonathan Hyslop as the keynote speakers.

> not stand in the limelight, the key roles being allocated to metropolitan statesmen on the one hand and native elites on the other. Our conference would like to counter-balance that neglect by focusing on the role played by common people and their experience, initiatives and organisations, in the dissolution of the British Empire. Marcel van der Linden once declared that 'the history of the British working class can only be written as a transcontinental one' [Marcel van der Linden, back cover of Billy Frank, Craig Horner and David Stewart (eds), *The British Labour Movement and Imperialism* (Newcastle upon Tyne, 2010)]. Sharing that belief, the organisers welcome papers that contribute to telling the history of the liquidation of the British Empire from below, and to putting the voiceless and the invisible back on the map.

Those were the ambitions: to consider labour in its widest possible definition, from the Labour Party headquarters studied by Rhiannon Vickers to the African trade unionists portrayed by Frederick Cooper to the rural rebels recovered from oblivion by the Indian Subalternist school.[3] Previous studies, we felt, had been too compartmentalised, too limited in their thematic or geographical scope. Time was ripe for a more comprehensive vision that would exclude no aspect of the labour movement and no area of the empire. The abstracts we received met many of our expectations and the crew we gathered was rich, composed of some of the best experts in the field, of a couple of PhD students and even of a labour activist. It is a collection of six of the talks given on that day (by Yann Béliard, Nicholas Owen, Matt Perry, Gareth Curless, Dave Hyde and Tom Sibley) that Neville Kirk and I have chosen to edit, together with three complementary chapters (by Marie Terrier, Quentin Gasteuil and Evan Smith) to form a volume largely concentrated on transnational actors and colonial workers.

In the introductory remarks that follow I will outline how the paths of imperial and labour histories, although they originally developed in separate spheres, have come to converge, before examining more precisely how that tendency has affected the understanding of British decolonisation per se. Highlighting the achievements and also the lacunae in the relevant historiography, I then sketch what makes this collection an original contribution to the collective efforts of historians so far.

[3] Rhiannon Vickers, *The Labour Party and the World*, vol. 1, *The Evolution of Labour's Foreign Policy, 1900–51* (Manchester, 2003); Frederick Cooper, *Decolonization and African Society: The Labor Question in French and British Africa* (New York, 1996); Ranajit Guha (ed.), *A Subaltern Studies Reader, 1986–1995* (Minneapolis, 1997).

When imperial and labour histories were separate continents

The connection between imperial and labour histories was not always on the agenda. It is still a work in progress, resulting from relatively recent and converging evolutions, as old habits and disciplinary silos die hard. 'Old' imperial history on the one hand, 'old' labour history on the other, were indeed for a long time indifferent to each other, to say the least. The most evident reason for this is of course that imperial history as an academic discipline grew long before labour history, the former developing at Oxford and Cambridge during the interwar years, while labour history's breakthrough had to wait until the 1960s and 1970s. Be that as it may, it is remarkable that the classical accounts of Britain's imperial expansion should have made so few references to working-class organisations. Although Charles Dilke published his first *Greater Britain* in 1869, the year following the foundation of the Trades Union Congress (TUC), and his second version in 1907, the year following that of the Parliamentary Labour Party (PLP), the growth of the labour movement was evidently not at the heart of his concerns.[4] John Seeley's *Expansion of England*, published just before that remarkable year, 1884, when both the Fabian Society and the Social-Democratic Federation (SDF) were formed, paid no greater attention to working-men's efforts to organise.[5] Anthony Froude's *Oceana*, although published in 1887, the year of the Bloody Sunday at Trafalgar Square, shared the same indifference towards the labour question.[6] The three authors mentioned above did write of the English or British 'people', but it was in a racial, not a social sense. The *Cambridge History of the British Empire*, published between 1929 and 1959, written by academics who tended to see the imperial experience with an indulgent eye and rarely leant towards the left, did not correct that omission.[7] And even the more recent best-sellers on imperial history leave class issues in the background.[8]

[4] Charles Dilke, *Greater Britain: A Record of Travel in English-speaking Countries during 1866 and 1867* (London, 1869); *Greater Britain: A Record of Travel in English-Speaking Countries, with Additional Chapters on English Influence in Japan and China, and on Hong Kong and the Straits Settlements* (London, 1907).

[5] John Robert Seeley, *The Expansion of England: Two Courses of Lectures* (London, 1883).

[6] Anthony Froude, *Oceana or England and her Colonies* (London, 1886). Although Froude claimed to have met all classes of people during his tour of South Africa, Australia and New Zealand, he was interested in the governors' opinion on his projected imperial federation, not in the servants' or the miners'.

[7] J. Holland Rose, A.P. Newton and E.A. Benians (eds), *The Cambridge History of the British Empire*, 8 vols (Cambridge, 1929–1959).

[8] Niall Ferguson, *Empire: How Britain Made the Modern World* (London, 2003); Jeremy Paxman, *Empire: What Ruling the World Did to the British* (London, 2011).

The fact seems unescapable: most of the literature on the history of the British Empire has traditionally focused, in a top-down manner, upon the views and actions of the establishment and elite groups and individuals who held the reins of power and control throughout the empire.[9] These were predominantly white, male and British. In many instances their traditional portrayal as being the 'great and good' who adhered to the assumed British peculiarity of enlightened and beneficent imperial rule is misleading. Along with their French, German, Belgian, Russian and other imperialist counterparts they often showed a capacity for arrogant, patronising, cruel, rapacious and coercive behaviour, notwithstanding their claims to the contrary, rather than being in practice fair-minded, tolerant, understanding, restrained and given to compromise. This top-down and idealised approach has also often been accompanied by a particular interest in these men and groups in the metropole, although the actions of the white male Britons who ran the formal colonies and their relations with indigenous colonial elites have also constituted important objects of study.

By contrast, the views and actions of the labouring and producing people – factory- and non-factory-based men, women, white and non-white, the skilled and non-skilled, the organised and unorganised, the more and less secure and the employed and unemployed in urban and rural areas – in relation to questions of empire, imperialism and colonialism have traditionally been of little or no concern. That is apart from their neglected and shadowy existence as supporters or opponents of the elite practitioners of imperialism and nationalism in both metropole and colony.

Alongside their top-down focus, most traditionalists mainly assumed that ideas, practices and influences flowed in relatively simple and one-dimensional ways from a superior metropolitan core to a subordinate periphery. Yet, as Wendy Webster has perceptively observed, this approach neglects and in the majority of cases completely ignores the ways and extent to which the formal colonies of dependence in particular, but also the increasingly self-governing 'white' dominions, shaped the nature and development of British society itself, for example in relations to questions of race, 'whiteness' and ethnicity.[10]

It was not until the British Empire reached its zenith, in the interwar years, that a couple of foreign historians underlined the interest one might find in studying the destinies of Labour and of Empire in relation to each other.

[9] Neville Kirk, *Labour and the Politics of Empire: Britain and Australia, 1900 to the Present* (Manchester, 2014), 5–7; P.J. Cain and A.G. Hopkins, *British Imperialism*, 2 vols (London, 1993); Ferguson, *Empire*.

[10] Kirk, *Labour and Politics of Empire*, 7–11; Wendy Webster, 'Transnational Journeys and Domestic Histories', *Journal of Social History*, 39.3 (2006), 653.

One was a French Liberal, Elie Halévy, in his *History of the English People*.[11] The other was a Chinese nationalist named Tingfu F. Tsiang, with his thesis entitled 'Labor and Empire: A Study of the Reaction of British Labor, Mainly as Represented in Parliament, to British Imperialism since 1880'.[12] In post-war Britain, even a prominent Marxist historian like Victor Kiernan tended to cling to the traditional top-down approach of imperialism, and it was not until the end of the twentieth century that more systematic efforts were made to bridge the gap between imperial history and labour history.[13] Similarly, in the field of British labour history, the imperial dimension was long overlooked. In the Webbs' and in Pelling's famous histories of British trade unionism, the indexes show no entry for the words 'empire' or 'imperialism'.[14] The same goes for the more recent studies published by Hamish Fraser in 1999 and Alastair Reid in 2004.[15] Admittedly, the general histories of the labour movement produced by G.D.H. Cole in the 1930s and 1940s and by A.L. Morton and George Tate in the following decade did bring the question of imperialism into the picture, but they were exceptions and did not lead to a thematic shift for labour historians.[16] E.P. Thompson was conscious that empire and imperialism should not be left out, but that statement did not reflect so much in his historical writings as in his political activism. On the whole, apart from E.J. Hobsbawm, it has to be admitted that the pioneers of British labour history tended to be rather insular in the scope of their research.[17]

This does not mean that, in the heyday of the British Empire, thinkers and politicians did not make connections between social questions in Britain and imperial expansion: on the contrary. From the last quarter of the nineteenth century to the Second World War, the consolidation

[11] Elie Halévy, *Histoire du peuple anglais au dix-neuvième siècle* (Paris, 1932). His six volumes were published in English under the title: *A History of the English People in the Nineteenth Century* (London, 1949–1952), including volume 5 entitled *Imperialism and the Rise of Labour, 1895–1905* (London, 1951).

[12] Tingfu F. Tsiang, 'Labor and Empire: A Study of the Reaction of British Labor, Mainly as Represented in Parliament, to British Imperialism since 1880', PhD thesis, Columbia University, 1923.

[13] Victor Kiernan, *The Lords of Human Kind: European Attitudes to Other Cultures in the Imperial Age* (London, 1969).

[14] Beatrice Webb and Sidney Webb, *The History of Trade Unionism* (London, 1920); Henry Pelling, *A History of British Trade Unionism* (Harmondsworth, 1963).

[15] Hamish Fraser, *A History of British Trade Unionism, 1700–1998* (Basingstoke, 1999); Alastair Reid, *United We Stand: A History of Britain's Trade Unions* (London, 2004).

[16] Neville Kirk, 'Challenge, Crisis and Renewal? Themes in the Labour History of Britain, 1960–2010', *Labour History Review*, 75.2 (2010), 162–80.

[17] E.J. Hobsbawm, *Industry and Empire: An Economic History of Britain since 1750* (London, 1968); E.J. Hobsbawm, *The Age of Empire, 1875–1914* (London, 1987).

of the Empire was seen in most quarters as beneficial for the British people and intrinsically positive for social cohesion. Encouraging the poor to emigrate to the White Dominions was considered as a remedy against the ill effects of the industrial revolution, while the possession of exploitable colonies was seen as fundamental to the provision of cheap food for the domestic labour force.[18] Even among those who contested the established order, for example radicals and republicans like Joseph Chamberlain and Charles Dilke himself, the building of the Empire was deemed to be a panacea. Other liberals, such as Richard Cobden and later John A. Hobson, came to see imperialism as a threat to the well-being of the British people, since it meant a colossal waste of capital in colonial wars and foreign investments. They considered all the money was needed at home for welfare reforms. One way or the other, links were drawn between imperial and social questions by many late nineteenth-century and early twentieth-century intellectuals. But they tended to think of the labouring masses as Britons in need of salvation rather than as autonomous agents, seeing industrial disputes as sowing the seeds of anarchy, not of an emancipated future. It is therefore hardly surprising that, in academia, imperial history and labour history should have developed as two separate fields. The mutation and rapprochement that did take place at the end of the twentieth century can be interpreted as the result of three different developments: the rise of New Imperial History, of post-colonial studies and of global labour history.

Connecting labour and empire

The 'social turn' of imperial history

Imperial history is no longer the preserve of military or diplomacy historians but has undergone an impressive renewal over the past thirty years, what one might call a sociological turn, thanks to historians such as John MacKenzie and Bernard Porter, who were among the first to tackle the question of the impact of Empire on British society. How did the possession of the biggest empire ever in the history of mankind affect Britain? MacKenzie and Porter came up with different answers, the former arguing that public opinion was manipulated into adhering to the ideology of imperialism (and that the labour movement's advocacy of an ethical imperialism led to class conciliation), the latter claiming that, in spite of propaganda, the masses,

[18] Froude, disgusted by the 'dreary routine of soulless, mechanical labour' he had witnessed in Birmingham and Glasgow (*Oceana*, 332), hoped migration towards the colonies of his imagined Commonwealth might help the British people regenerate through contact with natural beauty.

contrary to the upper and middle classes, remained largely indifferent to it.[19] What they had in common – a subject this book would like to pursue – is that both sought to look beyond the official attitudes of labour organisations, and attempted to grasp the feelings of the men and women in the street. Largely under their influence growing numbers of historians since the 1980s have addressed the very important issue of whether the British people largely embraced or were indifferent towards the vast mass of imperial literature, values, practices, iconography and propaganda to which they were routinely exposed and subjected.

In 2005, Andrew Thompson tried to move beyond the schism between 'minimalist Porterans' and 'maximalist MacKenzieites'. In *The Empire Strikes Back*, he argued that the Empire's impact upon Britain was 'pervasive', but that Britain's embrace of that empire was 'more tentative'.[20] Britons were influenced, whether they liked it or not, by the existence of the British Empire, yet Thompson was cautious about generalisations, if only because of the pluralism of British society. Contending that Empire was not only a concern of the ruling class, he concluded that the workers related to it with neither enthusiasm nor indifference, but with a sort of banal acceptance. He also insisted that the world of British workers should include the millions who migrated around the Empire and in all directions from the 1840s to the 1920s. In 2009, Thompson wrote: 'We need to look much more closely at the British labour movement's imperial involvements'.[21] That is precisely what our book tries to do.

Since the MacKenzie–Porter controversy and the Thompson synthesis, efforts to understand Empire from below have continued and this volume owes a lot to those diverse endeavours, which have developed both in Britain and abroad, in a truly transnational movement.[22] Some of the most

[19] John MacKenzie, *Propaganda and Empire: The Manipulation of British Public Opinion, 1880–1960* (Manchester, 1984); Bernard Porter, *The Absent-Minded Imperialists: Empire, Society and Culture in Britain* (Oxford, 2004). See also Catherine Hall (ed.), *Cultures of Empire. A Reader: Colonisers in Britain and the Empire in the Nineteenth and Twentieth Centuries* (Manchester, 2000).

[20] Andrew Thompson, *Imperial Britain: The Empire in British Politics,* c.*1880–1932* (Harlow, 2000); Andrew Thompson, *The Empire Strikes Back? The Impact of Imperialism on Britain from the Mid-Nineteenth Century* (Harlow, 2004); Andrew Thompson (ed.), *Britain's Experience of Empire in the Twentieth Century* (Oxford, 2012).

[21] Andrew Thompson, response to Trevor Harris's review of *The Empire Strikes Back?*, 11 Dec. 2009. *Reviews in History* (https://reviews.history.ac.uk/review/531), accessed 16 Aug. 2019.

[22] Clarisse Berthezène, Robert Boyce and Marie Scot (eds), 'Nouvelles perspectives historiographiques sur le monde britannique', *Histoire@Politique: Politique, Culture, Société. Revue électronique du Centre d'histoire de Sciences Po*, 11 (2010) (http://histoire-politique.fr/index.php?numero=11&rub=dossier&item=110), accessed 16 Aug. 2019.

interesting developments have concerned the study of colonial workers, of their plight as well as of their resistance. As an answer to Niall Ferguson's neo-conservative praise of the British Empire and its legacy, many historians have shed new light on how colonial people felt about British presence, offering useful academic counter-narratives. Before Ferguson had even embarked on his pro-imperial campaign, Barbara Bush was one of the first to underline the perpetual instability of the imperial order due to colonial agency.[23] Walking in her footsteps, Antoinette Burton too has argued that dissent rather than Pax Britannica was the norm.[24] Among the works that have recently addressed popular reactions to imperial domination, two broad-sweeping books stand out as particularly readable by a larger audience: John Newsinger's *The Blood Never Dried* and Priyamvada Gopal's much-acclaimed *Insurgent Empire*.[25] The growing attention paid to the Empire as perceived and experienced from below has not just been the result of individual efforts but has taken the shape of a truly collective enterprise, with solid teams of researchers going down that path. This can be illustrated by two examples among others. The Department of History at the University of Exeter has created an online Imperial and Global Forum, with weekly posts that never fail to be thought-provoking.[26] And the University of Bristol convened a conference in June 2010 entitled 'Scribblings from Below', which focused on 'subaltern groups in empire', on the 'less powerful and less privileged actors', looking for a less hegemonic imperial archive made of everyday writings such as diaries, letters, petitions, folk songs, suicide notes and graffiti – an important episode in the rediscovery of empire from a bottom-up perspective. The momentum given by the rise of New Imperial History at the end of the twentieth century is therefore still bearing its fruits. It is now considered legitimate, indeed indispensable, to examine the popular experience of empire, just as it is now deemed legitimate and vital to connect the study of the Empire at home with that of the Empire overseas.[27]

[23] Barbara Bush, *Imperialism, Race and Resistance: Africa and Britain, 1919–1945* (London, 1999).

[24] Antoinette Burton, *The Trouble with Empire: Challenges to Modern British Imperialism* (Oxford, 2015).

[25] John Newsinger, *The Blood Never Dried: A People's History of the British Empire* (London, 2006); Priyamvada Gopal, *Insurgent Empire: Anticolonial Resistance and British Dissent* (London, 2019).

[26] See their 'Blog of the Centre for Imperial and Global History at the University of Exeter' (https://imperialglobalexeter.com), accessed 17 Aug. 2019.

[27] See the concept of 'imperial societies' used by Christophe Charle in *La Crise des sociétés impériales, Allemagne, France, Grande-Bretagne (1900–1940): essai d'histoire sociale comparée* (Paris, 2001).

The post-colonial effect

The second strand that contributed to the unsettling of traditional imperial history was the rise of post-colonial studies in British and American universities, a development inseparable from the growth of history as a profession in Britain's ex-colonies. The post-colonial questioning of Western hegemony was initiated by Edward Said in the late 1970s and inspired a whole generation of researchers keen to contest the established vision of the British Empire as a benevolent entity. Mostly it has been among historians living in or coming from Britain's ex-colonies, who appropriated Marx's materialistic methods to study their people's history, that the most impressive leaps forward were made. The best illustration of this has been offered by the Indian 'Subalternists'. In the 1980s, explicitly embracing E.P. Thompson's 'history from below' philosophy, they produced the first analyses of Indian history giving a central place to workers' struggles, with an original focus on rural workers rather than on urban ones.[28] Their efforts were echoed in the 1990s by the work of Samita Sen, an Indian historian of the Marxist school.[29] With time the Subalternists tended to concentrate on cultural and intellectual issues rather than on economic and social ones, somehow limiting their heuristic value for labour history – an evolution aptly summed up by Matt Perry in his chapter.[30] Although many representatives of that current embraced the post-modern 'linguistic turn' in the 1990s and 2000s, their importance cannot be underestimated. By provincialising Britain, they made it impossible for anyone working on labour and empire to focus merely on British labour organisations and forget about the millions exploited in the colonies, be it in mines or on plantations, on the docks or on the railways. 'We give up neither Marx nor "difference"', insisted Dipesh Chakrabarty in 1995.[31] The dynamic character of the Association of Indian Labour Historians since its foundation in 1996 can clearly be linked to the impetus given by the Subalternist push. And the Subalternists played a crucial role in enlarging labour historians' understanding of class, inviting them to look beyond the white and male wage-earner, and embrace in their study of the

[28] The series *Subaltern Studies: Writings on South Asian History and Society* was published by Oxford University Press, except for volume 11, printed by Columbia University Press. Volumes 1–6, from 1982 to 1989, were edited by Ranajit Guha, the five following volumes, from 1993 to 2000, by other editors, notably Partha Chatterjee and Dipesh Chakrabarty. For an evaluation of their legacy and a rich bibliography, see Jacques Pouchepadass, 'Que reste-t-il des *Subaltern Studies*?', *Critique Internationale*, 24 (2004).

[29] Samita Sen, *Women and Labour in Late Colonial India: The Bengal Jute Industry* (Cambridge, 1999).

[30] See chapter by Perry in this volume.

[31] Dipesh Chakrabarty, *Provincialising Europe: Postcolonial Thought and Historical Difference* (Princeton, NJ, 2000).

working class both the formal and the informal sector.[32] For limiting the definition of the working class in the colonial and post-colonial world to urbanised and waged factory workers would mean excluding the bulk of the proletariat made up, in turns or simultaneously, of slaves and indentured workers, not to forget rural migrants and the self-employed.

Labour history's transnational move

The third development that encouraged a rapprochement between imperial history and labour history was the growth of global labour history at the turn of the twentieth and twenty-first centuries, notably under the tutelage of Marcel van der Linden and his colleagues at the International Institute of Social History (IISH) in Amsterdam.[33] That 'global turn' in labour history would not have been possible without the rise of global approaches in the historical profession in general as a means of overcoming the limitations of area studies.[34] Comparative history, as practised in the Cold War years, had been one way of moving forward, through the comparison between wide cultural 'areas'. The advantage was to denaturalise each of those areas, but the risk remained of considering those areas as self-contained entities, as essentially separate objects. World history as practised later in certain history departments in the USA presented another risk, that of smoothening differences and presenting teleological narratives. Instead, global history in its most fruitful form took the shape of transnational and connected history, where the purpose was not so much to paint new frescoes as to explore contacts and exchanges.[35] Rejecting Eurocentrism and methodological nationalism, a new generation of scholars strove to produce a more decentred account of history, which, without denying the conquest of the world by European powers between the fifteenth and the

[32] Rana P. Behal and Marcel van der Linden (eds), *Coolies, Capital and Colonialism: Studies in Indian Labour History* (Cambridge, 2006); Prabhu Mohapatra and Marcel van der Linden (eds), *Labour Matters: Towards Global Histories, Studies in Honour of Sabyasachi Bhattacharya* (New Delhi, 2009).

[33] Jan Lucassen (ed.), *Global Labour History: A State of the Art* (Berne, 2006); Marcel van der Linden, *Transnational Labour History: Explorations* (Aldershot, 2003); *Workers of the World: Essays toward a Global Labor History* (Leiden, 2008); Marcel van der Linden (ed.), 'Travail et mondialisation', special issue of *Le Mouvement social*, 241 (2012).

[34] For historiographical overviews, see Caroline Douki and Philippe Minard (eds), 'Histoire globale, histoires connectées: un changement d'échelle historiographique?', special issue of *Revue d'histoire moderne et contemporaine*, 54.4 (2007); Pierre-Yves Saunier, *Transnational History* (Basingstoke, 2013).

[35] Romain Bertrand, *L'histoire à parts égales: récits d'une rencontre Orient–Occident, XVIe–XVIIe siècle* (Paris, 2011); Sanjay Subrahmanyam, *Mughals and Franks: Explorations in Connected History* (Oxford, 2005).

twentieth centuries, attempted to reconstruct the dialectics of relationship and resistance.[36]

Quite a few labour historians were content to get on board the transnational ship as their objects, working people and their organisations, were international in essence. The monumental inquiry on dockworkers around the world that Sam Davies coordinated in the late 1990s is a brilliant illustration of that trend.[37] That enthusiasm, however, was not unanimously shared. British labour history remained fairly insular at first, although a series of conferences – in Coleraine in 2009, in Huddersfield in 2014 – managed to arouse interest and demonstrate the scientific benefits of transnationalism.[38] It took the efforts of Neville Kirk, whose comparative history of labour in Britain and the USA had shown the way, to put the transnational approach more firmly on the map, and the present book is part of that exercise in persistence. Kirk's plea for connected histories of labour, it has to be noted, has also always been a cautious one. Where van der Linden considers that the 'old' (pre-Thompsonian) and 'new' (post-Thompsonian) labour histories should now be subsumed into 'global labour history', Kirk has underlined both the promises and the pitfalls of the global paradigm, insisting on the necessity for labour history to always keep an eye on the local, the regional and the national – a concern expressed in similar terms by Canadian labour historian Bryan D. Palmer.[39] The bias towards the nation-state can indeed also be overcome by micro-studies of the trans-local kind, comparing situations across oceans without attempting to embrace too vast a space.[40]

Whatever the caveats, transnational labour history has already produced notable results that can only encourage further explorations. Yes, there are

[36] For an example of that approach, see Christopher Bayly, *The Birth of the Modern World, 1780–1914: Global Connections and Comparisons* (Oxford, 2004). Such decentring is defended with vigour by anthropologist Jack Goody in *The Theft of History* (Cambridge, 2006).

[37] Sam Davies et al. (eds), *Dock Workers: International Explorations in Comparative Labour History, 1790–1970* (Aldershot, 2000).

[38] Most of the papers given in Coleraine were published in *Labour History Review*, 74.3 (2009) and 75.1 (2010), in special issues edited by Neville Kirk, Don MacRaild and Melanie Nolan.

[39] Bryan Palmer, review of van der Linden's *Workers of the World*, in *Labour/Le Travail*, 65 (2010), 246–48. For critical evaluations of global labour history, see also Dorothy Sue Cobble, 'The Promise and Peril of the New Global Labor History', *International Labor and Working-Class History*, 82 (2012), 99–107; Adrian Grama and Susan Zimmermann, 'The Art of Link-Making in Global Labour History: Subaltern, Feminist and Eastern European Contributions', *European Review of History*, 25.1 (2017), 1–20.

[40] Sheldon Stromquist, 'Thinking Globally, Acting Locally: Municipal Labour and Socialist Activism in Comparative Perspective, 1890–1920', *Labour History Review*, 74.3 (2009), 233–56.

difficulties for academics claiming to write a global history of workers, notably linguistic and practical ones, as underlined by Fabrice Bensimon in his review of the special issue devoted to the topic by the French labour history journal *Le Mouvement social*.[41] But there is also a wealth of potentialities.[42] So-called 'old' labour history can be practised in original ways, with a study of working-class organisations on a broader scale than before. Steven Hirsch and Lucien van der Walt have attempted to do this for the syndicalist current.[43] And Steven Parfitt, after an exciting study of the British and Irish offspring of the North American Knights of Labor, is at present writing a global history of the Knights.[44] Worker rebellions are also being revisited through the transnational lens. Peter Linebaugh and Marcus Rediker have vividly charted the emergence and growth of a radical transatlantic seafaring proletariat during the eighteenth century (a forerunner of the radical artisan and factory-based working class of the early nineteenth century), highlighting both the structural conditions of their proletarian subjects and their agency, i.e., their power to exercise, albeit limited, influence over these conditions and the course of events.[45] Collecting data about strikes from all around the world over the *longue durée*, the network set up and coordinated by Dutch historian Sjaak van der Velden is providing researchers into labour disputes with an unprecedented tool.[46] Some of the most stimulating studies have dealt with one particular branch of production involving workers across continents, such as Emma Robertson's work on chocolate, or Anthony Cox's and Jim Tomlinson's books on jute.[47] Connecting York and West Africa in

41 Fabrice Bensimon, 'Pour une histoire transnationale du travail', *La Vie des Idées*, 16 Jan. 2014 (www.laviedesidees.fr/Pour-une-histoire-transnationale.html), accessed 30 Sept. 2019.

42 This is illustrated by Bensimon himself in his work on British lace workers in the Victorian age, on their multi-directional travels across the English Channel and their eventual migration to Australia. Fabrice Bensimon, 'Calais 1816–2016', *History Today*, 24 Oct. 2016 (www.historytoday.com/calais-1816-2016), accessed 17 Aug. 2019. See also his article 'British Workers in France, 1815–1848', *Past and Present*, 213 (2011), 147–89.

43 Steven Hirsch and Lucien van der Walt (eds), *Anarchism and Syndicalism in the Colonial and Postcolonial World, 1870–1940: The Praxis of National Liberation, Internationalism, and Social Revolution* (Leiden, 2010).

44 Steven Parfitt, 'Constructing the Global History of the Knights of Labor', *Labor. Studies in Working-Class History*, 14.1 (2017), 13–37.

45 Peter Linebaugh and Marcus Rediker, *The Many-Headed Hydra: The Hidden History of the Revolutionary Atlantic* (London, 2000).

46 Sjaak van der Velden, Heiner Dribbusch, Dave Lyddon and Kurt Vandaele (eds), *Strikes around the World, 1968–2005: Case-Studies of 15 Countries* (Amsterdam, 2007). The data gathered in that volume are completed year after year on the group's website, 'Labor Conflicts' (http://laborconflicts.socialhistory.org), accessed 17 Aug. 2019.

47 Emma Robertson, *Chocolate, Women and Empire: A Social and Cultural History* (Manchester, 2009); Anthony Cox, *Empire, Industry and Class: The Imperial Nexus of Jute*,

one case, Dundee and Calcutta in the others, they constitute daring and convincing attempts at pulling together the metropole and the imperial hinterland, at studying workers here and there as part of the same imperial working class shaped by the mechanics of global capitalism, made and unmade by one single process of class formation.

Empire and class: the ongoing debate

Interrogating the links between labour and empire is thus no longer an incongruous task, and labour historians have been well placed to bring their own contribution to the MacKenzie–Porter debate over the reality and extent of popular imperialism, all the more so as even New Imperial History has tended to favour histories influenced by the cultural turn and privileging the racial and gendered perspectives over the class one. The debate among labour historians has revolved around a central question: to what extent did the British labour movement and British workers at large act as loyal supporters of, or as staunch opponents to, British imperialism? In other words: was British labour internationalist at heart, reasoning on a class basis and guided by the interests of both 'white' and 'coloured' workers around the Empire, or did national identity take precedence and lead it to embrace the racist stereotypes that justified the oppression and exploitation of the 'non-whites'?

The contrasted, sometimes provocative answers given to the question were summed up in their complexity by Neville Kirk in 2003 and only an oversimplified version of the controversy can be presented here.[48] A flattering vision of labour's relation to the British Empire could be formulated as follows: created by the workers to resist the excesses of capitalism, the trade unions and the Labour Party played their role in the expansion of democratic values across the British world, denouncing whenever necessary the abuses of colonialism in Africa and Asia; their fight for a 'better imperialism' and the sense of responsibility of Labour governments in the twentieth century were crucial in making the transition from Empire to Commonwealth a relatively smooth one. Opposite judgements have of course been expressed, especially by Marxist

---

1840–1940 (London, 2013); Jim Tomlinson, *Dundee and the Empire: 'Juteopolis', 1850–1939* (Edinburgh, 2014). Cox's fascinating study firmly incorporates into its framework of analysis not only employers, governments and the state but also workers and their transnational and transcontinental connections.

[48] Neville Kirk, *Comrades and Cousins: Globalization, Workers and Labour Movements in Britain, the USA and Australia from the 1880s to 1914* (London, 2003); see, in particular, chap. 3: 'The Rule of Class and the Power of Race: Socialist Attitudes to Class, Race and Empire during the Era of "New Imperialism", 1899–1910', 149–218. The discussion is also addressed in Yann Béliard, 'Le Mouvement ouvrier britannique et l'Empire (1815–1931): ennemi intérieur ou loyal serviteur?', in Sylvie Aprile and Michel Rappoport (eds), *Le Monde britannique, 1815–(1914)–1931* (Neuilly, 2010).

militants and academics. In their view, because the trade union and Labour Party leaders were never firmly committed to the cause of international socialism, because they allowed themselves to be corrupted by the crumbs fallen from the British bourgeoisie's imperial banquet, they behaved mostly as auxiliaries of the British ruling classes and of their imperialist system, never lending anti-colonial revolts the support they deserved. Whether one favours one interpretation or the other, what is clear is that the labourist ideology that came to dominate the organised labour movement in Britain did not stand for the dismantling but for the reform of the British Empire. Rather than celebrate or deplore this, the task for historians is to account for and make sense of that moderation in imperial affairs. It is also to ask themselves to what extent the non-organised workers adhered to the pro- or anti-imperialist propaganda they were confronted with.

Kirk's overview did not put an end to the discussion, which continued with a vigorous dialogue between Jonathan Hyslop and William Kenefick over the political views of Scottish miners in pre-1914 South Africa, proving that there are no simple, straightforward or unilateral answers to the interrogation.[49] Sweeping generalisations about the British labour movement are always risky, if only because of its fragmented character. Being divided between its cooperative, trade union and political branches, between right-wing and left-wing tendencies, between its English, Welsh, Scottish and Irish poles, between its metropolitan core and its colonial and post-colonial offshoots, between officialdom and grassroots, there was no way its attitude towards the Empire and imperialism could be monolithic, all the more so as attitudes can change over time. The appeal of 'labour and empire' as a field of study lies precisely in that diversity. Applied to the period when Britain's empire started to crumble, the general questions stated above imply interrogating the attitudes of the British labour movement and of ordinary workers towards popular rebellions in the colonies and the decolonisation process more generally.

Labour and the end of the British Empire

If studying labour and empire in conjunction with each other is now generally accepted, the study of British decolonisation per se has rarely focused on the working-class dimension. From John Darwin to Ronald

[49] William Kenefick, 'Confronting White Labourism: Socialism, Syndicalism, and the Role of the Scottish Radical Left in South Africa before 1914', *International Review of Social History*, 55.1 (2010), 29–62; Jonathan Hyslop, 'Scottish Labour, Race, and Southern African Empire *c.*1880–1922: A Reply to Kenefick', *International Review of Social History*, 55.1 (2010), 63–81.

Hyam, remarkable studies of the process have been published over the years but, without neglecting the social aspects of decolonisation, they have seldom placed the question of class at their heart.[50] Some authors have examined the part played by class interests in the dissolution of the Empire, but from the point of view of the 'gentlemen capitalists' in the case of Cain and Hopkins, or of business more generally in the case of Nicholas White.[51] Their thorough scrutiny of the complex links between economic actors at the top of the social pyramid and political decisions in Downing Street and Whitehall has enhanced our knowledge greatly. But researchers shining the light on the lower strata of society in the metropole and the colonies have tended to put the stress on gender and race rather than on class relations whenever they have addressed the decolonisation era. Bush and Burton, for example, have both resurrected forgotten episodes of working-class resistance in the colonies, underlining the breadth of the workers' repertoire of action, with their resort to sabotage, desertion, boycotts, strikes, etc. But few books have taken the labour movement as their central focus. The passage below offers a brief overview of three key works.

P.S. Gupta (1975): paving the way

When Indian historian Partha Sarathi Gupta published *Imperialism and the British Labour Movement, 1914–1964* in 1975, his book was innovative in more ways than one, as Christopher Bayly underlined in his foreword to the 2002 edition.[52] This was not only because Gupta was probably the first post-Indian independence historian daring to write on a British topic but quite simply because no one so far had attempted to offer a comprehensive overview of how the metropolitan labour organisations in all their variety had related to imperial affairs.[53] The study was as dense as it was ambitious, since it covered not only the Labour Party but also the Independent Labour Party (ILP), the Fabian Society, the trade

[50] John Darwin, *The End of the British Empire: The Historical Debate* (Oxford, 1991); Ronald Hyam, *Britain's Declining Empire: The Road to Decolonisation, 1918–1968* (Cambridge, 2006).

[51] P.J. Cain and A.G. Hopkins, *British Imperialism*, 2 vols (London, 1993); Nicholas White, *Decolonisation: The British Experience since 1945* (London, 2014).

[52] Partha S. Gupta, *Imperialism and the British Labour Movement, 1914–1964* (London, 2002).

[53] A few years earlier David Goldsworthy had laid some foundations with his *Colonial Issues in British Politics, 1945–1961: From 'Colonial Development' to 'Wind of Change'* (Oxford, 1971). So had Bernard Porter, on an earlier period and in a more circumscribed area, with his *Critics of Empire: British Radical Attitudes to Colonialism in Africa, 1895–1914* (London, 1968).

unions and a myriad of other bodies, and analysed their attitudes over a full half century, whether Labour was in or out of office. At a time when labour history in Britain was prospering and often adopted a broadly Marxist outlook, Gupta explicitly rejected Lenin's analysis of the social and political effects of imperialism on the British 'labour aristocracy' and made critical use of the notion of 'class consciousness', taking his inspiration from Pelling rather than Thompson or Hobsbawm. Yet his overall estimation of Labour's colonial policy was not so different from what left-wing critics of the Labour Party contended: in its approach of imperial questions, the Labour Party had never really followed the principles of proletarian internationalism, adhering instead to a form of liberal imperialism inherited from Gladstone. Its criticisms of imperialism had been moral rather than scientific, owing more to Hobson or Edmund D. Morel than to Friedrich Engels or Rosa Luxemburg; the party's objective had always been to improve the situation in the Empire, not to dismantle it. Without attempting to analyse in depth how labouring people related to empire, Gupta mostly exonerated the British working class of racism, considering that colonial questions were hardly part of its everyday priorities compared to bread and butter issues. Unexpectedly, one of the strengths of the study was that (taking an object that might have seemed peripheral to the Labour Party's identity – its colonial policy) it showed how a close study of that policy was revealing as to the essentially non-socialist nature of the party's ideology and practice.

Almost half a century after its publication, Gupta's book can be praised for having stood the test of time. Some of its shortcomings were only due to the constraints weighing on the author at the time, in particular limited access to a number of official archives, others to the fact that his study did not go beyond 1964 – whereas British governments in the following decades, especially Wilson's, would still have much trouble decolonising. However, Gupta's focus being on the decision-making and policy-framing institutions of the movement, namely on the leaders of the Labour Party and the TUC, there were two areas where his book did leave room for other researchers to develop: the study of the radical left inside and outside Labour on the one hand, that of working-class attitudes towards imperialism, anti-colonialism and decolonisation on the other. A couple of important volumes published since his seminal work have helped, to a certain extent, to fill both those gaps.

S. Howe (1993): a focus on the radicals

If there is one work that has been a stepping stone for every contributor to this volume, it is Stephen Howe's *Anticolonialism in British Politics: The Left and the End of Empire, 1918–1964*, a book that, almost twenty years after Gupta's, moved historical reflection forward in several complementary ways.[54] Howe opened his study with a critique of 'the poverty of historiography' on British decolonisation, which at the time was still analysed essentially as a quiet transition from the Empire to the Commonwealth. Refusing that view, which mirrored most official standpoints, Howe recognised that decolonisation had been decided in high places but stressed that it had been under pressure from below, and occasionally from armed rebellion. Howe was also original in that he refused to treat labour and empire as separate spheres. Whereas Gupta had pursued the indispensable task of mapping out the colonial vision of important metropolitan bodies such as Labour and the TUC, Howe looked in more detail at anti-colonialists in the colonies and at their transnational connections with activists in Britain. He also painted a more complete picture by scrutinising organisations that Gupta had not placed at the centre of his study, notably the ILP, the Communist Party of Great Britain (CPGB) and the Movement for Colonial Freedom (MCF), inside which members of those parties and other activists coexisted from 1954 to 1964.

In his explanation of Labour's tepid anti-colonialism, Howe, building on the foundations laid by Gupta, highlighted key explanatory factors. One was the considerable influence of non-revolutionary critiques of imperialism upon British labour, in particular liberal radicalism and Christian pacifism.[55] Another factor was the initial moderation of the colonised themselves: whether in India or South Africa, the first nationalist leaders spoke out in favour of Imperial Citizenship and constitutional methods, not of the violent overthrow of British imperialism. Of further importance was the labour leaders' search for respectability and recognition from the British establishment. Why should Henderson, MacDonald, Attlee or Wilson have embraced fundamental anti-colonialism, when neither pressure from the rank-and-file nor solicitations from the colonised was strong? To become part of the state apparatus, to be accepted as a government party, Labour had to prove it could be a reliable guardian of imperial interests.[56] What Howe underlined more than Gupta was the activism of the left-wing tendencies inside or outside of Labour. He documented with unprecedented accuracy Labour's reluctance to stand for disengagement from

[54] Stephen Howe, *Anticolonialism in British Politics: The Left and the End of Empire, 1918–1964* (Oxford, 1993).

[55] On that topic, see two important books published after Howe's study: Paul Ward, *Red Flag and Union Jack: Englishness, Patriotism and the British Left, 1881–1924* (Woodbridge, 1998); Gregory Claeys, *Imperial Sceptics: British Critics of Empire, 1850–1920* (Cambridge, 2010).

[56] This is well illustrated by a twenty-four-page brochure written by the Labour Party's Advisory Committee on Imperial Questions in 1943: 'The Colonies. The Labour Party's Post-War Policy for the African and Pacific Colonies'.

the colonies: the party did not admit the principle of independence for the colonies until 1957, and even then support for nationalist forces was always conditional upon them being on the 'right side' in the Cold War, i.e., on the side of NATO and the USA.

Confirming Gupta's interpretation of Labour's extremely moderate anti-colonialism, Howe broke new ground in his close examination of the CPGB and of why the party, in spite of its initial defence of radical anti-colonialism, put that cause on the backburner from the mid-1930s to the late 1940s, with a short and dizzying parenthesis from 1939 to 1941. The leaders of the British party mostly adapted to the demands placed on it by a bureaucratised Comintern, which were motivated primarily by the twists and turns in Stalin's foreign policy, and from 1934 onwards by his search for support from the 'democratic empires' of Britain and France. Howe did not deny that the CPGB was a small party with limited resources at the centre of a mighty empire, which in its early days had had to fight against persecution from the state as well as against ostracism from the Labour Party and TUC 'officialdom'. But the sincere anti-colonialism of many members and cadres was not enough to counterbalance pressure from the Kremlin to adopt the Popular Front line, which led to the dissolution of both the League Against Imperialism (LAI) in 1937, after merely ten years of existence, and that of the Comintern itself in 1943.[57]

Howe's study thus shed new light on the success of Pan-Africanism among West Indian and African anti-colonialists, even among those who, like George Padmore and Chris Braithwaite, had been convinced and active communists. In their eyes, not only the Labour Party but also the CPGB was too opportunistic to be trusted.[58] They ended up championing a form of black nationalism which retained a certain socialistic tinge, but placed their hopes in a rising of the oppressed black masses around the world, not in a united action of the international working class which they now deemed highly improbable.[59] The moderation of many colonial nationalists, who identified

[57] Smith, in his chapter for this volume, summarises the historiographical debate. Since Howe's book, significant contributions to the history of the CPGB's anti-imperialism have been published. See Neil Redfern, *Class or Nation: Communists, Imperialism and Two World Wars* (London, 2005). See also Daniel Edmonds, Evan Smith and Oleska Drachewych, "Editorial: Transnational Communism and Anti-Colonialism", *Twentieth Century Communism. A Journal of International History*, 18 (2020), 5–13.

[58] This frustration is reminiscent of that of Indian nationalists towards European socialists prior to the First World War at the international congresses of Paris (1900), Amsterdam (1904), Stuttgart (1907) and Copenhagen (1910). See Ole Birk Laursen, 'Anarchist Anti-Imperialism: Guy Aldred and the Indian Revolutionary Movement, 1909–1914', *Journal of Imperial and Commonwealth History*, 46.2 (2018), 286–303.

[59] Christian Høgsbjerg, *C.L.R. James in Imperial Britain* (Durham, NC, 2014); Christian Høgsbjerg, *Mariner, Renegade and Castaway: Chris Braithwaite, Seamen's Organiser, Socialist and*

with the British upper classes far more than with the lower classes in their own country, is of course a key factor in explaining why cross-continental anti-colonial alliances, when they did take place, remained relatively aloof from socialist and communist influence. This was the case of the Indian–Irish Independence League (IIIL), formed in 1932, although colonial authorities saw its founders as Bolsheviks.[60] But the perceived unreliability of the British left could only nourish suspicion among those nationalist or working-class activists in the colonies who did have socialist leanings.

The British Labour Movement and Imperialism (2010): widening the scope

A third book – this one not a monograph but a collection of individual chapters, including one by Neville Kirk – has recently extended Gupta's and Howe's works: *The British Labour Movement and Imperialism*, edited by Billy Frank, Craig Horner and David Stewart.[61] Based on a conference held at the University of Central Lancashire, Preston, in 2008, the volume was path-breaking in its attempt to consider labour in its widest sense and make full use of the tools of transnational history – options that the authors of the present collection have also tried to stick to and exploit for the best. The chapters broadly confirmed three points already established by previous research: not all British workers were indifferent to imperial matters; their attitudes were not determined merely by narrow self-interest or absent-minded imperialism;[62] and the visions of Empire issuing from Labour Party and TUC headquarters were, at least until the late 1950s, suffused with paternalism, 'Kiplingism' and racial prejudice.[63] The conclusion that international class solidarity had not been a priority for Labour in the decolonisation period was inescapable. So was the fact that the small groups within the British labour movement who were supportive of popular uprisings in the colonies had little practical help to offer. For the editors, however, this did not mean that the efforts of those who had tried to build bridges should be

Militant Pan-Africanist (London, 2014). See also Theo Williams, 'George Padmore and the Soviet Model of the British Commonwealth', *Modern Intellectual History*, 16.2 (2019), 531–59.

60 Keith Jeffery, *Ireland, India and Empire: Indo-Irish Radical Connections, 1919–1964* (Manchester, 2008).

61 Billy Frank, Craig Horner and David Stewart (eds), *The British Labour Movement and Imperialism* (Newcastle upon Tyne: Cambridge Scholars, 2010).

62 See Hester Baron, 'Weaving Tales of Empire: Gandhi's Visit to Lancashire, 1931', in Frank, Horner and Stewart, *British Labour*, 65–88. The editors in their introduction rightly raise the question of the workers' 'limited media access to information about colonial developments' (3).

63 See, for example, Billy Frank, 'Labour's "New Imperialist Attitude": State-Sponsored Colonial Development in Africa, 1940–1951', 107–30; Mary Davis, 'Labour, Race and Empire: The Trades Union Congress and Colonial Policy, 1945–1951', 89–106.

forgotten. Their collection, which combines economic, social, political and cultural approaches, constitutes an invaluable study of those minorities who attempted to swim against the current.

Labour and decolonisation: a flourishing of inquiries

Since Gupta and Howe produced their classics, and thanks to the impetus they gave to further research, the historiography on labour and decolonisation has kept expanding. Tributes to Frederick Cooper's *Decolonization and African Society: The Labor Question in French and British Africa* (1996) abound in the following pages, and for good reason.[64] Cooper, indeed, was the first historian to explore in great depth the 'aggressive developmentalism' deployed by the Attlee government in Britain's African colonies and its determination to shape colonial trade unions according to the British model imagined by Sidney Webb, then Lord Passfield, in his 1930 memorandum on the question. Cooper was also the first to take waves of strikes in and across the colonies as an object of study in their own right, underlining how they become a permanent feature after 1918, and contrasting, in the post-1945 years, the disputes that were kept under control and those that, like in the Gold Coast, turned into emancipatory movements. Anti-colonialism too has been studied more closely, with one work towering over the field: Nicholas Owen's study of the British Left and India until 1947, now also a milestone for all researchers.[65] Owen's book renders more complex the picture offered by Howe thanks to the consultation of Comintern archives only made accessible after the dissolution of the Soviet Union.

Two areas that have recently attracted the attention of historians and have, as a side result, shed some light on labour and decolonisation, are the Labour Party's foreign policy on the one hand and British counter-insurgency on the other. Since 2000, Rhiannon Vickers, John Callaghan, and Paul Corthorn and Jonathan Davis have all taken a new look at Labour's discourse and practice in international relations.[66] Even though those studies adopt mostly a top-down approach and are not centrally concerned with the British Empire and Commonwealth, they have participated in enriching the conversation, if only by making researchers more sensitive to the wider geopolitical issues examined in Labour headquarters. So has the growing

[64] For references to Cooper's more recent work, see historiographical overviews offered by Curless and Hyde in this volume.

[65] Nicholas Owen, *The British Left and India: Metropolitan Anti-Imperialism, 1885–1947* (Oxford, 2007). His chapter in this volume re-examines some of the questions raised in his book using new primary and secondary material.

[66] Vickers, *The Labour Party and the World*, vol. 1; John Callaghan, *The Labour Party and Foreign Policy: A History* (London, 2007); Paul Corthorn and Jonathan Davis (eds), *The British Labour Party and the Wider World* (London, 2008).

literature on Britain's policing of the colonies, even when, like in Caroline Elkins's or Benjamin Grob-Fitzgibbon's works, it does not focus on the repression of working-class movements as such but on that of nationalist rebellion.[67] Their examples paved the way for historians such as Martin Thomas who are now scrutinising the policing of industrial disputes in particular. Like Cooper's, Thomas's work is fundamentally comparative.[68]

So it seems that the steps forward taken by the practitioners of New Imperial History and global labour history, although mostly taken separately, are now bearing fruit, in particular in the study of decolonisation. In 2015, Spencer Mawby produced the first synthesis on British decolonisation that devotes a whole chapter, and revealingly the final one, to 'Capital and Labour'.[69] This choice reflects the welcome increase in the number of studies concentrating on colonial workers, illustrated, for example, in the contributions of Curless and Hyde to this volume. Are the traditional lacunae apparent in much of the treatment of labour and decolonisation about to be filled? This can only be a cumulative process and the present book has no other aim than to participate in that progress.

* * *

Our study covers almost two-thirds of the twentieth century, from the days of High Imperialism to the moment when Britain had lost most of its colonies. The volume follows a chronological progression, with a focus in Part I – Contesting Imperialism (1910s–1950s) – on individual activists who, in distinctive ways, set about to destabilise the imperial status quo when the Empire was at its zenith. Part II – Labour, Decolonisation and Independence (1940s–1960s) – presents a series of case studies tackling working-class interventions in the phase of transition from British rule to colonial emancipation.

In terms of chronology, the two parts overlap slightly, as the shaking of Britain's imperial order started long before the end of the Second World

[67] Caroline Elkins, *Imperial Reckoning: The Untold Story of Britain's Gulag in Kenya* (New York, 2005); Benjamin Grob-Fitzgibbon, *Imperial Endgame: Britain's Dirty Wars and the End of Empire* (Basingstoke, 2011); David Anderson and David Killingray (eds), *Policing and Decolonization: Politics, Nationalism and the Police, 1917–65* (Manchester, 1992); David Anderson, *Histories of the Hanged: Britain's Dirty War in Kenya and the End of Empire* (London, 2005).

[68] Martin Thomas, *Violence and Colonial Order: Police, Workers and Protest in the European Colonial Empires*, 1918–1940 (Cambridge, 2012).

[69] Spencer Mawby, *The Transformation and Decline of the British Empire: Decolonisation after the First World War* (London, 2015), 119–43 and chapter 1 (18–42), 'Anti-Colonialism in the British Empire'.

War. In terms of themes and objects too, the two parts resonate with each other, as the militants who were active in the interwar years were part of transnational networks that often played a role in post-war events also. In other words, the twofold structure adopted here should not be interpreted as a wish to propose a binary vision: the British imperial and Commonwealth experiences examined here are plural. At the same time, placing labour in its widest sense and transnational activists and networks at the heart of our enquiry, we have sought to preserve a coherence of focus throughout the book.

Having said that, our exploration of labour, empire and decolonisation offers no unique interpretation, no single frame of analysis, whatever our common assumptions may be – in particular the rejection of exceptionalism and essentialism, and a preference for comparative and transnational approaches. It should also be added that, as a glance at the table of contents reveals, this collection does not claim to be an encyclopaedia of labour and decolonisation. It is too fragmentary for that, and the case studies it brings together are mere signposts on the road that may lead to the production of such an academic tool.[70]

Although the present book is necessarily selective in its subject matter and limited in its scope, it hopes to persuade the reader that it makes a new, original and useful contribution to the task at hand. It is hoped that further research will build upon and extend the foundations laid here. Helped by collaborative scholarly endeavours across the world, we will eventually be in a position to offer a truly comprehensive account of the important subject areas of labour, empire and decolonisation.

[70] It would be a useful complement to Immanuel Ness and Zak Cope (eds), *The Palgrave Encyclopedia of Imperialism and Anti-Imperialism* (Basingstoke, 2016).

I

Contesting Imperialism (1910s–1950s)

1

Annie Besant's Fight for Home Rule in India, 1910s–1920s

Marie Terrier

'Dear Sir, I am not taking any part in Labour movements', Annie Besant explained to Edward Pease, her former Fabian colleague, in 1895.[1] When she thus refused to join a committee supporting the locked-out French glass workers of Carmaux, she did not imagine that, ten years later, she would be at the forefront of political agitation in India and that she would have to deal with labour movements again.

When she began fighting for Home Rule in India, Annie Besant (1847–1933) was a well-known public figure. In England, she had been involved in the radical and socialist movements. From the mid-1870s, she had advocated land reform, denounced elite politics and even promoted republicanism. Her first criticism of British imperialism dates back to that period and is imbued with the values of reformist liberal radicalism that she consistently defended in her subsequent political struggles.[2] Because of her militant atheism and her defence of Neo-Malthusianism she was not considered a respectable woman. However, Annie Besant shared many of the evangelical values from her middle-class education. Her crisis of faith led her to search for an alternative morality to support human beings in their attempt to eradicate suffering.

In the mid-1880s, appalled by the misery of the working classes and convinced it was necessary to change radically the social and economic system, she adopted socialism. She joined the Fabian Society and helped the group define an evolutionary brand of collectivist socialism. In 1888, she defended the London matchgirls and supported their strike.[3] She came

[1] Fabian Society Archives, London School of Economics, FABIAN SOCIETY/A/6/1. Annie Besant to Edward Pease, London, 23 Oct. 1895.

[2] The introduction to this volume has underlined the influence of this reformist critique of imperialism on the future Labour Party's moderate approach in imperial affairs.

[3] Louise Raw has rightly stressed that many of the strikers were women in their twenties and thirties. She therefore refers to them as 'matchwomen' in Louise Raw, *Striking a Light:*

to collaborate with trade unionists, especially when they united to compel London School Board (LSB) contractors to respect trade union wage and working hours. In 1924, George Lansbury admiringly declared that, during her term on the LSB, she had been 'a "Pioneer" on behalf of organized Labour'.[4]

However, Annie Besant grew disillusioned with the socialist credo that economic reforms would cure all social ills. She considered that socialism could never become a reality until there was 'a real movement of self-sacrificing devotion'.[5] In 1889, she converted to theosophy in order to promote universal brotherhood thanks to moral and spiritual reform. Although her interest in social and political questions did not vanish, she focused on spirituality, especially when she became one of the leaders of the Theosophical Society. In 1895, she moved to India, which theosophists considered the motherland of spirituality. She adopted a traditional Indian lifestyle and decided to dress in a white sari in order to show her respect for Indian culture and her sympathy with India's suffering – white being the colour of mourning.[6] At first, Annie Besant mainly tried to revive Indian cultural and spiritual traditions.

However, on the eve of the First World War, she made her entry on the Indian political scene and became a leading figure of the nationalist movement. Many studies have been written on Annie Besant's militant activities in India. Mark Bevir worked on the genesis of her involvement, insisting on the political potential of theosophy.[7] Various books and articles presented her ideas and actions, underlining her courage and effectiveness.[8] Historians stressed her pioneering role in extending the nationalist movement and tried to understand her dramatic election as president of the Indian National Congress (INC or Congress), in 1917,

---

The Bryant and May Matchwomen and their Place in Labour History (London, 2009). For the sake of coherence with Besant's writings and with secondary sources on the subject, the traditional term 'matchgirls' has been retained here.

[4] George Lansbury, 'Annie Besant as a Politician', in D. Graham Pole, *Dr. Annie Besant: Fifty Years in Public Work* (London, 1924), 11.

[5] Annie Besant, *Annie Besant: An Autobiography* (London, 1893), 338.

[6] Muriel Pécastaing-Boissière, *Annie Besant (1847–1933): Struggles and Quest* (London, 2017), 269–70.

[7] Mark Bevir, 'In Opposition to the Raj: Annie Besant and the Dialectic of Empire', *History of Political Thought*, 17 (1998), 61–77; Mark Bevir, 'Theosophy as a Political Movement', in A. Copley (ed.), *Gurus and their Followers: New Religious Reform Movements in Colonial India* (New Delhi, 2000), 159–76.

[8] Joanne Stafford Mortimer, 'Annie Besant and India 1913–1917', *Journal of Contemporary History*, 18 (1983), 61–78; S.R. Bakshi, *Annie Besant: Founder of Home Rule Movement* (New Delhi, 1990); Jyoti Chandra, *Annie Besant: From Theosophy to Nationalism* (New Delhi, 2001); Kumar Raj, Devi Rameshwari and Romila Pruthi (eds), *Annie Besant: Founder of the Home Rule Movement* (Jaipur, 2003).

at the age of seventy. Other studies were more critical of her elitism and her attachment to the British Empire.[9] Hugh F. Owen and Mark Bevir were particularly interested in her Home Rule League (HRL) and its new forms of mobilisation.[10] Annie Besant's activities after 1918 have attracted less attention because most historians argue that she lost her influence when she refused to endorse the non-cooperation movement launched by Gandhi. At the end of the war, her promotion of legal means of agitation and constitutional reforms to obtain self-government within the British Empire were deemed too conservative for the younger generation of nationalists who therefore decided to follow more radical leaders. Nevertheless, Annie Besant's struggle extended well into the 1920s, as Arthur Nethercot, her biographer, showed.[11] Historians who study the relations between the British left and the Indian nationalist movement have also acknowledged Annie Besant's ongoing activity, especially her lobbying of the British Labour Party after the end of the war.[12] However, they have seldom analysed how Annie Besant addressed the Labour Party and how she tried to win over the grassroots in England. Her attitude towards the nascent labour movement in India is also rarely discussed, although one of her closest assistants, the manager of the Theosophical Publishing House and editor or several of her papers, B.P. Wadia, helped organise Madras workers. Based on existing historiography as well as on a selection of pamphlets and articles written by Annie Besant herself, this chapter will seek to shed new light on her fight for Home Rule in the 1910s and 1920s and show that it lay at the intersection of both imperial and labour history. The aim is to understand the global logic of Annie Besant's fight and to explore the way she connected her struggle for India to labour movements, both in England and in India.

[9] Daniel H.H. Ingalls, 'The Heritage of a Fallible Saint: Annie Besant's Gifts to India', *Proceedings of the American Philosophical Society*, 109 (1965), 85–88; Georges Fischer, 'Un trait d'union: Annie Besant (1847–1933)', *Tiers Monde*, 15 (1974), 341–55.

[10] Hugh F. Owen, 'Towards Nationwide Agitation and Organisation: The Home Rule Leagues: 1915–18', in Donald Anthony Low (ed.), *Soundings in Modern South Asian History* (Berkeley, CA, 1968), 159–95; Mark Bevir, 'The Formation of the All-India Home Rule League', *Indian Journal of Political Science*, 52 (1991), 341–56. The Home Rule League founded by Annie Besant sometimes bore different names, especially in its publications. However, the Home Rule League, the All-India Home Rule League and the Home Rule for India League all refer to the same organisation. For the sake of clarity, only the name 'Home Rule League' will be used hereafter.

[11] Arthur Hobart Nethercot, *The Last Four Lives of Annie Besant* (London, 1963).

[12] Georges Fischer, *Le Parti travailliste et la décolonisation de l'Inde* (Paris, 1966); Partha S. Gupta, *Imperialism and the British Labour Movement, 1914–1964* (New Delhi, 2002); Nicholas Owen, *The British Left and India: Metropolitan Anti-Imperialism, 1885–1947* (Oxford, 2007).

Promoting India's freedom within the Empire

Annie Besant moved to India as a theosophist determined to restore India's spiritual greatness. Originally, theosophists were little concerned about politics. However, the first aim of the Society was often interpreted as endorsing efforts to promote equality in the social and political spheres: it stated that theosophists were 'to form a nucleus of the Universal Brotherhood of Humanity, without distinction of race, creed, sex, caste or colour'. In London, theosophists focused on occultism and spirituality, although many were also personally involved in various progressive movements. In India, they devoted their energies to the promotion and reform of Indian culture and spirituality. Theosophists wanted to help India rediscover the greatness of its traditions because they considered that the teachings from the Aryan and Vedic times were the basis of all the civilisations of the world. India represented the last bastion against the creeping dangers of materialism. According to Annie Besant, 'it is the perpetual affirmation of spirituality as the highest good that is India's mission to the world'.[13] Mark Bevir showed that theosophists thus thwarted the official discourse of the Raj with its denigration of Indian religious traditions as obscurantist teachings leading to alienation and backwardness.[14] On the contrary, theosophists underlined the moral and spiritual superiority of Indian faiths, which insisted on duty and fraternity.

Britain's controlling of India was further challenged by theosophists' alternative history. They refused to present the arrival of the British as beneficial. They rather contrasted the dire present conditions to the ancient Indian civilisation they viewed as a golden age of purity and excellence. Annie Besant even urged the British to show more respect because: 'You are dealing in India with a civilization far older than your own'.[15] She also bluntly attributed India's economic decline to England's exploitation and misgoverning:

> What causes the famines? Partly the financial drain of the 'Home Charges' and the huge bureaucracy. Partly the destruction of the manufactures of India for the profit of Lancashire, the compulsory revelation of trade secrets, and the forcing on India of English methods of production. Partly the destruction of the communal system of land tenure, the imposing of

[13] Annie Besant, 'India's Mission among Nations', in *Essays and Addresses*, vol. 4, *India* (London, 1913), 2–3.

[14] Bevir, 'In Opposition to the Raj'; Mark Bevir, 'A Theosophist in India', in Rita S. Kranidis (ed.), *Imperial Objects: Essays on Victorian Women's Emigration and the Unauthorized Imperial Experience* (New York, 1998), 211–27.

[15] Annie Besant, 'Theosophy and Imperialism' (1902), in *Essays and Addresses* (London, 1913), iv. 83.

> the English system of landlordism, of rigid rents and taxes levied in money in lieu of the flexible indigenous system of proportionate rents and taxes paid in kind; partly the network of railways facilitating the buying up of crops and sweeping them away for export.[16]

According to her, the degradation was not only economic: it was also political and moral. The British had prevented Indians from developing the virtues necessary for self-government. Instead, they had brought their materialistic and individualistic values, best exemplified by the inferior condition of women and the degradation of the lower castes. The social and cultural reforms theosophists promoted were therefore presented as a return to the purity of ancient past. Although it is difficult to assess the influence of the theosophical discourse regarding British imperialism, it is interesting to note that among labour leaders who visited India, some, such as Ellen Wilkinson, also tried to go beyond the traditional prejudices about the colony, seeking instead to identify with India's plight and to draw on universal experiences in an attempt to build transnational solidarity.[17]

Theosophy arguably played a major role in Annie Besant's defiance of British rule in India. However, it is not only 'through theosophy'[18] that she became involved in the nationalist struggle. It is important to underline that theosophy did not necessarily lead to nationalism. For both ideological and strategic reasons, the founders of the Theosophical Society, Colonel Olcott and Madame Blavatsky, had promised the British authorities they would not become involved in Indian politics. It was only when Annie Besant became international president of the Theosophical Society in 1907 that she felt less committed by her predecessors' pledge. Additionally, few theosophists of British descent joined the nationalist movement. For example, Charles Leadbeater, an eminent theosophist who collaborated with Annie Besant in occult research, remained deeply attached to the British Empire in its traditional shape.[19] Some theosophists even regretted Annie Besant's association with the nationalist cause.[20]

Her actions in India were also deeply influenced by the radical and socialist ideals that she had formerly expounded. Her interest in India's plight had

[16] Besant, *Essays and Addresses*, iv. 186.

[17] See chapter by Perry in this volume.

[18] According to E.J. Hobsbawm, 'Annie Besant ... found her fulfilment and her major political role after 1890 as high priestess of Theosophy and – through Theosophy – an inspirer of the Indian national liberation movement'. E.J. Hobsbawm, 'Man and Woman: Images on the Left', in *Worlds of Labour: Further Studies in the History of Labour* (London, 1984), 100.

[19] Mary Lutyens, *Krishnamurti: The Years of Awakening* (London, 1975), 87. I would like to thank Muriel Pécastaing-Boissière for drawing my attention to this reference.

[20] See articles and correspondence on theosophy and politics in *The Theosophist* from 1914 to 1917.

been aroused in the 1870s and 1880s when she denounced the Jingo fever and was brought to study the government of India. While describing the 'English tyranny' in details, her motto had been 'Make India free'.[21] Afterwards, she never relinquished the radical ideal of self-government. However, her radical past also shaped her attachment to the Empire. Her attacks were focused on the failure of Britain to elevate the peoples of the Empire towards self-government, and she hoped that this institution could unite equal nations in a universal brotherhood. Encouraging Britain to change its attitude, she declared: 'Let us have an Imperialism, but let it be one of righteousness, of justice, of love and of truth'.[22] She believed that the Empire should be 'a Federation of Self-Governing Nations'.[23]

For Annie Besant, self-government had to be accompanied by a reform of the political organisation. She favoured a pyramidal structure based on the village *panchayat*, the traditional village council, which would be returned by universal suffrage. Representatives in the higher councils (the district board or municipal council, the provincial council, and the national Parliament) would be elected by educated people and by the members of the councils below them. In this meritocratic system, Annie Besant hoped to give power to educated and competent representatives. Above this national structure, India would be represented in 'the Imperial Council of the Empire' and the 'Imperial Parliament', which would conduct international policy only, leaving each nation to decide on its own economic, fiscal or social policy.[24] Like many Indian nationalists, including Gandhi, Annie Besant idealised the *panchayat* and wished to make it the basis of a self-governing nation. Whatever the level of government, she also wanted the executive to be accountable to an elected assembly. This idea of responsible government stood as a serious alternative to the British system in which the governors of the provinces were only accountable to the viceroy, who himself was only accountable to the Cabinet in London. At a time when India was not represented in the British Parliament, Annie Besant's proposal of an Imperial Parliament, where India would enjoy an equal status with Britain and the other dominions, was particularly daring.

Although Annie Besant focused on political reform, she was also concerned about economic issues. She never sought to defend a socialist agenda and she did not draw any definite economic scheme, but many of

[21] Annie Besant, *England, India, and Afghanistan* (London, 1879), 51.

[22] Besant, 'Theosophy and Imperialism', 206.

[23] Annie Besant, 'Federation' (1914), in *The Birth of New India: A Collection of Writings and Speeches on Indian Affairs* (Adyar, 1917), 70.

[24] Annie Besant, 'Indian Industries as Related to Self-Government', in *Wake up, India: A Plea for Social Reform* (Adyar, 1913), 123; Besant, 'Federation', 77.

the ideas she defended echoed her socialist past. As the vast majority of the population was composed of poor peasants often on the verge of famine, she wanted to encourage agriculture, mainly by reducing taxation and establishing communal ownership of the land. Although Indian industry was developing, she rarely mentioned it, preferring small-scale industry and Indian crafts. She was aware of the plight of indentured labour, used both in India and in Britain, and called for the abolition of this system. However, she did not defend any specific reforms such as minimum wage, an eight-hour day or Factory Acts to protect workers, as she had in the 1880s. According to her, it was only once India had gained self-government that its representatives could efficiently tackle these issues. Annie Besant seldom castigated capitalism by name, but she clearly criticised its results. Reviewing the economic situation in Britain, she asserted that 'it is but little to a nation that it stands as wealthy among the nations of the world, if the wealth be in a few hands and the makers of that wealth are plunged in the direst poverty'.[25] As a consequence, she wished to reunite capital and labour and showed interest in the cooperative movement and guild socialism.[26]

Annie Besant's actions were more definite and successful in the education field. In India, she took part in the foundation of schools, from primary schools to university. She drummed out that all castes, all religious groups, but also girls and young women should be educated. Her educational efforts, which have been well documented by her biographers, began when she arrived in Indian and continued during her political struggle.[27]

Annie Besant was also deeply attached to social reform, explaining that it should go hand in hand with political reform. The series of conferences she delivered in October and November 1913 to signal her political commitment was published under the title *Wake up, India: A Plea for Social Reform*. In September, she had also founded a group called the Brothers of Service. Their objective was to promote India's 'rising into ordered freedom under the British Crown' and to foster the union of the Indian nation thanks to social reform.[28] They pledged 'to disregard all restrictions based on Caste', 'to promote the education of the masses' and 'to ignore all colour distinctions in social and political life'.[29] They also pledged to fight against child marriage and to educate their daughters. *Commonweal*, the weekly paper that Annie Besant started in January 1914, was also meant to promote social and

[25] Besant, 'Indian Industries', 117.

[26] Annie Besant, *The Guild System as a Substitute for Trade Unionism* (Madras, 1921).

[27] Nethercot, *The Last Four Lives*; Pécastaing-Boissière, *Annie Besant* (in particular, 'Educational Reforms in India', 272–78).

[28] Annie Besant, 'Conference of Theosophical Workers at Adyar', in *Wake up, India*, 297.

[29] Besant, *Wake up, India*, 297.

political reform and its subtitle read: 'A Journal of National Reform'. In autumn 1919, while in London, Annie Besant announced the launching of a new paper called *United India* and described its editorial line:

> It will advocate Home Rule for India, but it will be far more than a political paper in the narrow sense of the word. It will concern itself with all the phases of India's national life and particularly with the uplift of the submerged classes of India, and social reform in its large aspects – the treatment of criminals, the flogging of adults for petty thefts, child marriage, the woman movement, and serfage among agricultural labourers.[30]

The paper disappeared rapidly for lack of readership and financing, but it testified to Annie Besant's deep concern about social questions in India. It is therefore possible to argue that she joined the nationalist struggle when she saw that it was impossible to carry out spiritual, educational and social reforms as long as India was not politically free.

Although Annie Besant's fight for women's rights was not at the core of her nationalist involvement, there is continuity between her feminist stance and her actions in India. In spite of a difficult context, she was an advocate – although sometimes cautiously – of women's rights in India.[31] Additionally, if her critique of imperialism was not as directly informed by her feminism as Sylvia Pankhurst's, it was nevertheless indirectly shaped by it.[32] As Joy Dixon showed, theosophy attracted many women who were in search of a spirituality that treated them on an equal footing with men and that could coincide with the moral and social causes they fought for.[33] There was therefore no contradiction but rather a form of integration of her feminist, theosophical and anti-imperialist discourse.

Legal agitation and constitutional reforms

On the eve of the First World War, the nationalist movement in India was weakened by repression and internal divisions. Since 1907, the Extremists had been excluded from Congress by the Moderates. Annie Besant deeply respected Gopal Krishna Gokhale, the leader of the Moderates, who accepted British authority while asking for more indigenous representation in the political institutions of India and aspired to develop liberal political

[30] Archibald Fenner Brockway, 'Mrs. Besant's Lead for India: Interview on the Demand for Home Rule', *Labour Leader*, 11 Sept. 1919. On Brockway's positions, see chapter by Gasteuil in this volume.

[31] For more details, see Pécastaing-Boissière, *Annie Besant*, 130–34.

[32] See chapter by Béliard in this volume.

[33] Joy Dixon, *Divine Feminine: Theosophy and Feminism in England* (London, 2001).

institutions on the British model in India. However, Annie Besant also felt close to the Extremists such as Bal Gangadhar Tilak or Bipin Chandra Pal, who were associated to the Hindu revival and demanded more ambitious political reforms. She showed particular interest in their message from the moment they refused to promote violence and terrorism. When Annie Besant became a member of Congress in January 1914, her main objective was to reunite the nationalist movement and to help it gain momentum. She also incited Congress to work with the Muslim League in order to elaborate joint proposals for self-government to be presented to Westminster.

Annie Besant criticised the INC for being a mere deliberative body and for restricting its demands to piecemeal political reforms. She used her own papers, *Commonweal* and *New India*, a daily she founded in July 1914, to promote Home Rule. When the war broke out, she also distinguished herself by refusing to suspend agitation. On the contrary, her motto became 'England's need is India's opportunity'. It meant 'opportunity not to weaken England, but to strengthen her; not to be a danger in her rear, but a protecting shield at her back'.[34] According to her, Indians should support the war effort. Simultaneously, they had to draw schemes of self-government to be submitted to England at the end of the war because she believed this period would be propitious to renegotiate India's position in the Empire.

In spite of her growing influence in the nationalist movement, Annie Besant failed to convince the INC to carry out a militant campaign on Home Rule. As a consequence, she began touring the country to promote her idea and she created her Home Rule League in September 1916. Tilak had created his own Home Rule League in April; it thrived in the East, around Poona and Bombay, while Annie Besant's was active in Madras and also established branches all over the country thanks to the theosophical network.[35] Among other eminent Congress leaders, Motilal Nehru and his son Jawaharlal both joined Annie Besant's league. Although Tilak's had more members, historian Hugh F. Owen considers that 'from 1914 to 1917 the pace was set for the Indian national movement by Annie Besant'.[36] To spread her ideas, she relied on the techniques of mobilisation that she had used in Britain: lecture tours, pamphleteering, journalism, reading groups and a national network of branches. Annie Besant's HRL recruited far beyond theosophical membership. It appealed to young people, most of them Brahmin and Western-educated. According to Hugh F. Owen, her

[34] *Commonweal*, 5 Aug. 1914, in Annie Besant, *War Articles and Notes* (London, 1915).

[35] Owen, 'The Home Rule Leagues'.

[36] Owen, 'The Home Rule Leagues', 165.

league brought an agitational style of politics and extended the nationalist movement, giving it a more national dimension.

In 1917, the nationalist agitation was stimulated by the international context – the Bolshevik revolution with the Comintern's support of anti-imperialist movements and the American entry into the war with the promise to defend self-government for all the European nations.[37] In the provinces, governors tried to repress Home Rule agitation. Peter Robb showed that, contrary to the governors, the viceroy and the British government refused to suppress a movement which advocated reforms peacefully.[38] For her part, Annie Besant argued that the call for Home Rule was not seditious. Nevertheless, in June 1917, the Madras government interned Annie Besant and her collaborators, George Arundale and B.P. Wadia. This internment proved counterproductive: it provoked a wave of indignation in which Extremists and Moderates united. To appease the situation, the British government and the viceroy convinced the governor of Madras to release them in September 1917. Due to her popularity, in December 1917, Annie Besant became the first woman to be elected president of the INC.

To understand Annie Besant's position from autumn 1917, it is necessary to underline the evolution of the political context. In August 1917, the new Secretary of State for India, Edwin Montagu, had expressed sympathy with the demands of the nationalists. He stated that the British government aimed at 'the gradual development of self-governing institutions with a view to the progressive realization of responsible government in India as an integral part of the British Empire'. Annie Besant was enthusiastic because it seemed that the bill Montagu wanted to prepare would match her expectations, granting India dominion status.

Therefore, in her speech to the annual meeting of Congress in December 1917, Annie Besant invited the nationalists to work with the British authorities, arguing that Britain's policy towards India had evolved in the right direction.[39] According to Hugh F. Owen, 'following her release, she turned her face against agitation and joined the Congress Moderates in rejecting passive resistance'.[40] Nethercot also considers that 'Mrs. Besant [changed] her mind'.[41] It rather seems that Annie Besant persisted in defending the same

[37] See chapter by Owen in this volume. On the communist influence in Bengal in the 1920s and 1930s, see Anthony Cox, *Empire, Industry and Class: The Imperial Nexus of Jute, 1840–1940* (London, 2013).

[38] Peter Robb, 'The Government of India and Annie Besant', *Modern Asian Studies*, 10 (1976), 107–30.

[39] Annie Besant, *The Case for India* (London, 1917).

[40] Owen, 'The Home Rule Leagues'.

[41] Nethercot, *The Last Four Lives*, 274.

objectives and strategies. She did not repudiate agitation, but the agitation she promoted was to be peaceful and legal. She warned that 'if [Home Rule] be not granted, an even more vigorous agitation will begin', but she never endorsed the strategy of passive resistance and civil disobedience that the Extremists were promoting with growing success.[42] Annie Besant hardly changed her discourse, but in a context of radicalisation of the nationalist movement, her position appeared more and more moderate. This does not imply that the declarations she made were not ambiguous and even contradictory. On the one hand, as a gradualist, she was willing to accept any reform, even if it was minimal. On the other hand, she continued to defend her ideal of complete self-government. The attitude of the British government was also ambiguous. Contrary to what she expected, the Montagu–Chelmsford report published in summer 1918 recommended a dual system of government called 'dyarchy'. Provincial assemblies would be in charge of education, health and agriculture. As for finance, justice and the police, they would remain in the hands of unchecked executives. In addition, the central government of India would remain responsible only towards Westminster. Many members in the INC and the Muslim League voiced their discontent. As president of the INC, Annie Besant said what its extremist majority wanted to hear: that the proposals were 'unworthy of England to offer and unworthy of India to accept'.[43] Although disappointed, many Moderates decided to accept these reforms and agitate for their extension. Annie Besant herself officially adopted their position, hoping that this would prevent them from leaving Congress. In the end, she not only failed to keep Congress united, but her strategy made her appear inconsistent.

From 1918, Annie Besant became increasingly out of tune with the Extremists, whose influence grew. She voiced her disapproval of Gandhi's strategy of civil disobedience and non-cooperation in protest at the passing of the Rowlatt Act in March 1919, which imposed serious limitations on civil liberties in the name of the fight against activities deemed seditious. Although Annie Besant rejected these repressive measures, she explained that the non-cooperation campaign could not remain peaceful as it encouraged the man in the street to disrespect the law. Given the multiple tensions and resentments in India, she predicted that this strategy would spiral into violence. When the army fired at a crowd in Delhi in order to end a riot, Annie Besant wanted to recall the danger of civil disobedience and declared that 'before a riot becomes unmanageable, brickbats must inevitably be answered by bullets in every civilized country'.[44] In April 1919, when the

[42] Besant, *The Case for India*, 27.

[43] Quoted in Nethercot, *The Last Four Lives*, 278.

[44] Nethercot, *The Last Four Lives*, 278.

army killed more than 350 unarmed demonstrators at Amritsar, this 'bullet for brickbats' statement was instrumentalised by her opponents to make her pass for a traitor. In addition, although she denounced repression, she argued that Gandhi and his followers bore much of the responsibility for this rise of violence.

When most branches of her Home Rule League now endorsed Gandhi's strategy, Annie Besant resigned and launched a new organisation, the National Home Rule League (NHRL), in 1919. As a delegate of this organisation, she went to London where she had been unable to go for the whole war. Among other activities, she attended sessions of the Select Joint Committee in charge of examining the Government of India Bill and she was even invited to present a memorandum and to make a statement at the end of July 1919. Her position was not as moderate as many historians have suggested. As she explained: 'we are endeavouring to make the Government Bill a real step towards responsible Government in India … and to make sure that it contains openings for the development in that direction in the future'.[45] She urged an enlargement of the electorate to include not only much of the working population, but also women. She criticised the principle of dyarchy, regretting that Indian ministers in provincial councils would have no 'power over the purse'.[46] She also wanted to increase the legislative powers of the Indian Assembly. Annie Besant's support of the bill was not unconditional: it was strategic. She repeated that it would be only a first step and that 'we shall trust ourselves to enlarge it later by action within the Assembly and by pressure outside'.[47] Back in India, she went to the annual conference of the INC held in Amritsar where she defended the Government of India Act – it had been voted in early in December. Even if some delegates accepted the idea of integrating the new institutions, her position became increasingly unpopular. In 1920, when Congress officially adopted the strategy of non-cooperation, Annie Besant refused to work with the organisation, at least for a short time.

She continued the fight, but her efforts now lay in drafting a constitution that would define the status of dominion for India. In the 1920s, this had also become the objective of the Moderates such as Motilal Nehru, who urged the British government to open new negotiations with the nationalists. In 1921, many Liberals and Moderates met at the Reform Conference Annie Besant organised.[48] She regained some influence in the

45 Brockway, 'Mrs. Besant's Lead for India'.

46 Brockway, 'Mrs. Besant's Lead for India'.

47 Brockway, 'Mrs. Besant's Lead for India'.

48 Annie Besant, *Presidential Address of the First Reform Conference under the Auspices of the National Home Rule League* (Madras, 1921); Annie Besant, *Winning Home Rule: The Presidential Address at the Second Reform Conference* (Madras, 1921).

nationalist movement as Gandhi was imprisoned and the boycott campaign was fleetingly on the wane. In the meantime, the Moderates had recaptured Congress and decided to run for election in the newly created institutions. In February 1924, a National Convention dedicated to writing a Commonwealth of India Bill began its work, with Annie Besant as secretary. In spring, she was sent to Britain in order to announce that the document would be ready to be introduced in Parliament by 1925. It was eventually completed but few among the INC accepted to back her scheme. In April 1925, the National Convention asked her to make another trip to Britain where her bill found scarcely more support than in India.

In spite of this failure and of her declining influence Annie Besant still agitated for dominion status. In 1927, when the British government decided to send the Simon Commission to India to review its political institutions, she joined the other nationalist leaders to call for a boycott because of the lack of Indian representatives. From June to August 1928, Annie Besant went to Britain to justify the boycott. To counterbalance the proposals of the Simon Commission, Congress leader Motilal Nehru organised an All-Parties Conference in January 1928. When Annie Besant came back from Britain in August, her name was added to the committee of seven members responsible for drafting a constitution which took up many of the proposals of her Commonwealth of India Bill. In December 1928, the INC adopted the Nehru Report, but warned that if dominion status was not granted within a year it would launch a mass movement of non-cooperation that would include strikes, political and economic boycotts, and non-payment of taxes. Predictably, Annie Besant disagreed with this strategy. She joined the National Liberal Federation (NLF) and continued to advocate dominion status. She opposed complete independence officially endorsed by Congress – now under the influence of Gandhi and Jawaharlal Nehru – in autumn 1929. She urged nationalist leaders to take part in the Round Table organised by the British government in 1930, but also demanded that dominion status, rather than the Simon Report, be discussed. Although she hoped to be selected as a delegate for this Round Table, she was not. She followed the discussions attentively but, because of her declining health, she finally withdrew from politics at the age of eighty-three.

Annie Besant was convinced that Indians should be involved in the political transition towards self-government, but she believed that dominion status had to be granted by the British Parliament. Her action was therefore two-sided: in India, she tried to unite the nationalist movement around constitutional reform and maintenance of India in the Empire; in Britain, she tried to influence lawmakers, taking advantage of the parliamentary growth of the Labour Party which she found supportive of Indian political freedom.

The appeal to British Labour

Annie Besant understood early that she could find a sympathetic hearing among labour circles. In 1910, the *Labour Leader* published her open letter to the authorities of the Raj in which she denounced racism and discrimination.[49] In spring 1914, while she was in Britain as a delegate of the INC, Annie Besant used her former socialist connections to organise meetings and conferences. She also tried, although in vain, to form a parliamentary group to promote Indian interests. She nevertheless persuaded Labour politicians and journalists to contribute to *New India* regularly. Her paper published articles and letters by influential members of the Labour Party such as Philip Snowden or David Graham Pole, but also by the suffragist Evelyn Sharp, or the editor of the *Labour Leader*, Archibald Fenner Brockway.[50] Her former Fabian comrades, Shaw and Webb, also sent a few pieces.

In spring 1916, as she was setting up the Home Rule League, she asked John Scurr, David Graham Pole (who was her personal solicitor) and George Lansbury to support her efforts. While Scurr and Pole both belonged to the Theosophical Society, Lansbury had been acquainted with theosophists and their defence of India from the 1890s: the branch of the Social Democratic Federation (SDF) that he launched in Bow and Bromley had often met at the East London Working Women's club founded by Annie Besant and other theosophists. Lansbury became secretary of the British Auxiliary of the HRL, which organised conferences but also published leaflets.[51] The books it published were prefaced by eminent Labour politicians.[52]

In 1917, the British Auxiliary was very active during Annie Besant's internment.[53] In the House of Commons, Labour MPs, such as Philip Snowden and Josiah C. Wedgwood, attacked the government policy in India and asked for her liberation. Her theosophist friends in England also helped publicise her cause.[54] By the end of the summer, she was acclaimed

[49] 'Mrs. Besant's Appeal', *Labour Leader*, 18 Mar. 1910.

[50] A member of the ILP since 1907, Fenner Brockway was a key figure in the fight against British imperialism in the interwar period and was often at odds with the Labour Party on imperial issues. See chapter by Gasteuil in this volume.

[51] For example, Home Rule for India League, *What India Wants* (London, 1916); Home Rule for India League, *The Waste of Loyalty* (London, 1916).

[52] For example, James Keir Hardie, *India: Impressions and Suggestions* (London, 1909); Lala Lajpat Rai, *Young India: An Interpretation and a History of the Nationalist Movement from Within* (London, 1917).

[53] George Lansbury, *The Persecution and Internment of Mrs. Besant* (London, 1917).

[54] See, for example, the letters by H. Baillie-Weaver, the general secretary of the Theosophical Society in England and Wales, and Emily Lutyens in the *New Statesman*, in July and August 1917.

as heroine of the Indian cause by the left-wing press. At the end of the war, she used the British Auxiliary to appeal to the British working classes. From India, she denounced the 'coercive legislation which outdoes that of any Continental Power'.[55] She explained the current radicalisation of the nationalist movement: 'As a dry matter of fact, India has lost faith in Great Britain. All the talk about fighting for liberty, about Self-Determination, about resistance to autocracy, is discounted by the grim fact that Britain denies in India all that she asks Indians to fight for abroad'.[56] She directly addressed British workers urging them to pressure their representatives into voting for self-government in India:

> I appeal to the British Democracy, to the sons of the fathers I have worked with to win their freedom. To the miners of Northumberland and Durham, in whose cottages I have slept and eaten; to the grinders of Sheffield; to the shoemakers of Bradlaugh's Northampton; to the pottery-makers in Staffordshire; to the cotton weavers and spinners in Lancashire; to the woolen weavers in Yorkshire; to the matchmakers, and dockers and unskilled labourers in East London who sent me to the School Board to win meals for their starving children. To them I appeal, old friends and fellow-workers, Socialists and Radicals, who love liberty and are creating a ruling Democracy. Help us share your Freedom.[57]

In her emotional conclusion, she reminded them both of her radical and socialist past, and of the recent events when India sent troops to fight in Europe. She reasserted her desire that India remain in the Empire while defending the principle of political equality: 'We do not wish to break away from you. … Accept us as brothers, as equals, for no longer will we live as dependents, as a subject Nation'.[58]

From June to November 1919, Annie Besant went to Britain to demand the widening of the Montagu–Chelmsford reforms, but also to secure the support of the Labour Party. She attended its annual conference and joined its Westminster branch at the end of June. Her choice was both strategic and ideological: on the one hand she hoped 'to serve India better by this adhesion'; on the other hand she asserted that this party 'embodies my lifelong ideals' of service and brotherhood.[59] She also rejoined the Fabian Society where she delivered a lecture on 'Socialism in India', explaining

[55] Annie Besant, *From Within the Iron Ring: Being an Appeal to British Labour* (London, 1918), 4.

[56] Besant, *From Within the Iron Ring*, 7.

[57] Besant, *From Within the Iron Ring*, 10–11.

[58] Besant, *From Within the Iron Ring*, 11.

[59] Letter first published in Lansbury's *Daily Herald* and reproduced in the *Labour Leader*, 26 June 1919.

that although modern socialism did not exist in India, Indian people were animated by the spirit of socialism. With other nationalist leaders, Annie Besant also toured the country, delivering conferences to Labour Party branches. In September, while he interviewed her, Fenner Brockway expressed his admiration and his enthusiasm: 'Before parting from Mrs. Besant, I ventured to say how glad we were to welcome her into the British Labour movement'. Reasserting her belief in socialism as the solution to poverty, she replied: 'I have worked always with the Labour Party. In India, I could not do much for the Party, but when I returned here I took my natural place in it again'.[60]

Annie Besant's popularity in labour circles caused concerns to the other members of the INC delegation in Britain. Tilak, for one, resented her undermining Congress opposition to the Government of India Bill.[61] Nevertheless, with Annie Besant, British labour leaders felt they were working with a like-minded reformer. Although she considered that India was ready for self-government, she did not totally reject the paradigm of political maturity, which deeply influenced the debate over Indian political reform in labour circles. Her plans, as those of most labour leaders, were also inspired by the British political model. Last but not least, Annie Besant opposed the strategy of non-cooperation that many labour leaders also rejected. The Labour Party adopted the same position as Annie Besant and the Moderates on the 1919 Government of India Bill: they encouraged Indians to work with the newly created institutions but also to continue agitation.[62]

In the early 1920s, Annie Besant's promotion of dominion status was supported by her labour allies who formed a National Conference to replace the British Auxiliary. Josiah C. Wedgwood, with whom she had corresponded since 1917, wrote *The Future of the Indo-British Commonwealth*, a book that she had asked him to write. According to Wedgwood, Britain had to abandon the old idea of Empire to become 'the centre of a Commonwealth of free peoples enjoying equal rights'.[63] In 1923, Wedgwood became president of a newly created Parliamentary Committee on India. In May 1924, as Annie Besant was in Britain to announce the drafting of the Commonwealth of India Bill, she helped form the British Committee on India Affairs (BCIA), with Lansbury as president and Pole as secretary. She was received by MacDonald, then Prime Minister, and by the secretary of

[60] Brockway, 'Mrs. Besant's Lead for India'.

[61] Owen, *The British Left and India*, 117.

[62] On the position of the Labour Party in this period, see Owen, *The British Left and India*, 120–22.

[63] Josiah C. Wedgwood, *The Future of the Indo-British Commonwealth* (Adyar, 1921), p. xv.

State for India, her former Fabian colleague, Sydney Olivier. She hoped that the Labour Party, who had formed a minority government, would support her plans. She also toured Britain to '[awaken] the country to a recognition of the fact that India is by no means asleep, and that she means to be heard'.[64] She explained the working of the National Convention, describing the tasks of its various committees and insisting on its representative character. She acknowledged the division of the nationalist movement but she was confident that the new constitution would finally satisfy everyone in India. She hoped that 'the British Government [would] take it up as a parliamentary measure' or that, at least, 'a group of members in the House of Commons will back it ... supported ... by a strong agitation in India'.[65] Annie Besant was convinced that the Labour Party would support her scheme. In July, its prominent leaders, Pole, MacDonald, Lansbury and Snowden, had praised her work during the celebration of her 'fifty years in public work'.[66] Unfortunately, MacDonald's government was in a weak position and fell in December 1924, before her document was completed. She nevertheless hoped that MacDonald or Wedgwood would present her Commonwealth of India Bill to Parliament, but the official line of the Labour Party was more moderate than she had anticipated. For their part, Congress leaders were extremely disappointed with the Labour Party: while in office, it had refused to organise a conference on constitutional reforms, as Motilal Nehru had asked, and it had backed repression against the non-cooperation movement in the provinces.

In October 1925, Annie Besant attended the Labour Party conference in Liverpool. Delegates adopted a resolution in favour of the drafting of a constitution by the Indian people in order to replace the 1919 Government of India Bill. However, they refused to support her Commonwealth of India Bill. Lansbury eventually presented it in the House of Commons in December 1925, but as a private member's bill. Although she must have been disappointed, Annie Besant never wavered in her faith in the Labour Party, casting a blind eye on its moderation and even its irresolute approach. In 1926, she continued to assert that salvation would come from the British Labour Party, which had already done much for India.[67] She did not acknowledge that although most Labour leaders seemed to defend the cause of India they did not share the same vision of the necessary reforms. From the 1900s to the 1920s, many Labour leaders such as Hardie, MacDonald, the Webbs, Scurr and Wedgwood visited India and talked with nationalist

[64] Annie Besant, 'India, a Dominion', *The Clarion*, 1 Aug. 1924.

[65] Besant, 'India, a Dominion'.

[66] D. Graham Pole, *Dr. Annie Besant: Fifty Years in Public Work* (London, 1924).

[67] Annie Besant, *India, Bond or Free? A World Problem* (London, 1926), 26.

leaders. However, few believed, as she did, that India was politically mature. The most prominent, such as MacDonald, Olivier or the Webbs, argued that social and educational reforms had to be carried out first. They feared that otherwise the masses would be at the mercy of the elites who dominated the nationalist movement. Most of them were anxious about building a labour movement in India which could follow the British model. To them, a period of apprenticeship appeared necessary to develop class consciousness and to get the workers to recognise the value of political representation to secure their rights.[68] In addition, the labour unrest that erupted in the aftermath of the First World War revealed that Annie Besant's vision of the labour movement in India did not exactly match theirs.

Ambiguous relations with the nascent labour movement in India

From 1918 to 1922, India was in political as well as social turmoil.[69] The workers' resistance to ruthless exploitation was not new, but this social agitation led to the first attempts at organising workers on a long-term basis.[70] Philanthropists and workers' leaders sought the support of nationalist circles, which they rarely obtained.[71] However, in Madras, they found sympathetic hearing among the nationalist leaders, most of whom were theosophists in that region. It is no coincidence that theosophists were thus appealed to. At the time, they voiced very progressive ideas and *New India* published articles on social questions, sometimes denouncing the exploitation of Indian workers by British employers. Annie Besant herself had shown interest in labour movements. In the summer of 1914, *The Theosophist* and *Commonweal* reported her support of the locked-out trade unionists in the building industry in London. Although she disagreed with the policy of the British labour movement, she declared: 'I cannot but sympathize with the spirit of all efforts to raise those who supply us with the necessaries of life to at least the minimum of comfort, health, education and refinement

[68] Nicholas Owen, 'British Progressives and Civil Society in India, 1905–1914', in Jose Harris (ed.), *Civil Society in British History: Ideas, Identities, Institutions* (Oxford, 2003); Owen, *The British Left and India*.

[69] In his case study, Cox has analysed this rising tension in Bengal in the jute industry. Cox, *Empire, Industry and Class*, 113–32.

[70] P. Chellathurai, 'The Context of the Russian Revolution in the Genesis of Labour Movement in Tamil Nadu', *Social Scientist*, 11 (1983), 47–56; Sanat Bose, 'Indian Labour and its Historiography in Pre-Independence Period', *Social Scientist*, 13 (1985), 3–10; Partha S. Gupta, 'British Labour and the Indian Left, 1919–1939', in Sabayasachi Bhattacharya (ed.), *Power, Politics and the People: Studies in British Imperialism and Indian Nationalism* (London, 2002).

[71] Cox, *Empire, Industry and Class*, 125.

necessary for any life deserving to be called human'.[72] She therefore helped the unionists form a cooperative of production whose first work was to complete the new headquarters of the Theosophical Society in London. Annie Besant also tried to attract British unionists' attention to the plight of indentured workers and asked them to welcome Indians in their unions 'and thus effectively checkmate the capitalists when they play off coloured labour in trade disputes'.[73] Although she addressed white trade unionists, her article could be read in India and her support of 'collective bargaining with the capitalist' to avoid starvation wages was not likely to pass unnoticed.[74]

In April 1918, the leaders of the Madras cotton mill workers asked Annie Besant and her colleagues for support when they tried to form an association to improve their conditions. Members of a religious group as well as nationalist leaders such as Kalyanasundaram had already compiled and publicised the workers' grievances. Wadia accepted to meet the workers of Buckingham and Carnatic Mills. Appalled by their conditions, he decided to serve them as a lawyer and to help them form a union. The Madras Labour Union (MLU) is considered the first modern trade union in India. For about four years, Wadia supported and advised the 5,500 workers in their fight punctuated with strikes, lock-outs, law suits and various pressures on the part of the employers. Although Annie Besant was not directly involved in the MLU, she supported the initiative. In December 1918, she accepted to preside over a public meeting meant to inform the Madras citizens on the lock-out of trade union workers. Earlier, in June 1918, she had also backed Wadia's effort to organise the rickshaw drivers in a union after their successful strike. In March 1919, she publicly supported the tramway drivers' strike and encouraged them to form a union. She also announced that she had encouraged the printing staff of *Commonweal* and *New India* to organise and join the newly created printers' union.

In May 1919, just before her departure for Europe, the MLU passed a resolution in order to 'request her to use her great influence on the British Labour Party to secure redress of the grievances of labourers and to assist their President, Mr. Wadia, in his efforts in that direction'.[75] At the end of the war, British Labour leaders, such as MacDonald and Scurr, showed great confidence in Annie Besant's potential for encouraging a labour movement in India and for leading what would become the Indian left.[76] Annie Besant herself had tried to explain that the nationalist movement had inspired

72 *The Theosophist*, July 1914.

73 Annie Besant, 'Indian Emigration and Trade Unionism', *Commonweal*, 24 July 1914.

74 Besant, 'Indian Emigration'.

75 B.P. Wadia, *Labour in Madras* (Madras, 1921), 151–52.

76 Fischer, 'Un trait d'union', 351.

the labour movement thanks to Wadia in Madras or Gandhi, who had supported the weavers' strike in Ahmedabad. She argued that nationalists were teaching the masses the principle of self-government and that thanks to Home Rule propaganda 'the workers all over India are beginning to resist capitalist oppression'.[77]

However, one of the Indian workers' most devoted mouthpieces in England was Wadia. In the beginning of August 1919, he was heard by the Select Joint Committee of the Houses of Parliament on Indian Reforms. He reported on the inefficiency of the Factory Acts to protect Indian workers and asked for the legal recognition of trade unions. In addition, Wadia urged the committee to 'enable the Indian labourer to send his own representatives to the Provincial Councils; [and] let all matters relating to his welfare and betterment be in the hands of responsible elected representatives'.[78] Due to this energetic defence of Indian workers, the Trades Union Congress (TUC) asked Wadia to write a memorandum on labour problems in India. Wadia and Besant were also invited to the TUC annual congress held in Glasgow in September 1919. Wadia explained that with the Indian Reform Bill, 'the voice of the poor factory labourer will … be drowned amid the droning of the machinery of the rich capitalist'.[79] He also urged British trade unionists to help their 'comrades in India' in their struggle to improve their conditions. In October 1919, he went to Washington, D.C. to attend the International Labour Conference thanks to the support of the British TUC and of Montagu. Back in India, Wadia continued the fight on behalf of Madras labour. As for Annie Besant, she still followed the evolution of the nascent labour movement: in October 1920, she and Wadia attended the first meeting of the All-India Trade Union Congress (AITUC), which soon affiliated to the International Labour Organisation (ILO).

In spite of these connections with the labour movement in India, Annie Besant's priority was the political struggle. For example, barely a year after the internment episode, she tried to encourage Wadia towards more moderation. She asked him to withdraw a statement that implied that the employers of the Buckingham and Carnatic Mills ill-treated their workforce. As Wadia was threatened with a suit for libel, Annie Besant feared that the authorities would support the employers and use any pretext to silence him. Insisting on the exclusive nature of the political struggle, she asserted that 'in the great struggle for Indian Freedom, we cannot spare our bravest soldiers from the battle-front except for the sake of that Freedom. The Labour struggle, important as it is, is, in this great campaign, a side issue.

77 Besant, *From Within the Iron Ring*, 10.

78 Wadia, *Labour in Madras*, 207.

79 B.P. Wadia, *A Memorandum on Labor Problems in India* (London, 1919), 9.

Winning Home Rule, Labour wins its Freedom'.[80] Annie Besant found it extremely difficult to define the role of the labour movement within the fight for Home Rule. She did not consider that the workers could play an active role in the process of political liberation. In a country with a high rate of illiteracy, she believed the masses were not mature enough to make political decisions. In addition, as a theosophist, she was not fully committed to democracy, preferring instead a hierarchical social order in which the moralised elites would carry out the necessary social reforms. Annie Besant's attitude was in tune with the mainstream nationalist movement which 'proved reluctant to use industrial labour as anything more than an auxiliary force in demonstration', as Anthony Cox explained.[81]

On the contrary, Wadia stressed the importance of developing a genuine labour movement in India.[82] He was convinced that political emancipation would not necessarily end exploitation because he saw that 'the rich classes … might any day ally themselves with the British capitalists'.[83] During the strikes that took place in Madras in 1918 and 1919, he became aware that 'unless something was immediately done to bring the labourer to power, he greatly ran the risk of being neglected under the new régime of reforms'.[84] According to Wadia, the success of the movement for political emancipation depended on the involvement of the masses. They had to be organised so that they could influence the nationalist movement in a more democratic direction. Wadia wanted Home Rulers 'to recognize the Labour Movement as an integral part of the National Movement'.[85] He then added: 'The latter will not succeed in the right direction of democracy if Indian working classes are not enabled to organize their own forces and come in to their own'.[86]

In 1921, Josiah C. Wedgwood praised Wadia as one of the most devoted workers for the 'organisation and emancipation' of labour in India.[87] He approved of Wadia's strategy to use laws and political institutions, especially the new legislative councils, to obtain the legalisation of trade unions and the passage of Factory Acts. This fight for legal recognition was all the more crucial as, at the end of 1920, the Madras High Court backed Buckingham

80 Wadia, *Labour in Madras*, 39–40.

81 Cox, *Empire, Industry and Class*, 125.

82 Communist militant M.N. Roy, who was most influential in Bengal, also sought to create a nationalist movement of workers and peasants that would be independent from the INC. See chapter by Owen in this volume.

83 B.P. Wadia, *Aims of the Labour Movement in India* (Madras, 1920), 3.

84 Wadia, *Aims of the Labour Movement in India*, 5.

85 Wadia, *Labour in Madras*, p. xvi.

86 Wadia, *Labour in Madras*.

87 Wadia, *Labour in Madras*, p. ix.

and Carnatic Mill's claim for damages due to the strike, and condemned Wadia and other union leaders for illegal combination. In the end, a compromise was reached between both parties, but Wadia had to sever his relations with the workers. Although Wadia published the story of the MLU the following year, he withdrew from the labour movement. At the end of 1921, he settled in the USA where he joined dissident theosophists and carried on his exegesis of Blavatsky's doctrines. The Court's ruling and Wadia's decision to leave India represented a serious blow for the British unionists and labour politicians who wished to help India develop a trade union movement on the British model.

Conclusion

Annie Besant's cooperation with the British Labour Party relied mainly on a shared strategy of constitutional reforms in order to transform the British Empire gradually. It also rested on a series of misunderstandings, most of them being overlooked for strategic reasons. The British Labour Party praised Annie Besant's work as it represented an alternative to non-cooperation. They also considered that, contrary to the Moderates, she 'went to the masses of the Indian people'.[88] That assumption has been challenged since.[89] Labour Party leaders overlooked the fact that she lost much of her popular support in the 1920s when she defended the Labour Party's line. In addition, many refused to acknowledge that she focused on political reforms and would not promote the British model of socialism and trade unionism in India. As for Annie Besant, she constantly overlooked the lack of unity within the British labour movement in general and of the Labour Party in particular so far as Indian reforms were concerned and she probably overestimated her personal influence on its policy.

With the benefit of hindsight, one could be tempted to conclude on her failure fully to associate the labour movements both in Britain and in India to the nationalist struggle. However, it is important to recall that this had not been her intention at first because she considered the labour movements as only auxiliaries in the fight for Home Rule. It therefore seems preferable to study her strategy and to underline the complexity of the context, with its multiple actors and organisations, its issues and its constraints. This allows one to see how her political struggle led her to appeal to the British Labour Party and made her aware that the nationalist movement was giving impetus to a labour movement in India.

[88] Brockway, 'Mrs. Besant's Lead for India'.

[89] Nethercot, *The Last Four Lives*, 275.

2

Sylvia Pankhurst vs the British Empire

The *Workers' Dreadnought* Experience, 1917–1924

Yann Béliard

On 8 March 1919, the *Workers' Dreadnought* published a letter signed by the president and the secretary of the Social-Democratic Party (SDP) of Dunedin, New Zealand, stating that it was 'the most advanced of any labour paper in the Empire'.[1] Mark Silverstone's and Arthur McCarthy's flattering judgement is hardly reflected by the discrete place allocated to the weekly, and more generally to Estelle Sylvia Pankhurst, by historians of British anti-colonialism and of the British left in their works.[2] The poverty of historiography on Sylvia Pankhurst has been partly counterbalanced, since the 1980s, by the publication of several biographies, all written by women.[3] But until the release of Katherine Connelly's *Sylvia Pankhurst* in 2013, none of them, however remarkable, granted the *Dreadnought* the weight it deserves, be it in Pankhurst's personal trajectory or in the broader political trends that shaped interwar Britain.[4] Admittedly, between 1917 and 1924,

[1] *Workers' Dreadnought*, 8 Mar. 1919. Hereafter in the footnotes the weekly is referred to as *WD*.

[2] In their pioneering studies, neither Stephen Howe (*Anticolonialism in British Politics: The Left and the End of Empire, 1918–1964*, Oxford, 1993) nor Nicholas Owen (*The British Left and India: Metropolitan Anti-Imperialism, 1885–1947*, Oxford, 2007) pays much attention to Sylvia Pankhurst. She receives hardly more coverage in histories of British communism, whether they are told from a Stalinist point of view (James Klugman, *History of the Communist Party of Great Britain*, vol. 1, *Formation and Early Years, 1919–1924*, London, 1968) or a Trotskyist one (Hugo Dewar, *Communist Politics in Britain: The CPGB from its Origins to the Second World War*, London, 1976). The same observation applies to the more recent study by James Eaden and David Renton, *The Communist Party of Great Britain since 1920* (Basingstoke, 2002).

[3] Hereafter, Estelle Sylvia Pankhurst will be referred to as Pankhurst.

[4] Katherine Connelly, *Sylvia Pankhurst: Suffragette, Socialist and Scourge of the Empire* (London: 2013); Barbara Castle, *Sylvia and Christabel Pankhurst* (Harmondsworth, 1987); Patricia Romero, *E. Sylvia Pankhurst: Portrait of a Radical* (New Haven, CT, 1987); Shirley Harrison, *Sylvia Pankhurst: Citizen of the World* (London, 2009); *Sylvia Pankhurst: The Rebellious Suffragette* (Newhaven, 2012).

the *Dreadnought* was far from being the labour weekly with the widest readership in the British world: with a circulation of about 10,000 copies, it could not compete in quantitative terms with the *Labour Leader* or the *Daily Herald*. But in terms of content, the *Dreadnought* stood out, in particular because of its advanced positions on colonial questions.

As a radically anti-colonial paper published in days when so many thought the British Empire would last forever, the *Dreadnought* deserves to be reappraised by historians of British labour and British decolonisation alike.[5] Indeed, although Pankhurst was expelled from the mainstream suffragette movement in January 1914 because of deep divergences with her mother Emmeline and her elder sister Christabel, she is still remembered mostly for her pre-war fight in favour of women's rights. As for those who celebrate the Pan-African engagement to which she devoted her last twenty years, they tend to overlook the fact that her anti-imperialism was, at a crucial moment in her life, inseparable from the communist perspective. As observed by June Hannam, 'her contribution to socialist and revolutionary politics has been taken less seriously' than her activities as a suffragette.[6] It is therefore that neglected aspect of her political involvement that this chapter addresses. The story of her life is sometimes presented as a succession of episodes with little sense of continuity.[7] But if there is one period when she was able constructively to 'put together the different strands of her interests', it is during the *Dreadnought* era.[8]

Examining the particular type of anti-imperialism defended in the columns of the *Dreadnought* between its creation in 1917 and its demise in 1924, this chapter is meant as a contribution to the rediscovery of the weekly founded and directed by Pankhurst in what were probably her years of most intense political activity. In a period marked by unprecedented levels of labour militancy, Pankhurst's paper offered its readers a political vision that distinguished itself from the other working-class publications on offer in Britain at the time by its commitment to the October Revolution and to the new brand of anti-colonialism advocated by the Bolsheviks via the Communist International. Although Pankhurst broke with the Communist Party of Great Britain (CPGB) in 1921, the *Dreadnought* was informed

[5] Mary Davis, *Sylvia Pankhurst: A Life in Radical Politics* (London, 1999); Wilma Boisnard, '"Travailler pour les autres": Sylvia Pankhurst, une rebelle aux causes multiples', in Véronique Molinari (ed.), *Droit des femmes, droit des autres: des féministes britanniques face aux autres exclus de la citoyenneté (1860–1930)* (Clermont-Ferrand, 2012), 111–54.

[6] June Hannam, 'Pankhurst (Estelle) Sylvia (1882–1960)', *Oxford Dictionary of National Biography* (Oxford, 2004; online edition Sept. 2015).

[7] The Wikipedia page about Pankhurst, which considers in turn 'Suffragism', 'Communism' and 'Support for Ethiopia', is typical of that segmentation.

[8] Hannam, 'Pankhurst', *ODNB*.

from beginning to end by a Marxist understanding of imperialism that gave it a distinctive colour. The sheer space devoted to imperial questions in its columns made it different from the labour weeklies printed in the Late Victorian and Edwardian era, and so did the varied angles from which British imperialism was denounced. It presented more than a moral or philanthropic variety of anti-colonialism. Traditional attacks on military interventions abroad were complemented with a critique of economic exploitation, of informal imperialism, and integrated within a systemic analysis of imperialism as a world order. The chapter studies two other features that made the *Dreadnought*'s anti-colonialism original: its attention to what imperial domination implied regarding women's conditions – a focus that owed a lot to Pankhurst's persistent feminist engagement – and its criticism of bourgeois nationalism in the colonies – a theme that she would later abandon in her move from communism to Pan-Africanism. The final part deals with the coverage of labour revolts in the Dominions and the colonies, and the innovative perception of Asiatic workers as the vanguard of the international socialist revolution.[9]

From 1917 to 1924: changing identities

Before taking a look at the *Dreadnought*'s coverage of imperial questions, it is necessary to briefly sum up its history. The paper was started as the *Woman's Dreadnought* by the East London Federation of Suffragettes (ELFS) on 8 March 1914, i.e., on the International Women's Day, a few weeks after its founder and leader Sylvia Pankhurst had officially declared this young branch independent from the Women's Social and Political Union (WSPU).[10] From 1914 to 1916, the *Dreadnought* was the voice of the ELFS, distinguishing itself from the mainstream of feminist publications by its support for the labour movement and its opposition to the war.[11] With 30,000 copies sold

[9] I wish to thank Matt Perry and the late Sam Davies for inviting me to discuss this work with their colleagues and students, respectively at Newcastle University (Apr. 2015) and Liverpool John Moores University (Mar. 2015). My gratitude also goes to Wilma Boisnard and Mary Davis for their precious feedback on earlier versions of this chapter.

[10] During the Great Labour Unrest (1910–1914), she had rooted her efforts in the East End, where she believed a mass mobilisation could be built among women workers and dockers. Against police interventions in the area she proclaimed the need for a People's Army. Eventually it was her speech on 14 Nov. 1913 at a rally in support of Jim Larkin and the locked-out Dublin dockers that caused her expulsion from the WSPU. See Sylvia Pankhurst, *The Suffragette Movement: An Intimate Account of Persons and Ideals* (London, 1931).

[11] Boisnard observes a contrast in the Pankhurst obituaries published in *The Times*: while Emmeline, Christabel and even Adela were excused for their resort to extreme methods in the pursuit of the suffrage, Sylvia was never forgiven for her Bolshevism.

every week, it was an immediate success. The ELFS renamed itself the Workers' Suffrage Federation (WSF) in March 1916, and the *Woman's Dreadnought* was renamed the *Workers' Dreadnought* in July 1917.[12] From July 1917 to August 1921, the *Dreadnought* continued its move to the left, as illustrated by significant changes on its front page. From 12 June 1918, the S in WSF stood for 'Socialist' instead of 'Suffrage'. On 20 July 1918, the *Dreadnought* changed its subtitle from 'Socialism, Internationalism, Votes for All' to the shorter 'For International Socialism'. By then Pankhurst had become one of the most vocal British advocates of the Bolshevik revolution and she transformed the *Dreadnought* into a tool for the construction of a British section of the Communist International. In 1919, the motto 'For International Socialism' gave way to 'Towards the Communist Party'. On 14 June 1919, the WSF presented itself as the 'WSF–Communist Party' for the first time, and on 26 June 1920, it gave up the WSF label completely, swapping it for 'Communist Party, British Section of the Third International (CP–BSTI)' until August 1921.

The changes in the headings of the *Dreadnought* do not tell the entire story. For Pankhurst disagreed with the Third International on key tactical issues. She did not believe that the future British Communist Party should ask for affiliation to the Labour Party, and she rejected participation in elections and in reformist trade unions. So when Pankhurst, on 19 June 1920, formed the first official Communist Party in Great Britain (the CP–BSTI), it was not recognised by Moscow and her backing in Britain was limited compared to that of the CPGB launched one month later, on 31 July–1 August 1920, around the British Socialist Party (BSP).[13] Could the CP–BSTI adhere to the CPGB to form a united Communist Party recognised by the Comintern, and what would become of the *Dreadnought* if unification took place? Those

[12] The WSF combined a series of welfare activities – the running of nurseries, schools and clinics, of cooperative shops and workshops, of cultural and recreational associations – with anti-war propaganda, all the while retaining a predominantly female leadership. See Sylvia Pankhurst, *The Home Front: A Mirror to Life in England during the First World War* (London, 1932).

[13] The biggest socialist organisation in Britain was the Independent Labour Party (ILP), with 35,000 members. It favoured a regeneration of the Second International over the foundation of a Third, so took no part in the construction of the CPGB, though hundreds of its members joined it. On the birth of the CPGB, see Raymond Challinor, *The Origins of British Bolshevism* (London, 1977) and Walter Kendall, *The Revolutionary Movement in Britain, 1900–21* (London, 1969). Pankhurst's risky voyage to Russia in July 1920 allowed her to discuss matters directly with Lenin, but not to change his views. She was one of the targets of his *'Left-Wing' Communism: An Infantile Disorder* (1920). For her tale of the encounter, see Sylvia Pankhurst, *Soviet Russia as I Saw It* (London, 1921). See also Andrew Thorpe, *The British Communist Party and Moscow, 1920–43* (Manchester, 2000).

issues were complicated by Pankhurst's arrest on 20 October 1920 after the paper published an article approving of a revolt on a British battleship.[14] Her imprisonment was a blow.[15] The *Dreadnought*, now run by her partner, Italian anarchist Silvio Corio, and her friend Nora Smythe, was on the verge of financial collapse. As for the CP–BSTI, it kept losing members to the Moscow-supported CPGB, until its provisional leaders decided it was time for the BSTI to join the CPGB, to adopt its official organ, *The Communist*, as their own, and give up the *Dreadnought*, or place it under CPGB control. None of those moves was acceptable for Pankhurst: on 22 January 1921, one week before the CP–BSTI officially joined the CPGB, the *Dreadnought* ceased to call itself the official organ of the CP. After her release from jail on 30 May 1921, Pankhurst adhered to the CPGB but was expelled from the unified party on 10 September for her refusal to hand over the *Dreadnought* to the party.

On 17 September 1921, Pankhurst announced to her readers that the weekly was about to close down. But instead of dropping it, she reshaped it one last time, as 'an independent Communist paper untrammelled by party bias'. Once the *Dreadnought* broke up with the Third International, it adopted a new subtitle: 'For International Communism'. In February 1922, the paper announced its alignment with the German KAPD. The reproduction of speeches by Bolshevik leaders was supplanted by letters from leftist activists, who described the Soviet Union as state capitalism and called for the creation of a Fourth International.[16] In June 1924, the *Dreadnought* came to a halt and, for about a decade, Pankhurst retired from

[14] Based on the report of an anonymous British sailor, the article called for solidarity with the Soviet Navy. Because she refused to inform the authorities about her sources, Pankhurst was charged with sedition under the Defence of the Realm Act. See 'Sedition: Sylvia Pankhurst. Imprisoned for publishing seditious articles (1920–1921)', The National Archives (TNA), Public Record Office (PRO), Home Office (HO) Papers, 144/1697/414256. See also 'File relating to Sylvia Pankhurst. Convicted at Mansion House on 23 October 1920 for publishing seditious matters and sentenced to six months' imprisonment (1920–1921)', PRO, HO, 144/1697/414256.

[15] A vehicle for her fight for freedom, the weekly published her photo on the front page on 6 Nov. 1920 (for her trial) and on 4 June 1921 (for her release). The 15 Jan. 1921 issue was devoted almost entirely to her prison declarations.

[16] See H. Görter's first editorial on 17 Apr. 1920 and his letters to Lenin in the following issues. See also A. Kollontai's series 'News from Soviet Russia', published from 22 Apr. to 19 Aug. 1921. Their Fourth International never took off and should not be confused with the one founded by Leon Trotsky in 1938. As time went by, anarchist militants or thinkers were referred to more and more frequently. The paper now adopted a different subtitle every week, and more and more often an apolitical one. In a period when working-class struggles were ebbing, Pankhurst now focused on humanitarian and societal subjects, such as the promotion of Esperanto, the Montessori approach to education, etc.

politics, devoting time to her family and literary activities.[17] All in all, the 1923 and 1924 *Dreadnoughts* are not as rich so far as imperial questions are concerned, so this chapter only makes cursory reference to the *Dreadnought*'s twilight years.

What do we know about the *Dreadnought*'s influence? Its core readership was formed by the members and sympathisers of the ELSF turned WSF, even though the paper was not its official organ. That East End milieu, comprising a strong proportion of women and foreign workers, could find in the columns of the paper a reflection of its activities.[18] The WSF held weekly meetings in the area, indoor or outdoor fixtures where the paper was on sale, as well as annual festivals, such as the Old Cockney Fair.[19] The price made the publication accessible.[20] But the readership was not confined within the boundaries of the East End. Subscribers could also be found in the provinces, more particularly in the mining communities of South Wales and Scotland, due to Pankhurst's long-time relationship with Keir Hardie. Judging by the letters received from the Dominions, Ireland or India, it is also clear that the *Dreadnought* appealed to labour circles overseas. Edited in the capital, read in the heart of working-class London, circulated across the British Empire, the *Dreadnought* was a paper that mattered, which explains why the authorities kept it under close surveillance and raided its offices, at 152 Fleet Street, over and over again.[21] The following analysis of the weekly's coverage of imperial questions, based on the consultation of the complete collection, i.e., about 5,000 pages published over a period of more than 350 weeks, is therefore also an answer to Chandrika Kaul's and John Callaghan's calls for research into how the press framed the discussion of empire.[22]

17 When the paper stopped, Pankhurst and Corio opened a café, then moved to Essex where, in 1927, Pankhurst, aged 45, gave birth to Richard, her only son.

18 The paper occasionally published announcements in Yiddish. See *WD*, 17 Feb. 1923.

19 *WD*, 15 Nov. 1919.

20 When it was founded, the weekly cost no more than one penny. Its price rose to two pence after a couple of months and was brought back down to one penny in 1922.

21 See 'Sylvia Pankhurst record file (1921–1938)', TNA, PRO, Metropolitan Police (MEPO) Papers, 38/36. See also 'Activities and biographical notes on Miss E. Sylvia Pankhurst (1950)', PRO, Foreign Office (FO) Papers, 371/80230.

22 Chandrika Kaul, *Communications, Media and the Imperial Experience: Britain and India in the Twentieth Century* (Basingstoke, 2014); John Callaghan, 'Editorial', *Socialist History*, 31 (2007).

Defying British militarism

The *Dreadnought* presented a critique of British imperialism that went beyond the call for a reformed Empire that was so common among pre-1914 socialists, a critique that combined the denunciations of militarism, political oppression and economic exploitation. The most visible component of the *Dreadnought*'s anti-imperialism lay in its systematic opposition to Britain's military interventions, whether abroad or within the remits of the British Empire. The weekly's militaristic title may seem a paradoxical choice. Built in the armament race with Germany, dreadnoughts were immense battleships, presumably unsinkable cruisers, the first of which was used by the Royal Navy in 1906. The choice of the title indicates that, far from advocating pacifism in the Quaker sense, Pankhurst in 1917 shared Lenin's idea that the imperialist world war could only be brought to halt by a worldwide class war against capitalism. That refusal to turn the other cheek was coherent with her political choices as a feminist, the *Woman's Dreadnought* having always backed the idea that women, in their fightback, should 'dread nought' and that the enemy's force should be met with force.

Founded to protest against the patriotic truce advocated by Emmeline and Christabel Pankhurst, the *Dreadnought* printed page upon page denouncing the Great War. A 1922 cartoon placed the words 'Germany, 1914–1918' at the top of a funeral crown made of Britain's 'righteous wars': 'America, 1814; France, 1815; China, 1842; Russia, 1854–56; New Zealand, 1865; Afghanistan, 1878–80; Transvaal, 1880; Egypt, 1882–89; South Africa, 1890–1902; Sudan, 1896; East Central Africa, 1897–99; Natal, 1906'.[23] The world war, that 'ignoble and mercenary battle of thieves', was interpreted not as an accident but as the logical continuation of Britain's struggle for global supremacy.[24] While a majority of labour publications had frankly embraced the war in August–September 1914, while the dissenting minority often remained tepid in its pacifism, the weekly launched a remarkable series entitled 'From the Trenches' to voice the suffering and anger of the Tommies, a series presenting the British army in a most unflattering light. That audacity explains why the *Dreadnought* was so frequently in trouble with the authorities, its immediate support for the October Revolution only making things worse.

Pankhurst and her comrades could only welcome the Bolsheviks' call for an immediate and general ceasefire: they shared the same condemnation of the ongoing war and the same conviction that their own empire was their first enemy, but also, more fundamentally, Lenin's party embodied

[23] *WD*, 20 May 1922.

[24] *WD*, 29 Dec. 1917.

the fight for workers' power that the WSF claimed to be leading on British soil. Significantly, it was just above the *Dreadnought*'s office on Fleet Street that the People's Russia Information Bureau (PRIB), founded by Pankhurst in September 1918, had its headquarters.[25] In late 1917 and early 1918, photographs and speeches of Bolshevik leaders occupied half the pages of the paper, which turned itself into the main British vehicle for Soviet views.[26] In particular, it informed its readers of the Bolsheviks' anti-imperialist decrees: the one on peace and the one on the rights of the peoples of Russia, both reproduced extensively. In exchange for that political support, the Soviet government provided the *Dreadnought* and the RPIB with financial support, and the Comintern sent a delegate to London in 1919 for the WSF's annual conference.[27] That loyalty to the new 'workers' fatherland' and the weekly's explicit disloyalty towards the Crown were two sides of the same unacceptable coin in the eyes of the Home Office.

Suspicion grew even stronger when the *Dreadnought* became involved in the Hands Off Russia campaign, a campaign that brought together members from the WSF, the BSP and the De Leonite SLP (Socialist Labour Party), united by their opposition to the sending of British troops against Soviet Russia. The paper, not content with a special Hands Off Russia issue on 28 December 1918, attacked British cruelty to Russian prisoners, championed 'red propaganda among the Tommies' and called for an anti-military strike.[28] The circulation of pamphlets by WSF member Harry Pollitt and others was at the origin of the boycott of the *Jolly George*, a ship the London dockers refused to load when they learnt it was about to transport weapons to Poland. The positive report on the operation in the *Dreadnought* was one of the reasons for Pankhurst's arrest and longest imprisonment. The paper's support for the Bolshevik revolution extended to its European replicas in Germany and Hungary, and news of the counter-revolution in the Central Empires and of 'white terror' in Russia and its periphery also received plentiful coverage.[29] All in all, the *Dreadnought*'s choice systematically to side with foreign revolutions against Britain's geopolitical and diplomatic interests made it, for the authorities, a publication to be watched.

[25] The RPIB, to which the Independent Labour Party (ILP) and the British Socialist Party (BSP) were affiliated, employed only four people. Its main task was to publish Bolshevik pamphlets.

[26] The *Dreadnought* published a series entitled 'News from Moscow' to keep the British reader updated with the forward march of the Russian Revolution.

[27] Pankhurst remained proud of that collaboration, even when she became disillusioned with communism.

[28] *WD*, 4 Jan. 1919, 21 July 1919 and 28 Feb. 1920.

[29] *WD*, 25 Jan. 1919 and 8 Feb. 1919.

At the same moment, British troops were intervening on another front, much closer to home, in a 'domestic' war against Ireland. In Easter 1916, the *Woman's Dreadnought* had been one of the only British periodicals to applaud the rising, with the publication of reports by WSF correspondent Patricia Lynch. A few years on, the editorial team did not flinch in its approval of Irish emancipation. A cartoon printed on 17 January 1920 showed a semi-naked man embodying the Irish nation tortured on a rack by a politician and a general, under the ironical heading 'self-determination of small states'. This was a reference to the British excuse for declaring war on Germany – the defence of defenceless Belgium – and to Wilson's Fourteen Points, the essence of which the British government claimed to share while doing its utmost to preserve its imperial belongings.[30] The *Dreadnought*'s views on imperialism were often expressed through cartoons. A common feature in the press of the time, they never occupied in the pages of the *Dreadnought* the same special space as Will Dyson's cartoons in the early *Daily Herald* (1912–1914). Yet their relative abundance can be related to Pankhurst's artistic sensibility, even though she did not sign any of them.[31]

'All the world does not want to be English!'

The stigmatising of military aggressions rested on a principled opposition to the very existence of the British Empire, to the control that the Union Jack exerted over one-quarter of the planet's surface and population. The indictment of administrative control over foreign territories was thus at the heart of the *Dreadnought*'s anti-imperialism. An Empire within the Empire, India was, unsurprisingly, the colony that received the largest coverage in the paper, with 'India for the Indians' as a leitmotiv.[32] Presenting its own counter-history of the colonisation of India, the *Dreadnought* reminded its readers of the 1877–1878 famine, in which 5 million people had died, and of the £30 million 'drained out of India' each year.[33] The political and economic

[30] As opposed to Ireland, the *Dreadnought* did not treat Wales and Scotland as colonies. Its 'Welsh notes', 'South Wales Notes' and 'Scottish Mining Notes' made no mention of national oppression, which makes Pankhurst's leftism different from John MacLean's. However, in an article imagining what would happen 'If Wales Went red', the paper anticipated that it would 'light a fire in Britain that could never be extinguished' (*WD*, 14 Jan. 1922).

[31] She was trained as an artist at the Manchester Art School, at the Accademia of Venice and the Royal College of Art in Kensington, and designed the WSPU's membership card long before the expulsion of the ELFS.

[32] Pankhurst's interest in India was long-lasting. See Sylvia Pankhurst, *India and the Earthly Paradise* (Bombay, 1926).

[33] *WD*, 29 Dec. 1917.

dimensions were always tied together, as in the 'Special Indian Supplement' published by the *Dreadnought* on 7 September 1917. The first two pages dealt with the Montagu–Chelmsford report, which the weekly repudiated with a resolution calling for its replacement by 'a scheme of genuine democratic self-government for India', while the other two pages, copiously informed by 'Indian comrades', focused on labour conditions. To the readers who might have felt indifferent to those far away matters, the *Dreadnought* assured: 'British workers, if you do not aid the Indian workers to raise themselves from their state of heavy oppression, you may shortly find their labour power used to oppress you'. The working conditions in the colony and the metropole were perceived as tightly connected, the threat for British jobs coming not from Indian workers, but from their low level of wages.[34]

Direct political control over the country was always an important theme, especially after the Amritsar massacre of 13 April 1919, to which the paper reserved its first page. Yet, in the weeks that followed, the weekly chose to focus on the deeper 'causes of the Indian unrest', identifying 'the repressive Rowlatt legislation' *and* 'the appalling poverty of the Indian people' as the key factors.[35] Two years after the massacre, the Amritsar story was brought back home by the weekly, with a cartoon entitled 'Amritsar the second'.[36] It showed a stereotypical British boss, smoking a cigar and threatening four trade unionists at his feet with a heavy baton. The message was, that if the authorities were ready to shoot rebellious Indians, they would not refrain from doing the same to labour rebels at home – a shock image to express the idea that workers in Britain and India shared the same enemies. The formation of the first Labour government in 1924 was no turning-point for India according to Pankhurst. In one of the paper's last issues, her editorial criticised MacDonald's 'so-called Indian reforms'.[37] She saw them as a mere excuse to refuse a round table and perpetuate the 'subjection and exploitation of 300 million people' by 'a government supposed to represent 47 million people of another race living on a distant island one-fortieth of its size'.[38] Less frequently the weekly evoked the peripheral regions of the Indian Empire, notably Afghanistan, Ceylon and Burma. The use of India as a springboard for British imperialism in the whole of Asia and even East Africa was exposed, the sorry state of the Indian army – in which two-thirds of the recruits were unfit for service – being read as a sign

[34] On the same theme, see 'A Menace to British Workers: How the Business Government Works in Britain, India and Burma', *WD*, 25 Jan. 1919.

[35] *WD*, 26 Apr. 1919.

[36] *WD*, 18 June 1921.

[37] *WD*, 29 Mar. 1924.

[38] *WD*, 8 Mar. 1924.

that there was 'much to be done in putting the British Imperial House in order'.[39]

The geographical scope of the articles dealing with the British Empire was not limited to the Indian peninsula. The paper once covered a strike in the Falklands that had led to the deportation by the authorities of British workers who had protested against the whaling companies employing them, companies they blamed for killing whales in unreasonably vast quantities.[40] This was an original instance of the *Dreadnought* combining social and ecological preoccupations, as it underlined in a visionary way the dire consequences of the imperialist thirst for profit on the planet's natural resources. Moving from the South Atlantic to the South Pacific, the weekly also incriminated the Colonial Office for its plans to re-indenture Chinese labourers on the island of Samoa, for less than 15 shillings a week, a project it equated to slavery.[41] A broad-sweeping article, 'How British Dominions are Governed', took a look at the undemocratically chosen bodies governing Nyasaland, South Rhodesia, South Africa, Uganda, Trinidad and Hong Kong, to waspishly conclude: 'So the British Empire civilises the world'.[42]

Whatever country it dealt with, the *Dreadnought* stood for the right of its people to ask for, and if necessary fight for, self-determination. 'Some in the Labour Party want to extend the Empire. We want to destroy it'.[43] The paper's line of thought on colonialism could not have been more bluntly expressed. Beside such tough talk, Pankhurst and her companions occasionally used humour to broadcast their aims. 'All the world does not want to be English!', one journalist joked.[44] And the weekly published a song entitled, 'We Love the Empire', ironically praising all the institutions it stood against:

We love the Empire, dear old Empire,
We love its sons so brave and true,
We love the Army and the Navy,
We love the blood that's 'royal blue',
We love the Church and Constitution,
We love the 'Lords' and 'Commons' too,
We love 'our country' and 'our nation',
We love the slaves, we do, we do.[45]

39 *WD*, 25 Aug. 1918.
40 *WD*, 29 May 1920.
41 *WD*, 17 July 1920.
42 *WD*, 8 May 1920.
43 *WD*, undated clipping.
44 *WD*, 11 Oct. 1919.
45 *WD*, 15 July 1922.

In a similarly light vein, a cartoon published on 12 July 1919 represented the British Empire as a crowned and crying snake – the archetypal symbol of evil – that had swallowed so many territories – Ireland, Egypt, India, Transvaal, Gibraltar and Canada – that it blurted: 'This is terrible. As if my digestion were not bad enough already'.[46] Two young boys, axes in hand, were shown running towards it, the one named 'Self-determination' following close behind the one named 'Bolshevism'. The message was transparent: the Empire's days were counted, and popular revolts led by the communists would play the key role.

Home and away, colonialism unveiled

Stephen Howe has argued that anti-colonialism in the United Kingdom was always more moral and emotional than based on a scientific knowledge of the economics of imperialism, that it was essentially coloured by the radical and philanthropic traditions more than by the Marxist one.[47] The *Dreadnought* is a compelling exception. Its indictment of British imperialism was not limited to the traditional denunciation of military enterprises overseas, which ethical socialists and radical liberals alike had already formulated in the Late Victorian age. It opposed them above all as the expression of Britain's ambition to retain its hegemonic position in the global economy, i.e., from a materialist standpoint characteristic of Marxism, condemning the domination of British capital over the world, whether it took the shape of direct rule or informal influence. It was indeed keen to remind its readers that Britain's supremacy did not rest solely on military occupation and administrative control, but that its grip on foreign countries relied also, if not primarily, on invisible but profound economic influence – what has come to be known as 'informal imperialism'.

According to the weekly, nowhere was Britain's hold more hypocritically imposed than in China, a country that was not officially a colony, but which gunboats had opened by force to Indian opium.[48] Closer to home, the 1920 Overseas Credit Scheme – a governmental plan to support investments in Eastern Europe – was analysed by Pankhurst as a tool to contain the advance of communism.[49] The export of British capital to Argentina

[46] The cartoon, by Arthur ('Art') Young, was initially published on 15 May 1919 in *Good Morning*, a radical periodical printed in the United States.

[47] See also Bernard Porter, *Critics of Empire: British Radical Attitudes to Colonialism in Africa, 1895–1914* (London, 1968) and Gregory Claeys, *Imperial Sceptics: British Critics of Empire, 1850–1920* (Cambridge, 2010).

[48] Arthur Finch, 'The Destruction of China's Independence: A Tale of Shame', *WD*, 21 June 1919.

[49] *WD*, 24 Apr. 1920.

was similarly denounced as a means of subordinating a nation whose independence was nothing but formal.[50] Special emphasis was laid upon the fight for raw materials. Shapurji Saklatvala, who in 1922 was to become the first communist MP ever and the third ethnic Indian MP, devoted a whole page to 'the new competition in Africa, India and China' over access to coal and iron.[51] The race for oil in the Middle East, in Mesopotamia and Persia came under even closer scrutiny, as the *Dreadnought* foresaw the possibility of an imminent world war between Britain and the USA over the issue.[52]

However daring, the unravelling of the manoeuvres of British capitalists abroad and the focus on finance were not new in socialist literature. A more groundbreaking aspect of the paper's anti-imperialist propaganda was the link it drew between the oppression of colonised people overseas and the racist treatment of foreign workers, especially when they were perceived as 'coloured', in the metropole. That connection was made possible thanks to African American writer Claude McKay, who was invited by Pankhurst to tackle the colour question *ad libitum*, both as a black man and as a communist. Boisnard has explored his production for the *Dreadnought* in detail, underlining the force with which he addressed the unemployed dockers 'who (had) been negro-hunting' and 'stabbing Negroes in the London dock area'.[53] In a series of ten falsely naïve questions, he demonstrated that they were barking up at the wrong tree and playing into the hands of the capitalist class.[54] The use of ethnic differences by the employers to split the working class was a leitmotiv: 'The capitalists soon forgive each other their mistakes. It is we workers who keep on hating each other on account of race differences, nationality and colour!'. But he also expressed confidence in the future:

> The spirit of rebellion ... is now being fostered by all Negroes subject to British imperial rule. ... Socialism should step in to bridge the gulf that has been created between the white and coloured workers by Capitalism. ... For who knows when the storm will break? When rivers of blood will flow, bearing the souls of white and black workers into eternity?[55]

McKay was particularly shocked to see racial prejudice broadcast by the *Daily Herald* when George Lansbury's paper published a letter by E.D. Morel reproving the allegedly beastly sexual behaviour of black troops in Germany:

[50] *WD*, 1 Feb. 1919.
[51] *WD*, 14 Feb. 1920.
[52] *WD*, 21 Jan. 1922.
[53] Boisnard, 'Pankhurst'.
[54] *WD*, 7 June 1919.
[55] *WD*, 7 Feb. 1920.

> I write because I feel that the ultimate result of your propaganda will be further strife and blood-spilling between the whites and the many members of my race, boycotted economically and socially, who have been dumped down on the English docks since the ending of the European War.[56]

An unusual report sent from Liverpool in 1923 described a case of local black sailors being 'scabbed' by an all-white crew, a scenario contradicting the stereotype of the 'scabbing foreigner'.[57] It was the weekly's merit, in a delicate period when the state, the shipowners and the National Seamen and Firemen's Union (NSFU) all fuelled anti-alien sentiment, to repeat that 'seamen white, brown and black' had the same interests, and that 'the dockers, instead of being unduly concerned about the presence of their coloured fellow workers, who like themselves are the victims of Capitalism and Civilisation, should turn their attention to the huge stores of wealth along the waterfront'.[58] For the *Dreadnought* team, the fight against capitalism could not be won so long as white workers were blinded by racism. Any serious fight against imperialism had to begin at home.

A systemic denunciation of imperialism

British imperialism was always the *Dreadnought*'s favourite target, both because the British Empire was the largest, and because Pankhurst and her friends believed it was their duty to 'fight their own bourgeoisie'. Yet the paper's anti-imperialism embraced all empires, as it conceived of imperialism as a globally oppressive structure. For instance, when British authorities published a Blue Book on German atrocities in South West Africa, the paper did not deny that atrocities had taken place, but it insisted that the publication was a tactical move to justify a British mandate over the territory, and focused on the banality of German crimes:

> Cruelty towards the subjugated native has been used by some members of every European nationality that has colonised, or has imported the peoples of another type of civilisation as workers. Individual atrocities are certain to be perpetrated as soon as one race has power to dominate another.[59]

56 *WD*, 24 Apr. 1920.

57 *WD*, 12 May 1923.

58 Claude McKay, writing under the pen name Leon Lopez, 'The Yellow Peril and the Dockers', *WD*, 16 Oct. 1920. See Jacqueline Jenkinson, *Black 1919: Riots, Racism and Resistance in Imperial Britain* (Liverpool, 2009) and Laura Tabili, 'Review of *Black 1919: Riots, Racism and Resistance in Imperial Britain*' (www.history.ac.uk/reviews/review/840), accessed 11 Feb. 2016.

59 'Germans in South West Africa', *WD*, 21 Sept. 1918.

The violence used by the French and the Russian governments within their own imperial domains was also under accusation, the weekly refusing to consider Britain's allies as less nefarious than her rivals. Even Wilson's United States of America, in spite of their proclaimed anti-imperialism, came under the *Dreadnought*'s fire. 'Mexico, Haiti, San Domingo, Nicaragua and Panama have all something to say about the benevolence of America', the paper observed in a detailed review of US interventions south of the border.[60] 'The moral of all this is that the great capitalist Empires cannot safely be trusted with absolute power over alien populations': such was the *Dreadnought*'s guideline.[61]

Imperialism was attacked for the oppression each European bourgeoisie imposed on its own colonised peoples, and more generally for the chaos and destruction that the never-ending rivalries between superpowers had produced with the outbreak of the world war. 'This clash of European armies ... is the outcome of competition between the Powers for the possession of those territories inhabited by Eastern and African people', the paper stated, following the analysis defended by Lenin in his *Imperialism, the Highest Stage of Capitalism* (1916).[62] The *Dreadnought*'s propaganda, in line with the Comintern's theses, argued that the 1918 Armistice would soon be followed by another world war, opposing yesterday's allies, i.e., the declining British Empire to the rising American one. The potentially explosive competition for control over the seas was represented, in a cartoon entitled 'The Rift in the Loot', by the confrontation between a triumphant Uncle Sam, standing above a trunk overflowing with 'war profits', and a humiliated, sobbing 'Mrs Britannia'.[63] The control of oil fields in the Middle East was another sore point, and 'Blood for Oil' was a recurring nightmare in the paper's columns.[64] But a war provoked by the struggle for cotton, or even, more classically, for territorial conquests, was not excluded.[65] As early as 1919, the *Dreadnought* had printed a cartoon showing a 'rickshaw boy' – in fact a conscripted worker – pulling two heavy and smiling statesmen carrying the flag of 'Imperialism' in the direction of 'the next war'.[66]

[60] 'The Benevolence of America', *WD*, 13 Jan. 1923. The US government was also criticised for its repression of pacifists, syndicalists and communists. 'Letters from an American Communist', *WD*, 17 and 24 Jan. 1920; 'Under the Stars and Stripes', *WD*, 14 Apr. 1923.

[61] 'Lynch Law in Ceylon', *WD*, Dec. 1917.

[62] *WD*, undated clipping.

[63] *WD*, 18 Jan. 1919.

[64] 'Oil and Politics', *WD*, 21 Jan. 1922; 'Oil and the War Clouds', *WD*, 30 Sept. 1922; 'Oil and the Troubled Waters of the World', *WD*, 7 Aug. 1920.

[65] 'War Still Threatens', *WD*, 7 Oct. 1922; 'War Preparing – and Why: Cotton and the War Clouds', *WD*, 14 Oct. 1922.

[66] *WD*, 10 May 1919.

Rivalries but also collusions between rival powers were pinpointed – for example, the secret understandings the British government had signed before the war with Russia against India and the ones it had signed with Japan against China and Korea.[67] As for the League of Nations and its promotion of Wilsonian anti-imperialism, the *Dreadnought* rebuked it as a sham. The fact that it was promoted by South African General Smuts, notorious for his crushing of a general strike in 1913–1914, was one reason among others to mock it as 'the League of Capitalism'.[68] The mandate scheme, because it gave such obvious advantages to British and French interests, came under particularly critical scrutiny.[69] The nail in the coffin was a passionate poem by an Indian, rejecting the plundering of 'the backward blacks of half the world in the name of goodwill and peace on earth' that the League would allow.[70] Logically enough, Pankhurst did not take the International Labour Organisation (ILO)'s pretence to bring about fairer industrial relations around the world any more seriously. The ILO, like the League of Nations, she perceived as a camouflage for the winning powers' appetites. The *Dreadnought*'s critique of imperialism, British and otherwise, was therefore an original and wide-ranging one. Beyond the negative judgement on European and US domination, it also entailed a positive appreciation of all the struggles erupting in the colonies, be they led by women, nationalists or workers – three identities that often overlapped.

Solidarity with women's struggles in the colonies

The *Dreadnought*'s anti-imperialism was also original in the importance granted to gender. Admittedly, between 1917 and 1924, Pankhurst was, first and foremost, a communist, with workers' power as her compass, and her championing of the women's cause receded into the background.[71] But

[67] Arthur Finch, 'Criminals Behind the Scenes: The Fruits of the Anglo-Japanese Alliance', *WD*, 13 Nov. 1920. The disclosing of Russia's secret pre-war treaties by the Bolsheviks was emulated in Britain by the *Dreadnought* with the publication, on 9 Feb. 1918, of a supplement showing the projected arrangements on a world map.

[68] *WD*, 18 Jan. 1919. A few weeks later (*WD*, 29 Mar. 1919), a cartoonist invented the following dialogue between two stereotypical bosses: '(1) What do you think of the League of Nations? (2) Oh! "Capital," my boy, "Capital"!'.

[69] *WD*, 29 Mar. 1919. 'The Scandal of the Mandates: The League of Nations Exposed', *WD*, 26 June 1920.

[70] M.O. Abbassi, 'League of Nations', *WD*, 19 Apr. 1919.

[71] Davis contends that Pankhurst's call for household Soviets led by women reflected an acceptance of the sexual division of labour – a possible inheritance of syndicalism's gender-blindness. See 'The Liberation of Mothers and Socialisation of Houses', *WD*, 3 July 1920.

the *Dreadnought* did remain a woman's *Dreadnought*. Revealingly, the only picture illustrating the CP–BSTI's provisional programme on the paper's front page on 3 July 1920 was that of a woman with her newborn baby crying over the start of 'another war' – a sign that Pankhurst never jettisoned her feminist ideal. She was one of the rare female activists, alongside Clara Zetkin and Alexandra Kollontai, to combine socialism and feminism, and look at colonial questions with particular attention to women's plight.[72]

Several of the *Dreadnought*'s articles on India highlighted how the traditional oppression of women had not been alleviated but perpetuated by British domination. In a sceptical presentation of the Settlement Scheme supposed to put an end to the system of recruitment of indentured labourers from India in the tropics, the paper explained: 'The Indian woman is not yet a human being in the eye of the Government. … Women unaccompanied by their families will not be assisted', and regretted that India '(had) yet produced no suffragettes'.[73] On numerous occasions, the weekly denounced the violence inflicted by British troops upon Indian women because of their participation in protests against excessive taxes: the burning of a woman in Gujarat during the destruction of her village;[74] the beating and shooting of many others in Bundi during a punitive military operation.[75] The *Dreadnought* was careful not to portray women merely as victims but also as agents of change. In its coverage of the Egyptian revolt of 1919 against British rule, based on reports from *Le Populaire* and *L'Humanité*, their part in the rebellion was underlined: 'The women have even torn off their veils, broken the gratings of the harems, and gone out in the streets to demonstrate. In Cairo, 20,000 of them have joined the demonstrators'.[76] The importance granted to female agency in the field of politics could lead the weekly to surprising obliterations. When the Provisional Executive Committee for General Zionist Affairs sent the paper a letter explaining that there would be 'no need for "Votes-for-Women" campaigns in the new Jewish State that (was) to be established in Palestine', equal suffrage being accepted as 'a matter of course by the pioneers', the editors published it in full without any comments – ignoring the ways in which the Balfour Declaration penalised the Arab population and served the cause of British imperialism.[77]

[72] In different ways, so did Annie Besant and Ellen Wilkinson. See chapters by Terrier and Perry in this volume.

[73] '"Settlement" Scheme for Indians', *WD*, 3 Sept. 1917.

[74] 'A Massacre of a Peaceful People', *WD*, 20 May 1922.

[75] 'Rajputana States Letter', *WD*, 1 Sept. 1923.

[76] 'Egyptian Awakening', *WD*, 5 Apr. 1919.

[77] 'Woman Suffrage in Palestine', *WD*, 31 Aug. 1918.

To keep her readers informed about women's conditions around the British Empire, Pankhurst relied to a large extent on external sources but was occasionally capable of producing original reports thanks to her own transnational network. This is vividly illustrated by the article 'Women Workers in Limerick', based on interviews conducted by the *Dreadnought* correspondent with local lace and mattress workers, and hiding none of the disturbing truths: the precarious terms of employment, the lack of washing facilities, the absence of any woman factory inspector, the low level of wages, the bleeding fingers, underfeeding and premature ageing.[78] The report celebrated the women's moves towards the Irish Transport and General Workers' Union (IT&GWU), the very union Pankhurst had supported in 1914 against her family's advice, with no reference to the national oppression of the Irish. For the *Dreadnought*, economic exploitation always came before questions of nationality, although it did attempt more than other labour periodicals to tie those dimensions together.

The *Dreadnought* was able to provide its readers with news from Australia's female anti-imperialists thanks to Pankhurst's connection with an expatriate sharing her world vision: her younger sister Adela, who had emigrated from Britain in 1914 owing to discomfort with their mother Emmeline's and their elder sister Christabel's autocratic ways as well as with their rejection of the labour movement.[79] In Australia as in Britain, the anti-war minority grew louder after 1916. Its progress was reported in the columns of the *Dreadnought*, using *The Socialist* – the Victoria Socialist Party's official organ, published in Melbourne – as a complementary source of information.[80] What emerges from the reports is the importance of female mobilisation in the anti-war agitation, and Adela's leading role in it. Women were at the forefront, as keepers of the family budget unable to cope with the rising food prices. The Women's Peace Army (WPA) called for the Nationalist government to put an end to speculation by controlling the price of foodstuffs and distributing them to working-class families.[81] But Prime Minister Billy Hughes, who had succeeded Andrew Fisher in 1915, believed the mechanics of supply and demand should be left untouched.

[78] 'Women Workers of Limerick', *WD*, 24 May 1919.

[79] Adela shared Sylvia's socialist and feminist convictions, but not her antiracism: she embraced the White Australia policy advocated by the mainstream of the Australian labour movement, preaching a racialised and racist view of womanhood. See Joy Damousi, *Women Come Rally: Socialism, Communism and Gender in Australia, 1890–1955* (Melbourne, 1994).

[80] *The Socialist*, founded by Tom Mann during his stay in Australia, became a promoter of whiteness after his departure in 1909. See Neville Kirk, *Transnational Radicalism: The Connected Lives of Tom Mann and R.S. Ross* (Liverpool, 2016), especially Part III ('Womanhood, Whiteness and War', 179–252).

[81] *WD*, 16 Feb. 1918.

Besides, wartime legislation forbade demonstrations of more than twenty people. As a consequence, a series of massive protests in front of the Federal Parliament – one thousand women on 9 August and twice that figure a fortnight later – led to Adela being arrested, fined and sentenced to nine months' imprisonment.[82] The extensive agitation that followed, pioneered by the Australian Socialist Women's League (SWL), also found its place in the *Dreadnought*, which sided with the so-called 'seditionists and disloyalists' against the War Precautions Act.[83] After that movement, the weekly's articles about Australia focused on industrial topics rather than on women and imperialism, but still came under a female signature: A.W. for Adela Walsh, as Adela Pankhurst married a leader of the sailors' union, Tom Walsh, one of the founding members of the Communist Party of Australia (CPA) in 1920. Still a herald of women's emancipation, she devoted a full article to the CPA's position on prostitution.[84]

Informed coverage of women's conditions in South Africa was also made possible by the *Dreadnought*'s connections overseas, in this case through a male correspondent, W.H. Andrews, and a female one, Chris Barnet, two internationalists about to found the South African section of the Third International (CP–SASTI).[85] Both complained that 'the women's movement in South Africa' was virtually non-existent, that there was 'no sign of activity among Socialist or Labour women', and both agreed on the diagnosis. Because of the abundance of native workforce, most manual jobs, be it in agriculture, in the industry or in domestic service, were occupied by blacks, who weren't allowed to form trade unions, and the war had not caused the number of white women workers to soar. They tended to remain outside of the labour market and be 'more parasitic than in all-white communities', so that unions of women workers had never materialised. Even the suffrage movement was lagging behind its British counterpart: white women could not imagine asking for 'adult suffrage', as it would enfranchise the totality of African and Indian adults. But without the backing of black women, no mass movement comparable to the metropolitan one seemed possible.

[82] 'Coercion and Profiteering in Australia', *WD*, 24 Nov. 1917.

[83] The *Dreadnought* was surprisingly uncritical of one of the reasons given by Australian activists to protest the war: that it might lead to 'the white races ... being exterminated' (*WD*, 24 Aug. 1918). The only tangible sign that Sylvia disapproved of Adela's views was her refusal to reproduce her sister's numerous articles on 'Australia's colored problem'.

[84] *WD*, 26 Feb. 1921. Like Sylvia, Adela was to turn away from communism, but sooner and more sharply: in 1928, she founded the Australian Women's Guild of Empire; and during the Second World War, in the name of Australian nationalism, she advocated the severing of ties with Britain and the signing of a separate peace with the Japanese Empire.

[85] W.H. Andrews, 'South African Socialism and the War: Women Workers', *WD*, 16 Feb. 1918; Chris Barnet, 'The Women's Movement in South Africa', *WD*, 4 Jan. 1919.

On top of that, the voting rules varied from province to province, the Cape being socially rather than racially exclusive like Transvaal, further complicating the adoption of a common claim. On a humorous note that proved her disdain for so-called 'British civilisation', Barnet concluded: 'We are somewhat in advance of the Patagonians, but a long way behind the Eskimos'. More seriously, she added that a growing number of Dutch women ('woefully ignorant and easy of exploitation') were entering factories and that a female labour movement might emerge from that group.[86] As for Andrews, he concluded that 'the woman and the coloured problems will only be solved by … the social revolution. Organisation by women is no solution, nor is organisation by race. The organisation of the future must be organisation on *class* lines'. Although those were not Pankhurst's words, they aptly sum up her weekly's principles.

However essential the feminist strand, Pankhurst's loyalty to the cause of women did not make her tender towards female activists with whom she disagreed politically. The *Dreadnought*'s treatment of Annie Besant is a case in point.[87] Being one of the pillars of the Indian Home Rule Movement, she appeared often in the paper, but in reports that were mostly unflattering. In the aftermath of the Amritsar massacre, having explained that, faced with 'mob rule', the government of India was justified in using machine guns, she was denounced as 'a very strong Imperialist', supportive of 'British suzerainty'.[88] Such was also the judgement expressed on the weekly's first page a few weeks later, in a long article entitled 'Mrs. Besant, India and Labour'.[89] Besant's answer to the paper's accusations was published extensively but was immediately followed by Pankhurst's harsh comments: 'She was rather a rebel herself, once – in the days of long ago!' but 'it (was) useless to expect from her an enlightened regard for the oppressed Indian masses'. The attacks, crudely expressed, were not gratuitous: during the war, Besant had supported the recruitment of Indians into the British army and on the colonial question in India she was now a moderate in terms of both goals and means, believing that the connection with the British Crown should be preserved and that Gandhi's tactics were too provocative and created an atmosphere too favourable to Bolshevik propaganda not to be repressed. Whatever sympathy Pankhurst may have had for the Besant of the late 1880s, Besant's recent interventions in favour of the restoration of

86 That prognosis was later confirmed by the important role played by women in the 1922 rising on the Rand. See Jeremy Krikler, *White Rising: The 1922 Insurrection and Racial Killing in South Africa* (Manchester, 2005).

87 On Annie Besant's relation to India, see Terrier's chapter in this volume.

88 *WD*, 26 Apr. 1919.

89 *WD*, 28 June 1919. The quotations that follow are from the same article.

law and order both in the metropole and in India meant she could only be perceived by Pankhurst as a class enemy, 'a Tory', 'an individualist with a capitalist outlook', '(believing) in the caste system, the rule of the many by the few', not as someone entitled to speak out in the name of 'Indian Labour' and certainly not as a sister in arms.

A *Dreadnought* interview with Constance Markievicz, although far from being so negative, reveals the same prevalence of political convictions over female solidarity.[90] The Countess had much in common with Pankhurst: a childhood free of material hardship, an artistic training, early sympathy for the toiling masses soon translated into political involvement within the ranks of the labour movement, not to forget sustained pro-suffrage activism.[91] Yet the feminist question was quasi-absent from the interview, the only mention of women's specific experience being in relation to the physical and mental torture inflicted upon female Republican prisoners in the Irish Free State jails. The questions asked concentrated mostly on the fight between the Republicans, the side Markievicz belonged to, and the Treatyists, which she insisted were supported by the British state. Although the *Dreadnought* too sympathised with the ideal of a united Irish Republic and refused any legitimacy to the Free State institutions, it also underlined everything that Markievicz and Pankhurst did *not* have in common. As a Minister of Labour in the Irish government between April 1919 and January 1922, Markievicz 'had taken a part in damping down' industrial disputes, her role being 'to arbitrate between employers and employed in the interests of Irish unity'. And when asked about her views on communism, she answered that her model was also anti-capitalist, but based on 'the old Gaelic civilisation', a perspective which the *Dreadnought* dismissed as follows: 'In this we totally disagree with her', the only possible 'Workers' Republic' in Ireland would be 'a Communist Republic', or else 'the Irish Republic (would) be as far from Communism as the Republics of France, Germany or the United States'.[92] Here we touch upon another distinctive feature of the *Dreadnought*'s anti-imperialism: its refusal automatically to categorise the bourgeois enemies of British rule as friends of the colonial working class.

90 *WD*, 10 Mar. 1923. The quotations that follow are from the same article.

91 Markievicz's part in the 1913 Dublin lockout and the Easter Rising of 1916 inspired respect on the part of the *Dreadnought* team, as shown by the article published on its front page on 23 June 1917.

92 The year before, because Markievicz had rejected the Treaty partitioning Ireland, the *Dreadnought* had expressed a more laudative opinion, affirming that 'she alone repeated the 1916 slogans, saying that she stood for the Workers' Republic and the Co-operative Commonwealth'. *WD*, 14 Jan. 1922.

Critical support for Irish anti-colonialism

Beyond the systemic critique of imperialism and the attention paid to women's problems across the Empire, the variety of anti-colonialism defended by the *Dreadnought* was also characterised by its support for each and every struggle that weakened British domination. Logically enough, that support went to labour rebellions rocking the imperial boat but also, more problematically, to forces that situated themselves on the terrain of national rather than social emancipation. For that reason, the weekly's siding with what it termed 'bourgeois nationalists' was always complemented with warnings about their potential betrayals of colonial workers and calls for the necessity of independent class organisation. The unconditional support for any nationalist revolt defying British rule distinguished the *Dreadnought* from the imperial loyalism often expressed at the time by the Labour Party and the TUC. As for the critical outlook on nationalist leaders, it helped the paper not to fall into a pitfall that has been common on the left ever since the European empires started to decline: blind adherence to this or that anti-colonial leader, with little regard for how his policy affected the colonial proletariat. Having already analysed that positioning in a study of the *Dreadnought*'s coverage of South African affairs, I have chosen here to concentrate instead on its approach to the Irish question, which, in spite of all the contextual differences, was built on the same underlying assumptions.[93] To inform its readers about Ireland, the editorial team chose, as it did for South Africa, to publish articles signed by local activists rather than by the London headquarters.

Inspired by Marx, the *Dreadnought* considered the attitude towards the Irish question as a central criterion to judge British labour organisations' commitment to proletarian internationalism and to the cause of socialism. Refusing to take sides with those fighting for independence from the British tether was seen as a sign of complicity with the British ruling classes and their state. British workers needed to understand that 'British rule in Ireland (was) the cornerstone of their own house of bondage'.[94] 'Your Empire' is not yours, the paper insisted, but 'the Empire of Lloyd George and King George – for, of course, you are only workers in the Empire – you do not own any part of it'.[95] The paper was therefore extremely critical of the TUC, of the Labour Party, and of their past and present attitudes. In Easter 1916, there had been Labour Party ministers in the British government that had 'doomed James

[93] Yann Béliard, 'A "Labour War" in South Africa: The 1922 Rand Revolution in Sylvia Pankhurst's *Workers' Dreadnought*', *Labor History*, 57.1 (2016), 1–15.

[94] Captain White, 'Ireland, Marx and Internationalism', *WD*, 22 Mar. 1919.

[95] F. O'Brien, 'Patriotic Ireland: An Open Letter to British Trades Unionists', *WD*, 4 Dec. 1920.

Connolly to death', and they had not pronounced a word of protest.[96] More recently, at the very moment when an 'imperial rape of the Irish people' was being perpetrated, Arthur Henderson had declared that Ireland should not 'be lost to the British Empire'.[97] That continuity was proof enough, for Pankhurst and her companions, that the so-called Labour Party, 'fed, fat and contented', was in fact 'an Imperialist Labour Party', pretending to 'see a Socialist Empire looming in the future', when it was merely '(carrying) on the old game of imperialism'.[98] The party's avowed impotence in front of the Black and Tans' crimes, and later its acceptance of the Treaty dividing Ireland in two, were interpreted as further signs of that complicity.[99]

> On Imperial policy, which is the bedrock on which British governments are founded, the Labour Party is irreproachable from the Court and Capitalist standpoint. … The call for international class and Trade Union solidarity falls on deaf ears … when a question of Imperial etiquette is involved.[100]

The weekly showed no mercy on the Irish Labour Party either, as its 'Yellow Fakirs' refused to condemn a Treaty that mutilated the Irish nation.[101] Even the IT&GWU was criticised for its betrayal of its founding fathers' patriotism, as its call for a general strike 'for peace' on 24 April 1922 was an implicit condemnation of the Republicans.[102] The 'scabs' officially leading the Irish labour movement were 'endeavouring to keep clear from the Treaty controversy' when, like Jim Larkin from his prison in North America, they should have been 'repudiating the Treaty and all association with the British Empire, and declaring for a Workers' Republic'.[103] The only position acceptable for the *Dreadnought* was that of the Communist Party of Ireland (CPI): full support for independence and a categorical rejection of partition. In a daring reversal of British paternalism, an editorial even argued that 'English Labour must … learn of Ireland, imitate its zeal and take flame from its devotion'.[104]

[96] Joseph McDonnell, 'Why Irish Labour Demands National Independence', *WD*, 30 Mar. 1918.

[97] 'The Martyrdom of Ireland', *WD*, 9 Oct. 1920; 'Ireland: What It Calls Self-Determination', *WD*, 7 Feb. 1920.

[98] 'The Martyrdom of Ireland'.

[99] See also 'Policy of Communists and Labour Party', *WD*, 27 Nov. 1920. The Labour Party's scheme, Dominion Home Rule, was decried as 'pseudo-self-determination'. See also 'War with Ireland? Labour Party Support?', *WD*, 29 Oct. 1921.

[100] 'The Outlook after the Election: The Irish Executions', *WD*, 25 Nov. 1922.

[101] Wobbly, 'The Four Courts', *WD*, 29 Apr. 1922.

[102] Rank-and-Filer, 'The Irish Strike and Lock Out', *WD*, 13 May 1922.

[103] *WD*, 14 Jan. 1922.

[104] *WD*, 30 Mar. 1918.

Backing those who fought 'to be free of an Empire, to be free of the suzerainty of a King', however, could not be the final word.[105] Time and again the periodical explained that the replacement of British exploiters by Irish ones would bring no solution to the labouring majority: 'Political freedom for Ireland is all very well, but the worker must not be exposed to a system of despotic industrial control by an Irish Republic'.[106] Sinn Féin (SF) was characterised as a party representing 'small capitalists' and 'would-be capitalists', but neither Irish workers nor the landless peasants: 'The Sein Feiners are not fighting for a Workers' Republic, but an Irish Republic; they are not Red Guards but Green Guards'.[107] The *Dreadnought* used a South African comparison to identify the typical rural supporter of Irish nationalism, speaking of 'the back-veld type of Sinn Feiner', as opposed to the working-class Sinn Feiner.[108] The Irish Republican Army (IRA) did comprise a number of urban militants who, calling themselves Larkinites or Bolsheviks, saw an 'identity of aim and interest between genuine Irish nationalism and International Socialism'.[109] One of the *Dreadnought*'s major correspondents in Ireland, 'Wobbly' – a pen name indicating sympathy for if not affiliation to the Industrial Workers of the World (IWW) – went so far as to evoke 'a strong minority of reds' inside the IRA executive, and a situation that resembled 'the early stages of the Russian revolution', a judgement that Pankhurst, in an unusual display of internal dissension, allowed herself to call 'nonsense' in the comment she printed alongside the report.[110] Admittedly, the SF leadership's attitude towards labour claims was sometimes so tolerant that it could be assumed it would never turn against the workers. The situation was ambiguous enough for the *Dreadnought* to feel the need to ask the question: 'Will Sein Fein Go Red?'.[111] But its answer was a definite no, whatever branch of the nationalist movement the paper looked at. The Michael Collins fraction, at the head of the Free State, was not long in sending in troops to reclaim the factories for their legal owners in those numerous cases when workers' soviets had taken control.[112] Theirs was evidently 'an employers' Free State'.[113] As for Eamon De Valera, his 'Document 2' defended the principle of cooperation in terms so vague that it could hardly be taken for a socialist manifesto. For all its heroism, the

105 'Ireland Unfree', *WD*, 16 Dec. 1922.

106 J. O' Hagan, 'Irish Labourers and the Class Struggle', *WD*, 10 July 1920.

107 'Ireland and the Government', *WD*, 24 Apr. 1920.

108 White, 'Ireland, Marx and Internationalism'.

109 White, 'Ireland, Marx and Internationalism'.

110 *WD*, 29 Apr. 1922.

111 'The Martyrdom of Ireland'.

112 'The Soviets in Cork', *WD*, 18 Feb. 1922.

113 'No Freedom for Workers in the Irish Free State', *WD*, 21 Jan. 1922.

occasional protection given to working-class initiatives by the anti-Treaty faction was therefore analysed as circumstantial rather than ideologically motivated.[114] In 1922, the *Dreadnought* deplored that Connolly's Irish Citizens' Army (ICA), launched during the Dublin lockout of 1913, was severing its links with the labour movement to become a mere appendix of Republicanism.[115] To those readers tempted by Wobbly's optimism, the editors repeated: the 'bourgeois nationalists' would sooner or later try to 'efface the class struggle', as they were 'tactically as well as theoretically opposed to Communism'; 'the militant Nationalists are definitely opposed to working-class emancipation'.[116] The Republicans' rebuttal of CPI collaboration in the fight against the Treaty was another sign that the communists needed to 'sow their own seed' if they wanted the anti-imperial struggle to lead to a 'Red Republic'.[117]

'Mere Republicanism will not provide a change of system', declared Jim Larkin in an interview for the *Dreadnought* shortly after his release from US jails.[118] Sharing that point of view, the weekly tried to tell its readers about every working-class struggle in Ireland that went beyond nationalist aims. It noted that Ireland was 'seething with proletarian unrest' and hoped that 'the peasantry and proletariat of Ireland may turn Red to-morrow'.[119] This might have sounded too triumphal if so many collectivist experiences had not taken place. The seizure of workplaces by what the workers themselves called 'soviets' was not a rarity, occasionally leading to the takeover of a whole town and area.[120] Although power never remained for long in the soviets' hands, the experience, which did lead to economic advances, was deemed 'of inestimable value' and celebrated as the path British workers should follow.[121] 'The Irish Soviets are purely the work of the humble rank and file', the paper claimed, praising the Irish worker for being 'more consciously "Bolshevik" than many theorists'.[122] That was, to a certain extent, an exaggeration. They were maybe communists in practice, and certainly 'the deed (was) outstripping the word'.[123] But they were in general

114 'Workers' Control in Ireland', *WD*, 12 Aug. 1922.

115 Wobbly, 'The Four Courts'.

116 *WD*, 29 Apr. 1922.

117 'The Irish Revolution', *WD*, 4 Mar. 1922.

118 'An Interview with Jim Larkin', *WD*, 29 Mar. 1924.

119 'The Soviets in Cork'; 'The Martyrdom of Ireland'.

120 'The Truth about the Limerick Soviet', *WD*, 22 May 1919; 'Irish Workers Seize Thirteen Creameries', *WD*, 29 May 1920; 'A Tipperary Soviet', *WD*, 11 Mar. 1922.

121 'Boring from Within', *WD*, 18 Feb. 1922.

122 'Workers' Control in Ireland', *WD*, 12 Aug. 1922; O' Hagan, 'Irish Labourers and the Class Struggle'.

123 'Workers' Control in Ireland'.

not convinced of the doctrine to the point of joining the CPI, which, in spite of that wave of labour militancy, rapidly lost ground to the nationalist current. The *Dreadnought*, once Pankhurst was expelled from the CPGB, became increasingly critical of the CPI, calling its official programme 'a Fabian Scheme'.[124] Nonetheless, in its approach of Irish anti-colonialism, it remained faithful to its original Marxist view:

> To Communists, the question of Ireland's Independence is only important because the workers in an independent Ireland would be more free to learn that their real enemy is Capitalism, and because the break-up of the British Empire means the destruction of a great bulwark of the capitalist system.[125]

Labour in the Dominions, or paradise lost

What is remarkable about the *Dreadnought*'s coverage of events in Australia and New Zealand is how it contrasted with the vision of a 'workers' paradise' so prevalent in the labour press before the First World War.[126] The war, because it caused pressure to enforce conscription in Dominions that had once seemed more progressive than the Mother Country and free of Old World constraints, was indeed a turning-point in the state's relation to the labour movement. The weekly told its readers of the Illegal Associations Act that, in June 1919, allowed the Australian government to ban the IWW, deport those of its leaders born abroad, and thus prevent a general strike in Sydney.[127] Adela Walsh, née Pankhurst, noted the xenophobic propaganda used to attack the Seamen's Union leaders: they were accused of being 'imbibed with foreign notions' when they decided to launch a strike against conditions on Australian ships. She too highlighted the repression endured by labour activists, by her communist husband Tom Walsh in particular.[128] A report on the prolonged mining strike at Broken Hill in 1920 conveyed the same image of a country where life for the workers was far from free and easy, where the authorities and the employers were at least as inflexible as in the metropole.[129] According to the 'impressions on this particular part of the British Empire' sent by an anonymous correspondent, Australia was

124 'Communism v. Reforms: Mistakes of the Communist Party of Ireland', *WD*, 9 Sept. 1922.

125 'False Pretences Towards Ireland', *WD*, 3 Sept. 1921.

126 Neville Kirk, 'The Australian "Workingman's Paradise" in Comparative Perspective, 1890–1914', in *Comrades and Cousins: Globalization, Workers and Labour Movements in Britain, the USA and Australia from the 1880s to 1914* (London, 2003), 59–148.

127 'Australian News', *WD*, 21 June 1919.

128 Adela Walsh, 'The Australian Shipping Strike', *WD*, 18 Oct. 1919.

129 'The Class War in Australia', *WD*, 18 Sept. 1920.

a 'capitalist Eldorado' where the farmers lived 'under the heel of the Banks' and where the majority of Labour men sitting in the federal House were 'grafters of the first water', submitted to a Labour premier, Billy Hughes, who had just been 'presented with £27,000 last week for efforts in saving the Empire'.[130] An illustration of that devotion to British imperialism, the correspondent underlined, was the expulsion of Member of the Legislative Assembly (MLA) Mahon for his scourging of Britain's military intervention in Ireland.

As for nearby New Zealand, a land that, socially and politically, could also be perceived as more advanced than Britain prior to the war, another correspondent went so far as to describe it, 'from a militant working-class standpoint', as 'one of the worst (countries) in the world'.[131] The employers' attacks were frontal, he wrote; progressive literature was virtually banned. Speaking about the official Labour leaders, he explained: 'We used to call them "yellow" but I think they are pure white'. For, like most of their Australian counterparts, they had not tried to oppose the war, and had let down one of their representatives in Parliament, Patrick Webb, who had campaigned against conscription and been sentenced to months of hard labour for his disloyalty. A letter from John McDonald, the secretary of the Workers' Industrial Propaganda League (WIPL), painted so 'rotten' a picture of the social situation in his country that the conclusion was inevitable – 'emigration (was) no solution':

> Let the workers of the Old Dart stay where they are, and agitate, educate and organise for the betterment of their conditions and the overthrow and abolishment of the wage-system and capitalism, which is the cause of all the wrongs and miseries afflicting the workers, including the apparent necessity of emigration.[132]

All in all, the British Empire territories of the antipodes as they appeared in the pages of the *Dreadnought* were anything but a workers' haven.[133] And the imperialist war into which they had been plunged was blamed for the evils now affecting Australasian society, from influenza to unemployment and industrial strife.

Canada is a New Britain that figured less prominently than Australia and New Zealand in the columns of the *Dreadnought*, as the paper lacked

130 'Bolshevism in Western Australia', *WD*, 5 Feb. 1921.

131 'From New Zealand', *WD*, 8 Apr. 1922.

132 John McDonald, 'Open Letter to British Workers', *WD*, 16 Oct. 1920.

133 As denounced by the *Dreadnought* decades before it became a public scandal, it was not a paradise either for the dozens of poor British boys and girls sent there every year 'to develop the Empire', i.e. to work as 'indentured wage-slaves … alone and friendless … for unknown masters'. *WD*, 24 Feb. 1923.

permanent correspondents there. The shape taken by the social movements there owed little to the subordinate status of the country, and the longest articles devoted to the Canadian Dominion were a series of three comprehensive reports on the Winnipeg general strike of 1922, narrating the dispute from its start on 15 May until the defeat of the 'Winnipeg Soviet' at the end of June – reports from which the question of imperialism was virtually absent.[134] But the articles did enhance the part played by the Great War in the revolt, during which the demobilised soldiers formed a Parliament of their own and demonstrated in their thousands. Like in Australasia, the strike leaders were accused of being of foreign origin or under foreign influence, their supposed disloyalty to the Crown being pinpointed as their major crime.

Colonial workers as the revolutionary vanguard

For lack of local correspondents, the *Dreadnought* published a significantly smaller number of articles on Britain's crown colonies than on the Dominions and Ireland. Yet the place granted to workers' struggles in the Indian Empire and the territories under direct British rule was symbolically important. 'From all around the Empire comes news of revolt; only here in Britain a heavy apathy holds the oppressed masses', lamented the paper in early 1922.[135] A strike of several weeks in Hong Kong, involving seamen but also servants and bank employees, had just succeeded in obtaining an increase in wages, in spite of the British government's extreme response. The union headquarters had been raided, the labour leaders thrown into jail and their associations declared illegal. To break the strike, the authorities ('O benignant British rule!') had allowed the recourse to compulsory labour and released Chinese gangsters to intimidate the strikers.[136] The very severity of the reaction comforted Pankhurst and her comrades in seeing the labour movement in the Far East as possibly more vigorous and therefore more threatening than its European cousin for the stability of imperialist capitalism as a world system. 'Industrialism is spreading fast in the East, and bids fair to eclipse Western methods in the early future', the paper proclaimed a few months later, drawing the lessons from the movement.[137] The British seamen present in the harbour having accepted to be used as

[134] 'The Winnipeg Soviet. Part One', *WD*, 26 July 1919; 'The Winnipeg Soviet. Part Two', *WD*, 2 Aug. 1919; 'The Winnipeg Soviet. Part Three', *WD*, 9 Aug. 1919. The paper only mentioned in passing the most important female figurehead, Mrs Helen Armstrong.

[135] *WD*, 11 Mar. 1922.

[136] *WD*, 11 Mar. 1922.

[137] *WD*, 22 July 1922.

strike-breakers, it seemed the European trade unions were no longer showing the way, leading the *Dreadnought* to wonder: 'Why is the Anglo-Saxon race so lacking in solidarity?'.

Prior to the First World War, it seemed only natural for labour activists around the world to consider that the overthrow of capitalism and its replacement by socialism would begin in the countries that had been the first to undergo the industrial revolution, therefore in Europe and North America. The less industrialised parts of the world would eventually follow, if their case was considered at all. The Russian Revolution of 1905, and more importantly that of 1917, had challenged that vision, and showed that even in a land with 80 per cent of peasants, a highly concentrated working class could play an essential political role. The workers of a backward country could be at the vanguard – an observation generalised and theorised at the first Comintern congresses, and applied by the *Dreadnought* to the British colonies, in particular to 'the Jewel in the Crown'. In 1919, the weekly heralded 'Labour's awakening in India'.[138] It reported that 'amidst great difficulties workers and peasants' unions (were) being formed', unions capable of putting 100,000 mill hands out on strike in Bombay, despite the sending in of policemen and soldiers, capable, also, of organising their own type of soviet ('sabha' was the term used). 'Let the workers of Europe extend their assistance to the workers of India': the *Dreadnought*'s invitation to its readers reflected the paper's attachment to proletarian internationalism. But the lexical field of 'assistance', which still implied some form of Western or Northern superiority over the East and South, was seldom used, the stress being more and more on the colonial workers' own potential. The *Dreadnought* journalists also contended that the Indian working class, because it was present in the subcontinent but also in South Africa, Kenya, the West Indies and the metropole, was now a transnational force to be reckoned with.

When the *Dreadnought* incited the British worker to financial solidarity with Indian Labour, for example on the eve of the first All-India Trade Union Congress (AITUC) to be held on 22 August 1920, the argument of 'fraternal generosity' was balanced with that of 'self-defence'.[139] Donations would help Indian militants, of course, but more fundamentally they should be motivated by the sense that workers in India and the metropole shared common interests: 'The lower condition of Indian Labour is the future doom of the British workers', argued one article, citing J.E. Potter Wilson, the general secretary of the Workers' Welfare League of India. The AITUC would be led by Annie Besant, who was not exactly a *Dreadnought* favourite,

138 *WD*, 1 Feb. 1919.

139 *WD*, 14 Aug. 1920.

and the weekly had already denounced some Indian leaders on the railways as spineless negotiators. Still, the weekly felt it could only encourage the creation of a body representing hundreds of thousands of so far barely organised workers. Two articles published in 1920 reflected the *Dreadnought*'s confidence in India as a springboard for the international socialist revolution. In 'India and Bolshevism', a local correspondent compared the social structure of India with that of pre-revolutionary Russia, and concluded that, in Asia, India was 'the (country) most prepared for Socialism'. Using an argument that was borrowed from the populists rather than from the Bolsheviks, he described the traditional village structures as 'akin to Sovietism'. More in line with the teachings of Marx, he mocked those who saw Lenin's hand behind all acts of rebellion great and small, when 'Bolshevism (would) be quietly brought into India ... by British exploiters' themselves. Equally optimistic was M.N. Roy's editorial, 'Proletarian Revolution in India'.[140] In an epic evocation of the 1857 and 1873 revolts up to the present 'unprecedented series of strikes', the Indian communist defended the idea that 'bourgeois democrats' in India were 'insignificant' compared to the masses of 'disinherited toilers', so that, 'even if the first stage of the Revolution in India (was) fought under a nationalist banner ... the revolutionary ferment in India (was) bound to express itself through a proletarian mass movement, which (would) put an end to class rule under any form, and usher the Communist State'. The 1947 scenario was quite different. But it is revealing of the *Dreadnought*'s positive appreciation of the colonial labour movement that it should have printed such hopeful prose on its first page. The publication of the Indian strike statistics for years 1921 to 1923 could only reinforce the readers' impression that something grand was brewing in the East, that labour protests against British imperialism in India could play the same role the October Revolution had played in pushing forward a global upsurge against capitalism.[141]

For all the attention paid to anti-colonial revolts in Ireland, India and elsewhere, for all the sympathy expressed towards them, the *Dreadnought* showed no traces of what would later be called 'third-worldism'. Pankhurst is known for having embraced the cause of Ethiopian independence, for her protests in the 1930s against the Italian invasion and against British plans to turn the country into a protectorate. After Corio's death in 1956, she even moved to Ethiopia where, due to her support for Emperor Haile Selassie's regime, she was granted a state funeral on 27 September 1960 and was buried. But of that late adhesion to bourgeois nationalism, one

[140] *WD*, 11 Sept. 1920. On M.N. Roy's links with Russian and British communists, see chapter by Owen in this volume.

[141] 'Indian News', *WD*, 28 July 1923.

finds no harbingers in the pages of the *Dreadnought.* Some have sneered at the apparent lack of intellectual coherence that this demonstrates. But this chapter merely wishes to underline the coherence that did prevail between 1917 and 1924 in the *Dreadnought*'s analysis of bourgeois anti-colonialism. Leaders such as Gandhi or De Valera were treated with little indulgence, as men to be supported in their duel with the British Empire, but in the long run not worthy of the workers' confidence.[142] In her challenge of imperialism, Pankhurst made sure that her followers would not automatically consider the Empire's enemies as their comrades.

Conclusion

According to John Callaghan, it was inadequate access to information about the colonies that limited awareness of imperialism in the metropole. If it was indeed ignorance that fuelled 'popular imperialism', then the *Workers' Dreadnought* can be said to have provided a precious alternative to the sanitised views of the Empire still prevailing at the end of the First World War. Of course, communism having been described as the longest footnote in modern British history, it would be easy to discard Pankhurst's publication as merely a footnote in the footnote, and easier still to argue that, in the process leading to the liquidation of the British Empire, the part played by the *Dreadnought* was minute. It is nonetheless a periodical that deserves to be rescued from oblivion – because it brought to thousands of working-class readers, whether male or female, whether metropolitan or colonial, news from the Empire they could not have been aware of otherwise; and because it offered a critique of British imperialism at once fierce and sophisticated, incorporating feminist preoccupations and warnings against bourgeois nationalism in the colonies. The *Dreadnought*'s anti-colonial objectives came fifth in a list of six 'principal aims' introducing its 'Provisional Resolutions Towards a Programme' for the foundation of a Communist Party in Great Britain:

> The breaking-up of all empires, since these are instruments of capitalist oppression and exploitation, and the establishment of a world federation of Communist republics, and the consequent abolition of all racial and national barriers. Whoever lives and works in a Soviet republic is entitled to all the rights of citizenship.[143]

That perspective, diverging widely from the dominant ideology, was surely a minority one. Representing John Bull as a 'champion baby killer' and

[142] Irish and Indian nationalism were often studied in connection with each other. See 'India Going Sinn Fein', *WD*, 7 Jan. 1922.
[143] *WD*, 3 July 1920.

a 'holder of world records' in the sport of mass massacre was not the mainstream vision of the day.[144] Neither was the argument that 'the great empires will be disintegrated and the bursting forth of the small nationalities will hasten the world's progress to the eventual Socialist confederation of all peoples'.[145] That language placed the paper at odds with the Labour Party and the TUC leaderships, which in September 1914 had agreed, like the mainstream suffragettes, not to disturb the war effort, and later participated in the recruitment campaign.[146] Yet the *Dreadnought* did have an impact, and a legacy.

With the global rise in labour militancy that followed the wartime strikes, the soldiers' mutinies and the October Revolution, the weekly reflected, especially in the first half of its brief existence, the preoccupations of many a rank-and-file worker, in one of those exceptional moments when social protest in the metropole and overseas seemed to be converging. Admittedly, the space devoted to imperial questions in the *Dreadnought*'s pages diminished over the years. In 1923 and 1924, anyone in search of information about social movements in the Empire was more likely to find it in the *Workers' Weekly*, the official organ of the CPGB, as it now benefited from the Comintern's global network, while Pankhurst's milieu was shrivelling.[147] But that does not mean that the *Dreadnought*, in its most dynamic phase, was not an inspiration for the rest of the revolutionary press, be it *Plebs* or other periodicals more directly related to the CPGB, such as the *Communist Review* or the *Labour Monthly*. Indeed, as noted by Mary Davis, the *Dreadnought* was 'refreshingly unsectarian' and 'distinguished itself by its verve, openness and internationalism'.[148] Few activists outside of the WSF circles explicitly admitted being intellectually indebted to Pankhurst.[149] The fact that Pankhurst chose to adhere to the Labour Party in 1948, while one of the major reasons for her split with the CP had been

[144] *WD*, 8 Nov. 1919.

[145] Pankhurst, 'Empire and Nationality', *WD*, 1 June 1918. The second half of that article is an enthusiastic summary of Trotsky's pamphlet *War or Revolution*.

[146] The *Dreadnought*'s reports on the post-war Labour Party gatherings (29 June 1918 and 23 Nov. 1918) and TUC conferences (20 Sept. 1919 and 20 Dec. 1919) were highly critical.

[147] Printed from 10 Feb. 1923 until 1927, the *Workers' Weekly* reached a circulation of 50,000 copies per week, a level never attained by the *Dreadnought*. It was the continuation of *The Communist* (the weekly published by the CPGB from 29 July 1920 until June 1923), which was itself the successor of *The Call*, the weekly edited from 24 Feb. 1916 by the internationalist BSPers who had refused Hyndman's nationalistic course.

[148] Davis, *Pankhurst*, 58.

[149] Pankhurst's arrogance is paramount in accounting for that lack of recognition. The Special Branch agents keeping an eye on her were not so mistaken when they reported: 'Miss Sylvia Pankhurst wants her own way'; 'No one has yet succeeded in working amicably with Sylvia Pankhurst'. 'Sylvia Pankhurst record file (1921–1938)', TNA, PRO, MEPO, 38/36.

her refusal to join Labour, did not help. But she was interested in and critical of the British Empire before many others and her anti-colonial views were to become commonplace on the left, inside the CPGB as well as inside the ILP.[150]

If only for that reason, it is hard to disagree with June Hannam's judgement that 'Sylvia Pankhurst made an important contribution in her own right to radical politics during the twentieth century' and it is hoped that this chapter has confirmed that 'her lengthy involvement in political life deserves serious consideration'.[151] Further explorations of Pankhurst's anti-colonialism would need to look at her copious correspondence, the many books she published on related topics and her work as the editor of the *New Times and Ethiopian News* from 1936 to 1956, and of the *Ethiopian Observer* from 1956 until her death in 1960.[152] How similar or how different her later anti-colonialism was from her views during the *Dreadnought* years is a question that still requires in-depth study.

[150] That was true for about a decade, until 1935, when they embraced 'popular front' politics and chose to play down, if not to ditch, the anti-colonial theme.

[151] Hannam, 'Pankhurst', *ODNB*. Such serious consideration has been confirmed recently. The Sylvia Pankhurst Memorial Committee is running a campaign to raise a statue in her honour and Rachel Holmes has just published a truly monumental biography (*Sylvia Pankhurst: Natural Born Rebel*, London, 2020).

[152] The International Institute of Social History (IISH) in Amsterdam and the Women's Library in London both hold sizeable collections of her letters.

3

Alliances from Above and Below

The Failures and Successes of Communist Anti-Imperialism in India, 1920–1934

Nicholas Owen

The theme of this book is the part played by 'working people' in the decolonisation of the British Empire. The primary theme of this chapter concerns the campaigning of the Communist Party of Great Britain (CPGB) and its attempt to recruit British workers in solidarity with the Indian struggle. India is chosen because it was the dominant imperial question of the interwar period. It was the location, with Egypt and Ireland, of a triple crisis of empire towards the end of the First World War: a crisis which, unlike the other two, was not stabilised but continued to erupt for the next thirty years until independence was achieved in 1947. The Communists are chosen because they made the most significant attempt to organise a popular anti-imperialism in interwar Britain. Like all attempts to recruit the British public for anti-imperialism, however, the Communists' effort was a mixed success, never really achieving the mass support they sought. Close study of its successes and failures might therefore help us in defining the forms and limits of popular anti-imperialism.

In doing this, we need to distinguish between three possible obstacles to a mass anti-imperialism in Britain. First, we must examine the problem presented by *compromising interests* – the possibility that certain sections of British industry were so reliant on imperial trade that their workforces could not afford the loss of empire and were consequently hostile to campaigns that undermined it. Secondly, there is the problem of *low salience* – the possibility that levels of public interest in imperial matters were so low that there was no scope for significant metropolitan campaigns of anti-imperialist solidarity. Thirdly, we should consider the problem of *poor political articulation* – that neither interests nor public attitudes were insuperable obstacles to such campaigns, but that their potential was badly handled by political leaders.

Economic interests were *indeterminate*: that is, they had no single, directional implication for the recruitment of British workers for anti-imperialism. A good example is the recession-hit cotton industry, threatened by both the Gandhian boycott of cotton and the emergence of competition from low-wage Indian mills. The cotton workers' problem was the impossibility of knowing for sure what would be gained, and what lost, were India to achieve self-government.[1] Their unions accordingly favoured neither the use of imperial power to refuse protection to the Indian market nor the transfer of industrial policy to Indian hands before the franchise was widened and trade unionism was stronger. Rather, they favoured the ending of the cotton boycott and higher wages and strengthened trade unionism in the Indian mills, by *whichever political means* were more effective. This made them potential allies of Congress campaigns for self-government, if they promised to end the boycott, protect the unions, improve wages and conditions and restore – or better yet develop – the Indian market for British exports. On the other hand, the very same considerations made the unions fearful that too early a concession of self-government would merely reward the unregulated Indian millowners who paid for Congress campaigns at the expense of both their Indian workforces and British jobs. So there was scope for going slow too. In other words, the interests at stake were significant, but also inconclusive in their political effect on campaigns.

The same can be said of low salience. From Bernard Porter's work we know that imperial planners had consciously avoided stimulating the interest of working-class Britons in imperial matters.[2] Levels of popular ignorance of the facts of empire were legendary. But ignorance did not necessarily demobilise. As any student of contemporary opinion on questions such as the European Union or immigration knows, ignorance of the facts is no impediment to strong feeling and political mobilisation. It was possible to rally the public, but only by starting where they started, in a position of considerable ignorance, but with feelings about what was acceptable, and identities and self-perceptions which could be engaged in support of (or opposition to) what their co-nationals did. These *might* – again, the indeterminacy is important – form the basis for campaigning, if they were framed in the right way. By the same token, even if low salience ruled out *mass* popular campaigns, it did not rule out more restricted campaigns of solidarity. These could thrive in conditions of apathy, if only because the apathetic lacked the energy to oppose them, provided that they were neither expensive nor problematic for issues of greater salience.

In short, this left the heavy lifting to the political entrepreneurs, and to parties like the British Communists. It was their task to *articulate* anti-imperialism:

[1] Nicholas Owen, *The British Left and India: Metropolitan Anti-Imperialism, 1885–1947* (Oxford, 2007), 4–5, 152–58, 184–89.

[2] Bernard Porter, *The Absent-Minded Imperialists: Empire, Society and Culture in Britain* (Oxford, 2004), 194–226.

to frame it in ways which meshed with economic interests, resonated with existing sets of beliefs and feelings and also fitted with the other priorities of their movement. Like the support offered by other metropolitan parties and movements, the support of the CPGB for anti-imperialism was therefore indirect and conditional. But this does not mean its anti-imperialism was necessarily weak. Practically all interwar metropolitan anti-imperialism was like this. Almost no one was an anti-imperialist first and foremost, but only when (and only if) anti-imperialism spoke in some way to other values and primary loyalties they held. What mattered was the closeness of fit between these primary objectives and the anti-imperialism.

To complicate matters further, there were, in the period I examine here, four significant sets of political actors: (1) the Communist International; (2) the Indian émigré revolutionary groups directed by – or in rivalry with – the Bengali revolutionary M.N. Roy, to whom Comintern initially assigned its Indian work; (3) the Communist Party of India (CPI) founded by Roy in October 1920; and (4) the CPGB itself, which was given, first informal, and from 1925 to 1934, formal, responsibility for Communist work in India. We also have to consider other actors not under Communist control but with whom these four wished or were obliged to work. In India, these included nationalist movements such as the Indian National Congress, as well as peasant and labour struggles. In Britain, they included the trade unions, the other parties of the left and the various groups of resident Indians, especially merchant marine sailors and Indian students. Internationally, they included international bodies such as the Red Trade Union International (RILU), the League Against Imperialism (LAI) and further groups of expatriate Indian nationalists and anti-imperialists. Communist anti-imperialism, in short, was not a single unified movement, but took a reticulated form as a transnational agitational network.

Roy and the Comintern

The support international Communism might offer the Indian anti-imperialist movement was first fully discussed at the Second Congress of Comintern in July 1920, which was attended by Roy.[3] The main question was what attitude to take to the newly militant Gandhian Congress. Should Communists lend support to Congress on minimal conditions, as a means of undermining Britain, with Communism itself held over for a later struggle? Should they try

3 See Comintern, *Workers of the World and Oppressed Peoples, Unite! Proceedings and Documents of the Second Congress, 1920*, ed. John Riddell (London, 1991); John P. Haithcox, *Communism and Nationalism in India: M.N. Roy and Comintern Policy, 1920–1939* (Princeton, NJ, 1971), 11–19.

and take over Congress, and if so, should they undermine its leadership 'from below', by organising mass movements of workers and peasants, or 'from above', by persuading elements of the existing leadership to come across? Or should they denounce Congress altogether and build their own independent revolutionary movement? Lenin had argued in *Imperialism, the Highest Stage of Capitalism* (1917) that super-profits of imperial trade made it possible for the bourgeoisie to bribe the upper strata of the proletariat and thereby to foster the success of reformist social democratic parties. Revolution in the imperial states might therefore be assisted by giving support to movements in the colonies which sought to break the imperialists' grasp on them, even if they were bourgeois-democratic movements and not revolutionary ones.[4] In 'backward Europe', Lenin had written in 1913, the bourgeoisie resisted social progress, allying itself to all that was 'outdated, moribund and medieval', while in 'advanced Asia' it stood at the head of a 'mighty democratic movement [in which] … hundreds of millions of people were awakening into life, light and freedom'.[5] Lenin's own original draft theses for the Second Congress therefore argued for the obligation for Comintern to support bourgeois-democratic liberation movements, provided that the embryonic forms of future proletarian movements were not thereby aborted.[6]

Roy, however, had different aims: first, to persuade Comintern to take India seriously; and secondly, to ensure that it did not uncritically back Congress. He tried to achieve the first aim by an exaggerated argument that European capitalism now rested mainly on its colonies, and that, as a consequence, revolution in Europe depended upon a prior colonial revolt. Lenin and Comintern rejected this, forcing Roy to water down his claim such that it stated merely that colonialism provided one source of capitalist strength, and that only in combination with a proletarian revolution in the capitalist homelands could colonial revolt topple capitalism. However, in his second aim, Roy was more successful. He argued that although the cooperation of the bourgeois-democratic movements might be temporarily useful, it and the revolutionary movement represented 'contradictory forces'. Wartime industrialisation and repression had created a class-conscious Indian proletariat five million strong, with a further thirty-seven million landless peasants whose growing unrest might be harnessed for revolutionary purposes. Cooperation with Congress, therefore, should be only temporary, and designed to create space for the development of an independent movement of workers and

[4] V.I. Lenin, *Imperialism, the Highest Stage of Capitalism* (1917), in V.I. Lenin, *Collected Works*, 47 vols (Moscow and London, 1960–1980), xxii. 185–304.

[5] V.I. Lenin, 'Backward Europe and Advanced Asia' (1913), in *Collected Works*, xix. 99–100.

[6] Lenin's original and amended 'Theses on the National and Colonial Questions' (1920) are in Riddell, *Workers*, 211–16, 283–90.

peasants. Otherwise Congress would use workers and peasants to force the British out, but thereafter turn on them. The failure to organise separately from the start would then prove costly. The Comintern did not fully accept this position and insisted on strengthening the commitment to work with bourgeois-democratic movements in the short term. But it agreed with Roy that the 'foremost and necessary task' was an independent one: the organisation of the peasants and workers for Communism.[7]

A further decision of the Second Congress was to organise and fund this anti-imperialist activity, not directly, which would have been exceedingly difficult, given Congress distrust of Russian Bolshevism and the defensive strength of the British authorities, but through the intermediary of Indian émigré groups, who claimed to possess the necessary contacts. This, however, forced Communist anti-imperialism through the choked and twisted channels of émigré politics. The war had not been kind to the émigrés. Cut off from directly influencing the struggle in India, they had fought instead for the only means of indirect influence: the patronage of their hosts. Émigré politics was characterised by bitter factional rivalries over these thin spoils, which were readily worked upon by the secret police of the various European capitals. Long years of this dispiriting work had lowered the ambitions of most of the émigré groups, which had by 1918 largely given up hopes of influencing events in India itself, and were absorbed instead in the struggle for a purely local recognition and the raising of their standing within the wider expatriate community.

Into this small, poor world, the sudden irruption of Bolshevik interest and money came as a disturbing opportunity, promising to transform a group's prospects at a stroke. There were several rival groupings to consider. Moscow's first instinct was to fund Chattopadhyaya's longstanding group of revolutionaries in Berlin, with their superior connections to India. Contra Roy, Chatto doubted the prospects for Communism in India. Despite growing proletarianisation, India remained an overwhelmingly agricultural society in which lines of class were overlain by significant caste and religious divisions. Chatto proposed conditional support of Congress as the quickest means of destroying British imperialism. This, rather than social revolution, should be the 'first charge on the Communist International'.[8] There was also

[7] For Roy's draft theses and the Commission's amendments to them, see Riddell, *Workers*, 218–24, 846–53, 865–69.

[8] Russian State Archive of Socio-Political History, Moscow (hereafter RGASPI) 495/68/37, Berlin Group, 'Theses on India and the World Revolution', 1921. See also 'Organization and Scheme of Indian Work', 1921, same file, and RGASPI 495/68/64, Bhupendranath Datta, 'The statement and memorandum in regard to the works to be carried on in India', 1921.

a 'Tashkent' group of revolutionaries, consisting of *mujahirs* who had worked as part of a German plot to destabilise British rule in India during the war, and had allied with revolutionary Communists in 1919. Its programme was Pan-Islamist and nationalistic in orientation, although it shared the Berlin group's pessimism concerning Roy's 'left communism' as inappropriate for an India in which labour organisation was new and weak.[9]

Roy saw off these rivals less because of his ultra-left strategy, which remained controversial, but because of his demonstration of total loyalty to Comintern and his commitment to disciplined party organisation. He had already enjoyed the benefits of this strategy in 1919 when the patronage of the Bolshevik emissary to Mexico, Michael Borodin, had enabled him to gain valuable Bolshevik recognition for his own Mexican Communist Party – an affair of some six members – over its larger rival. Roy persuaded the Bolsheviks that Chatto's group were nationalist rather than revolutionary, an impression reinforced by Comintern's own investigations.[10] '[I]ntellectual anarchism is the predominant characteristic of the Indian emigrants', Roy told Comintern. 'Discipline is a thing absolutely unknown to them'.[11] Once his own position was secure, Roy felt confident enough to invite the Berlin group to join his own, and to use their refusal as further evidence of their lack of commitment.[12] The 'Tashkent' group were also criticised by Roy for their Pan-Islamism and indiscipline. The implications of Pan-Islamism for Soviet control elsewhere, and the *muhajirs*' plans to destabilise India's northern frontiers, which were diplomatically embarrassing while the Soviet Union was negotiating a trade treaty with Britain, pushed them out of Comintern calculations by the end of 1921. Although at the Third Congress in July of that year, India was relegated in importance, Roy was at least in charge of it.[13]

[9] RGASPI 495/68/45, Acharya to Comintern Secretariat, 30 Aug. 1921; RGASPI 495/68/31, Abdur Rabb Barq to Chicherin, 29 July 1921.

[10] Gene D. Overstreet and Marshall Windmiller, *Communism in India* (Berkeley, CA, 1959), 31–34, 36–37; Nirode K. Barooah, *Chatto: The Life and Times of an Indian Anti-Imperialist in Europe* (New Delhi, 2004), 158–60; National Archives of India, New Delhi (hereafter NAI), Home-Political Proceedings, Deposit Series, June 1921, no. 54, Report of Director, Intelligence Bureau, Government of India (hereafter DIB Report), n.d.; RGASPI 495/68/5, Roy to Horner, 2 Apr. 1921.

[11] RGASPI 495/68/69, Roy to Eastern Secretariat, 20 July [1921?].

[12] RGASPI 495/68/37, 'Report about Indian National Group in Moscow', [1921?].

[13] 'Extracts from the Resolution of the Third Comintern Congress on the Report of the Executive Committee, 29 June 1921, in Jane Degras (ed.), *The Communist International, 1919–1943: Documents*, 3 vols (London, 1956–1965) (hereafter Degras, *Comintern*), i. 226–29.

The CPI and Roy

However, the effort to build an effective revolutionary movement in India through émigrés proved very difficult. Although the Bolsheviks had money to spend, they had almost no way of controlling what was done with it. In Bengal, Roy relied upon his surviving contacts in the pre-war revolutionary movement, but elsewhere he had never met most of the people he was forced to use as agents. While they were happy to take his money to rebuild their own revolutionary organisations, many were unpersuaded by Roy's new faith in Communism.[14] Most of the sums provided by Comintern went on propaganda and newspapers rather than the direct organisation of workers and peasants.[15] Some of it went on facilities that would have been hard to defend to Comintern: in one case, a new house.[16] When a British Communist visited secretly in 1925, Roy's agents refused to meet him partly because they feared that he had been sent by Comintern to check on the misuse of funds.[17]

Furthermore, although Roy formally accepted the need to engage with Congress, his approaches were perfunctory and designed to expose its failings to Comintern as the prelude towards building his own independent mass party. 'To revive the Congress is an almost hopeless task', he wrote privately in December 1922. 'It appears to be politically dead'.[18] However, it was slow work to persuade Congress supporters to abandon Gandhian non-violence in favour of Communism. Some of Roy's allies therefore tried to define an Indian form of Communism, which Roy regarded as hopelessly parochial.[19] 'I am suspicious of the type of labour organisers that clamour for funds and decry revolutionary literature as … useless [and] … even denounce it as "outside interference". … You need political direction from the leaders of the world movement much more urgently than funds', he told them.[20] Singaravelu's response to Comintern discipline, Roy complained to the more

[14] Haithcox, *Communism*, 29; British Library, Oriental and India Office Collection (OIOC), Indian Political Intelligence Records (hereafter IPI), L/PJ/12/47, DIB Report, 7 Mar. 1923; IPI, L/PJ/12/48, DIB Report, 10 June 1923.

[15] IPI, L/PJ/12/47, Report of Indian Political Intelligence (hereafter IPI Report), 11 and 21 Nov. 1922; 10 May 1923.

[16] Sir Cecil Kaye, *Communism in India* (New Delhi, 1925; repr. Calcutta, 1971), 12–13; Philip Spratt, *Blowing Up India: Reminiscences and Reflections of a Former Comintern Emissary* (Calcutta, 1955), 34.

[17] Sir David Petrie, *Communism in India, 1924–27* (New Delhi, 1927; repr. Calcutta, 1972), 96; IPI, L/PJ/12/246, IPI Report, n.d.

[18] IPI, L/PJ/12/140, Roy to Singaravelu, 12 Nov. 1922.

[19] Overstreet and Windmiller, *Communism*, 55–58, 77–81, 89.

[20] IPI, L/PJ/12/48, Roy to Shamsuddin Hassan, [1923?], DIB Report, 31 Oct. 1923.

loyal Dange, was 'we know everything, let us alone ... give us help and keep your mouth shut'.[21] Roy's efforts to get literature into India and to organise a rival party to Congress were also hampered by the penetration of his new organisation by the British intelligence machine, improved during the war, and now adapted to combat Bolshevik efforts.[22] With the ports and passes carefully watched, it was hard to get agents into India. All those who had been trained in Tashkent and Moscow were picked up as they arrived and his correspondents were kept under surveillance. As a result, by the end of 1923, nearly all Roy's agents were under arrest. They were tried and convicted at Pesahawar in 1923 and Kanpur in 1924.

This swift collapse casts light on the nature and problems of the networked structures of anti-imperialism, discussed elsewhere in this book.[23] In much contemporary thinking, networks are a sign of strength. Their advantage is that they are resilient in the face of attack. Activities and resources can be relocated when the network comes under pressure. But it is easy to miss their vulnerability. The network relies on activists knowing which nodes and which parts of the network are compromised. If they do not, the network's integrity is only as strong as each of its nodes. It can be destroyed through the opening provided by a single weakness. The very same imperial and global structures and opportunities which permitted the networking of the anti-imperialists were also those through which information and activity flowed to *counter and disrupt* them. Indeed, in this instance at least, the more networked the anti-imperialism was, the more easily it was to penetrate it, because the connections made it easier to track subversive activity from one location to the next. As it had been for the Ghadr, the Communists' networked structure was both strength and weakness. At times, it enabled anti-imperialists to support each other, elude capture, and so forth; but it also permitted the network's opponents to make the connections needed to arrest large numbers of anti-imperialists and prosecute them in mass 'conspiracy' trials. Without the conspiratorial evidence the network itself had produced it would have been impossible to connect them all together.

At the Fifth Comintern Congress in 1924, the mood was therefore more sober. Revolution in Germany having failed, Comintern was now prepared to put more efforts into its eastern work. '[A]mple funds', Roy wrote to his wife, 'would now be available'.[24] But Roy's organisation was evidently

[21] IPI, L/PJ/12/48, DIB Report, 7 Nov. 1923.

[22] Richard Popplewell, *Intelligence and Imperial Defence: British Intelligence and the Defence of the Indian Empire, 1904–1924* (London, 1995), 306–17.

[23] See, in particular, chapters by Gasteuil and Smith in this volume.

[24] IPI, L/PJ/12/49, IPI Report, 23 Apr. 1924 and Secret Intelligence Service, Northern Summary, 13 May 1924.

not ready to receive fresh aid, so Comintern insisted on closer contact with the nationalist movement. Worse still for Roy, it decreed that direct contact should be made between the British Communists and the Indian movement.[25]

The Comintern and the CPGB

The involvement of the CPGB was partly intended by Comintern to provide some of the reliability and professionalism that Roy and his agents had been unable to supply. The CPGB's metropolitan location, as a primary node in the network, made it the best place from which to attack the empire. But no less importantly, the CPGB's involvement would also recruit resources within Britain for anti-imperialism. True, the CPGB's early output on colonial questions had been characterised by moral or humanitarian rather than Marxist criticism, and muddle on the crucial question of whether British workers gained or lost from empire.[26] But by 1924 the Communists had developed a more scientific analysis which located imperialism as the basis of capitalism in its current stage and were therefore able to place the colonised and British workers in a single interpretative frame.[27]

The CPGB also brought metropolitan anti-imperialism a level of commitment that it had hitherto lacked. This mattered. The organisational challenge for metropolitan anti-imperialism, after the turn away from Britain instigated by Gandhi, was how to recruit and motivate supporters when they were no longer speaking for Indian nationalism. The Communists had effective answers to this challenge, in their distinctive sense of vocation. Communist life was characterised by hyper-activity: an endlessly inventive proliferation of organisational initiatives: study groups, campaigns, pamphlets and conferences. This was combined with a cadre structure which permitted synchronised and nationwide activity directed from the top, something anti-imperialists had never achieved before. The CPGB was in design not a loose, horizontal affiliation of mutually affable individuals, like other anti-imperialist groups, but a vertically integrated and hierarchical structure. This deterred the individual defaulting and foot-dragging, which generally characterised other metropolitan

[25] Overstreet and Windmiller, *Communism*, 69–72; 'Draft Resolution of Comintern Presidium', 4 Apr. 1924, in Purabi Roy, Sobhanlal Datta Gupta and Hari Vasudevan (eds), *Indo-Russian Relations, 1917–1947: Select Documents from the Archives of the Russian Federation*, 2 vols (Calcutta, 1999), i. 183–85.

[26] Stephen Howe, *Anticolonialism in British Politics: The Left and the End of Empire, 1918–1964* (Oxford, 1993), 56–57.

[27] Stuart MacIntyre, *Imperialism and the Labour Movement in the 1920s* (London, 1975), 17.

campaigns. No other organisation could have ordered a national Meerut Week campaign, culminating in 20,000 demonstrators in Trafalgar Square, as the CPGB did in 1930, or insisted that its local parties, no matter how small, established colonial sections.

The CPGB's activism on the Indian question was, at least at first, positively affected by a further distinctive feature of Communist anti-imperialism: its ultimate subordination to an international organisation. The precise effects of this arrangement have been the subject of extensive debate in recent years.[28] In this case, the effects were mixed. Comintern probably helped to neutralise national sentiment about empires, providing a common framework of analysis and even action within which specific struggles could be situated, with supporting propaganda, training and funds. Without Comintern's prodding it seems certain that less would have been done. However, Comintern was always and increasingly under the direction of the Soviet Union, its activities directed above all to the protection of the Soviet state. Heavy financial dependence on Comintern funding further limited the autonomy of the CPGB. Control was never total: the erratic nature of Comintern advice on Indian questions permitted a certain looseness of application. Had the CPGB obeyed Comintern instructions to bring Roy to Britain to stand in the 1924 General Election, he would have been arrested and deported to India, where he had been convicted in his absence earlier in the year. Questions of immediate tactics remained the responsibility of the national sections. One CPGB member cheerfully observed that the Party did not defer to the Soviet Union on colonial or Indian matters, because 'we knew far more than they did'.[29] Certainly, too, there were recognised CPGB authorities on Indian questions, such as the Dutts, Saklatvala and Robin Page Arnot. But, as was to become clear later on, even tactical questions were reviewed by Comintern, and wider strategy was a matter of direct instruction.

The main source of disagreement between Comintern and the CPGB on India concerned the problem of salience. The CPGB believed that even though its cadres could be ordered to march for India, new recruits among British workers seemed likely to be alienated from the Party through being forced to campaign on matters which meant little to them. At the Second Congress, Lenin reported that Tom Quelch of the British Socialist Party (BSP) had said that, in any colonial rising, the 'ordinary British worker would regard it as treason to help the dependent peoples to rebel against

[28] For a critical survey, see John McIlroy and Alan Campbell, '"Nina Ponomareva's Hats": The New Revisionism, the Communist International, and the Communist Party of Great Britain, 1920–1930', *Labour/Le Travail*, 49 (2002), 147–87.

[29] Malcolm MacEwen, *The Greening of a Red* (London, 1991), 114.

British rule'.[30] Although the British delegation later claimed that Quelch had not meant this to be an excuse for inactivity, it had not gone down well. Radek had argued that the sympathy of the colonised masses would be needed to ensure that a future British revolution was not starved out. This sympathy, and Comintern approval, could not be won by protest meetings and articles in the press, but only 'the [British] number of comrades thrown into prison for agitating in the colonial countries'.[31] The role favoured by the CPGB, however, was initially less directly interventionist than Comintern had demanded. It was twofold, J.T. Murphy argued: to forge links for 'simultaneous proletarian action' with the colonial revolutionary movement in the colonies, and to create a movement within Britain capable of challenging the imperialists at home.[32] Even this programme, however, was held back by financial pressures in an organisation with low membership that prioritised work in the depressed areas of industrial Britain.[33] The CPGB's own view, despite Comintern's prodding, was that while India mattered, it could never be the lever that would detach British workers from their primary allegiances to the unions and the Labour Party.

The CPGB and Roy

Neither the CPGB nor Roy found it easy to work with each other. Immediately after the Second Congress, they had agreed that the CPGB would provide support for Roy's agents in India by sending them literature and propaganda; and also train and send agitators to India, 'legally or illegally', to assist them in building their movement. At home, the CPGB would agitate among British workers to alert them to the interdependence of the revolutionary movements in India and Britain, and recruit and train resident Indians, especially sailors and students, to work for Communism on their return to India.[34] The British work was initially entrusted to Shapurji Saklatvala, the ex-ILP activist who was soon to be elected as MP

[30] McLaine's speech and Commission on the National and Colonial Questions, in Riddell, *Workers*, 262–63, 865–69; *The Communist*, 26 Aug. 1920.

[31] Radek's speech, in Riddell, *Workers*, 230–34.

[32] Murphy's speech, in Riddell, *Workers*, 270–71.

[33] Andrew Thorpe, *The British Communist Party and Moscow, 1920–43* (Manchester, 2000), 65–66, 104–5, 146.

[34] The National Archives (TNA), KV2/612, McLaine to Saklatvala, 7 Aug. 1920; 'Indian Delegation to Saklatvala and R. Palme Dutt', 9 Aug. 1920, in Roy, Gupta and Vasudevan, *Indo-Russian Relations*, i. 22–25; RGASPI 495/68/5, Roy to Secretary of the British Communist Party, 9 Aug. 1920, 'Practical Measures for Coordinating the Indian Revolutionary Movement with the Proletarian Revolution in England', 12 Aug. 1920; NAI, Home-Political Proceedings, Deposit Series, Oct. 1920, no. 81, DIB Report, n.d.

for Battersea North. Within a few weeks of exchanging correspondence with Roy, however, Saklatvala's enthusiasm had been chilled by a police raid on his house. It was 'very obvious', the police inspector reported, 'that he is a red-hot Bolshevik'.[35] The authorities considered deporting Saklatvala to India, but decided against it, on the grounds that, as the government of India's Director of Intelligence put it, 'we have more to fear from Indians returning to India from Europe than from agitators in the country'.[36] Nevertheless, the experience seems to have shaken Saklatvala. He wrote what the security service described as a 'whimpering kind of letter' to the detectives who had raided his house, sympathising with their concern about 'revolutionaries' and turning in the secret letter he had received from Roy, whom he claimed not to know.[37]

Saklatvala thereafter confined himself to the legal work of building a united front through critical but friendly approaches to Congress leaders and moderate trade unionists in India.[38] He argued that Roy's hopes for proletarian revolution in India were premature and favoured an alliance from above with Congress.[39] He also urged the Indian Communists to get closer to the nationalist movement.[40] In May 1921, Roy's wife Evelyn visited London and reported that Saklatvala's moderate allies would never come across to revolutionary work. 'We must find younger and bolder material to work with', she told Comintern.[41] She also gave £2,000 to Saklatvala to support this work, but the money mysteriously disappeared, with the Roys claiming that it had been misappropriated by British Communists, and Saklatvala that Evelyn Roy had never handed it over.[42] Saklatvala wrote to Comintern to complain about Evelyn Roy's indiscipline and his suspicions that she was a spy. Thereafter, unsurprisingly, very little, if any, money was sent to Communists in Britain from the funds which Comintern

[35] TNA, KV2/612, Report on Papers and Correspondence Taken on 18th October [1920] from 51 Lebanon Park, Twickenham, the house of Shapurji Saklatvala, n.d.

[36] NAI, Home-Political Proceedings, B series, Jan. 1921, nos. 306–7, DIB Report, 5 Dec. 1920.

[37] TNA, KV2/612, Kell to Hose, 15 Dec. 1920.

[38] Jawaharlal Nehru Memorial Library, New Delhi, Papers of the All-India Congress Committee, AICC 4/1921, Saklatvala to Motilal Nehru, 3 Mar. 1921.

[39] TNA, KV2/613, Note on Saklatvala, 24 Nov. 1920.

[40] TNA, KV3/19, Saklatvala to Singaravelu, 13 Mar. 1924.

[41] RGASPI 495/68/57, Evelyn Roy to Comintern, [1921?]; Evelyn Roy, 'Report of Trip to Germany, France and England', 7 Aug. 1921, in Roy, Gupta and Vasudevan, *Indo-Russian Relations*, i. 92–95; National Museum of Labour History, Manchester (hereafter NMLH), CPGB Archive, Politburo minutes, 17 Sept. 1923.

[42] IPI, L/PJ/12/46, IPI Reports, 1 Nov. 1921, 24 Aug., 7 and 9 Dec. 1922; NAI, Home-Political Proceedings, Deposit Series, Oct. 1920, no. 81, DIB Report, n.d.

had provided Roy.[43] This provided the CPGB with an additional reason for inaction. The CPGB told Roy's agent that it was 'too busy to do the Indian work' itself unless someone else paid. 'No part of the grant given to the British Communist Party by the Comintern', it had insisted, 'could be expended on India'.[44]

Partly as a result of these rivalries, and partly because the CPGB remained privately convinced that British workers would respond better on industrial questions than on colonial ones, little activity resulted.[45] In March 1922, Moscow called for the CPGB to launch a 'well-organised and long term action to support the revolutionary movements in India and Egypt'.[46] But, although there was talk in October 1922 of establishing a Colonial Committee as agreed with Roy in 1920, nothing came of it, and despite regular detailed suggestions from Roy, and further proddings from Comintern, the CPGB seems to have done little more than publicise Roy's leaflets.[47] Reporting in April 1924, it had to confess that its Colonial Committee was not yet established, and that colonial questions only arose in an ad hoc way at Politburo meetings.[48] Roy complained of its inefficiencies, ignorance, inattentiveness, and especially of the need to break the alliances Saklatvala was building with mere reformers in India.[49] He wrote to Radek to complain that Saklatvala was 'a careerist pure and simple' and his activities 'not those of a Communist'.[50] For his part, Saklatvala insisted that Roy should play no part in negotiations with his Indian contacts.[51]

43 RGASPI 495/27/5, Saklatvala to Comintern Praesidium, [1921?]; IPI, L/PJ/12/46, IPI Report, 7 Dec. 1922.

44 IPI, L/PJ/12/49, IPI Report, n.d.

45 'Report of the Work and Organization of the Indian Communist Party, 1921', in Roy, Gupta and Vasudevan, *Indo-Russian Relations*, i. 82–85.

46 'Resolution of the ECCI on the Eastern Question', 4 Mar. 1922, in Degras, *Comintern*, i. 326–27; 'Theses on the Eastern Question Adopted by the Fourth Comintern Congress', Nov. 1922, in Degras, *Comintern*, i. 382–93.

47 NMLH, CPGB Archive, Sub-Executive minutes, 22 Sept. 1922; Executive Committee minutes, 13 Oct. 1922; Politburo minutes, 28 Feb. and 14 Mar. 1923; IPI, L/PJ/12/179, 'Report on Revolutionary Organizations in the UK', 10 Apr. 1924.

48 TNA, KV3/24, Secretary [unknown] to Inkpin, Control Commission, 8 Apr. 1924; RGAPSI 495/100/260, Tom Bell, Report to Colonial Commission, 26 Mar. 1925.

49 RGASPI 495/68/5, Roy to Executive Committee of the CPGB, 1 Feb. 1921; Roy to Saklatvala, 28 Feb. 1921; RGASPI 495/68/104, Roy to CPGB, 29 Mar., 12 June, 15 and 26 Aug., 21 Nov. 1923; Roy to Newbold, 10 July 1923; Roy to Dutt, [1923?]; TNA, KV3/28, Evelyn Roy to Dutt, 20 and 21 Mar. 1924; TNA, KV3/30, Roy to Politburo, CPGB, 25 May [1924?].

50 RGASPI 495/68/104, Roy to Radek, 16 Aug. 1923 and Roy to Secretary, CPGB [no day given] Aug. 1923.

51 TNA, KV3/30, Saklatvala to Macmanus, 3 May 1924.

Matters came to a head at the Fifth Comintern Congress in 1924, as Zinoviev had warned the CPGB they would.[52] Manuilsky attacked the CPGB for its poor record: 'Do our British comrades think that the revolutionary process begins with the English proletariat liberating itself and then in the capacity of a Messiah carrying deliverance to the colonial peoples?', he asked.[53] The Party had done 'as good as nothing' to help.[54] The Fifth Congress gave a new priority to the anti-imperialist movement, to the need to work with anti-imperialists even where they were bourgeois, and also to the role of Communists in the imperial centres. 'The British Party', Comintern now resolved, 'must make its activities imperial in scope'.[55] Roy welcomed this publicly but criticised the tendency of *Kommunistischen Imperialismus:* the propensity of the metropolitan Communists to dominate the anti-imperialist struggle.[56]

The CPGB Colonial Committee was finally set up on a firm basis in November 1924, and over the following year reported considerable progress: weekly meetings, a campaign on the Kanpur trial (the prosecution of Roy's Communists), improved contacts with London-based Indians and Indian sailors, a planned East–West conference to bring Indian trade unionists to London and an exploratory visit to India by one of its leaders, Percy Glading.[57] However, from the Committee's minutes and its correspondence with Roy it is clear that there were serious weaknesses in this work, many due to the unresolved rivalries with Roy's organisation. The CPGB refused to have Evelyn Roy on its Colonial Committee, or to work under the direction

52 TNA, KV2/1183, Zinoviev to Stewart, 30 Apr. 1924.

53 Quoted in Haithcox, *Communism*, 42.

54 John Callaghan, 'The Communists and the Colonies: Anti-Imperialism between the Wars', in Geoff Andrews, Nina Fishman and Kevin Morgan (eds), *Opening the Books: Essays on the Social and Cultural History of British Communism* (London, 1995), 6.

55 'Concrete Tasks of the Most Important Sections of the CI: England', July 1924, in Degras, *Comintern*, ii. 155–56; Sixth Plenum, 'Resolution on the English Question', 4 Mar. 1926; Seventh Plenum, 'Resolution on the Situation in Britain', Dec. 1926, in Degras, *Comintern*, ii. 262–65, 314–19; RGASPI 495/100/291, 'The Colonial Commission of the CPGB', [1926?].

56 M.N. Roy, 'Imperialist Plunder, Corruption of the English Proletariat and Conditions of Revolution in England', 20 June 1924, in M.N. Roy, *Selected Works*, ed. Sibnarayan Ray, 4 vols (Oxford, 1987), ii. 286–90.

57 RGASPI 495/100/188, CPGB Colonial Committee, 22 Dec. 1924; RGASPI 495/100/260, CPGB Colonial Committee, 5 Mar. 1925; RGASPI 495/100/260, Report by Tom Bell to Colonial Commission, 26 Mar. 1925; 'Report of Progress by CPGB Colonial Department', 26 June 1925, in *Communist Papers: Documents Selected from Those Obtained on the Arrest of the Communist Leaders on the 14th and 21st October, 1925*, Cmd 2682, 1926, doc. 41; TNA, KV3/20, CPGB Colonial Department to Eastern Department, ECCI, 19 and 26 June 1925.

of Roy's International Bureau. It insisted on its own responsibility for making recommendations to the Politburo about colonial policy: there would be no 'dictation from outside'.[58] The Kanpur campaign was embarrassingly weak. The defence fund claimed to have raised £60, but apart from £1 from George Lansbury and 10 shillings from James Maxton the rest had come from Roy. Only £22 was sent to India since the rest had already been spent on the campaign itself. Since M.A. Jinnah wanted £2,000 to act as defence counsel, this made little impression.[59] The CPGB's leaflets on Kanpur were also ignorant and inaccurate in attacking the Colonial Office rather than the India Office for the trial and deploring British actions at Chauri Chaura (where Indian nationalists had killed Indian policemen).[60] The East–West conference failed to come off, although Roy believed that in inviting moderate trade unionists it was pointless and out of keeping with Comintern instruction to seek revolutionary potential in the Congress movement.[61]

The CPGB also quarrelled with Roy over Indians in Britain. The Colonial Committee initially rejected Roy's suggestion it should recruit a subcommittee of expatriate Indians, but then faced with an independent move to establish one, reluctantly agreed to set one up. This was the Indian Bureau, comprised of Clemens Dutt, Saklatvala and four other Indians, including M.A. Khan and A.C. Banerji.[62] The CPGB disliked this arrangement, since the Bureau contained non-party members, refused political direction, and sought direct contact with Moscow. This was contrary to the practice of democratic centralism adopted by the Party, by which the relationship with Moscow had to run through the leadership. Comintern accepted the CPGB's advice on this question and told the Indian Bureau that it must work in conjunction with the Colonial Committee of the CPGB as well as Roy.[63]

[58] RGASPI 495/100/261, 'Resolution of the International Colonial Bureau on Colonial Work in Great Britain', 23 Oct. 1924; RGASPI 495/100/260, C.P. Dutt, 'Notes on Visit to the Colonial Bureau, Paris', [Oct. 1924?]; RGASPI 495/100/188, Colonial Committee Reports, 6 and 24 Nov. 1924; RGASPI 495/100/260, Colonial Committee Report, 5 Mar. 1925; Report of Colonial Bureau, 3 Apr. 1925, in Roy, Gupta and Vasudevan, *Indo-Russian Relations*, i. 199–200.

[59] Kaye, *Communism in India*, 98–100; Petrie, *Communism in India*, 56; KV3/30, Macmanus to C.P. Dutt, 2 May 1924.

[60] IPI, L/PJ/12/180, India Office discussion of the CPGB Kanpur leaflets, various dates, 1925.

[61] RGASPI 495/100/260, CPGB Colonial Committee, 6 Nov. 1925; Petrie, *Communism in India*, 266–70; 'Report of Colonial Activities', [1925?], *Communist Papers*, doc. 46; TNA, KV3/33, Field to Macmanus, 8 Aug. 1925.

[62] RGASPI 495/100/188, CPGB Colonial Committee, 15 Dec. 1924; RGASPI 495/100/260, CPGB Colonial Committee, 23 Feb. 1925.

[63] 'Suggestions of Indian Comrades in London', [1925?], Dutt et al. to CPI European Bureau, 6 July 1925, and reply, 15 Sept. 1925, in Roy, Gupta and Vasudevan, *Indo-Russian*

But relations remained strained. Saklatvala believed that Banerji was a government spy. The CPGB leadership thought that members of the Indian Bureau were really working for Roy.[64] They attempted to control its interactions, excluding Banerji from the party offices and demanding to vet the correspondence between Bureau members and Roy. This was attacked by Khan at a meeting in Amsterdam attended by the CPGB's London organiser, Roy and Comintern's west European director Henrik Sneevliet, in July 1925. Roy, although he was careful not to side directly with the Bureau, argued that the dominance of Indian work by the CPGB 'smack[ed] of imperialism' and 'a desire of maintaining … prestige'.[65] Nevertheless, the evidence suggests that the CPGB's fault was less 'bossing' than pessimism and 'footdragging', as Clemens Dutt privately acknowledged.[66] The party, his brother R.P. Dutt concluded the same year, was not ready to discuss imperial questions and should focus on points of immediate agitation.[67] Hugo Rathbone told Roy of a typical CPGB response to one of his Indian initiatives:

> [I]t really is bloody awful. The replies to all proposals as to action in defence of your child was: no, we have gone to pieces there – anyway action on another subject has failed, how can this one succeed[?] Can't put any more burdens on our overburdened collection. … What's the use of starting a new action on something that will be bound to fail … Anyway there are no speakers and who's to come to listen to them if there were etc etc … Then comes the final touch: the pol[itical] letter … was suggested – the answer was what's the use, no one reads them anyway.[68]

The CPGB and the CPI

The Amsterdam meeting was also attended by Glading, who reported on his recent visit to India. This was the first successful CPGB effort to contact Indian Communists, an earlier attempt having failed when its emissary was arrested on arrival due to a leak from Roy's office.[69] Glading reported

Relations, i. 202–5; IPI, L/PJ/12/342, Meerut Committal Order, Prosecution Document P2379–1, 97, n.d.

64 They were certainly seeking advice from Roy. See RGASPI 495/68/186, Banerji to Narinda, 21 Dec. 1926 and 'J' [J.C. Dutt?] to 'R' [M.N. Roy?], 3 Dec. 1926.

65 'Colonial Conference held at Amsterdam, July 11th and 12th, 1925', *Communist Papers*, doc. 42.

66 IPI, L/PJ/12/50, IPI Report, 15 July 1925; Thorpe, *British Communist Party*, 110.

67 TNA, KV3/23, R.P. Dutt to Politburo, 21 Feb. 1925.

68 RGASPI 495/68/285, Rathbone to Roy, 31 Jan. 1928.

69 Kaye, *Communism in India*, 21; RGASPI 495/100/188, Colonial Committee, 22 Dec. 1924; NMLH, CPGB Archive, Politburo, Newbold to Inkpin, with minutes of

that Saklatvala's contacts had proved unreliable and unbiddable, and that hardly any of Roy's tiny yet factionally divided band of Indian Communists had made any progress with the labour movement. Glading nonetheless believed that there was scope for a mass party if the right organisation were put in place, under CPGB control.[70] Hence the CPGB decided to dispatch its union organisers to India under cover to help develop and direct the Indian trade union movement.[71] The miner George Allison arrived in India in April 1926 on a forged passport but after working for nine months was arrested and sentenced to eighteen months for the forgery and subsequently deported. He was replaced in September 1927 by the engineering worker Ben Bradley.

Glading had also suggested that British Communist students be sent out as 'live wires' to galvanise the labour movement, and in December 1926, Philip Spratt, a Cambridge graduate, was sent. It was hard to prevent British Communists like Spratt from obtaining visas for India, since unlike the Indian revolutionaries, they were not generally known to the India Office before they were sent. 'Our system is of course mainly designed to keep undesirable *aliens* out of India', the India Office noted in 1927.[72] Its extraordinary proposal that some 6,000 British Communists should all have their passports restricted to keep them out of India was defeated by the Home Office and Foreign Office which insisted that class exemptions were organisationally impossible and politically hard to defend.[73]

The CPGB emissaries put their efforts not into the CPI but Workers and Peasants Parties (WPPs) to swamp the Congress from below and carry it towards revolution. For Roy, such movements were at best a way of demonstrating the indifference of Congress to economic questions, but for the CPGB they came to mean working alongside Congress to radicalise its campaigns.[74] By the end of 1928, considerable progress had been made: the Bengal WPP, which had been set up shortly before Allison's arrival, was followed by another in Bombay which was an important factor in building

meeting, 8 Apr. 1924. For the first attempt [Charles Ashleigh], see IPI, L/PJ/12/101 and L/PJ/12/246.

70 TNA, KV3/33, Pencil notes of Glading's correspondence from India, probably made by Macmanus for CPGB Colonial Committee, n.d.; IPI, L/PJ/12/50, IPI Report, 15 July 1925.

71 RGASPI 495/68/179, 'The Plan of Action of the Colonial Commission of the Communist Party of Great Britain with Regard to India', [1925–1926?].

72 IPI, L/PJ/12/312, 'Note on British Communists' Entry into India', 26 Apr. 1927.

73 TNA, PRO, HO, 144/22404, Minutes of inter-departmental conference on restricting passports of British Communists travelling to India, June 1928; TNA, PRO, HO, 144/10693, Peel to Joynson-Hicks, 27 Feb. 1929, Chamberlain to Peel, 15 Mar. 1929.

74 RGASPI 495/68/205, 'Proposals re Indian Work', 14 Apr. 1927 and C.P. Dutt to Tivel, 21 Apr. 1927.

labour unrest in the Bombay textile mills and the railways. At the national trade union congress in December 1928, the Communists also managed to defeat the moderate leadership's proposal to affiliate to the Amsterdam socialist International Federation of Trade Unions (IFTU) rather than the Communist RILU, and to work through the British TUC.

However, these successes sidelined Roy's CPI, whose contribution the emissaries regarded sceptically. Allison, like Glading, had found that there was little evidence of Communism beyond the intellectual and petty bourgeois classes. He bluntly told the CPI that its pamphlets were a waste of time, and that it should get on with capturing the trade unions.[75] He also tried to get the CPI to break its links to Roy and leave all the questions of affiliation and international correspondence to him.[76] Saklatvala, who visited India openly in 1927, initially refused to meet the CPI on the grounds that it was not properly affiliated to Comintern. He labelled it a 'concordia of naïve petty bourgeois intellectuals' and criticised its distance from Congress and over-dependence on Roy, suggesting that it should merge itself into the WPP, and the latter affiliate itself not, as Roy wished, to the Berlin-based League Against Imperialism (LAI) but to the CPGB-controlled Minority Movement.[77] He had even, to Roy's horror, urged Gandhi to take up the leadership of the WPPs.[78] Spratt was more tactful, but he too was surprised to find the CPI consisted of so few members and had done so little to build a mass movement.[79] The future, he told Clemens Dutt, lay in unions affiliated to Communist-controlled WPPs, not the CPI.[80]

The CPI resented what it saw as an attempt to close it down or push it into alliance with Congress. It protested to Comintern about Saklatvala's

[75] Petrie, *Communism in India*, 117; Spratt, *Blowing Up India*, 32, 36; RGASPI 495/68/186, 'Don' [Allison?] to Comintern, 8 and 9 Oct. 1926; RGASPI 495/68/285, Note by D[onald] C[ampbell] for [C.] Dutt and [M.N.] Roy, 13 Aug. 1928.

[76] RGASPI 495/68/204, Anonymous CPI member to Comintern, 6 Jan. 1927, and C. Dutt et al. to Tivel, 4 Aug. 1927.

[77] Saklatvala's own records are in British Library, OIOC, Saklatvala Papers, MS Eur D1173. His instructions are in RGASPI 495/68/178, Comintern to Comintern representative, London, 31 Dec. 1926. See also RGASPI 495/68/101, Saklatvala to Ghate et al., 18 Jan. 1927; RGASPI 495/68/230, 'Saklatwala [*sic*] in India', 28 Feb. 1927; Petrie, *Communism in India*, 109–10; Gangadhar Adhikari (ed.), *Documents of the History of the Communist Party of India*, 8 vols (New Delhi, 1971–1982), iii. 31.

[78] Saklatvala to Gandhi, 17 Mar. 1927, in M.K. Gandhi, *Collected Works*, 100 vols (New Delhi: Government of India, 1960–1994), xxxiii. 486–87.

[79] Spratt, *Blowing Up India*, 35.

[80] RGASPI 495/68/285, Spratt to Dutt, 13 Jan. 1928; RGASPI 495/68/205, 'Meerut Committal Order', Prosecution document P1008, Dutt to Spratt, n.d., 112–13 and Dutt to Tivel, 21 Apr. 1927; Dutt to Tivel, 19 May 1927, in Roy, Gupta and Vasudevan, *Indo-Russian Relations*, i. 238.

snubs to its leaders both directly and also through Clemens Dutt, seconded by Comintern to work with Roy in the hope of reducing the friction between him and the CPGB.[81] Roy complained that the 'British party starts from the assumption that since they have not done anything in India, nothing whatsoever exists there, and that they must begin the whole thing'.[82] He instructed the CPI that they must be 'stricter in their relations with the new British comrade [Bradley]' who was supposed to work under their direction. '[I]f he assumes an attitude of superiority as Campbell [Allison's codename] did, he should simply be reminded of his position and … asked to go away'.[83] The CPI itself should follow the direction of Roy's Foreign Bureau, not the CPGB.[84] In Moscow, his associates commented sourly on the CPGB's uncritical endorsement of Congress positions.[85]

At the same time, however, Roy and Clemens Dutt were both aware of the CPI's weaknesses. It was, they accepted, not interested in developing the WPPs and lacked a proper sense of their importance, regarding them as 'a fad of the Britishers which they have promised to humour'. It had not developed any satisfactory means of controlling them from outside. Besides this inactivity, the CPI was also insufficiently aware of the need to take orders from Moscow even if it disliked them, fearing that to formalise its position as a section of Comintern would invite repression.[86]

Allegations of 'bossing' were a continual refrain in the 1920s. 'The viewpoint of the Indian national revolutionaries', Agnes Smedley had written in 1921, 'is opposed to any work with any English party, Communist or otherwise. Every English person to them is either an enemy or a potential enemy … It is a commonplace saying among them that since all other British parties have failed to "manage" India, the Communist Party now intends

[81] RGASPI 495/68/205, General Secretaries, CPI, to Saklatvala, 16 Jan. 1927, and C.P. Dutt to Roy, 26 Jan. 1927; RGASPI 495/68/204, Anonymous CPI member to Comintern, 4 and 21 Jan. 1927; Anonymous CPI member, Report to the Indian Commission, 18 May 1928, in Roy, Gupta and Vasudevan, *Indo-Russian Relations*, i. 298–302; C.P. Dutt and Muhammad Ali, Report on Organisational Work in India, 16 Mar. 1927, in Roy, Gupta and Vasudevan, *Indo-Russian Relations*, i. 234–36.

[82] Roy to Petrov, 30 Dec. 1925, in Roy, Gupta and Vasudevan, *Indo-Russian Relations*, i. 205–6; RGASPI 495/68/240, Maurice [Ali?] to Richard [Roy?], 28 Sept. 1927; RGASPI 495/18/590, Rathbone, 'Statement on the Spratt Case', 19 Dec. 1927; RGASPI 495/60/132, 'Erklarung zum Fall Spratt', [1928?].

[83] Roy to Maurice [Ali?], 18 Oct. 1927, in Roy, Gupta and Vasudevan, *Indo-Russian Relations*, i. 245–46.

[84] Sir Horace Williamson, *India and Communism* (Calcutta, 1933), 128–30.

[85] Meeting of Anglo-American Secretariat of Comintern, 10 Jan. 1928, in Roy, Gupta and Vasudevan, *Indo-Russian Relations*, i. 247–63.

[86] RGASPI 495/68/205, Dutt and Ali, 'Report on Organisational Work in India', n.d.; C.P. Dutt to Roy, 26 Jan. 1927 and Dutt to S.V. [Ghate], 1 May 1927.

to try its hand'.[87] But hostility to British Communists, Tom Bell countered, was not the feeling of the Indians in India, but only of the émigré groups.[88] The émigrés needed to maintain themselves as Comintern's link to India, without which they had little function, and the CPI wished to preserve itself against efforts to control it. Charges of bossing were one means of doing so. There is slight evidence that the work of the CPGB emissaries was resented on this score by others, especially the trade unionists in India among whom they worked. Unlike practically all other British activists, the CPGB emissaries generally worked in solidarity with their Indian counterparts, sharing the risk of persecution, arrest and imprisonment and leading by example. Expertise offered on these terms was not generally resented.[89]

The new line

The CPGB strategy for India, however, was brought to an end through the course of 1928. This had less to do with events in India than factional disputes in the Soviet Union, which drove sympathetic figures in Comintern leftwards to avoid Stalin's attack on Bukharin and right deviationism. At the Ninth Plenum, in February 1928, Comintern had instructed the CPI to construct a broad anti-imperialist front ('middle classes, intellectuals, petty bourgeoisie, peasantry') and, as representatives of the proletariat, to exercise hegemony over it.[90] Yet at the Sixth Congress, in the middle of 1928, it was decided that the Communists should demarcate themselves clearly from nationalists and organise the Indian peasants and workers under the leadership of an unveiled Communist Party. There were also incoherent but effective attacks on the thesis, argued by Roy and the CPGB, that India was industrialising under British rule. Instead, Comintern insisted that imperialism *retarded* the growth of industrial capitalism in India. Critics who pointed out that, if true, this also retarded the necessary conditions for a self-reliant Communist Party got nowhere. At the subsequent Indian Commission, even Bukharin attacked the CPGB for exaggerating the revolutionary potential of Congress protests.[91] This was resisted by both the

[87] Agnes Smedley, 'Note for Small Bureau of Comintern', 5 Aug. 1921, in Roy, Gupta and Vasudevan, *Indo-Russian Relations*, i. 86–92.

[88] 'Minutes of the Indian Commission', 6 Aug. 1921, in Roy, Gupta and Vasudevan, *Indo-Russian Relations*, i. 140–42.

[89] RGASPI 495/42/4, Masut to the Indian Commission, 19 Apr. 1928.

[90] Ninth Plenum, 'Resolution on India', 15 Feb. 1928, in Roy, Gupta and Vasudevan, *Indo-Russian Relations*, i. 268–69.

[91] Bukharin, 'Speech to Indian Commission', 17 Aug. 1927, in Roy, Gupta and Vasudevan, *Indo-Russian Relations*, i. 238–39; Bukharin's notes on Roy and Page Arnot's proposals, in Roy, Gupta and Vasudevan, *Indo-Russian Relations*, i. 270–76.

CPGB, and even Roy, who now believed that the WPPs had potential that the CPI could exploit if it could only take charge of them.[92] As nationalist unrest began to grow in response to the Simon Commission, and inch towards civil disobedience, the opportunities for joint work seemed to be opening up, just as Comintern was closing them down.

This change of direction owed much to Stalin's exploitation of the debacle in China, where a strategy of supporting the nationalist Kuomintang had backfired disastrously when the nationalists turned on the Communists once they had been assisted to power. However, it was also a consequence of the weaknesses of the WPP strategy evident *before* the Sixth Congress. The WPPs looked as though they were growing, but in reality they were being carried along by spontaneous outbursts of labour unrest, which they did not control.[93] '[W]e are still backward', Spratt had confessed in January 1928. 'Our numbers do not increase and our organization is very defective'.[94] As a consequence, rather than capturing Congress from below, the WPPs lobbied it from a position of weakness. Strikes remained under the control of moderate leaders, who struck deals with local Congress leaders, leaving the Communists in the cold. The nationalists, Spratt lamented, took over the labour demonstrations that the WPP had organised and refused to let Communists speak at them.[95] While Clemens Dutt and Roy still valued the WPPs, they agreed that it was now time for the CPI to emerge from behind them, so as to criticise them when they merely acted as the left wing of the Congress.[96]

This position was not identical to, but also not *irreconcilable* with, the Sixth Congress decision that the WPPs should be continued but controlled by an independent CPI operating at a greater critical distance from Congress.[97] Such a repositioning might have been useful, especially at times when Congress temporised, as at the time of the Gandhi–Irwin

[92] Roy on Bukharin's 'Amendments to the Indian manifesto', 8 Mar. 1928, in Roy, Gupta and Vasudevan, *Indo-Russian Relations*, i. 276–78.

[93] RGASPI 495/42/3, 'Stenograph of Indian Commission', 19 Apr. 1928, and 'Points to be Specially Stressed in the Letter to S[pratt] and B[radley]', n.d.; RGASPI 495/42/4, Masut to Indian Commission, 19 Apr. 1928.

[94] RGASPI 495/68/285, Desmond [Spratt?] to Comintern, 17 Feb. 1928, and Spratt to Comintern, 23 Feb. 1928.

[95] RGASPI 495/68/285, Spratt to Dutt, 13 Jan. 1928, John [C. Dutt?] to Richard [Roy?], 26 Jan. 1928, and Spratt [?] to Page Arnot, 27 Oct. 1928; Petrovsky, 'The Tactical Tasks of the Communists in India', 10 Apr. 1928, in Roy, Gupta and Vasudevan, *Indo-Russian Relations*, i. 280–83.

[96] C.P. Dutt, 'Draft Resolution on the Indian Question', 30 Apr. 1928, in Roy, Gupta and Vasudevan, *Indo-Russian Relations*, i. 284–96.

[97] 'Theses on the Revolutionary Movement in Colonial and Semi-colonial Countries', 1 Sept. 1928, in Degras, *Comintern*, ii. 526–48.

Pact. But Comintern instructions received at the end of 1928, more or less simultaneously with the news of the Sixth Congress, demanded not merely the unveiling of the CPI, but also the 'determined and relentless exposure' of Congress.[98] The American Communist Jack Johnstone spent late 1928 in India reporting to Comintern, and concluded that the CPI was failing to capitalise on the workers' energies for radical politics, which were all being run into the WPPs and benefiting Congress rather than the Communists.[99] The CPGB and Roy, by contrast, wanted to preserve the WPPs and to remain open to the opportunities presented by a radicalising Congress. But the 10th Plenum, in July 1929, hardened the line, insisting that the WPPs be liquidated. This destroyed the flexibility towards which the CPGB and Roy had been working, putting the emissaries in a weak position to make gains from the civil disobedience campaign that Gandhi was about to launch, which they were ordered to denounce as merely a sham fight.[100] The CPI had less trouble accepting the new line, which reflected its own preference for attacking the nationalists and its lack of commitment to the WPPs. Its complaints of 'bossing', however, were not heeded.[101] The CPGB remained in charge of enforcing the new line, as well as developing its metropolitan work more energetically.[102] The question, in any case, became theoretical as the British authorities moved in March 1929 to arrest the CPGB emissaries and CPI leaders and put them on trial for conspiracy at Meerut.[103] The fate of the Indian revolution, Manuilsky told Comintern in February 1930, now lay 'in the hands of the metal workers of Manchester and the Scottish miners'.[104]

[98] 'Extracts from a Letter from the ECCI to the All-India Conference of Workers' and Peasants' Parties', 2 Dec. 1928, in Degras, *Comintern*, ii. 557–64.

[99] RGASPI 495/68/322, 'The Situation in India', 11 Sept. 1928; Johnstone to ECCI Eastern Secretariat, 12 Feb. 1929; Report to Jack [Johnstone?], n.d.

[100] 'Comintern Draft Resolution on India', 25 Mar. 1930, in Roy, Gupta and Vasudevan, *Indo-Russian Relations*, ii. 79–95.

[101] 'Meerut Prisoners to Comintern', 18 May 1929, in Roy, Gupta and Vasudevan, *Indo-Russian Relations*, ii. 43–46.

[102] 'Resolution on Organisational Work in Regard to India', 13 Feb. 1928, in Roy, Gupta and Vasudevan, *Indo-Russian Relations*, i. 263–67; Roy et al. to Comintern, 29 Apr. 1928, in Roy, Gupta and Vasudevan, *Indo-Russian Relations*, i. 283–84; Pavel Mif to CC, CPGB, 3 Oct. 1929, in Roy, Gupta and Vasudevan, *Indo-Russian Relations*, ii. 54–55.

[103] John Saville, 'The Meerut Trial, 1929–33', in Joyce Bellamy and John Saville (eds), *Dictionary of Labour Biography*, vol. 7 (London, 1984).

[104] 'The Meeting of the Enlarged Presidium of the ECCI', Feb. 1930, in Degras, *Comintern*, iii. 98–102.

The Meerut campaign in Britain

The 'new line' forced on the CPGB was, however, far from straightforward to explain to the metal workers, miners or indeed other British workers. As India erupted in civil disobedience, the party was forced to argue not merely that Congress was uninterested in social revolution, which was easily shown, but that it was not serious about getting rid of the British either. To Robin Page Arnot, the keenest member of the Politburo on the application of the new line to India, Gandhi's salt march was simply a stunt, and even his imprisonment intended to delude his followers into thinking he really opposed imperialism at all. However, the district parties found this line very hard to take. Encouraged by the centre to develop their Indian work, they tended to enthuse uncritically about the civil disobedience movement.[105] Some Politburo members shared their unease. Gallacher argued that, whatever his bourgeois leanings, Gandhi was at present more of a threat to the British than to the revolution.[106] Page Arnot stamped firmly on this tendency at a meeting of the newly purged Central Committee of the party in June 1930. The line being taken by some of the districts was 'totally wrong … a mass of confusion'. The Indian revolution could not be under way because the proletariat was not in charge of it, and Gandhi's purpose was only to stifle its emergence in the interests of the bourgeoisie.[107]

The adoption of the 'new line' also cut a swathe through the network of alliances that the CPGB was developing not only in India but also in Europe and Britain. It destroyed the League Against Imperialism (LAI), the international anti-imperialist front launched in 1927 which had briefly brought together Indian nationalists such as Jawaharlal Nehru and Subhas Bose and European socialists.[108] In Britain, the CPGB first took over and then destroyed the London Branch of the Indian National Congress (INC), established in June 1928 by ILP India expert Tarini Sinha and C.B. Vakil with Nehru's blessing.[109] Such destruction was quite intentional: the Communist hope was to draw in non-Communists, then force a split at a suitable moment, blame the non-Communist elements for it, and harvest the recruits for their own organisations. There was parallel destructiveness over the Meerut trial. The CPGB had established a Meerut Defence

105 IPI, L/PJ/12/382, Scotland Yard Report, 11 June 1930.

106 NMLH, CPGB Archive, Politburo minutes, 10 May 1930.

107 NMLH, CPGB Archive, Central Committee minutes (hereafter CC), 1 June 1930.

108 John Saville, 'Reginald O. Bridgeman' and 'The League Against Imperialism', in Bellamy and Saville, *Dictionary of Labour Biography*, vol. 7; Jean Jones, *The League Against Imperialism* (London, 1996).

109 Owen, *British Left and India*, 213–14, 226.

Committee on united front 'from above' lines, including the ILP, left-wing Labour MPs and non-Communist trade unionists. However, at the 10th Plenum in July 1929, this strategy was criticised by Comintern officials. Page Arnot accepted that it had been a bad mistake to involve the 'pseudo-left' leadership. He called for a campaign 'from below' based in the factories, run by a network of activists developed alongside local sections of the LAI, serviced by a reinvigorated Colonial Department at CPGB headquarters.[110] Circulars were duly sent to the districts and local parties urging activity for a Meerut Week in March 1930, and the establishment of new committees based on the factories which excluded the leaders of the ILP and reformist trade unions.[111] The Meerut Defence Committees should be reconstituted into Hands Off India Committees, committed not merely to aiding the prisoners, but of preparation for a proper revolution in India.[112]

However, CPGB anti-imperialism in the period of the 'new line' never really got beyond the destruction of the existing organisations. The widening 'from below' Page Arnot had demanded to replace the departing 'pseudo-lefts' did not occur. This failure provides a useful test of the rival claims of low salience and poor political articulation. On the face of it, the Meerut trial certainly was politically salient: indeed, it aroused considerable public disquiet among British workers. According to the Labour leaders, Clement Attlee and George Lansbury, it came up at every meeting, a claim amply supported by the volume of correspondence received by the Labour Party international department.[113] Although Walter Citrine, TUC General Secretary, argued that no genuine trade union question was involved, it is evident from his correspondence too that a significant section of non-CP union opinion had been aroused.[114] Indeed, since it involved British as well as Indian trade unionists, Meerut secured the CPGB a hearing in British trade union circles which was otherwise hard to obtain in the period of sectarianism. The length of the trial, the conditions under which the prisoners were kept and the harassment of labour organisers all resonated

[110] NMLH, CPGB Archive, CC minutes, 12 Jan. 1930; IPI, L/PJ/12/382, Scotland Yard Report, 22 Jan. 1930.

[111] IPI, L/PJ/12/382, CPGB Secretariat to DPCs, LPCs and comrades in charge of colonial work, 20 Jan. 1930.

[112] NMLH, CPGB Archive, Politburo minutes, 15 and 20 May 1930; CC minutes, 1 June 1930; IPI, L/PJ/12/382, CPGB Colonial Department to all districts, 21 Aug. 1930, and Scotland Yard Reports, 14 May, 11 June and 23 July 1930.

[113] British Library, OIOC, Sir Samuel Hoare Papers, MS Eur E240/3, 620–28, Hoare to Willingdon, 3 Mar. 1933.

[114] NMLH, Labour Party Archive, William Gillies Correspondence, WG/IND/102, Citrine to Henderson, 16 May 1929; Modern Records Centre, University of Warwick, Trades Union Congress Archive, MS 292/954/29, Note on Meerut, 10 Jan. 1930.

powerfully among British workers: 'the stories of brutal repression', the Politburo was told, 'arouse … their indignation'.[115]

On the other hand, it is also evident that this opinion was unformed, easily put off by a strong countering argument from informed opponents, and dissipated quickly without stimulation.[116] The Meerut campaign was a top-down affair, only catching fire when sparked from the centre or where it could win the support of the non-Communists. There was little *spontaneous* protest from below. When the CPGB asked what the local parties wanted included in its Charter (1930) not a single mention was made of the empire or India.[117] When it offered to pay for leaflets on Meerut, it only received a single reply.[118] British Communists had too little knowledge of the Asian communities in their own districts.[119] The districts were sternly told of the need to 'root out the opportunist attitude to colonial work as something extra'. They 'must re-act energetically and on their own initiative to all important news from India'.[120] But they waited for instructions from the centre, and when they got them, demanded literature, speakers and organisers, rather than developing any local capacity.[121] When repression of Congress began again at the start of 1932, the Politburo was told that 'not … a single resolution … from any group of workers' had been received.[122]

Why was this? The CPGB took the task of party education seriously, and its army-like structure helped it to do so. But it seems to have elicited the response familiar in armies: formal compliance with orders, but foot-dragging and almost no grass-roots initiative. The leaflets were printed and the hall booked, but few came. This in turn was partly a consequence of sectarianism. CPGB campaigns had worked best when Communists had been the loudest voice in broader organisations. But the useful energies that Meerut had aroused on the fringes of the CPGB and among non-party workers had vanished when the CPGB split and destroyed the elite organisations that it had built up. The party itself, Glading complained towards the end of 1931, had done 'practically nothing' over Meerut: it was 'dead in relation to the trial', relying wholly on the efforts of the remaining non-Communists.[123]

115 NMLH, CPGB Archive, Politburo minutes, 21 Aug. 1930 and 13 Feb. 1931; CC minutes, 12 Jan. 1930 and 1 June 1930.

116 NMLH, CPGB Archive, CC minutes, 12 Jan. 1930; Politburo minutes, 24 July 1930.

117 NMLH, CPGB Archive, Politburo minutes, 4 Sept. 1930.

118 NMLH, CPGB Archive, CC minutes, 12 Jan. 1930; IPI, L/PJ/12/381, CPGB circular to local parties, 12 Apr. 1929.

119 NMLH, CPGB Archive, Politburo minutes, 21 Aug. 1930.

120 IPI, L/PJ/12/382, Scotland Yard Reports, 11 June and 23 July 1930.

121 NMLH, CPGB Archive, Politburo minutes, 21 Aug. 1930.

122 NMLH, CPGB Archive, Politburo minutes, 9 Jan. 1932.

123 NMLH, CPGB Archive, Politburo minutes, 1 Oct. 1931, 5 Nov. 1931.

Only four of the local Meerut Defence Committees agreed to be reconstituted as Hands Off India committees, and the departure of the non-Communists left them much poorer and little more than 'the Party meeting itself under another name'.[124] Indeed, there was not a single factory-level Hands Off India Committee.[125] The British Section of the LAI was an elite organisation par excellence: it also had no factory-level presence at all, only one trade union affiliate (the Furnishing Trade Association) and no functioning Indian section. It also had little support outside London: fewer than half its affiliates were outside the capital, and these were mostly miners' branches under CPGB control.[126] The Meerut Defence Committee, in its early non-sectarian phase, had raised around £1,000. In early 1932, as a CPGB-only affair, it made a fresh appeal, but not a single factory sent a contribution, and the sum raised was £3.[127] When one of the Meerut prisoners, Lester Hutchinson, broke with his colleagues over whether to welcome the renewal of Congress civil disobedience, Page Arnot insisted that he be expelled from the group.[128] Since this entailed withholding the funds raised by the CPGB for his defence, it prompted Hutchinson's mother, a powerful presence in the CPGB in Manchester, one of the brighter spots in the Meerut campaign, to set up a rival organisation to support the prisoners.[129] By the time the CPGB lifted its sectarian approach, there was little trust left. In late 1932, with the Meerut prisoners due to be sentenced, the CPGB set up a Prisoners Release Committee on a broader basis. But of 130 letters sent out to potential non-Communist supporters, only a few even received a reply, and these were conditional or non-committal. At its initial meeting, only four people turned up.[130]

[124] NMLH, CPGB Archive, CC minutes, 1 June 1930; 'Plan for Reorganising and Enlivening the British Section of the League Against Imperialism', 11 Aug. 1930, with Politburo 1930 papers; Politburo minutes, 1 Oct. 1931.

[125] NMLH, CPGB Archive, Politburo minutes, 21 Aug. 1930.

[126] NMLH, CPGB Archive, Politburo minutes, 17–18 July 1930 and 13 Feb. 1931; 'Plan for Reorganising and Enlivening the British Section of the League Against Imperialism'.

[127] NMLH, CPGB Archive, Politburo minutes, 4 Feb. 1933; IPI, L/PJ/12/345, IPI estimates of the Meerut Fund, 17 Sept. 1932; L/PJ/12/273, Report of 3rd LAI Annual Conference, 1933 and Scotland Yard Report, 22 Nov. 1933.

[128] NMLH, CPGB Archive, Politburo minutes, 14 Jan. 1932; TNA, KV2/1021, Bradley to Glading, 1 Jan. and 17 Nov. 1932.

[129] IPI, L/PJ/12/272, Scotland Yard Reports, 17 Mar. and 4 May 1932; IPI, L/PJ/12/343, Bradley and Spratt to Bridgeman, 29 May 1930; IPI, L/PJ/12/344, Usmani to Dutt, 18 and 25 July 1930, Thengdi to Hare, 18 July 1930, Thengdi to Saklatvala, 25 July 1930, Thengdi to Bridgeman, 24 Oct. 1930, Bradley to Hare, 18 July 1930; IPI, L/PJ/12/345, Bradley to Glading, 1 Jan. and 5 May 1932, and Bradley to Bridgeman, 19 May, 7 July and 4 Aug. 1932.

[130] NMLH, CPGB Archive, Politburo minutes, 4 Feb. and 9 Mar. 1933.

Indian residents in Britain

A further area of CPGB activity casts additional light on the difficulties of articulating metropolitan anti-imperialism. It concerned the recruitment of Indian residents in Britain, especially sailors and students. The hope was that they might agitate in Britain while living there, or act as couriers or Communist agents in India or elsewhere in the world. Indian sailors made up about a quarter of the British merchant marine. They suffered lower pay, worse working conditions and job security than their white counterparts, as well as regulations which prevented them from competing with white sailors for work.[131] They had been targeted for anti-imperialist work since 1920, but the anti-Communism of the dockers' unions and language problems had hampered the effort.[132] Following racial disturbances in several British ports, the TUC passed resolutions in 1923 and 1924 calling for an end to the employment of Asiatic sailors on British ships and the repatriation of unemployed Asiatic sailors in British ports.[133] In 1925, it and the National Seamen and Firemen's Union (NSFU) were rewarded with the 1925 Coloured Alien Seamen's Order, which forced Indian sailors to obtain special certificates which restricted their employment rights and on-shore movements unless they could provide evidence of British citizenship. This discrimination prompted fresh efforts by the CPGB to capture the Indian sailors for Communism.[134] Under the direction of N.P. Upadhyaya, the Indian Seamen's Union (ISU) managed to build its membership from 310 in August 1926 to 1,500 by July 1927 and 6,000 by 1930, with branches not just in London, but Cardiff, Glasgow and Liverpool.[135]

The ISU was Communist-dominated: its members could not afford subscriptions, so it was entirely paid for by the CPGB. Its executive comprised three Indian sailors and six CPGB and Minority Movement

[131] See Laura Tabili, *'We Ask for British Justice': Workers and Racial Difference in Late Imperial Britain* (Ithaca, NY, 1994) and Gopalan Balachandran, *Globalizing Labour? Indian Seafarers and World Shipping*, c.*1870–1945* (New Delhi, 2012).

[132] IPI, L/PJ/12/143, IPI Reports, 18 May, 2 June and 17 July 1923; L/PJ/12/231, IPI Report on 'K.S. Bhat', n.d.; RGASPI 495/68/104, Roy to Banerji, 23 Apr. 1923, [May 1923?] and 18 May 1923.

[133] Trades Union Congress, *Annual Conference Reports* (1919), 331; (1923), 411–12; (1924), 445–47.

[134] RGASPI 495/100/260, CPGB Provisional Sub-Committee on Indian Sailors, 2 Feb. 1925, and Colonial Committee, 16 Feb. 1925; RGASPI 495/100/260, CPGB Colonial Committee Reports, 5 Mar. and 6 Nov. 1925; RGASPI 495/68/186, 'J' [J.C. Dutt?] to Andrew, 28 Oct. 1926.

[135] IPI, L/PJ/12/233 and 234, IPI Reports on Upadhyaya and Indian Seamen's Union, various dates; TNA, KV3/33, Upadhyaya to Macmanus, 1 Sept. 1925.

representatives. Its members proved valuable as couriers, carrying banned literature and communications from the CPGB to and from the CPI. But its capacity for industrial action was weak. While the NSFU cooperated closely with the employers in the Shipping Federation and secured recognition and gains through a generally non-militant position, most famously in its non-observance of the 1926 General Strike, the ISU was not recognised and, sensitive to the precariousness of the Indian sailors' livelihoods, never risked a strike in a British port. Moreover, the India Office had proved unexpectedly the defender of the Indian sailors in the negotiation of the 1925 Order, against the Board of Trade and the Home Office. This was why the Indian sailors, unlike the Chinese, did not have to register as aliens, but only to obtain certificates. This was, of course, still discriminatory, but the difference of status that had made even this imperially grounded concession possible did not go unnoticed by the Indian sailors and made them to a certain degree dependent on their claimed privileges as British imperial subjects.

Efforts to break down the barriers between British and Indian sailors were largely unsuccessful. British sailors generally failed to support campaigns for equal pay.[136] The dock towns, other than London, were not areas of CPGB strength, and the district committees there usually unaware of the grievances of the Indian sailors, partly owing to language difficulties.[137] A report by Allison for RILU in 1930 noted that the Indians objected to having to be members of two unions and refused to take action for any except their own grievances.[138] Upadhyaya also resented being told by the CPGB to produce Indian sailors for its marches and demonstrations.[139] Efficient dockyard policing also made it hard for the CPGB to get its message across. Even the CPGB agitators in the London docks could do little more than to 'throw the leaflets down the hold and run'.[140]

In the organisation of the Indian sailors, the CPGB favoured approaches by their co-nationals, and instructed its Indian Bureau to make this one of their principal activities. But the lines of class were not so easily bridged. Upadhyaya told a Comintern representative in 1925 that he got support from the British members of the CPGB but nothing from the Indian Bureau.[141]

136 See John Manley, 'Moscow rules? "Red" unionism and "class against class" in Britain, Canada, and the United States, 1928–1935', *Labour/Le Travail*, 56 (2005), 9–50.

137 NMLH, CPGB Archive, Politburo minutes, 21 Aug. 1930.

138 RGASPI 534/7/48, Allison, Report to RILU Colonial Bureau on Indian Seamen's Union, [1930?].

139 IPI, L/PJ/12/233, IPI Report on Indian Seamen's Union, 17 Oct. 1928.

140 NMLH, CPGB Archive, CC minutes, 1 June 1930.

141 'Colonial Conference held at Amsterdam', *Communist Papers*.

He resented the derogatory term 'Lascars', which the Gower Street [i.e., London University] Indians used when referring to Indian sailors.[142] For their part, the Indian sailors refused to join the student-dominated London Branch of the INC because 'an average Indian student would never even speak to an East End Indian'.[143] Harry Pollitt also complained that 'many of the students from colonial countries confined their activities to the West End of London' and were unwilling to work among Indians in the East End.[144]

In any case, at least in the 1920s, the CPGB found it hard to recruit Indian students. There was a large pool. The British undergraduate population in the 1920s was about 42,000, of which 1,800 Indians (some 4 per cent) formed the largest overseas component.[145] Many were politically active and debates in university Indian societies (the university *majlis*) almost invariably found majorities for the Congress position.[146] On the other hand, outside the *majlis*, many Indian students were circumspect about expressing their political views, and some adopted inconspicuousness or a thoroughgoing integration. The *majlis* was only rarely a base from which assaults were easily made on other views, but rather a protected space, created by under-confidence on the part of Indians and exclusiveness on the part of the British, which sustained a belief that Indian students were cliquish or aloof.[147] When in Oxford the Vice-Chancellor tried to insist that Indian students promise not to work for Communism, there was a vote of protest in the Oxford Union. But the Indian students themselves were divided: a majority of them, it was reported, voting for the Vice-Chancellor's

142 IPI, L/PJ/12/233, IPI Report on Upadhyaya, 19 Feb. 1930.

143 IPI, L/PJ/12/233, IPI Reports on Indian Seamen's Union, 28 Mar. 1929, 12 Feb. and 23 July 1930, 18 Mar. 1931.

144 IPI, L/PJ/12/275, Scotland Yard Report of LAI Annual Conference, 25–26 Jan. 1936; *Daily Worker*, 27 Jan. 1936. See also IPI, L/PJ/12/272, 'Summary of Draft of Resolution Prepared ... for the Central Committee of the British Young Communist League', [1931?] and Scotland Yard Report, 4 May [4 Mar.?].

145 V. Carpentier, *Historical Statistics on the Funding and Development of the UK University System, 1920–2002* (SN 4971), UK Data Archive, Essex, July 2004; Shompa Lahiri, *Indians in Britain: Anglo-Indian Encounters, Race and Identity, 1880–1930* (London, 2000); Sumita Mukherjee, *Nationalism, Education and Migrant Identities: The England-Returned* (London, 2010).

146 See, for example, *Indus. The Journal of the Indian Students' Union*, 2.9 (Mar. 1923); 2.11 (May 1923); 6.3 (Dec. 1926); *Report of the Committee on Indian Students 1921–22* (London, 1922).

147 Lahiri, *Indians in Britain*, 117–21; K.P.S. Menon, *Many Worlds: An Autobiography* (London, 1965), 54; S.W.R.D. Bandaranaike, 'Memories of Oxford', in his *Speeches and Writings* (Colombo, 1963), 12–75; G.K. Chettur, *The Last Enchantment: Recollections of Oxford* (Mangalore, 1934), 145–70; K.M. Pannikar, *An Autobiography* (Madras, 1977), 14.

position.[148] The Vice-Chancellor's first attempt to summon Indian students to meet him so that he could instruct them in loyalty was disrupted by a smoke-bomb; yet the second, at least by his own account, evinced murmurs of appreciation for the imperially grounded sentiments he expressed.[149] A report of the Oxford *majlis* found among the CPGB's papers during police raids in 1925 showed detailed analysis of the political composition of the student body, and plans for converts to be interviewed by Saklatvala before their return to India.[150] However, the list contained few promising recruits, and some of these were regarded as too committed to Gandhism or possessing only a theoretical interest in socialism. 'Groups of [Indian] students were always timid of being approached', Tom Bell reported in 1925, and shied away as soon as the CPGB was mentioned.[151] The Colonial Committee planned Communist study circles, but the Young Communist League (YCL) report for 1925 suggested that very little such work had been done.[152] When the CPGB directed students to campaign in May 1930, one local CP was told that the Indian students were too fearful of the authorities to take the work on.[153] The CPGB also had to fight off rival claims for the students' political support. Its anti-Gandhian stance, Saklatvala told the Politburo, was working 'very effectively' to limit the CP's influence among students.[154] The Indian Students' Hostel in London voted in 1931 to expel its Communist members for heckling visiting Indian politicians. When Harry Pollitt had addressed it, he had criticised Indians for failing to live up to their radical speeches.[155]

However, in the 1930s, in line with a wider radicalisation of student opinion, Indian students were easier to recruit. The CPGB had disbanded the Indian Bureau in 1929.[156] But in 1932, Comintern, keen that attacks

[148] Chinmohan Sehavanis, 'Communism at Oxford in the Mid-Twenties', in Barun De (ed.), *Essays in Honour of Prof. S.C. Sarkar* (New Delhi, 1976); 'Our Oxford Letter', *Indus*, 5 (Apr. 1926), 7.

[149] *Report of the Committee on Indian Students*. See also the minutes of evidence at British Library, OIOC, Official Publications series, India Office Records, IOR/V/26/864/13, Indian Students (Lytton) Committee 1921–22: Part 2 Evidence, 21–22.

[150] 'Report on the Composition of the Oxford Majlis', June 1925, *Communist Papers*, doc. 40.

[151] RGAPSI 495/100/260, Tom Bell, 'Report to CPGB Colonial Commission', 26 Mar. 1925.

[152] 'Report of Meeting of CPGB Colonial Committee', 15 Dec. 1924, *Communist Papers*, doc 43.

[153] IPI, L/PJ/12/382, Scotland Yard Report, 28 May 1930.

[154] NMLH, CPGB Archive, Politburo minutes, 17–18 July 1930.

[155] IPI, L/PJ/12/42, Scotland Yard Reports, 23 July, 20 Aug., 3 Sept. and 15 Oct. 1930, 13 May 1931.

[156] RGASPI 495/68/307, 'Letter Concerning Indian Work in Great Britain', 3 Oct. 1929.

on Congress should come from Indians in Britain, not white British Communists, proposed a secret bureau of three Indian Communist students and one representative of the CPGB. It would work among students and sailors, tap the funds of rich Indians, ship literature to India and recruit fellow Indians who would then return to India as trained Communist agents.[157] The London Indian Group (LIG) was duly set up at some distance from the party, so as not to arouse suspicion, with Communist instruction provided by a British CPGB tutor, but no contact permitted with the CPGB leadership. The LIG students resented their exclusion from party work, but were told by Glading and Rust that they had to learn patience and prepare for their return to India.[158] They were not satisfied, however, and in 1932 and 1934 complained about the incompetence and indifference of the CPGB and the *Daily Worker* on Indian questions.[159] In the *Communist Review*, one of them argued that there was 'a tendency to postpone the raising of the anti-imperialist question on important occasions', and 'even when the question is raised it is very often dealt with in a mechanical, general and lifeless manner'.[160] When the CPGB refused the LIG's request for a new booklet, on the grounds of its expense and difficulty for British workers, it broke ranks and wrote directly to Comintern.[161] This was followed by a further complaint in 1936, when two meetings with Bradley failed to satisfy them that they were being taken seriously as Communists.[162] These flaws were acknowledged privately by the Politburo and some of the Indians were brought on to the CPGB Colonial Committee.[163]

Here, as with the Indian sailors, difficulties were arguably created by questions of status among activists. Such aspects of social movements have usually been regarded as trivial matters of cultural difference, or just poor manners. In some movements, this may be true, but in movements

157 TNA, HW, 17/77, Comintern to CPGB (CBP15), 20 Feb. 1932; TNA, HW, 17/71, Comintern to CPGB (CC77), 16 Sept. 1932.

158 Nirmal Sen Gupta, *The Influence of Communism among Indian Students in London* (Calcutta, 1989).

159 'P' to Chatto and others, 13 Aug. 1932, in Roy, Gupta and Vasudevan, *Indo-Russian Relations*, ii. 179–80; Indian Communists' Group to Secretariat, CPGB, 9 Apr. 1934, in Roy, Gupta and Vasudevan, *Indo-Russian Relations*, ii. 224–25.

160 An Indian Comrade, 'The Anti-Imperialist Struggle in Britain', *Communist Review*, July 1934, 113–16.

161 'Submission to Comintern by Communist Group of Indians in Great Britain', 4 Sept. 1934, in Roy, Gupta and Vasudevan, *Indo-Russian Relations*, ii. 226–27.

162 RGASPI 495/16/34, Statement of the Indian Members of the CPGB, [Sept. 1936?].

163 TNA, KV2/1021, Bradman (Campbell) at Politburo, 4 May 1934; Report on Percy Glading, n.d.; TNA, KV2/1037, Note on Pollitt's activities, 9 Aug. 1934; IPI, L/PJ/12/274, IPI Report on 'League Against Imperialism and Connected Communist Activities', 4 July 1934.

which seek to transform the respect in which some (but not all) activists' identities, backgrounds, and capacities are held, they are close to essential. The same year, these sensitivities were also raised by Saklatvala on his return from a visit to the Soviet Union. Saklatvala had been impressed by Communist work in the Asian and Trans-Caucasian Republics.[164] He had, he wrote, usually held his tongue over the CPGB's poor attitude to Indian work in the past, 'fearing that it might be an over nationalistic tendency in myself'. But he now felt status differences were 'a defect which ought not to exist inside the Communist Party'. Even local parties could be unaware of the struggles of the Indian sailors against harassment by employers and the police. 'Many things happen ... [there]', he wrote, 'and members of the Party and of the unemployed workers' movement, living right in the locality know nothing about it, can give me no information, and have no plans of even friendly contacts or any desire to learn of the situation'. In the united front organisations which the Communists, in line with the latest shift of Comintern strategy, now favoured, white Labour MPs and bourgeois radicals were being recruited, but not Indians. Indian students were not invited into the homes of the Communist leaders, as they were by liberals and retired officials running bourgeois welfare campaigns. Grassroots party members themselves felt no special involvement in anti-colonial work. This was resented by the Indians, and although Saklatvala acknowledged such resentment could be 'exaggerated and unnecessarily hostile' it reflected a natural sense of frustration and disappointment at their exclusion.

Conclusions

The vanguardism of the Communist Party was both asset and liability. As a substitute for the leadership and influence that Gandhi had removed from the metropole, it helped to solve anti-imperialism's organisational dilemma. But this came at a price: the reappropriation of leadership from the Indian movement. The CPGB leaders were unembarrassed about their wish to be, as Saklatvala himself had put it earlier, the 'tail that wags the [Congress] dog'.[165] Indian nationalism, Page Arnot argued, was 'not something to repress, but something to raise to a higher level'.[166] For nationalists, however, if not for Communists, this created a tension in alliances, for leadership on such terms often entailed the subordinating of the needs of the Indian

[164] RGASPI 495/100/938, Shapurji Saklatvala, 'A Few Thoughts on Party Work', n.d.; *Daily Worker*, 20 July 1934.
[165] IPI, L/PJ/12/441, Scotland Yard Report, 9 Dec. 1931.
[166] NMLH, CPGB Archive, CC minutes, 1 June 1930.

movement to Communist demands. Communist anti-imperialism tended to be intolerant of local variations at the periphery, and suspicious of spontaneous, premature or apparently undisciplined mass actions which they did not understand.

Marx's writings seemed at the time to support such a stance for although they vigorously attacked imperialism as hypocritical and exploitative they also argued that Britain had to fulfil a 'double role in India, one destructive, the other regenerative – the annihilation of the Asiatic society and the laying of the material foundations of western society'.[167] Later, as Robert Young has argued, there was to emerge a reworked 'tricontinental' Marxism, bringing Marxism and national liberation into a dialectical, but productive relationship.[168] But although with the benefit of hindsight it is possible to catch sight of such reworkings quite early – at the 1920 Baku Congress and in the work of Sultan-Galiev, for example – these were rudimentary developments before the 1940s and, even then, not influential in India. Marxist categories were generally imported into India from Europe ready-packed rather than developed indigenously, and matters such as religion, linguistic divisions and the dominance of agriculture were given relatively little attention.

Communist anti-imperialism, in short, was to be *applied* to India, and, while Indian views were useful so as to enable the application to be made successfully, nationality and experiences were unimportant in the formulation of the application itself. Even Bradley's leadership in Meerut prison was described by Usmani, a fellow Indian prisoner, as exhibiting a 'distinct governing lust'. '[M]ost of our group have not yet cast off their timidity and the habit of being governed', Usmani told C.P. Dutt. 'Bradley with these people looks like "His Excellency" the Viceroy with his Council'.[169] Such stern authority was tempered by real solidarity, for Bradley was, after all, in prison with the Indians, not trying to direct the movement from afar. But nonetheless it made it clear who was in charge and why. When the CPGB recruited Indians in London, it did not do so in order to hear them speak for India. This was not because it believed them incapable of so doing but because the Communist Party was not intended to be a representative party at all. It recruited all its members for instruction, in order to assign them tasks, not because it wished to represent their views. In this limited sense alone, the Communist Party was colour-blind. Indians such as Saklatvala and the Dutt brothers were given leadership roles in the Communist Party,

[167] See Aijaz Ahmad, 'Marx on India: A Clarification', in his *In Theory: Classes, Nations, Literatures* (London, 1992).

[168] Robert Young, *Postcolonialism: An Historical Introduction* (Oxford, 2001).

[169] IPI, L/PJ/12/344, Usmani to Dutt, 18 July 1930.

but their Indianness was almost wholly irrelevant to their progress in the party, either negatively or positively.

This was at odds with an important element of Indian nationalism: its commitment to self-directed and self-reliant national struggle. It also suggests an important and often neglected aspect of efforts to understand metropolitan anti-imperialism. Decolonisation was not only a matter of what the British might do for the colonised but also of what the colonised wanted done for them. Terms such as sympathy, help and solidarity are not neutral terms: they define distinct relationships between those who act and those who benefit.

The unstated assumption of much work is that demand from the colonised was constant and unproblematic. Anti-colonial movements in the colonies, being distant, weak and needy, must, it is implied, have wanted all the external help they could get. The only important question was whose help they got, and on what terms. What this neglects is a lively debate among constituents concerning the value or necessity of the services of adherents. The neglect has occurred for two main reasons.

First, the best known anti-colonialists in the West were those who for the most part favoured such services, even if some of them insisted on tough terms for their delivery. They spoke to the colonisers, understood them, moved relatively frequently to and from the colonial metropole, and so forth. Those whose anti-colonialism was not expressed in English or other global languages, nor much addressed to audiences outside the colony, are less well-known outside their own countries. Their scepticism concerning the desirability of appeals to outsiders is therefore easily missed.

Secondly, neglect has occurred because until recently most models of colonial relations have been structured by the binary relationship between metropole and colony. Older metropolitan-centred models saw anti-imperial ideas – whether nationalist, or liberal or indeed Communist – radiating outwards from the metropole, stimulating responses on the colonial periphery. They privileged those actors who responded most clearly, whether through imitation or challenge, to the stimulus. Nationalist models of colonial relations were hardly less binary. They privileged actors who first drew strength from and stimulated their own incipient nation, and then turned outwards to face their occupier. In both models, those who faced in other directions, or turned their faces away altogether, have been harder to see. They are now more of a presence in the histories of national movements. But they have yet to be properly acknowledged as significant absences in the history of metropolitan anti-colonialism.

4

'The Lingua Franca of the Bangle'

Ellen Wilkinson, the Indian Nationalist Movement and British Labour, 1932

Matt Perry

In autumn 1932, Ellen Wilkinson, best known as the leader of the Jarrow Crusade and Attlee's Minister of Education, visited India. Until recently, anti-imperialism has been perhaps one of the most misunderstood and neglected dimensions of Wilkinson's career.[1] Thus, her novel *The Clash* has been criticised for displaying no awareness of colonialism and racism.[2] By contrast, Wilkinson's involvement in the cause of colonial liberation and anti-racism was long-standing. The British and Indian press, personal papers and India Office sources allow insight to examine the relationships between Wilkinson, the Indian nationalist movement and the British state. Wilkinson's relationship with India might be located within a critical examination of difference, considering the micro-level interplay between cultural difference and transnational contentious politics. Wilkinson provides an interesting case in point: rather than denying or evading difference, cultural contrasts (and crucially their social and political ramifications) suffuse Wilkinson's visit and her writing about it. Finally, the significance of this Indian visit in Wilkinson's intellectual and political itinerary is evaluated and how she incorporated her Indian experiences into her view of a world facing economic crisis, political instability and war.

During the interwar period, despite formal sympathy for the Indian people, the Labour Party's anti-imperialism disappointed Indian nation-

[1] For recent scholarship, see Paula Bartley, *Ellen Wilkinson: From Suffragist and Communist to Government* (London, 2014); Matt Perry, *'Red Ellen' Wilkinson: Her Ideas, Movement and World* (Manchester, 2014); Laura Beers, *Red Ellen: The Life of Ellen Wilkinson, Socialist, Feminist, Internationalist* (Boston, MA, 2016); Barbara Bush, 'Feminising Empire? British Women's Activist Networks in Defending and Challenging Empire from 1918 to Decolonisation', *Women's History Review*, 25 (2016), 499–519.

[2] M. Keith Booker, *The Modern British Novel of the Left* (Westport, CT, 1998), 307–9. For comment on 'backward races', *North Eastern Daily Gazette*, 30 Mar. 1928. On West African 'superstition', *Daily Mail*, 9 Apr. 1931.

alists and their British supporters.[3] Partha Sarathi Gupta proposed that Labour's desire to govern, the advice of ex-colonial administrators and the lack of a theory of imperialism caused these apparent failings.[4] Conversely, Edward Said attributed such weaknesses to an orientalist consensus wherein normative assumptions, stereotypes, conventions, symbolic representations and discourses reproduced Western domination, subsuming within it even those who appeared to criticise Empire.[5] Genealogically stretching back to Derrida's *Writing and Difference* (1967) and, despite their divergences, underpinning Said's *Orientalism* (1978), the concept of cultural difference has assumed the status of a master category within post-colonial studies. From the vantage point of Indian historiography, difference played a crucial role in Subaltern Studies' drift from Thompsonian Marxism to post-structuralism.[6] Thus, Chakrabarty criticised Hobsbawm's *Primitive Rebels* (1959) – a text that pioneered peasant studies and history from below – for its elitism (as a consequence of his 'not yet' historicism) towards the peasants who required civilising lessons from the West.[7] Chakrabarty's argument rests in part on the differentiated temporalities implicit in contrasting religious and secular belief systems. Failure to recognise this results in homogenisation and universalist assumptions. Systematising difference yet further, Partha Chatterjee characterised the nature of the British Raj as 'the rule of colonial difference'.[8] Encounters – Homi Bhabha pessimistically argued – between those from the metropolitan power and

[3] Mesbahuddin Ahmed, *The British Labour Party and the Indian Independence Movement, 1917–1939* (London, 1987); K.C. Arora, *Indian Nationalist Movement in Britain, 1930–1949* (New Delhi, 1992). This ambiguity regarding Empire was a feature of wider Labour foreign policy and attitudes within the Labour and Socialist International. See E.J. Hobsbawm, 'Working-Class Internationalism', in Frits von Holtoom and Marcel van der Linden (eds), *Internationalism and the Labour Movement* (Leiden, 1988), 3–16; Rhiannon Vickers, *The Labour Party and the World*, vol. 1, *The Evolution of Labour's Foreign Policy* (Manchester, 2003); John Callaghan, *The Labour Party and Foreign Policy: A History* (London, 2007).

[4] For a rejection of the labour aristocratic thesis, see Partha S. Gupta, *Imperialism and the British Labour Movement, 1914–1964* (London, 1975).

[5] Edward W. Said, *Orientalism* (New York, 1978).

[6] Criticising post-colonialist accounts of the Marxist category of abstract labour as homogenising (as an automatic consequence of being a universalising force) and therefore the inadequacy of Marxism to deal with racial difference. Vivek Chibber, *Postcolonial Theory and the Specter of Capital* (London, 2013), 130–51. Locating the philological gap in Chibber's argument regarding the influence of Heidegger and Nietzsche, see Timothy Brennan, 'Subaltern Stakes', *New Left Review*, 89 (2014), 67–87.

[7] E.J. Hobsbawm, *Primitive Rebels: Studies in Archaic Forms of Social Movement in the 19th and 20th Centuries* (Manchester, 1959); Dipesh Chakrabarty, 'Minority Histories, Subaltern Pasts', *Postcolonial Studies*, 1 (1998), 15–29.

[8] Partha Chatterjee, *The Nation and Its Fragments: Colonial and Postcolonial Histories* (Princeton, NJ, 1993), 10.

the colony constituted 'a process of misrecognition where each point of identification is always a partial and double repetition of the *otherness* of the self'. He thereby rules out the very possibility of any form of transcendence or negation of difference.[9] Vasant Kaiwar, however, has proposed such 'fetishism of difference' has led to an analytical, conceptual and methodological impasse in Subaltern Studies.[10] He argues that the research project has become mired in abstraction and its political implications foreclose the possibility of genuine (past or prospective) transformative politics beyond fragmentary empowerment at the micro-level. Such an emphasis upon difference can be found in writing on the interactions between the metropolitan left and revolutionaries in the colonies. For Nicholas Owen, the British left's support for Nehru rather than Gandhi stemmed from cultural assumptions of metropolitan superiority.[11] More sympathetic to such efforts, Kumari Jayawardena surveyed the interactions between Western women and South Asia under colonial rule.[12] She recovered British women revolutionaries who challenged British rule and raised class and gender in an Indian context. Demonised by the authorities, their local reception was contradictory. When they identified with the Indian cause, they were viewed as 'goddesses'. When they criticised South Asian culture on the grounds of gender or tradition, they were viewed as 'devils'. This debate evidently poses serious dilemmas for scholars of transnationalism. Trying to purge Eurocentrism from old labour history, Marcel van der Linden has called for rebuilding labour history with a widened category of the subaltern worker (not exclusively the wage-labourer of the USA and Europe) that recognises the multiple cultural specificities of capitalist relations.[13] Moreover, moving from the false alternatives of Eurocentric capitalist stages of development and culturally autonomous development, a trend within Indian labour history has embraced transnational themes of itinerant labour, seafarers and migrants.[14]

[9] Homi K. Bhabha, *The Location of Culture* (New York, 1994), 138–39.

[10] Vasant Kaiwar, *The Postcolonial Orient: The Politics of Difference and the Project of Provincialising Europe* (Leiden, 2014). An analogy might be drawn with the quite different critique provided in Rita Felski, 'The Doxa of Difference', *Signs*, 23 (1997), 1–21.

[11] Nicholas Owen, *The British Left and India: Metropolitan Anti-Imperialism, 1885–1947* (Oxford, 2007).

[12] Kumari Jayawardena, *The White Woman's Other Burden: Western Women and South Asia During Colonial Rule* (London, 1995).

[13] Marcel van der Linden, *Workers of the World: Essays toward a Global Labor History* (Leiden, 2008), 363–66.

[14] Rana P. Benhal, Chitra Joshi and Prabu P. Mohapatra, 'India', in Joan Allen, Alan Campbell and John McIlroy, *Histories of Labour: National and International Perspectives* (Pontypool, 2010), 290–314.

Trip to India, autumn 1932

In autumn 1932, Wilkinson travelled to India along with Monica Whately, Leonard Matters and V.K. Krishna Menon on the India League's behalf.[15] The trip's rationale was to secure 'reliable witnesses' to inform British public opinion of the 'truth about India'.[16] The Indian National Congress's civil disobedience campaign and the British colonial government's repressive ordinances provided the background. Originally, the intention was to send a group of four, including two MPs. The organisers were 'specially anxious' to persuade Wilkinson, who had already secured permission for unpaid leave from her union duties, because of her flare for publicity and her British and American press contacts.[17]

The visit occurred at a delicate moment in the Indian struggle. The global economic slump strained the interdependent underpinnings of the British and Indian economies and these pressures manifested in the Ottawa negotiations over trade within the Empire, the boycott of British imported goods and the Lancashire cotton strike. When the Simon commission rejected independence in May 1929, Congress launched a campaign of civil disobedience (1930–1931). Cycles of protest entwined with the sequence of Round Table Conferences of British and Indian representatives (November 1930–January 1931, September–December 1931 and November–December 1932). The government was gauging reaction to the 'communal award' announced in August 1932 that reorganised the electoral system according ethnic-religious constituencies. The award exacerbated tensions, especially in the Punjab and Bengal, or along caste (particularly amongst the Untouchables) or gender lines.[18] By autumn 1932, repression seemed to be having its toll as protest was declining. Gandhi's fasting compensated for the decline of mass disobedience.[19]

Wilkinson and her party arrived in Bombay (Mumbai) on 17 August 1932. From there, the trip covered enormous distances. They journeyed from Bombay to Madras via Pune, spending a fortnight in the Madras Presidency with a week in Madras city. This leg of their visit extended as far south as Calicut. They then took in Orissa, Bengal, Assam, the United Provinces, the Punjab and the North-West Frontier. Their return to Bombay

[15] 'Denouncing the Trip', *Daily Worker*, 14 July 1932.

[16] India League Appeal from Bertrand Russell, C.F. Andrews, H.J. Laski, E. Pethick-Lawrence and J.F. Horrabin, 12 July 1932.

[17] Newcastle University Special Collections (NUSC), T.D.W. Reid Collection, Home Political (HP), 1932–1940, XII, 2, M.G. Hallett to Sir Samuel Findlater Steward.

[18] *Madras Weekly Mail*, 25 Aug. 1932.

[19] On the effect of 300 arrests in Bombay in August, see *Times of India*, 3 Sept. 1932.

went via Delhi, the Sind (including Karachi) and Gujarat. They stressed that they interviewed all shades of opinion, not only Congress activists but also government officials, other political organisations, trade union leaders, employers and women's organisations. After nearly seven weeks, the delegation's tour of India ended in Bombay on 7 November.

The filter of colonial legitimacy and the movement's cultural-political diversity

The authorities tried to use the filter of colonial legitimacy – combining a rationalising discourse and censorship – to alter the perceptions of the investigators. The authorities explicitly desired to keep the delegation 'on the leash'. Despite the authorities providing senior officials to interview, the India League delegation succeeded in going beyond this. Thus, the Bengal secretariat of the government of India complained that the investigators saw the area 'largely through Congress spectacles'. It was one of many such complaints. Congress spectacles were unnecessary, however, as on several occasions police officials indiscreetly divulged the brutality of British rule. On the day after their arrival in Bombay, Whately and Wilkinson interviewed Sir Patrick Kelly, of Bombay Police Head Office. He quizzed them about receiving Congress money and denied them access to political prisoners. Kelly did admit the use of whips for jail discipline, on pickets and during communal disturbances. He advised them that they would only hear truthful accounts from government officials.[20] The authorities failed to prevent the delegation from access to prisons or from seeing violent repression of demonstrations. Wilkinson regaled *Daily Herald* readers with her cunning in gaining prison access, despite the authorities' determination to prevent this. When told a man's prison was no place for an Englishwoman, she countered that if it was not fit for a woman to see, it was not fit to keep a man in and that she would tell the world this. She gained access to eight jails, including the 'beating jail' of Rae Bareli (meeting children aged eight given six-month sentences for distributing leaflets and pulling a train's communication cord).[21] On 11 September, Wilkinson and her colleagues witnessed the police ruthlessly beat a student demonstration in Calcutta so as to disperse it.[22] The intelligence report on their first week in India insinuated that Congress had attempted to 'stage a *lathi* [five-foot

[20] NUSC, Reid Collection, HP, 40 12, Kelly to Clee, 18 Aug. 1932.

[21] *Daily Herald*, 15 Feb. 1933.

[22] Monica Whately, Ellen Wilkinson, Leonard W. Matters and V.K. Krishna Menon, *Condition of India: Being the Report of the Delegation Sent to India by The India League in 1932* (London, 1933), 182.

cane baton] charge for the delegation's edification'.[23] The 'stage-managed' demonstrations and peaceful protesters being culpable for the violence inflicted upon them was a recurrent trope of both the police authorities in India and the British government to undermine the delegation. Police officials in Madras sought to undermine their findings, highlighting to their superiors that opinion was stage-managed, that interviewees were coached, as well as underlining the visit's brevity and superficiality. They even cast doubt on *lathi* scars shown to the delegates.[24] The most vivid experience of repression that Wilkinson saw herself was in Mardan (North West Frontier Province, NWFP).[25] In a guest house, Wilkinson interviewed witnesses about an incident when seventy villagers were killed in May 1930, asking the police who were accompanying her to leave while she did so. Police roughly beat the crowd that assembled outside with *lathis* and rifle butts.[26] Wilkinson witnessed it all from the first floor veranda. Armed police even surrounded and threatened Wilkinson's chauffeur. While playing all this down, local police reports admitted the use of force. Not forewarned of the delegation's presence, the local police were arresting those leaving the guest house, believing a meeting of the *Khudai Khidmatgars* (KK, the Servants of God, or the Red Shirts as they became known) to be inside. A plain clothes police officer rescued the situation, bringing orders for the armed reserve to withdraw. Later on, Wilkinson complained to Mardan's Joint Deputy Commissioner that a man was beaten with his hands tied behind his back. The next day, Wilkinson and Menon, upset by the Mardan events, visited senior Peshawar police officials. After the incident, the authorities withdrew permission for them to visit Haripur Central Prison. Reporting on the visit to the NWFP, local officials congratulated themselves that – the Mardan incident notwithstanding – little occurred that could not be denied. They had provided Wilkinson with government officials and loyalists to talk to and she had enjoyed the 'social and sight-seeing side of her visit', with the result that the tour 'has probably done more good than harm from the Government's point of view'.[27] However, official

23 British Library, IOR/L/PJ/12/448, Extract of weekly report of the Director, Intelligence Bureau, Home Department, Government of India, Simla, 15 Sept. 1932, no. 36. *Lathis* were three- or five-foot canes issued to police which could inflict vicious even fatal blows.

24 Whately et al., *Condition of India*, 183.

25 On the repression, see Mukulika Banerjee, 'Justice and Non-Violent Jihad: The Anti-Colonial Struggle in the North West Frontier of British India', *Études rurales*, 149–50 (1999), 181–98; Irfan Habib, 'Civil Disobedience 1930–31', *Social Scientist*, 25 (1997), 43–66.

26 Whately et al., *Condition of India*, 415–25.

27 NUSC, Reid Collection, HP, 40 12, Secret Report: Visit to the NWFP of Miss Wilkinson and Menon, 18 Oct. 1932. Report of the Assistant Superintendant of Police, Mardan.

investigations into the Mardan incident confidentially stated, despite local police denials, that Wilkinson's accusations 'must be accepted as true'.[28] A handwritten comment in the confidential official correspondence about her investigation into a riot and repression in Chittagong provided another backstage admission of Wilkinson's veracity, noting: 'I am afraid we may have trouble over this, which will be a pity as the Govt of Bengal have got away with it so easily'.[29] With the tour drawing to a close, in interviews with police officials, Wilkinson encountered the official formula of the 'possibility of occasional abuses' after Congress 'provocation'. When she remarked on the widespread anti-government discontent, this was blamed on 'lying and poisonous propaganda'.[30] A substantial part of the investigation was concerned with the contested claims about incidents when the authorities fired into crowds. Official figures for 1932, which did not include all incidents, admitted 29 occasions of the police or army firing into the crowds with 80 fatalities and 308 injured.[31] The commission investigated such events in Kohat (NWFP), Benares, Tarapore (Bihar and Orissa), Tehatta (Bengal), Hashanbad and Musaffarpur.[32]

With the cooperation between the Congress leadership and the delegation, the problem of an elitist Congress filter might equally skew the perspectives of the delegation homogenising their understanding of the movement. Congress provided guides and interpreters and it would be impossible for Wilkinson to comprehend India and the entire complexity of its social movements in such a visit. Wilkinson also gained access to the Congress leadership. Wilkinson's transnational connections within the international women's movement played a role in her visit to Gandhi in jail. Pressing to see suffragist and acquaintance Sarojini Naidu, Wilkinson gained permission to enter Yerwada jail (in Pune, Maharashtra), accompanying Naidu's daughter.[33] The authorities had sentenced Naidu to one year's imprisonment for leaving Bombay for Delhi despite a ban on movement. After Gandhi's arrest, she had taken over leadership of a march on a salt works with hundreds of Congress volunteers. Entry into the prison allowed Wilkinson to visit Gandhi who

[28] NUSC, Reid Collection, HP, 40 12, Civil Secretariat, NWFP, to Hallett, 15 Nov. 1932.

[29] NUSC, Reid Collection, HP, 40 12, Bengal Secretariat to Hallett, 17 Oct. 1932. British Library, IOR/L/PJ/12/448, Confidential: Copy of a DO no. 1088 PSD, from the Government of Bengal to the Government of India, Home Department, 17 Oct. 1932.

[30] NUSC, Reid Collection, HP, 40 12, confidential note, R.L. Ritter, 30 Oct. 1932; note, 31 Oct. 1932.

[31] Whately et al., *Condition of India*, 186–87.

[32] Whately et al., *Condition of India*, 185–91. The press was denouncing Congress women at Benares for fabricating a lathi charge. See *Madras Weekly Mail*, 25 Aug. 1932.

[33] *Time and Tide*, 7 Jan. 1933.

had just began his fast over Untouchability.[34] He had telegrammed to see Wilkinson. They discussed Congress's cotton boycott and the poverty of the Indian peasant who depended on extra income from hand-weaving.[35] She believed that jailing Gandhi was folly as no lasting settlement could be agreed without him. Only strengthening peasant devotion for him, the government might be forced to deal with the less moderate Nehru.[36] The visibly weakened Congress leader's courage deeply impressed Wilkinson. Despite her criticisms of his political judgement, he had the power to 'grab one by the heart'.[37] Wilkinson cabled the *Daily Herald* condemning separate electorates as Untouchables perceived this policy as perpetuating their status as well as relaying a message from Gandhi.[38] Wilkinson neither experienced nor presented a homogeneous nationalist movement. In the British press, she praised the unnoticed work of women activists who challenged Untouchability in the temples and at the wells.[39] Untouchability was a recurrent dimension of her visit. On their first day in India, the delegation had met Rajbhoj, a leader of the 'depressed classes'.[40] The communal award divided the leaders of the Untouchables with Ambedkar preferring separate electorates but Rajah and Congress preferring joint ones.[41]

Towards the end of their tour, on 20 October, she and Menon met with Gandhi for a second time; on this occasion, after his release, at his *ashram* (spiritual retreat) in Ahmedabad.[42] There, Wilkinson mixed with prominent Congress leaders planning the next stage in the Untouchables campaign and involved herself in the immediacy of Indian political contestation. On 24 October, she gave a speech at an Anti-Untouchable League 'bhajan'

[34] *The Englishman* (Calcutta), 19 Sept. 1932. Gandhi threatened to starve himself to death should the British not withdraw separate electorates for Untouchables. Geraldine Forbes, *Women in Modern India* (Cambridge, 1999), 134.

[35] *Northern Daily Telegraph*, 10 Oct. 1934.

[36] On Ellen Wilkinson's support for Nehru, see Library of the Society of Friends, Friends House, TEMP MS 46 13, Agatha Harrison to Ellen Wilkinson, 13 Oct. 1935; Harrison to Nehru, 20 Oct. 1935; Nehru's engagements, 26 Jan.–6 Feb. 1935. Thanks to Nicholas Owen for this lead. Also, Matt Perry, *'Red Ellen' Wilkinson: Her Ideas, Movements and World* (Manchester, 2014), 197–98 nn. 172–81.

[37] *Daily Herald*, 7 Dec. 1932.

[38] *India Bulletin*, Oct. 1932; *Times of India*, 16 Sept. 1932.

[39] *Star*, 25 Nov. 1932; Whately et al., *Condition of India*, 129–34; Christophe Jaffrelot, *Dr Ambedkar and Untouchability: Analysing and Fighting Caste* (London, 2005). On the Women's Association of India's resolution for the immediate eradication of Untouchability, see *The Englishman*, 19 Sept. 1932.

[40] *The Statesman*, 26 Aug. 1932.

[41] *Madras Weekly Mail*, 25 Aug. 1932.

[42] *Times of India*, 21 Oct. 1932.

in Ahmedabad, at which she negotiated cultural difference by describing herself as an English Untouchable for being a trade union official.[43] This exemplified her repeated framing strategy of identification as an act of solidarity rather than an egocentric preoccupation or as part of an autobiographical narrative. Such a transposition of self and other was symptomatic of Red Ellen's wider public persona of public virtue and abnegation.

Her engagement with the Untouchables campaign had a further significance: her experience of the diversity of the movements in India. As well as this campaign, in Chittagong, Wilkinson attended a meeting of the Swadeshi (consumer boycott) movement, which had not met for a year as a consequence of a ban.[44] She also encountered women's campaigning, student activism, Indian trade unionism and in the turbulent North West Frontier Province the non-violent KK, a pro-Congress Muslim mass organisation of Pathan ethnicity led by Abdul Ghaffar Khan, the 'Frontier Gandhi'.[45] Bengal illustrates Wilkinson's chameleon-like ability to talk to the authorities and revolutionary nationalists. Wilkinson, who knew Sir John Anderson, the Governor of Bengal, personally, stayed the weekend at Government House in Darjeeling. Opposition to British rule in Bengal had taken the form of assassination of British officials, especially the police. Up to September 1932, according to the *Madras Weekly Mail*, from the beginning of 1931, there had been 67 'outrages' and 9 'murders'.[46] Shortly before the arrival of the India League delegation, the Bengal legislative council had passed anti-terror legislation speeding up trials.[47] Despite possible terrorist attack upon him, Anderson accompanied Wilkinson to the Bazaar; his courage impressed her greatly.[48] Indicative of Wilkinson's engagement with the breadth of this multifaceted conflict, she also spoke with the lawyer Sham Lal. He had represented the renowned communist revolutionary Bhagat Singh, who was

[43] *Times of India*, 27 Oct. 1932.

[44] *Times of India*, 14 Sept. 1932.

[45] Mukulika Banerjee, *The Pathan Unarmed: Opposition and Memory in the North West Frontier* (Oxford, 2000), 57. Contrast this account with the reporting in the contemporary British press that claimed that 'mob savagery' had instigated the violence, with three British soldiers killed and an armed car set alight and that troops had behaved splendidly. No mention of 200 deaths of demonstrators is made, though the use of machine guns was admitted (*The Times*, 24, 25 and 26 Apr. 1930).

[46] *Madras Weekly Mail*, 8 Sept. 1932. On 24 September, Bengali revolutionaries had attacked the Assam-Bengal Railway European Institute killing one European and injuring eight (*The Englishman*, 26 Sept. 1932). In mid-August, two were killed in another attack in Chittagong (*Madras Weekly Mail*, 25 Aug. 1932).

[47] *The Englishman*, 5 and 12 Sept. 1932. This paper wanted a mandatory rather than discretionary death sentence.

[48] *The Clarion*, 17 Mar. 1934; James Arthur Salter, *Slave of the Lamp: A Public Servant's Notebook* (London, 1967), 110.

executed after the Lahore conspiracy trial.[49] Singh had assassinated a police officer in retaliation for the death at police hands of Lala Lajpat Rai on a non-violent protest against the Simon Commission.

Madras workers and Dehli students: political affinities, cultural differences

If one of the charges against such investigations was that a Congress filter always mediated Wilkinson and the Indian people and that she acted as a passive observer of events she could not herself comprehend, there were occasions when Wilkinson had direct access to the movement and acted as an intermediary between Indian and British radicals. This opened the possibility of cultural and political transfers between these groups. This had two aspects: first, when Ellen Wilkinson directly addressed Indian railway workers and students, and secondly, on her return home when she addressed the social movements of the UK relaying her Indian experiences. These moments of transnational mediation help understand her relationship to cultural difference.

Reporting on her experience in Madras, Wilkinson sought a dialogue between British and Indian workers through her journalism in her union's magazine *New Dawn*. There, she met Shiva Rao, who she had first encountered at the League Against Imperialism (LAI) founding conference in Brussels. He took her into the working-class quarter of Perambur, with its appalling housing conditions. She was then taken to an outdoor meeting of the railway workers' union. The All-India Railwaymen's Federation (AIRF) had been preparing a strike since early August.[50] She described the poverty of Indian workers as an international scandal, advocating complete self-government but observing that freedom would never be real unless India's workers achieved complete economic freedom. The only solution to the evils of capitalism, she observed, was the international solidarity of the working classes.[51] Challenging the assumptions about India amongst her readership and cleverly using familiar cultural references, she discussed her young interpreter in the workshops. He was a trilingual union executive member who ran a labour college class and read *Plebs*: 'ability to read the *Daily Mail* is not the only test of human intelligence'.[52] Such careful deployment of the familiar was calculated to stir instincts of British trade unionists. She then visited a textile

[49] Whately et al., *Condition of India*, 83.

[50] *Madras Weekly Mail*, 11 Aug. 1932; *Times of India*, 26 Oct. 1932. On spread of strike, see *Madras Weekly Mail*, 3 Nov. 1932.

[51] *Times of India*, 2 Sept. 1932.

[52] *New Dawn*, 25 Feb. 1933, 79–80.

mill, where pay and conditions were yet worse.[53] Again exploring prejudices, she observed: 'These textile workers seemed poor and therefore less intelligent than the railwaymen. I expect that was simply because they were half-starved. The wages were scandalous'. With arguments analogous to those she used for working women during the Great War, she reflected that the inefficiency of 'native' workers (her own quotation marks) had its roots in overwork and poor pay. At the textile mill, Wilkinson witnessed the Indian women workers' plight. Nearly all being married, they had their children with them, bearing the twin burdens of childcare and wage-earning. No wonder they lacked the 'kick and spirit of the railwaymen'. Wilkinson sought through these cameos to contest the preconceptions about colonial women and workers. Her support for Indian nationalism was inflected with class and gender politics and sought to overcome the cultural distance between British and Indian workers. Ending her article on a campaign that was gaining support in the British trade unions despite some resistance from right-wingers, the Meerut prisoners, she noted, were trying to organise precisely such textile workers. The right's objection that the Meerut prisoners were communists was a smokescreen and she appealed to NUDAW (National Union of Distributive and Allied Workers) branches for support. She had witnessed Indian jails and could only shudder at the prospect of transportation. She concluded: 'We, as British workers, cannot afford to regard Indian labour conditions as having nothing to do with us'.

Wilkinson and Menon arrived in Delhi on 17 October. The following day, Wilkinson spoke to 125 students in Hindu College Hall.[54] Her speech played self-consciously with cultural difference. Her talk both subverted and transcended difference on the grounds that it served imperialist ends. Moreover, she pointed to the artificiality of difference, of presumed superiority inherent in colonial stereotypes, and that this could be overcome through the establishment of Indian nationhood. Combining humour, internationalism and sympathy for the Indian cause, she stressed how much India and Britain had in common, and that she hoped for future peace between the two countries, working together for the common good. She observed – to considerable laughter – that 'the only people more commission-ridden than Indian people were the British miners: if only one could live on commissions both would be the best fed people in the world'. Using a vivid metaphor Churchill later made famous, 'an iron curtain' separated the Indian and British peoples since the ordinances and accurate news of India could not get through. Their tour's object was to overcome this barrier.

[53] On such conditions, see Forbes, *Women in Modern India*, 167–71.

[54] NUSC, Reid Collection, HP, 40 12, H.V. Thomson to Hallett, 3 Nov. 1932; *Hindustan Times*, 19 Oct. 1932.

She articulated a powerful internationalism: 'I shall be ashamed of my country if when we go back and tell them what we have seen, something is not done'. She remarked that Indians would win independence themselves and she believed India to possess immense possibilities. Using cross-national comparison, she challenged the anti-Indian stereotype of being absorbed in religion and incapable of handling machinery, observing that the 'stage Irish' disappeared from the music halls once Ireland had achieved statehood. Telling how a government official had said that he hoped that she would meet the best Indians, she noted that 99 per cent of the best Indians seemed to be in jail. The meeting's chair, Chirani Lal Paliwal, had recently served a six-month prison sentence for being in possession of unauthorised literature.[55] She concluded that she hoped that the repression would soon be over.

Disputed claims and an audience in the social movements in the United Kingdom

Official impressions of Wilkinson throughout the trip were relatively favourable, certainly more so than impressions of her colleagues: she appeared to be broad-minded, although not making any pretence to impartiality, and behaved sensibly. Clearly, she charmed official opinion. At the same time, official correspondence explored strategies to undermine the delegation. Officials dismissively reported that Wilkinson 'does not know very much about India, but wants to become popular with Indians and wishes to identify herself with Indian aspirations'.[56] Such observations fuelled efforts to discredit the investigation as Indian nationalist propaganda.[57] In the Commons, Hoare argued that Congress was manipulating the visitors: 'scenes were stage-managed for this delegation and … from start to finish they saw this carefully arranged side of the picture'.[58] Hoare had briefed the cabinet on Wilkinson's visit, during which he alleged 'demonstrations were staged to entice the police into making *lathi* charges'.[59] Privately, officials singled Wilkinson out as an effective advocate for the Indian cause due to her careful reasoning, eloquence and media contacts. Thus, rather than deny the practices she exposed, they laid the responsibility with the victims.

[55] NUSC, Reid Collection, HP, 40 12, Superintendant C.H. Everett, Delhi CID, confidential note, 25 Oct. 1932.

[56] NUSC, Reid Collection, HP, 40 12, [illegible] (Lucknow) to C.M. Trivedi, Deputy Secretary to the Government of India, 3 Nov. 1932.

[57] *Daily Express*, 29 Nov. 1933; *North Mail*, 29 Nov. 1933.

[58] Hansard, House of Commons, vol. 273, col. 1260 (22 Dec. 1932).

[59] The National Archives (TNA), Cabinet (CAB) Papers, 24/234, Secretary of State for India, Confidential appreciation of the political situation in India, 24 Oct. 1932.

The trip certainly concerned the authorities. Hoare's office provided the cabinet with a point-by-point refutation.[60] Hoare publicly dismissed Wilkinson's investigation as a Potemkin tour.[61] Thus, the government instrumentalised cultural difference, insisting that it prevented genuine connection or insight on the part of the commission. She responded that he intended this 'perfect excuse of the ages' to deflect her charges of police brutality and the loss of consent for British rule.[62] Had her companions adopted the procedures of official commissions, they would not have ascertained a realistic idea of the Indian situation. Admitting Congress (and non-Congress) assistance, the delegation remarked that some who had helped them had consequently been arrested and official obstruction necessitated reliance on such help. Along with the rest of the Conservative press, following Hoare's line of attack, Wilkinson was condemned in the *Daily Mail* for trivialising the question of Untouchability after her speech describing herself as an English Untouchable.[63] Criticism came from the left as well. The India League suffered from the ILP's acrimonious disaffiliation from the Labour Party. Denouncing any connection with the Labour Party, Fenner Brockway resigned from the India League executive on 20 October.[64] Saklatvala added to criticisms of the India League and Congress.[65]

While true that Wilkinson occasionally idealised Indian spirituality conforming to a common stereotype, her anti-imperialist propaganda and movement-building should not be taken for her private analysis. Wilkinson deployed devices to establish for a transnational audience a shared purpose, a mutual comprehensibility and frames that could build transnational movements. She thus proposed identifications of universal resonance: heroes, youth, trade unionists, women and class. She subverted difference to make common cause – as she did in describing herself when in India as an 'Untouchable' in England for being a trade unionist. She acknowledged her own initial prejudices about the cultural practices such as ritual bathing or using cow dung as polish or the lack of chemist shops, but equally criticised the 'fussy' luxury of Europeans in India.[66] She also took some pleasure in

[60] TNA, CAB, 24/234, Secretary of State for India, Confidential appreciation of the political situation in India, 24 Oct. 1932; TNA, CAB, 24/235, Secretary of State for India, Confidential appreciation of the political situation in India, 21 Dec. 1932.

[61] *Daily Mail*, 23 Dec. 1932.

[62] *Star*, 2 Dec. 1932. See also rejection of charge of being a conducted tour: Whately et al., *Condition of India*, 10–11; *Manchester Guardian*, 6 Dec. 1932; Whately doing the same, *India Bulletin*, December 1933.

[63] *Daily Mail*, 29 Oct. 1932.

[64] *Madras Weekly Mail*, 21 Oct. 1932.

[65] *Times of India*, 24 Oct. 1932.

[66] *Star*, 25 Nov. 1932.

challenging Indian attitudes as well, sporting bangles in colours associated with the depressed classes and being seen in a marketplace with Indian men who were friends rather than servants. The humble bangle illustrated the dialectical quality of her transnational solidarity, simultaneously discovering, recognising and seeking to transcend cultural difference. Bangles provided a 'lingua franca' between her and Indian women she encountered in a marketplace; she admired their jewellery, yet she had initially misunderstood and had to learn the caste code of the bangles.

On 21 November, on their return, the delegation briefed the press about their experiences. Wilkinson praised the 'mental ability, philosophic outlook, and grasp of political affairs' that she found in Indian villages. By contrast, the communal award sought to reinforce old cleavages and discredit Indian claims to nationhood. Despite this, she argued, British repression was generating Hindu–Muslim unity.[67] The India League organised a conference held in Kingsway Hall, London WC2, on 26 November.[68] The 475 delegates called for an immediate end to repression and an amnesty as a preliminary step to transferring power to the Indian people. The police report noted that Wilkinson's speeches were 'a totally different calibre' from those of other speakers, with an 'undeniable' appeal, 'and it may be said that if she and Bertrand Russell toured the country on behalf of the India League, without the collaboration of the other members, they would gain many converts to their point of view, even from among the sceptical'. Her afternoon speech tackled the myths of Britain's civilising mission and Indian nationalist ingratitude. Britain was an alien power that had broken indigenous economic and social structures. India, as its great monuments attested, was not a backward country (as ideological justifications of imperial rule suggested) but a ruined one.[69] For all the talk of European progress, India was now an overwhelmingly agricultural country that could not feed itself and the signs of development such as roads and rail were for European car owners and maintaining imperial rule. She regarded Gandhi's movement as the nation's future. The government had no right to strangle this in the name of the British people. She catalogued the follies of British rule: jailing 20,000 leaders of a progressive movement, closing down *ashrams*, destroying handlooms and failing to eliminate leprosy. She envied India's magnificent leaders and the unvanquished spirit of its masses. For her, India was a great country and had a philosophical depth that England lacked. She concluded that a free India would make a valuable contribution to world culture. In her evening speech, she analysed Congress, which was

[67] *Manchester Guardian*, 22 Nov. 1932.

[68] British Library, IOR/L/PJ/12/448, Report on India League conference, 26 Nov. 1932.

[69] Thomas R. Metcalf, *Ideologies of the Raj* (Cambridge, 1998).

multi-religious and thus a potential instrument of national freedom. She recounted 'in moving language' her interview with Gandhi during his fast. She explained Gandhi's achievement in breaking down Untouchability: his fast and Indian women's activism was bringing about a social revolution. She said that she believed the British government to be acting in crass and unforgiveable stupidity rather than deliberate cruelty, concluding that hope for the future lay with the nationalist movement.

The India League organised a Manchester meeting a fortnight later, at which Wilkinson challenged Hoare's claims of Congress stage-management. He could not deny the police outrages seen with her own eyes. Indeed, a district commissioner told her: 'Oh well, after all we have so many people in prison. It is much better to give them a thorough beating and send them away'. She also observed that while the ordinances remained, the boycott of British imported textiles would continue, with Lancashire suffering as a consequence. Questioned about the Labour government's record, she said that the beatings and ordinance rule were shameful. The solution lay with Gandhi's release and a negotiated settlement with Congress.[70]

Wilkinson spoke on her Indian experiences on other occasions. She evoked strong emotion, particularly when talking of the beatings perpetrated there.[71] She took the Indian question to Soroptimist Clubs, Women's International League of Peace and Freedom (WILPF) branches, Methodist Church events, Labour and nationalist organisations in Manchester, Birmingham, Brighton and London.[72] On 5 January 1933, she blended the exotic and the political to intrigue her audience at the Felling Labour Club, telling of her elephant ride and the government's policy of repression against Congress.[73] Although targeting the current government, Wilkinson did criticise the Labour government's record on India at the Labour Women's Conference.[74] Tailoring her case for the women's movement, she talked about the 'new women' of India who were challenging age-old convention while retaining their own cultural sense of femininity.[75]

70 *Manchester Guardian*, 12 Dec. 1932.

71 NUSC, TDWR, Frida Laski to Reid, 10 Aug. 1971.

72 *Brighton World*, 11 Feb. 1933; *Northern Echo*, 12 June 1933; *Birmingham Post*, 13 Feb. 1933; *Northern Daily Telegraph*, 10 Oct. 1934.

73 *Woodford Times*, 6 Jan. 1933.

74 Report of the National Conference of Labour Women, Brighton 14–16 June 1932, 39–40; *Manchester Guardian*, 15 July 1932.

75 *Northern Echo*, 12 June 1933; *Birmingham Post*, 13 Feb. 1933; *Northern Daily Telegraph*, 10 Oct. 1934; Mrinalini Sinha, 'Gender in the Critiques of Colonialism and Nationalism: Locating the "Indian Woman"', in Sumit Sarkar and Tanika Sarkar (eds), *Women and Social Reform in Modern India* (Bloomington, IN, 2008), 452–73.

Wilkinson wrote about the arbitrary ordinance rule, unaccountable police powers and special non-jury courts.[76] With 18,000 officially in jail, she contended in the *Manchester Guardian* that a negotiated lasting settlement in India necessitated an amnesty for political prisoners. Their conditions were atrocious, visibly breaking the health of Nehru and others that she knew. India's prisons signified monotonous food, overcrowding, beatings and the 'standing handcuffs' torture (hung by their wrists from a beam above their heads).[77] The revelations about this torture technique caused angry letters to the Foreign Office and some embarrassment as the authorities could not deny its use.[78]

Wilkinson also contributed to the mission's 534-page report, *Condition of India* (1933), which outlined the government's muddled policy of reform and repression.[79] It catalogued the repressive government ordinances that suspended civil liberties and examined the methods of police rule, even used against women and children, which included shooting unarmed demonstrators or charging with *lathis*, mass arrests and awful prison conditions. It exposed the government's mendacity and the widespread support that existed across different social classes and religious communities for self-rule and for Congress. The Indian authorities recommended *Condition of India*'s prohibition to the Secretary of State for India as a 'very dangerous' text that would 'have a considerable sale in India and do much mischief'.[80]

Conclusion

Despite the visit's relative brevity, her route, personal encounters and reportage resisted a homogenisation of the Indian nationalist movement read from its leaders and the urban elite. While praising Gandhi's courage and indispensable contribution to building a mass movement, Wilkinson certainly inclined towards Nehru in the way Nicholas Owen has described. Explicitly rejecting any intrinsic British superiority, her support for Nehru was strategic: both on cultural grounds (being most comprehensible to

[76] *Daily Herald*, 3 Jan. and 15 Feb. 1933.

[77] *Manchester Guardian*, 30 Dec. 1932.

[78] British Library, IOR/L/PJ/12/449, Jeffrey Williams to Hoare, 12 Jan. 1933; *New Clarion*, 14 Jan. 1933; D. Graham Pole (Chairman and Hon. Sec. of British Committee on Indian and Burman Affairs) to Hoare, 12 Jan. 1933; WDC [Croft] replies on Hoare's part, 18 Jan. 1933; a second reply of WDC, 18 Jan. 1933. Pole to D. Croft, 19 Jan. 1933; Departmental note, to Peel, Seton, Croft, 27 Jan. 1933.

[79] Whately et al., *Condition of India*.

[80] British Library, IOR/L/PJ/12/449, Telegram, Home Department, Government of India to the Secretary of State for India, 25 Mar. 1934. On the ban, see *Daily Mail*, 31 Mar. 1934.

her British audience) but also political ones, believing, rightly or wrongly, that his politics was more suited to contesting a global capitalist order. Wilkinson's Indian trip reveals the complex problematic of framing transnational contestation, particularly one that bridges a metropolitan–colonial divide. Her vivid rhetoric (of 'iron curtains', 'English Untouchables', 'the lingua franca of the bangle') both acknowledged and sought to transcend difference. Her concern was to connect contentious politics across frontiers. In so doing, she adopted a variety of framing strategies or modes of address: the familiarisation of the foreign, the defamiliarisation of the mundane; the injustice frame; the subversive quality of humour; the identification with the other as a conscious act of solidarity rather than artificially essentialised identity of the (collective) self; equality and shared interest counterposed to enforced and constructed difference. Where some Subaltern Studies scholars have emphasised that British radicals and Indian peasants lived in different world historical epochs, we might turn to the thought of Walter Benjamin, Wilkinson's contemporary, for a solution to the problem posed by the putatively different temporalities separating her and those she encountered in India. In *Theses on the Philosophy of History*, he spoke of the 'moments of danger' or the 'now time' that could 'make the continuum of history explode', drawing together the revolutionary pasts and presents.[81] Just as she confronted the complexity of the constituency of Indian nationalism, her purpose was to draw together the self-emancipatory agency in India in all its multiplicity with the Labour, trade union and women's movements in Britain. In so doing, although its impact should not be exaggerated, it appears, even from hostile witnesses, that Ellen Wilkinson attained an apparent, perhaps exceptional, receptiveness for an anti-imperialist message from her British audiences and was received favourably by her Indian nationalist hosts. In her own mind, India might well spark a further cycle of international revolution as Russia had done fifteen years earlier.[82]

As such, India initiated a second radicalisation of her own politics in the early 1930s. Moreover, as she was to repeat on several occasions, what was happening in the NWFP discredited the received wisdom that fascism could not take root in British political culture. Thus, her project was to connect those confronting imperialism across conventional boundaries. Having just witnessed the German elections of July 1932, Wilkinson's sense of an approaching 'moment of danger' gave this a special urgency. Her desire for unity and her internationalism were therefore not reducible to processes of homogenisation and Western universalism. This global context was no less

[81] Walter Benjamin, 'Theses on the Philosophy of History', in Walter Benjamin, *Illuminations* (New York, 1969), 261.

[82] *Plebs*, Dec. 1930.

significant for the prospects of an independent India. The stakes, so far as Wilkinson perceived them, tied the Indian people, British labour and those she had met in Germany together in a world beset by crisis and threatened by fascism and war.

From a wider historiographical viewpoint, in order to revalorise the experience and agency of transnational actors working in anti-imperialist movements, we might reject thinking of cultural(–temporal) difference as an always insuperable obstacle if we are to give proper weight to the actions of these movements. Moreover, rather than a Eurocentric manoeuvre to elevate the role of European activists, this allows greater understanding of subtle global connections, cultural transfers and the impact of revolutionary nationalist movements on metropolitan political cultures. Equally, in line with the observations in the introduction to this volume of essays about an over-romanticised view of labour and imperialism, these contacts and relationships should not be overstated, reified or essentialised. They depended upon sometimes fragile and contingent global networks of solidarity, political conjuncture and patterns of contestation.

Across the threshold of the Second World War, Wilkinson's position on British imperialism and India had changed dramatically. Within cabinet, she urged the 'safeguarding of B. [British] interests' – a phrase she would formerly have deemed to be code for the private interests of British capital – and even went so far as to propose 'the arrest of Gandhi, etc.', to avoid circumstances 'suggesting we're being stoned out'.[83] Moreover, Attlee's government viewed her erstwhile companion of 1932, Krishna Menon, who became India's High Commissioner to London in early 1947, as 'a serious menace to security'.[84] Wilkinson's anti-imperialism had traversed a divide in 1940 that was symptomatic of her political trajectory more generally. Thus, her ultimate political destination should not obscure her earlier anti-colonial radicalism, with India being a principal case in point.

[83] TNA, CAB, 195/4, Cabinet Notes, 14 May 1946, 193; TNA, CAB, 195/4, Cabinet Notes, 5 June 1946, 232–33.

[84] Paul M. McGarr, '"A Serious Menace to Security": British Intelligence, V.K. Krishna Menon and the Indian High Commission in London, 1947–52', *Journal of Imperial and Commonwealth History*, 38 (2010), 441–69.

5

A Comparative and Transnational Approach to Socialist Anti-Colonialism

The Fenner Brockway–Marceau Pivert Connection, 1930s–1950s

Quentin Gasteuil

While British anti-colonialism is a subject area of huge potential, large parts of it have yet to be explored. This is certainly the case in terms of its international ramifications, and comparisons and connections with other imperial areas. The purpose of this chapter is to focus upon one such example of these connections and comparisons: the fight against colonialism in general and in the British and French Empires in particular conducted by two important socialists, Fenner Brockway (1888–1988) and Marceau Pivert (1895–1958). Brockway, a key British figure in the opposition to British colonial rule before and after the Second World War, led a fight for nearly thirty years alongside French activist Pivert. From 1930 onwards, the two men embodied, in the United Kingdom and in France respectively, a revolutionary socialist current (a 'Socialist Left'), within or on the margins of the Labour Party and the Socialist Party – French Section of the Workers' International (Parti socialiste – Section française de l'Internationale ouvrière: PS–SFIO).[1] In the interwar period, Brockway was a central figure in the Independent Labour Party (ILP), which he had joined in 1907. In 1947, he joined the Labour Party without abandoning his beliefs, interests and previous networks. Pivert joined the SFIO in 1924 and remained on its left wing. Excluded from the SFIO in 1938, he then founded the Socialist Party of Workers and Peasants (Parti socialiste ouvrier et paysan: PSOP), before rejoining the SFIO when it was reconstituted in 1946. He remained a member until his death.[2] On the national level, the influence exerted by Brockway and Pivert on their

[1] The French Socialist Party was usually just called 'la SFIO', which is the acronym used in this chapter.

[2] Fenner Brockway, *Towards Tomorrow: The Autobiography of Fenner Brockway* (London, 1977); Jacques Kergoat, *Marceau Pivert, 'socialiste de gauche'* (Paris, 1994).

political families was variable. However, from the 1930s to the 1950s, they were among the leading figures of a European network sharing broadly the same conceptions of socialism that they advocated. That milieu never ceased to structure and reconstruct itself, to nourish exchanges and foster collective forms of action transcending national boundaries. This current was united, despite inevitable nuances and divergences, by a deep commitment to individual liberties, as well as by a vision of revolutionary socialism that combined internationalism, anti-Stalinism and the fight for peace. It was also an anti-colonialist variety of socialism, as Brockway, Pivert and their followers were involved, for three decades, in a long struggle for the emancipation of colonised peoples. In many ways, the relationship between the two men, from their first joint actions to Pivert's death, is representative of the militant internationalism of this European network. In addition, its study can illuminate the terms of their original anti-colonialist commitment, one that sought to transgress borders, and was seen as a logical extension of political struggles within the framework of the nation-state.[3] The multiple links between these two militants, examined through the transnational lens, allow us to go beyond the study of their interpersonal relationship and to grasp the larger phenomena embodied by their collaboration.[4] The Brockway–Pivert connection indeed merits attention in several ways. These embrace concrete practices, political options and repertoires of actions, personal and collective initiatives, the junction of two individual trajectories and the international structuring of a distinctive socialist and anti-colonialist orientation.[5] The present chapter addresses all these aspects.[6]

[3] The introduction of the present publication highlights the diversity of the relationships between labour and empire. The Brockway and Pivert anti-colonialist stances embodied one distinctive aspect of that diversity.

[4] According to Robert Frank's synthetic definition, the transnational approach focuses on 'relations and circulations existing beyond frontiers and involving not states but societies, networks, individuals' and on 'the capacity for those cross-border relations and circulations to transcend the "national"'. Robert Frank, 'Relations internationales', in Claude Gauvard and Jean-François Sirinelli (eds), *Dictionnaire de l'historien* (Paris, 2015), 591.

[5] The rich concept of 'repertoire of actions' elaborated by Charles Tilly has been defined in its simplest sense by Michel Offerlé as 'a means of action … or the array of means of action actually used or usable by an organization or a movement … by a social category'. Michel Offerlé, 'Retour critique sur les répertoires de l'action collective (XVIIIe–XXIe siècles)', *Politix*, 81 (2008), 182.

[6] In this chapter, all the translations of documents originally in French are by the author and the editors of the volume.

Companions under the banner of internationalism

It is difficult to date the first meeting between Brockway and Pivert, but the two men seem to have known each other since the late 1920s.[7] However, it was not until 1930, inside the International Bureau for Socialist Revolutionary Unity (Bureau international d'unité socialiste révolutionnaire: BIUSR), aka the London Bureau, that the collaboration between them became close.[8] This structure, of which Brockway's ILP formed an essential pillar, gathered parties or currents who shared a common position between reformist socialism and Stalinist Communism, between the Second and the Third Internationals. The Revolutionary Left (Gauche révolutionnaire: GR), which Pivert had founded in September 1935, as a tendency inside the SFIO, was not allowed officially to join another international organisation apart from the Labour and Socialist International, but it did enjoy close links with the London Bureau. The links were even greater after Pivert and his comrades were expelled from the SFIO in June 1938, when they founded the PSOP.

The London Bureau was concerned primarily with issues such as the war in Spain, fascism, the Soviet Union and the position to be taken against the risk of a European war.[9] However, the organisations composing the Bureau did not forget the colonial question. They denounced British and French governmental repression in their respective imperial territories and affirmed the right of colonised peoples to declare their economic and political independence, and resist the injustices inflicted by imperial rule. They proclaimed their support for those populations' struggles and called for the revolutionary socialist movement to engage resolutely in the anti-imperialist struggle. That choice implied the development of links with the national liberation movements in the colonies and the encouragement of socialist and trade union activities in the imperial territories. The London Bureau's activities also helped build links between metropolitan and colonial activists. The Brussels conference, held from 31 October to 2 November 1936, was attended by delegates from the British Colonial Liberties Group.[10] And the report of the Congress specified that the Bureau had close contacts with revolutionary socialist groups in India, Ceylon and

[7] John McNair, 'Two Great Comrades', *Socialist Leader*, 14 June 1958, 3.

[8] The London Bureau, whose origins date back to the 1920s, was progressively structured between 1933 and 1935. See Michel Dreyfus, 'Bureau de Paris et bureau de Londres: le socialisme de gauche en Europe entre les deux guerres', *Le Mouvement social*, 112 (1980), 25–55.

[9] The information below, unless otherwise mentioned, is from Michel Dreyfus, 'Bureau de Londres ou IVe Internationale? Socialistes de gauche et Trotskystes en Europe de 1933 à 1940', PhD thesis, EHESS and Paris Nanterre University, 1977.

[10] This was a small organisation which regrouped, on British soil and around Pan-Africanist leader George Padmore, both metropolitan and colonial activists. See

Egypt.[11] What is more, the Paris Conference of 19–25 February 1938 was attended by trade union, community and political representatives from the Middle East, African and Asian territories of the two colonial Empires.[12] When, in 1939–1940, the Bureau transformed itself into the International Workers' Front Against the War (Front ouvrier international contre la guerre: FOI), then into the International Revolutionary Marxist Centre (Centre marxiste révolutionnaire international: CMRI), the desire to maintain and develop anti-colonialist networks remained a central element.[13]

In the days of the London Bureau, Brockway was already, within the British left, one of the most active leaders in the field of anti-colonialism. Thus he was able to bring to the international structure his experience, knowledge and networks, which could serve as resources for the political actions led by his European peers. Presumably, Brockway, pushing in the same direction as a newcomer inside the GR, French anti-colonialist Daniel Guérin, played a key role in making Pivert more sensitive to the colonial issues he had so far tended to neglect.[14] Indeed, it was not until the second half of the 1930s that the colonial question acquired a central importance in Pivert's political thought and action, consistent with his pre-existing revolutionary and internationalist perspectives. Brockway and Pivert, as well as their London Bureau counterparts, then professed a type of anti-colonialism mainly articulated around the denunciation of colonial atrocities and the defence of self-determination for colonised peoples. Their case for an internationalist and socialist struggle against colonialism was underpinned, and reinforced, by its interpretation as one of the logical outcomes of capitalist oppression. All in all, their anti-colonialism was not closed in on itself, but seen as part of the battle for socialism that must be conducted globally. For them, victory against colonial domination would

---

Susan D. Pennybacker, *From Scottsboro to Munich: Race and Political Culture in 1930s Britain* (Princeton, NJ, 2009), 93–94.

[11] International Bureau for Revolutionary Socialist Unity (IBRSU), *A Lead to World Socialism: Report of Revolutionary Socialist Congress, Brussels, October 31st–November 2nd 1936* (London, 1936), 2–3.

[12] IBRSU, *A New Hope for World Socialism: The Resolutions Adopted at the Revolutionary Socialist Congress, Paris, February 19th–25th, together with the Introductory Speeches* (London, 1938), 2; John McNair, 'Towards Revolutionary Socialist Unity', *New Leader*, 4 Mar. 1938, 4–5.

[13] Fenner Brockway, *Inside the Left: Thirty Years of Platform, Press, Prison and Parliament* (London, 1942), 290–91.

[14] Daniel Guérin, *Front populaire, révolution manquée* (Paris, 1963), 229. Pivert did have links of his own with Messali Hadj's 'Etoile nord-africaine' from at least 1934, and one of his closest friends, Louis Caput, was a socialist militant in Indochina.

be only a first step towards freedom, the second and final step being the end of capitalism and the actual establishment of socialism.[15]

The positions defended by Brockway in the mid–1930s were basically in harmony with those of the ILP. Since the 1920s, the party had become more and more critical and radical regarding the colonial theme, and so had he. The attitude of the Labour Party vis-à-vis the Empire, especially during the two governmental experiences of 1924 and 1929–1931, was key in influencing this shift to the left. The colonial policy of the Labour Party in the interwar period was not only of little interest to ordinary members of the party but also cautious and limited. Rather than opposing British imperialism per se, it sought to 'rid the … Empire of any lingering connotations of coercion and repression', to develop a more enlightened, reformist and more consensual form of imperial rule or government, based upon the application of what Ramsay MacDonald called an 'imperial standard'.[16] In keeping with this perspective, it sought to promote imperial economic development and to spread self-government, gradually, throughout the Empire. But this extension was based upon highly racialised and paternalist assumptions and conditions. In general terms, the European subjects of the Empire, as in the Dominions, were viewed as possessing higher capacities and, as such, more deserving of self-government, than their colonised counterparts considered as less developed. Yet the Labour Party also maintained that there were colonised populations more developed than others. For example, Indians were better considered than Africans and, as such, more capable and worthy of self-administration and government – albeit, practically, at some unspecified point in the future.[17] At the same time, Labour's leaders, especially MacDonald, J.H. Thomas and Lord Passfield (Sidney Webb), were keen to demonstrate that, as a responsible governing party, Labour would defend the interests and the integrity of the Empire, if necessary against local uprisings regarded as irresponsible or irrational.[18] As Stephen Howe has noted: 'Disillusion among ILP activists with the performance of the government in 1924 was the starting point for the evolution of a more independent, and sharply critical, ILP view of Labour colonial policy … With the entry into office of the second Labour

[15] See, for instance, the resolution on the anti-colonial struggle ('The Fight Against Imperialism') adopted at the Paris Congress of February 1938: IBRSU, *A New Hope*, 35–38.

[16] Neville Kirk, *Labour and the Politics of Empire: Britain and Australia, 1900 to the Present* (Manchester, 2014), 141.

[17] On Labour and India, see Nicholas Owen, *The British Left and India: Metropolitan Anti-Imperialism, 1885–1947* (Oxford, 2007).

[18] In the present volume, Marie Terrier's chapter on Annie Besant offers an insight into the complex relationship between Labour leaders and Indian nationalist movements during the 1920s.

government, ILP discontent moved into outright opposition'.[19] The ILP's disaffiliation from the Labour Party in 1932 saw it adopt a more unqualified and more outspoken anti-colonialist stance. As we will observe in more detail below, Brockway was to the fore in the articulation of this minority labour-movement position.

Within the SFIO, Pivert's ideas in the second half of the 1930s did not win over the majority of leaders and activists either. Like their British counterparts, these leaders and activists showed only superficial and vague interest in colonial issues. The Socialist Party, although it protested against colonial abuses, was imbued with the notion of the 'civilising mission'. In the 1920s it claimed that, in opposition to the imperialism of capitalists and military leaders, a socialist colonial policy should bring progress to the greatest number possible. The exploitation of raw materials should be done on cooperative and socialist lines, colonised peoples should benefit from this exploitation and from the 'lights' of European culture and knowledge, the international scale should be favoured instead of the national one for the colonial supervision and development. Broadly speaking, the economic and social developments in the colonies should strive to avoid all capitalist evils and their consequences. However, this idea of a positive and socialist colonisation and an accurate socialist way to deal with the colonial questions was 'hardly developed and almost always contradictory, hesitant and nuanced in the extreme for the sake of synthesis'.[20] Gradually, in the 1930s, the party's doctrine became clearer, although colonial issues remained a minor topic in the political mind of the socialists. The party finally accepted both colonial occupation as well as its capitalistic dimensions as facts. Consequently, the main claims tended to shift to more familiar ground, addressing concerns that were aligned with positions the socialist movement was more familiar with, such as the development of professional, social and civil rights for the colonised. The ultimate objective, which from then on became the official party line, was to achieve 'assimilation'; that is to say the complete inclusion of the colonial populations and territories into the French cultural, political, economic and juridical framework. It stems from these political outlooks that colonial independence was overwhelmingly rejected by the party. Independence was considered as a simplistic answer to intricate problems,

[19] Stephen Howe, *Anticolonialism in British Politics: The Left and the End of Empire, 1918–1964* (Oxford, 1993), 68–69.

[20] Gilles Morin, 'Les socialistes et la colonisation, 1920–1939', *Revue de la Bibliothèque nationale*, 38 (1990), 43. See also Manuela Semidei, 'Les socialistes français et le problème colonial entre les deux guerres (1919–1939)', *Revue française de science politique*, 18.6 (1968), 1115–54.

as it would mean giving populations considered not yet able to govern themselves over to capitalist, bourgeois, feudal or reactionary greed. Pivert's creation of the Revolutionary Left in 1935 allowed those socialists who were the most critical vis-à-vis colonial issues to come together in a single organisation, albeit still in the SFIO. But it was mainly the split and the creation of the PSOP which symbolised the radicalisation of the socialist left, and that of Pivert, on these topics. The expectations were massive after the electoral victory of the Left in 1936 and the coming of the socialist leader Léon Blum as Prime Minister. However, the absence of fundamental changes regarding the colonial condition in the Empire during the Popular Front governments (1936–1938), coupled with the repression unleashed against the nationalist movements in the colonies, contributed – among other dissensions – to the tension and then the break between the SFIO and Pivert. Like Brockway, Pivert ended up at odds with the main party of the non-communist left. Like his British comrade, this opposition was after a leftward shift from the majority position, partly due to the disillusion of the exercise of governmental power.

The meeting of those two men also represented the meeting of two militant groups. Close ties were developed between the ILP and the Revolutionary Left (and later the PSOP), especially on the eve of the Second World War. French activists travelled to England and their British counterparts to France on several occasions. At the end of January 1939, Daniel Guérin was delegated by the PSOP to attend the anti-colonial exhibition organised by the ILP in London and the African International Bureau in the same city. There he created links with men such as the Kenyan leader Jomo Kenyatta and the Pan-Africanist George Padmore, both friends of Brockway.[21] A few days later, in Paris, in the presence of Brockway, his ILP comrade John McNair and other 'anti-imperialist delegates', a new meeting was arranged.[22] According to Guérin, who seems to have acted as both the GR's and the PSOP's representative in charge of colonial issues with the British, 'the cooperation between the anti-imperialists based in London and those based in Paris was already proving fruitful'.[23] These relationships also took a written shape in the form of an exchange of letters and newspapers. Much information about the situation in the British Empire and the political action of the ILP can be found in *La Gauche révolutionnaire* and *Juin 36*, two papers directed by Pivert.

[21] Bruno David, 'Récurrences et figures de l'autonomie ouvrière: histoire sociale du "pivertisme" (1935–1940)', PhD thesis, EHESS, 1996, 255.

[22] Guérin, *Front populaire*, 321.

[23] Guérin, *Front populaire*, 321.

Relevant material in the ILP's *New Leader* was often quoted.[24] But those publications also offered exclusive articles – for example, one by Francis Ambrose Ridley on the revolutionary challenges to British imperialism,[25] and another by Brockway himself on the conflict between Jews and Arabs in Palestine.[26] In May 1939, Brockway responded in the columns of *Juin 36* to an article by Daniel Guerin which had been published the month before.[27] In a similar way, *The New Leader* offered its readers articles about political events in France and French socialism. These were often related to the deeds and words of the GR and the PSOP, whose positions were relayed and praised by the weekly.[28] *The New Leader* also made a point of including articles on French colonial questions.[29] They were written sometimes directly by French activists,[30] but they could also be produced by a Paris correspondent.[31] Finally, joint initiatives were undertaken. In January 1939, a British Centre Against Imperialism (BCAI) was founded thanks to the ILP's efforts. It brought together metropolitan organisations and groups

[24] For example: 'Aspects de la lutte ouvrière internationale', *La Gauche révolutionnaire*, 20 Oct. 1935, 4–5; 'Le point de vue de nos camarades anglais de l'ILP', *Juin 36*, 30 Sept. 1938, 3; 'Courageuse déclaration de nos camarades de l'ILP', *Juin 36*, 11 Nov. 1939, 4.

[25] Francis-Ambrose Ridley, 'La Grande Frayeur de Neville Chamberlain', *Juin 36*, 7 Oct. 1938, 4. The author argued that Chamberlain only signed the Munich agreements for fear of the world revolution, a revolution that, if the war was to become global, was bound to destroy the British Empire from the inside, and to overthrow its ruling classes.

[26] Fenner Brockway, 'La Guerre en Palestine', *Juin 36*, 21 Oct. 1938, 3. Brockway denounced those he considered as capitalist, imperialist and feudal oppressors trying to divide and rule over the Jewish and the Arab workers. He called for both communities to unite in favour of a single, egalitarian and socialist Republic.

[27] 'Réponse de Fenner Brockway à *Juin 36*', *Juin 36*, 12 May 1939, 4.

[28] Fenner Brockway, 'The Popular Front is Dead – Long Live the Revolutionary Front!', *The New Leader*, 28 Jan. 1938, 4–5; 'Revolutionary Left Leads in France', *The New Leader*, 15 Apr. 1938, 5.

[29] See, for instance, Fenner Brockway's article about French repression in Tunisia: 'French Imperialism', *The New Leader*, 14 Jan. 1938, 5.

[30] G. Lenglet, 'What Happens When Working-Class Parties Administer Imperialism: A Warning from France', *The New Leader*, 11 Feb. 1938, 4–5. The author described the situation in French North Africa and denounced the repression used by the Popular Front government against the Moroccan, Algerian and Tunisian peoples. He called on revolutionary socialists to express their support for the colonised and to save the honour of the French labour movement since it had been tainted both by the socialist government and by its communist supporters.

[31] 'If Socialists Run Capitalism, They Must Suppress Colonial Revolt', *The New Leader*, 20 Jan. 1939, 3. Here again, the balance sheet of the Popular Front government in the colonies was presented as a very negative one. The author argued that it was impossible for a government that had decided not to attack the capitalist order to put an end to colonial oppression, even if it called itself left-wing.

formed by activists from the colonies, with the purpose of 'coordinating the various movements of liberation'.[32] A few months later, in April 1939, an Anti-imperialist Liaison Centre was created around the PSOP in Paris. Its goal was to do the same kind of work as the BCAI inside the French Empire, in close collaboration with its London counterpart. Delegates from the ILP and the International African Service Bureau (IASB) attended the founding conference of the French Centre. In all probability Brockway and Padmore were among them.[33]

For Brockway and Pivert alike, these links were valued as a means both to reinforce and to enrich the anti-colonialist actions that each of them was undertaking within his own national sphere and to expand their perspectives beyond borders. Those bonds also reflected the importance both men attached to internationally coordinated efforts and eventually the global reach of anti-colonialism. Moving to and fro across the Channel, John McNair of the ILP played a pivotal role. Indeed, he had lived in France between 1911 and 1923, and between 1925 and 1936.[34] During both periods he acquired a very good command of French and maintained political and personal relations with several French activists. He was therefore the right man in the right place to encourage and promote joint work, especially as he was omnipresent at Brockway's side and was on friendly terms with Pivert. McNair became general secretary of the ILP in 1939. As we will observe below, his international and transnational importance significantly increased during the 1940s and 1950s.

By the late 1930s, the essential terms of the relationship between Brockway and Pivert were visible. Three practical pillars of their anti-colonialist internationalism can be distinguished: the maintenance and development of a large network, the exchange of information and the establishment of a common political framework. These largely influenced the initiatives taken by the two men before, during and after the Second World War. Although the sources are scarce for the interwar period, the abundant correspondence between Brockway and Pivert from 1940 onwards enables us to imagine what it was like in the preceding years.[35] Arriving in the USA on 23 August 1939, Pivert was given the mission to remain there should the war break out, and to keep one of the two international secretariats of the FOI alive. Because his visa was not renewed by the American authorities, he was forced to leave New York for Mexico, where he settled at the end of July 1940, as did so many other European socialists in exile. He would not return to France until April

[32] Guérin, *Front populaire*, 320.

[33] 'Front ouvrier international contre la guerre', *Juin 36*, 5 May 1939, 4.

[34] Brockway, *Inside the Left*, 294.

[35] This correspondence is in the Marceau Pivert papers (559AP), kept at the 'Archives nationales' (hereafter AN) in Pierrefitte-sur-Seine, France.

1946. However, his links with the ILP and Brockway were not severed; quite the contrary.[36] The exchange of letters was still regular, and when Brockway was not able to it was McNair who wrote. Brockway and McNair also sent their political literature – *The New Leader*, *Left* and *Between Ourselves* – to Pivert, as he was sure to circulate it among the other exiles.

During the Second World War, the difference between the Labour Party and the ILP was still pronounced in terms of colonial questions. The participation of the Labour Party in Winston Churchill's government from May 1940 was crucial here. Clement Attlee's party, indeed, was forced to defend the integrity of the Empire against its detractors, while at the same time attempting to show that Labour constituted a progressive force that had not been contaminated by the ministerial fellowship with the Tories.[37] Labour's proposals primarily related to the economic and social development of the colonial territories. Politically, the party's policy boiled down to the promotion of international supervision of the management of the colonies. This supervision should be granted to a body shaped on the model of the Mandate Commission of the League of Nations, although in an improved form.[38] The party's leaders certainly intended to give India the status of 'self-governing dominion' at the end of the conflict, but without yielding to the immediate demands of the nationalists.[39] Except for this later case, all in all, political improvements within the Empire by the means of self-government and the end of 'trusteeship' were absent from Labour's agenda during the war. Broadly speaking, just like in the interwar period, colonial issues remained secondary in the minds of party leaders, and this was reflected in the party's work between 1939 and 1945. The production of policy recommendations continued from the party's dedicated internal structures and from its margins, while few activists attempted to draw renewed attention on the Empire during annual conferences.[40] But the

[36] For instance, Brockway wrote to his French comrade: 'I think you know without any assurance from us the close and affectionate sense of solidarity we have with you … and your work all the time. We feel towards you just as though you were in our own headquarters working with us here. Your office in Mexico is just another section of our movement, and we want to help you, as we know you want to help us, at every opportunity' (AN, 559AP29, Fenner Brockway to Marceau Pivert, 31 Oct. 1941).

[37] Ray M. Douglas, *The Labour Party, Nationalism and Internationalism, 1939–1951* (New York, 2004), 183.

[38] Labour Party, *The Colonies: The Labour Party's Post-War Policy for the African and Pacific Colonies* (London, 1943).

[39] Partha S. Gupta, *Imperialism and the British Labour Movement, 1914–1964* (London, 2002), 262–68.

[40] It was especially the case of the Labour Party Advisory Committee on Imperial Questions and its members, who were already very active during the interwar years.

Second World War brought neither colonial issues nor innovations in this field to the forefront of Labour's political interests.[41] Moreover, the Labour Party's commitment to governmental participation can also be considered as a brake to any daring and sustained initiative, given the context of a war where the overwhelming priority was Britain's power, security and victory. At the same time, some of the party's leaders expressed what were clearly imperialist ambitions, with Ernest Bevin being a case in point. As Ray Douglas pointed out:

> The impulse to defend the government's custody of the Empire against its numerous domestic and foreign detractors combined with war-heightened patriotic sentiment had lent by the middle of the conflict a distinctly Kiplingesque flavour to the pronouncements of Labour ministers, who unexpectedly discovered hidden virtues in a system they had formerly condemned as the quintessence of capitalist exploitation.[42]

Meanwhile, the socialist prospects of the London Bureau network were moving in a very different direction, under both Brockway's and Pivert's influence. They were embodied in the concept of the 'third political camp' (sometimes called the 'third front' or 'third force') in which colonised peoples occupied a place of prime importance. Indeed, early in the war, the FOI formulated the analysis that the conflict had stemmed from the rivalry between two kinds of imperialisms: capitalism and dictatorship. Socialism had therefore to encourage the emergence of a third camp: 'We are the Third Camp – the Camp uniting oppressed people from all around the world, uniting those who die for nothing, uniting the colonial slaves that modern slave traders compete for, uniting widows and orphans, the hungry and the destitute, THE CAMP OF THE WORLDWIDE SOCIALIST REVOLUTION!'.[43] In this perspective, the conjunction of socialist revolution in the metropolis and in the colonies had to be encouraged.[44] To this end, Brockway and his comrades in exile made a point of maintaining and developing links with organisations that had their roots in the colonies.[45]

41 Howe, *Anticolonialism*, 134–39.

42 Douglas, *Labour Party*, 187.

43 Front ouvrier international contre la guerre, Manifeste, 'Ouvriers et soldats allemands!', June 1940. One month later, Pivert would describe the Third Camp as springing from 'the ranks of those who are engaged in an internal struggle against the two great Camps, from the pain endured by starving civilians, from the muted revolt of oppressed peoples, from the servitude and humiliation of persecuted races, from the vast masses of colonial peoples who are being treated like cattle' (quoted in Kergoat, *Marceau Pivert*, 183).

44 AN, 559AP29, Fenner Brockway to Marceau Pivert, 31 Oct. 1941.

45 AN, 559AP4, Fenner Brockway to Julian Gorkin, 25 Sept. 1940.

The question of the contacts with the colonised activists is revealing of Brockway's and Pivert's internationalist conceptions. Indeed, beyond the British or French 'nationality' of the colonies in question, they considered their respective resources as a common good that everyone should be able to use to hasten the emancipation of dominated populations, wherever they were. The British and French imperial logics were intermingled, as evidenced by several examples. 'We would like to have direct connections with our friends in India. Is it really impossible for you to ask them to send us their publications? That region of the world, as one might have guessed, is raising more and more attention', Pivert wrote to Brockway in early 1942, in a letter transmitting some information he had gathered about Indochina and Morocco.[46] McNair also contributed to these exchanges, as evidenced by this query Pivert made: 'Will you try to find out from [George Padmore] what has happened to Faure, from the League for the Defence of the Negro Race?'.[47] Emile Faure was a Senegalese activist with contacts throughout the French Empire. In addition, to expand the area of their common network, McNair asked Pivert to provide him with a list of his contacts in Africa and Asia.[48] When Pivert complied and forwarded to Brockway a number of contacts that had been recommended to him, they were located in Trinidad, Tobago and Barbados, i.e., British territories.[49] In Brockway's and Pivert's post-war commitments, these colonial interlocutors would prove to be very important.

Anti-colonialists in search of a structure

As explained above, Brockway's and Pivert's interest in the people under colonial domination was inseparable from the concept of a 'third camp'. During the war years, that idea became more and more prevalent in the political thought of the two men and after 1945 it was the structuring of what they now called the 'third international force' that guided their activity. Their first battle was fought on the field of European integration, because of the new international configuration. According to them, the creation of two rival blocs in the context of the Cold War could only lead to a new world war. The battlefield would be Europe, so it was necessary to organise the third international force around the construction of a socialist Europe, capable of fighting on two fronts, to resist the deadly dangers weighing on her.[50] Thus,

[46] AN, 559AP29, Marceau Pivert to Fenner Brockway, 25 Jan. 1942.

[47] AN, 559AP29, Marceau Pivert to John McNair, 1 Oct. 1941.

[48] AN, 559AP29, John McNair to Marceau Pivert, 17 June 1943.

[49] AN, 559AP29, Marceau Pivert to Fenner Brockway, 4 Sept. 1943.

[50] Jonathan Schneer, 'Hopes Deferred or Shattered: The British Labour Left and the Third Force Movement, 1945–49', *Journal of Modern History*, 56.2 (1984), 197–226;

at the initiative of the ILP, two international meetings were held in 1947, on 22–23 February in London and on 21–22 July in Montrouge, France. These led to the creation of the Movement for the United Socialist States of Europe (MUSSE – in French Mouvement pour les Etats-Unis socialistes d'Europe: MEUSE).[51] The new body was largely framed by Brockway, Pivert and their peers. Pivert became its president after the congress in Montrouge, and Bob Edwards, one of the leading figures in the ILP since the 1930s, was elected vice-president. As for McNair, he was one of the two secretaries of the organisation. However, Brockway and Pivert considered that this socialist Europe could only represent a third international force in connection with the colonial territories. That idea, explicitly formulated from the formation of MUSSE, took a concrete form when it organised the Congress of the Peoples of Europe, Asia and Africa (CPEAA) in Puteaux, France, on 18–21 June 1948.[52] In many respects, this event is indicative of how Brockway, Pivert and their friends then engaged in favour of colonised populations, by fully integrating them into their fight for a third international force and for peace.

In the run-up to the Congress, MUSSE tried to gather together the largest possible panel of organisations. Towards this end it invited metropolitan as well as colonial groups to participate. Brockway, as the president of the organising committee, hand in hand with Pivert, endeavoured to mobilise their networks to make the event a success. Both men kept abreast of their progress through frequent contacts and, whenever possible, French and British comrades worked closely together. For example, when George Padmore expressed his reluctance to bring in the Pan-African Federation to the Congress of the Peoples, because of the ambiguous positions he attributed to the SFIO, McNair asked Pivert to send him the latest resolutions of the party so as to reassure Padmore and prove to him that the SFIO had changed.[53]

Bruce-D. Graham, 'Choix atlantique ou troisième force internationale?', in Serge Berstein, Frédéric Cépède, Gilles Morin and Antoine Prost (eds), *Le Parti socialiste entre Résistance et République* (Paris, 2000), 157–65.

51 Wilfrid Loth, 'The Mouvement socialiste pour les Etats-Unis d'Europe (MSEUE)', in Walter Lipgens and Wilfried Loth (eds), *Transnational Organization of Political Parties and Pressure Groups in the Struggle for European Union, 1945–1990: Documents on the History of European Integration* (Berlin, 1991), 277–318. The movement's name changed several times: Mouvement pour les Etats-Unis socialistes d'Europe (MEUSE) [Movement for the United Socialist States of Europe, MUSSE], Mouvement socialiste pour les Etats-Unis d'Europe, Mouvement démocratique et socialiste pour les Etats-Unis d'Europe. To simplify, only the earliest name, MUSSE, is used here.

52 Anne-Isabelle Richard, 'The Limits of Solidarity: Europeanism, Anti-Colonialism and Socialism at the Congress of the Peoples of Europe, Asia and Africa in Puteaux, 1948', *European Review of History*, 21.4 (2014), 519–37.

53 AN, 559AP29, John McNair to Marceau Pivert, 12 Mar. 1948.

Padmore's feelings were understandable, as the post-war SFIO was generally cautious on colonial questions: it recommended a federal association that would be part of the French Union, rejected all claims of independence and still displayed assimilationist tendencies. In addition, the SFIO had participated in governments pursuing policies that perpetuated colonial rule. However, the arrival of the Left at the head of the party in 1946 meant that anti-colonialist activists like Pivert were now also in charge, which allowed – at least for a while – more advanced goals and harsher criticisms to be expressed in the imperial field.[54] This joint action brought success. Although Padmore did not attend the congress, his comrade Peter Abrahams did so in the name of the Pan-African Federation. Pivert also sought to obtain unequivocal support from the SFIO for his international initiative and asked the British to do the same with the Labour Party.[55] The SFIO agreed to support the event but insisted that the socialists present at the Congress – and there were many of them – would only be representing themselves. In the case of the Congress taking decisions or displaying political orientations, the party would not be committed to follow them. The Labour Party seemed even more reserved. If some Labour MPs gave their backing, the party itself was represented by two members only, Fenner Brockway and Betty Hamilton, who were both compelled to sit merely as individuals and not as Labour Party representatives.

The Labour Party's extreme caution was understandable, given its modest colonial policy since the 1945 landslide and Clement Attlee's accession to Downing Street. Certainly, the achievement of independence in India, Pakistan, Ceylon and Burma was to the Labour government's credit, and it did introduce some constitutional progress in the Gold Coast. However, the maintenance of the integrity of the Empire, so crucial to the buttressing of British power, remained the key aim for a government that refused to engage itself in more widespread self-determination and independence for the colonies. Once Labour was in office, its wartime calls for an international supervision of the colonies petered out. This exposed the UK to international criticism, particularly in the United Nations. Moreover, Labour strove not so much for political reforms as for a policy of colonial economic and social development. However, that development hardly appeared as a priority compared with domestic issues, and the expected

[54] Gilles Morin, 'De l'opposition socialiste à la guerre d'Algérie au Parti socialiste autonome (1954–1960): histoire d'un courant socialiste', PhD thesis, Paris 1-Panthéon Sorbonne University, 1991, 101–20.

[55] AN, 559AP48, Marceau Pivert to Fenner Brockway, Bob Edwards and John McNair, 2 Jan. 1948.

progress failed to materialise in the colonial territories.[56] The discrepancy was therefore notable between Labour's actual policy and Brockway's designs and ambitions. Although he returned to the Labour Party in 1947, his ideas were in harmony with those of the Labour left, not with those of the majority of MPs and ministers.

To reach out to the widest possible audience, the organisers did not limit themselves to addressing people living in the French and British Empires. For instance, Brockway urged Dutch socialist Jef Last to inform the anti-colonialist organisations he was acquainted with in the Dutch-dominated territories.[57] The wide colonial networks of Jean Rous, a French anti-colonialist who was close to Pivert and worked as the secretary of the preparatory commission of the congress, were also instrumental in securing the presence of a large contingent of delegates from the French Empire, especially from North Africa (the Maghreb).[58] To put into practice the egalitarianism that was advocated, the invitation papers for the congress displayed the names of the European, African and Asian organisers on equal footing, with no prominence given to the Europeans – Brockway, Bob Edwards and Frenchman Claude Bourdet.[59] In quantitative terms, the Congress of the Peoples was undeniably a success: more than 300 delegates and personalities representing Africa, Asia, Europe, North America, South America and international organisations replied to the call.[60] This is an illustration of the strength and depth of the socialist and anti-colonialist networks that Brockway, Pivert and their comrades could mobilise in their political struggles. The numerous interventions during the conference sessions comprised an economic report and a political one, both shaped around the necessity of a 'third international force'. The economic report had been prepared under the patronage of Bob Edwards, the political one under Brockway's.

But things did not go as expected by the European organisers. According to historian Jean-Pierre Biondi, 'between the representatives of the colonised peoples and the representatives of the colonising peoples, the discussion quickly turned sour'.[61] In fact, several points of disagreement undermined

[56] Partha S. Gupta, 'Imperialism and the Labour Government of 1945–1951', in Jay Winter (ed.), *The Working Class in Modern British History: Essays in Honour of Henry Pelling* (Cambridge, 1983), 99–124.

[57] AN, 559AP42, Fenner Brockway to Jef Last, 18 Dec. 1947.

[58] Pierre Chevalier, 'Jean Rous (1908–1985): une vie pour le socialisme et la décolonisation', PhD thesis, University of Perpignan, 1999, 706–7.

[59] AN, 559AP38, 'Invitation au Congrès des peuples d'Europe, d'Asie et d'Afrique', n.d.

[60] *Report of the First International Conference of the Peoples of Europe–Asia–Africa Against Imperialism* (London, 1948), 5–14.

[61] Jean-Pierre Biondi and Gilles Morin, *Les Anticolonialistes (1881–1962)* (Paris, 1992), 286.

the 'third force' position that Brockway and Pivert had hoped to be adopted. For example, the delegates from the colonies wished to emphasise national liberation, for which they sought direct support. In so doing they played down the importance of the overall international situation and struggle. They were wary of their European interlocutors, whom they still identified with colonisation, and who did, sometimes, speak in a paternalistic manner. Moreover, they were unwilling to take a stand vis-à-vis the two blocs, especially not against the Soviet Union, believing they could find points of support for their own struggles on the Soviet side.[62] It was essentially this unwillingness that wrecked Brockway's and Pivert's unitary ambitions. In August 1947, Brockway had already warned Pivert that there was a risk in attacking the USSR too bluntly if the goal was to ally with the colonised over a common project.[63] In October 1947, he had made that concern very clear to other members of the organising committee.[64] Here a clear limit to the kind of anti-colonialism professed by European revolutionary socialists appears, even though it may have been less obvious in the case of Brockway. In spite of their numerous contacts with the colonised and the sincerity of their anti-colonialism, they were strongly influenced by their metropolitan tropism and their anti-Stalinism. The concept of 'third international force' could only meet the needs of colonised militants very partially, as they were ready to accept support from all horizons, without the caveats expressed by the Europeans, who were much more sensitive, for obvious reasons, to the bipartition of the world.

All in all, because this international meeting was exceptional in so many different ways, it cannot be considered a failure across the board. It brought together activists from all around the world who shared a common will and was a milestone in international political campaigns against imperialism. Moreover, discord was present but not omnipresent among the organisations of colonised peoples. In the aftermath of the congress, a permanent organisation was created, the Congress of Peoples Against Imperialism (COPAI). This was successful in uniting many of the organisations present in Puteaux. Jean Rous was its first secretary and Brockway its first president. In the latter's own words, 'this was a turning point in [his] life'.[65] The newly created COPAI established its office at 41 Boulevard Magenta in Paris. It was the same address as the Socialist Federation of the Seine (more or less equivalent to the Paris branch of the SFIO), headed by Pivert, who sat from the start on the international committee of the new

62 Richard, 'Limits of Solidarity', 528–31.

63 AN, 559AP29, Fenner Brockway to Marceau Pivert, 7 Aug. 1947.

64 Richard, 'Limits of Solidarity', 528.

65 Fenner Brockway, *Outside the Right: A Sequel to 'Inside the Left'* (London, 1963), 43.

organisation. In addition, the Socialist Federation of the Seine, as such, joined as an 'individual' member.

Subsequently, COPAI deployed its action in the directions it had initially set: making resolutions on French and British colonial territories, organising congresses and meetings, establishing regional centres in Asia and Africa, lobbying, and travelling to produce original surveys.[66] In addition, the organisation allowed its anti-colonialist militants, whatever the territory concerned, to circulate information, in particular via its newsletter, and also enabled connections between activists to survive.[67] COPAI's correspondents in the colonies were numerous, and the networks cut across imperial segmentation. Once again, what stands out is the deep-rooted internationalism of the Brockway–Pivert variety of anti-colonialism. For example, the congress in Puteaux was the starting point of Brockway's deep interest in the French colony of Madagascar.[68] COPAI's political positioning remained in line with that advocated at the Puteaux conference: the key values remained self-determination; cooperation for economic and social development; the interdependence of metropolitan and colonial struggles; internationalism and the 'third international force'.[69]

One should not, however, overstate the importance of the new movement, whose regional headquarters were in Paris and London. As Stephen Howe has observed: 'Soon the COPAI's story ... was one of decline and fall from its original high hopes. Neither the International Committee ... nor the Paris Centre ... seems ever to have functioned effectively. The London organisation had rather greater success, but never broadened into the kind of international anti-colonial crusade to which Brockway had aspired'.[70] For the international committee, there was a shortage of both money and volunteers, the ability to act was quite limited and, to make things worse, public activity was sometimes repressed. For example some COPAI meetings that had been planned in France were banned.[71] Too soon, the London centre proved to be the only one that was really active and Pivert himself, apparently overwhelmed with more urgent matters, gradually distanced himself from the organisation after 1949. Ultimately Jean Rous was the only Frenchman with a sustained interest in COPAI, of which he remained the regular correspondent. As for Brockway, acting as COPAI's president and in line with the Puteaux declarations, he was still very active and deployed

66 *Bulletin du Mouvement pour les Etats-Unis socialistes d'Europe*, Nov. 1948, 10–13.

67 Richard, 'Limits of Solidarity', 532.

68 Brockway, *Outside the Right*, 126.

69 Howe, *Anticolonialism*, 180–81.

70 Howe, *Anticolonialism*, 179.

71 Richard, 'Limits of Solidarity', 532.

many of his anti-colonialist actions from London. It was then with Rous, not with Pivert, that his exchanges were the richest. A fundamental difference between Brockway's anti-colonialism and Pivert's appears: for Brockway it was always a fundamental part of his militant commitment, while for Pivert, anti-colonialism seems to have been one cause among others, a cause that was likely to be muted depending on the vagaries of the political situation.

Characteristics and implications of a multifaceted relationship

If the actions taken jointly by the two men are a fundamental aspect of their relationship, it was also based on daily exchanges and smaller projects that had concrete and practical dimensions. These elements became particularly visible after the war. Even before the war, the publication of newspapers and reviews occupied an important place in their shared repertoires of actions. During the Second World War and immediately after the conflict, initiatives of various kinds were taken to disseminate publications that would embody their internationalism and anti-colonialism. From Mexico, Pivert managed the FOI newsletter. While it was a relatively little known paper with restricted diffusion, and that disappeared in 1942, it did collect a lot of information on colonial topics, embracing a large number of territories. The newsletter devoted plenty of space to the publications sent by Brockway from London, and the opposite was also true: the information gleaned through other channels by Pivert for the newsletter was used by the British in their own publications.[72] From Mexico, Pivert was acting as a living hub for the revolutionary international news that Brockway and the other FOI instigators wished to broadcast. A similar paper attempted to take over after the war, in an ephemeral way: *Informations Internationales. Bulletin de liaison des socialistes révolutionnaires européens* (International Informations. Liaison Bulletin of European Revolutionary Socialists). Directed once again by Pivert, it was published between September 1946 and summer 1947 only. Another type of publication was also envisaged. From the end of 1946, the idea of a collective European journal emerged. Brockway asked Pivert to be responsible for France, while he would be in charge of England.[73] The idea was appealing but did not lead to anything concrete.

At the same time, a project with nearly identical contours was carried by Pivert. With his *Socialisme et Liberté* (Socialism and Liberty), he was hoping to bring together, within a publication with an international appeal, contributions from around the world. The project included the prospect to afford the struggles in colonial territories the importance they merited. The

[72] AN, 559AP29, John McNair to Marceau Pivert, 2 Sept. 1942.

[73] AN, 559AP49, Fenner Brockway to Marceau Pivert, 14 Nov. 1946.

magazine was finally launched in February 1948 and had a multinational political committee. It included Pivert, among others, for France, and on the British side, Brockway rubbed shoulders with some leading figures of the Labour left, such as Michael Foot and Ian Mikardo. Among the contributors the same orientation was manifest. This was reflected, for example, in the contributions of John McNair, Richard Crossman and Walter Padley. The political sensitivities of all these activists, as well as the expected contributions from Jayaprakash Narayan, George Padmore and Jean Rous, indicated the importance to be attached to colonial questions.[74] Still, the experience quickly proved too ambitious for the handful of militants involved. *Socialisme et Liberté* disappeared after a few months without having given much attention to specifically colonial questions. In its three issues the magazine included only three brief items explicitly devoted to these questions. Two were written by Frenchmen, rather than the intended wide range of international anti-colonialists, and the third consisted solely of a compilation of messages of support received at the Puteaux Congress.[75]

These failed attempts led the British and the French activists to return to a simpler *modus operandi*: national publications based upon international and anti-colonial news supplied by domestic and foreign correspondents. This required an abundance and wide range of correspondence and the sustained exchange of newspapers and magazines. From his British comrades Pivert received more or less regularly *The Socialist Leader*, *Tribune*, *Left*, *Forward*, the *New Statesman and Nation* and *The Freethinker*. Excerpts dealing with the situation in the British colonies appeared, usually in the form of snippets, in the three periodicals Pivert was in charge of successively from 1946: *Masses* (1946–1948), *Correspondance Socialiste* (*CS*, 1947–1950) and *Correspondance Socialiste Internationale* (*CSI*, from 1950). Their columns also included the information given to him directly by his correspondents. For example, in *Masses*, Pivert informed his readers about the agricultural and food situation in the province of Madras. The information for this piece had come from 'a cable addressed to Fenner Brockway by Professor Ranga, representing the Hindu Congress on the International Food Board'.[76] This confirms that Brockway and Pivert never ceased to swap information, but it also reveals that they tried to make full use of the extensive news provided by their colonial contacts. At the same time, Pivert regularly sent his own publications to Brockway, McNair and his British comrades. These

[74] *Socialisme et Liberté*, Feb. 1948, 2.

[75] Jean Rous, 'Aux côtés des peuples d'Outre Mer', *Socialisme et liberté*, Feb. 1948, 22; Paul Rivet, 'Faites la paix en Indochine', *Socialisme et liberté*, Mar. 1948, 22; 'Messages des peuples d'Asie et d'Afrique', *Socialisme et liberté*, July 1948, 12–13.

[76] 'Informations internationales – Indes', *Masses*, Dec. 1946, 14.

included *Masses*, *CS*, *CSI*, *La Revue Socialiste* or the SFIO's internal bulletin, publications to which some of them actually subscribed. This allowed them to glean information about events within the French Empire and to circulate it. 'I note that you have also written a special article for *Masses* which I have … read carefully and I am giving particulars of this article to our colonial friends', McNair wrote to Pivert in April 1947.[77]

These exchanges also included articles written specifically for their foreign friends. Although Brockway did not have time to contribute regularly to *CSI*, he did provide occasional contributions.[78] One illustration was given in January 1953, when Pivert published an article in *CSI* that was signed by Brockway as the chairman of COPAI, entitled 'Why Ferhat Hached was assassinated'.[79] It referred to the death, in December 1952, of one of the main Tunisian trade union leaders. This article illustrates once more how porous imperial borders could be in the eyes of Brockway and Pivert. Even though Brockway was presented as the president of COPAI, he was also presented as a 'Labour MP', that is as a Briton speaking on a case concerning another imperial power, namely France. The article did not appear by chance. Brockway had met Hached in Puteaux in 1948 and again in Tunisia in 1951 at the Congress of the UGTT (Union générale des travailleurs tunisiens, the Tunisian trade union organisation). A friendship had developed between the two men.[80] This, however, was not the first time that Pivert had published a British opinion on a French colonial question. He had already reproduced, in April 1951, an article from *Tribune* and another from the *New Statesman and Nation* on the Moroccan question.[81]

Brockway and Pivert drew symbolic and practical resources from these exchanges to give their anti-colonialism strength, legitimacy and an international scope. For instance, Pivert used examples taken from the British Empire to press for improvements in the French colonial territories. This transnational borrowing also enabled him to argue that his anti-colonialism knew no borders, and that his own struggle was part of a larger one. This was the case with a *CSI* article that Brockway devoted to the question of autonomy measures granted to Ghana, as well as to Nkrumah's political

[77] AN, 559AP29, John McNair to Marceau Pivert, 8 Apr. 1948.

[78] AN, 559AP29, Fenner Brockway to Marceau Pivert, 18 Sept. 1950.

[79] Fenner Brockway, 'Pourquoi Fehrat Hached a été assassiné', *CSI*, Jan. 1953, 5.

[80] Brockway, *Outside the Right*, 115.

[81] 'Opinion socialiste britannique sur la situation au Maroc', *CSI*, Apr. 1951, 11–12. The *Tribune* article denounced the violent and authoritarian policy implemented in the Moroccan protectorate by General Juin – the Governor General – vis-à-vis the Sultan and the nationalists. The article in *New Statesman and Nation* presented the military importance of Morocco for the USA, and how this was leading the Americans to arbitrate the tense game between the French and the Moroccans.

and social achievements. At the end of the article Pivert wrote on behalf of the editorial board: 'What a lesson for the French colonialists who refuse self-government to the Tunisian people!'.[82] However, one should not overestimate the importance of colonial issues in the exchanges between Brockway and Pivert. Although they occupied a far from insignificant place, they were set alongside information dealing primarily with national issues, or international issues not directly related to the colonial empires.

The links between Brockway and Pivert constituted one aspect of their wider political networks. Pivert was not Brockway's only French contact; and the reverse was also true. Brockway's close bonds with Jean Rous, especially within COPAI, and their collaboration over emerging causes inside the French Empire, are a clear illustration of this.[83] In addition, the many initiatives Brockway and Pivert undertook in common, and even their daily transnational operating modes, acted more as vectors of interpenetration and co-construction than a strictly interpersonal relationship. They introduced metropolitan and colonial activists to each other, who, once they were acquainted, did not always need to consult them anymore and then used to bypass them. Therefore, as a duo but also independently of each other, they played within the wider European revolutionary socialist milieu the role of hubs, of nodes, promoting meetings, exchanges and circulations among militant networks. If these multiples bridges did not concern the anti-colonialist cause exclusively, they were fully embodied within this framework.

In addition to the examples already mentioned, there is another, long-running one that illustrates these entanglements perfectly. While George Padmore was close to Brockway, for a long time he hardly knew Pivert. In August 1946, McNair informed Pivert of Padmore's presence in Paris and urged him to make contact with him.[84] The two men met and did more than just that. 'I have established contact between George Padmore and Viet Nam: he visited President Ho Chi Minh just after my own visit to him',[85] Pivert wrote to McNair. Pivert had obtained the right to visit thanks to Louis Caput.[86] Following Padmore's meeting with Ho Chi Minh, the Pan-Africanist leader informed Pivert that he would write a report for *The Socialist Leader* and send him a copy. He also told Pivert that he had given the Frenchman's address to Ranga, an Indian socialist, so that

[82] Fenner Brockway, 'La Côte-de-l'Or garde sa gauche: Nkrumah montre le chemin', *CSI*, June 1953, 13.
[83] Chevalier, 'Jean Rous', 740–48.
[84] AN, 559AP29, John McNair to Marceau Pivert, 14 Aug. 1946.
[85] AN, 559AP29, Marceau Pivert to John McNair, 8 Sept. 1946.
[86] AN, 559AP4, Hoang Minh Giam to Marceau Pivert, 5 Sept. 1946.

Pivert and Ranga might meet. Padmore also gave Ranga the address of the Vietnamese delegation in Paris, so that he too could have a meeting with Ho Chi Minh.[87] When Pivert's Vietnamese friends then came to London, they were therefore able to reactivate direct contact with Padmore.[88] They no longer needed Brockway, MacNair or Pivert to act as intermediaries. In this case, Pivert's role as a go-between was part of a quid pro quo: 'It would be great if, on your side, you could ask the Hindu comrades[89] to send me all their documentation directly every time they send it to you, at the *Socialist Leader*. Or when a cable arrives, could you make me a copy of it, so that I may publish fresh news from India in our press?',[90] Pivert asked McNair the first time he came knocking on his door. McNair apparently saw nothing wrong with putting Pivert directly in contact with the Indian friends of the British. When Pivert wrote to Jayaprakash Narayan for the first time, a little over a month later, he introduced himself as follows: 'Dear Comrades, I am a French socialist of the internationalist and revolutionary left, friend of Fenner Brockway and John Mac Nair [*sic*]'.[91] He then asked the Indian socialists to collaborate with *Masses*. Moreover, thanks to Brockway, who had recommended him, Pivert was also able to meet the Indian socialist B.P. Sinha in Paris at the end of 1946.[92] Thereafter the connection between Pivert and the socialist movement in India flourished. When Rammanohar Lohia contacted Pivert in 1954 with a view to launching a global monthly magazine, the Frenchman advised him to go to Brockway, the latter having expressed his appetite for a similar idea two years earlier.[93]

Brockway and Pivert continued to meet frequently up to the late 1940s, especially as members of MUSSE and COPAI. Mostly, it was the British who travelled to France and until 1950 Brockway visited Paris two or three times a year. These journeys always provided an opportunity to see Pivert. In turn, the latter visited England at least once a year between 1946 and 1948. As already mentioned, the two men met, for example, at the inaugural meeting of MUSSE in London on 22–23 February 1947. On 20 September 1948, they were side by side on the platform at a meeting organised in Wimbledon by the group 'Victory for Socialism'. The latter brought together

[87] AN, 559AP49, George Padmore to Marceau Pivert, 7 Sept. 1946.

[88] AN, 559AP4, George Padmore to Marceau Pivert, 29 Oct. 1946.

[89] Pivert often used this term for 'Indian'. He referred here to the contacts of his British friends in India.

[90] AN, 559AP29, Marceau Pivert to John McNair, 8 Sept. 1946.

[91] AN, 559AP49, Marceau Pivert to 'Comrade Jai Prakash Narain, Calcutta (and to all the friends of the Socialist Party like Suresh Vaidya)', 16 Oct. 1946.

[92] AN, 559AP49, Fenner Brockway to Marceau Pivert, n.d. (probably Nov. 1946). See also *Informations internationales*, Dec. 1946, 1.

[93] AN, 559AP73, Marceau Pivert to Rammanohar Lohia, 9 Dec. 1954.

former members of the ILP, now working inside the Labour Party, to talk about the United Socialist States of Europe. These circulations were part and parcel of the extensive system of networking mentioned above. Indeed, for his COPAI activities, Brockway often travelled to see Jean Rous, and meeting Pivert was not the main purpose of those trips.[94] Furthermore, Jean Rous also travelled several times to England with the same goal.[95] These meetings were also an opportunity to maintain close relations with representatives of the organisations of colonised peoples attached to COPAI. As for European commitments, when the MUSSE board visited London, without Pivert, in December 1947 to meet with their British counterparts, Brockway organised a meeting with activists from the colonies.[96]

Finally, the practical dimension of the relationship between Brockway and Pivert was tied to the fundamental question of the language used. Brockway did not speak French, and wrote letters to Pivert in English. As for Pivert, at least from his exile in New York in 1939–1940, he could cope with English. However, when writing to Brockway, he mainly used French. Because McNair was omnipresent alongside Brockway and had a command of both languages, the link between the two men could be maintained partly thanks to him. Pivert's letters were systematically translated by McNair for Brockway and then often circulated among their British friends.[97] This was also the case in terms of the articles written by Pivert for his British correspondents. McNair's translational skills were combined with tireless commitment, deep political intelligence and an impressive organisational capacity. In addition, he was bound to Pivert by a very real friendship. All these attributes help to explain why he became and remained so crucial to the exchanges between Brockway and Pivert and their wider British and French networks and organisations.

Fighting side by side: new promises and final commitments

In terms of collective anti-colonialist action, the early years of the 1950s were relatively quiet compared with the late 1940s. Relations between Pivert and Brockway were mainly characterised by the exchanges mentioned above. They were nonetheless active in their separate spheres. Brockway, elected an MP in 1950, quickly specialised in colonial matters in the House of Commons. He now had a new forum to express the growing demands of the colonised. During this period of time the influence of the COPAI network

[94] AN, 559AP29, Fenner Brockway to Marceau Pivert, 18 Sept. 1950.

[95] *Bulletin d'information du Congrès des peuples contre l'impérialisme*, Jan.–Feb. 1949, 3–4.

[96] AN, 559AP29, John McNair to Jacques Robin, 24 Nov. 1947.

[97] AN, 559AP42, John McNair to Marceau Pivert, 3 Feb. 1948.

on Brockway's speeches is marked.[98] In the meantime, he made several trips to colonial territories, both British and French (where he had many friends), and even had contact with relatives of Pierre Mendès France, then *Président du Conseil* (head of the government). Indeed, after Mendès France had granted internal autonomy to Tunisia, for fear of an escalation in violence, his collaborators contacted Brockway – who had just travelled to the protectorate – to know his opinion on the mindset of the Tunisian militants.[99] As for Pivert, he gave less importance to colonial questions. Certainly, he was a tireless opponent of war in Indochina and wanted appeasement in Tunisia, but other issues occupied most of his political agenda, chief among them being the fight against German rearmament within the framework of the European Defence Community.

It was from 1954 until Pivert's death in 1958 that anti-colonialism, in different forms, got back to a prominent place in the relationship between the two men. The initiative came from England. In a context of tensions within the British Empire, a new structure was established in April 1954: the Movement for Colonial Freedom (MCF).[100] Promoted and led by Brockway, and partly emerging from the ruins of the British branch of COPAI, it would from then on play a key role in the seizing of colonial questions on the British left. As in the days of COPAI, Brockway was the President. Douglas Rogers and Joseph Murumbi acted as General Secretaries. The MCF, which 'functioned less as research body than as a crusade',[101] was clear about its aims. It inherited from COPAI demands for the right of all peoples to independence and a precise timetable for its achievement, development assistance, the rejection of exploitation and discrimination and the adoption of an internationalist outlook.

The birth and success of the MCF were bound up with the developments in the Labour Party vis-à-vis colonial questions. The 1950s saw a gradual change in the mentality of the party in terms of its attitudes to political issues in the territories under British rule. The positions of the Labour left on these topics, which were more advanced than the average opinion of party leaders, enjoyed growing appeal. One of the most dominant of these positions was that the colonial population should have the right to choose their own fate. According to those on the Labour left, the debates over colonial issues could no longer only be about the degree of reforms but also had to give greater

[98] Brockway, *Outside the Right*, 75 and 155–56. On some of the campaigns that Brockway led or supported in the early 1950s, see Howe, *Anticolonialism*, 196–214.

[99] Brockway, *Outside the Right*, 118.

[100] Howe, *Anticolonialism*, 231–88.

[101] David Goldsworthy, *Colonial Issues in British Politics, 1945–1961: From 'Colonial Development' to 'Wind of Change'* (Oxford, 1971), 324.

focus to the nature of colonial relationship. Gradually, its members also gained control of bodies within the Labour Party concerned with colonial matters.[102] How can one explain these changes and new perspectives in the party members' colonial attitudes? One answer might be that Labour's return to the opposition benches enabled a more radical stance, while the rising challenges inside the Empire itself – due to the crisis situation in several colonial territories such as in Kenya or in British Guiana – were also significant factors. In this 'favorable' context the MCF was successful in bringing colonial matters to greater prominence, especially in Parliament, and in persuading significant numbers of Labour members to adopt its views. Brockway played a central role in this process by becoming, from his election to the Commons, 'a parliamentary leader for the anticolonial left' and 'a central face and the best-known British anticolonialist'.[103] In his memoirs, written in 1963, he recorded these changes within Labour and the Parliamentary Labour Party: 'The increase of interest and knowledge among Labour Members has been remarkable. At first I suppose I drafted more than half the questions put by Labour MPs to the Colonial Secretary; I would provide each with a brief. Now I do not do this for any colleague. We have twenty or thirty MPs, well informed and vigilant, all of whom know their subject'.[104] Pivert did not have the same importance within his own party as his British counterpart but had more and more the same concerns. Indeed, at the very same moment, he was becoming increasingly interested in the emergence of the Third World movement, in which he thought he could spot the stirrings of the third international force that he had never stopped hoping for. The creation of the Asian Socialist Conference (Rangoon, January 1953), like the Bandung Conference (April 1955), encouraged him in this direction. Indeed, Pivert could discern in these events the combination of a remaining possibility of a left-wing, international solidarity and the refusal of a division of the world into two opposing camps.

The context was increasingly conducive to the recommencement of joint activities on the part of Brockway and Pivert. At the end of 1954, during a discussion at Claude Bourdet's house, Brockway asked Pivert to establish a new organisation that would be the French branch of the MCF.[105] To Brockway's delight, Pivert and Jean Rous accepted the proposition.[106] Pivert's ambitions were similar to what they had been in the COPAI days: 'What we will be able

102 Howe, *Anticolonialism*, 219–30.

103 Howe, *Anticolonialism*, 169.

104 Brockway, *Outside the Right*, 156.

105 AN, 559AP29, John McNair to Marceau Pivert, 27 Oct. 1954.

106 AN, 559AP29, Fenner Brockway to Marceau Pivert and Jean Rous, 3 Dec. 1954.

to do now is coordinate our efforts better and provide an opportunity for an internationalist rehabilitation, because the problems of the real emancipation of colonial peoples are closely linked to those of peace and of the liberation of workers everywhere'.[107] In March 1955, Douglas Rogers came to Paris at Pivert's invitation to talk about the MCF before the Zimmerwald Circle, an association of which he was a member and that was close to the magazine *La Révolution prolétarienne*.[108] During his stay in the French capital, an initiative committee was created, which was transformed in May into a new organisation connected with the MCF: the Mouvement justice et liberté outre-mer (MJLOM – the Movement for Justice and Freedom Overseas). Two months later, an initiative of another kind also reflected this renewed collective activity. Brockway and Pivert spoke as a tandem during an international symposium in Oxford in July 1955 on the prospects of socialism. The session which they were responsible for was entitled 'Socialism and the Problems of Colonial and Underdeveloped Areas'.[109]

Although it shared the political platform of the MCF, the MJLOM put more emphasis on the educational dimension of its actions: it wanted to promote in particular exchanges between metropolitan and colonial militants, and to disseminate its ideas widely through public campaigns, seminars and debates.[110] Here, Pivert's influence was notable, as was Brockway's on the MCF. With repertoires of actions of their own, they were able, in their individual ways, to influence the style of activities of their respective organisations. Pivert opened his columns to Brockway, to inform his readers of the activity of the MCF and encourage them to use it as an example to develop the MJLOM.[111] However, the latter never experienced the prestige and the dynamism of its British counterpart, and dwindled during the second half of 1957.[112] In fact, the French anti-colonialist environment was rapidly faced with turmoil, due to new developments in the war in Algeria. After the General election in January 1956, the SFIO's leader Guy Mollet became the new *Président du Conseil*. Contrary to his electoral promises, Mollet went further in waging war. He dragged with him the majority of the Socialist

[107] AN, 559AP38, Marceau Pivert to Fenner Brockway, 19 Mar. 1955.

[108] 'Troisième camp', *CSI*, Apr. 1955, 26. Founded in 1925, *La Révolution prolétarienne* was a syndicalist, anti-Stalinist and internationalist review. A forum for diverse tendencies inside the labour movement, it was among the first publications to express an interest in colonial questions, and to consider them with a critical eye.

[109] AN, 559AP30, Oxford Conference Programme, 16–18 July 1955.

[110] *Bulletin d'informations du Comité d'initiative pour un Mouvement pour la Justice et la Liberté Outre-Mer*, May 1955.

[111] Fenner Brockway, 'Au service de la plus grande révolution de notre temps', *CSI*, May 1957, 5–7.

[112] AN, 559AP74, Jean Rous to Marceau Pivert, 30 Dec. 1957.

Party, and his deeds contributed to a hardening of the anti-war movements' positions. Moreover, even if they were equally struggling against military action, these movements were not all advocating the same policy towards the Algerian situation. In this context, the MJLOM failed to unite within its ranks opponents of the conflict as well as, from 1956, opponents of the SFIO leadership.

It was around this colonial conflict that the Brockway–Pivert collaboration regained its former force. On the Algerian question, Pivert quickly became Brockway's and the MCF's referent. Pivert had been a long-time follower of Messali Hadj, the Algerian nationalist leader, as well as a tireless campaigner for his release from prison. In February 1955, Brockway asked his French comrade to organise a meeting with Messali during his own planned visit to France.[113] To that end, Pivert activated his contacts and eventually turned towards Yves Dechezelles, one of his socialist friends, who was Messali's lawyer.[114] Pivert also informed the MCF about different aspects of the war in Algeria. For example, he was in contact with Léon Szur and Mary Klopper, two South African activists who were very active in the British organisation. So while the MCF was preparing a brochure in 1957 on Algeria, Klopper asked Pivert for documentation and information. Among the issues she wished him to consider, the conflict between the two nationalist organisations, the National Liberation Front (Front de Libération Nationale: FLN) and the Algerian National Movement (Mouvement National Algérien: MNA), occupied a major place.[115] Essentially, due to a disagreement over whether the armed struggle for independence should be launched immediately or not, the split between the FLN and the MNA at the beginning of the war in Algeria quickly took the form of a fratricidal struggle for dominance in the nationalist movement. The main difference between the FLN and the MNA was not programmatic (as their claims were essentially the same) but had to do with the question of allegiance or not towards the figure of Messali Hadj.[116] While the MNA was in favour of this course of action, the FLN was opposed to it. The issue of the conflict between the FLN and the MNA dominated the correspondence between Pivert and the MCF during the following year, although the letters also included more general information on Algeria.[117]

113 AN, 559AP29, Fenner Brockway to Marceau Pivert, 23 Feb. 1955.

114 AN, 559AP73, Marceau Pivert to Yves Dechezelles, 26 Feb. 1955.

115 AN, 559AP73, Mary Klopper to Marceau Pivert, 20 Jan. 1957.

116 The FLN and the MNA, while fighting the French, were engaged in an all-out war with each other. It led to the FLN's victory over its rival after some 10,000 men were killed and 23,000 men were wounded. Guy Pervillé, *La guerre d'Algérie* (Paris, 2012), 114–15.

117 AN, 559AP73, Marceau Pivert to Mary Klopper, 30 Jan. 1958; Mary Klopper to Marceau Pivert, 7 Feb. 1958; Marceau Pivert to Mary Klopper, 21 Mar. 1958.

This continued interest in the FLN–MNA conflict was no coincidence, because it did hold, during this period, a special place in Pivert's commitment against the war in Algeria. Indeed, he remained invariably favourable to the Messalist MNA, while from the end of 1955 most French support for Algerian nationalism was invested in the FLN. Overall, both the FLN and the MNA maintained a distant relationship to the traditional labour movement. They both saw it as a Western offspring in which they did not identify the features of their national struggle for independence. Thus, the support by the French militants to one Algerian organisation or the other was not determined simply by an ideological proximity. Pivert's preference for the MNA stemmed from a variety of factors: his fidelity to Messali Hadj; his conception of the MNA as being, anyhow, closer to socialism than the FLN (based on Messali's deeds and words in the 1930s); his sympathy for those he considered as the victims, in a conflict he compared with the attacks against his friends from the Workers' Party of Marxist Unification (Partido Obrero de Unificación Marxista: POUM) by the Communist Party during the Spanish Civil war; and his rejection of the practices and claims of the FLN. This approach was more the result of instinct, intimate determinants and personal feelings rather than that of a cold political analysis. For this reason, it was neither obvious nor spontaneous for his British interlocutors, who analysed the situation with a less passionate outlook. In fact, the MCF refused at first to choose between the FLN and the MNA. The requests made to Pivert therefore represented a major challenge for the French activist: his siding with the MNA and his place within the French anti-colonialist network could have been considerably strengthened by support from the powerful British organisation. Still, at the end of 1957, Pivert's ambitions to bring the MCF on his positions had failed: the British organisation, although it was still refusing officially to choose, only maintained an effective link with the FLN, arguing that the MNA lacked activity and representativeness.[118]

This rivalry between the two organisations was also the cause of an incident that occurred in Athens during the international Anticolonial Congress organised in November 1957 by the Greek Anticolonial League.[119] Brockway and Pivert, accompanied by their British and French delegations, were present, embodying respectively the MCF and the MJLOM. On the second day the FLN delegation refused to stay if the MNA delegate was not

[118] Howe, *Anticolonialism*, 236.

[119] That event was officially organised by the MJLOM, the MCF and the World Council for Colonial Liberation (WCCL). The WCCL had been created, on Brockway's initiative, after the World Conference for Colonial Liberation, held in Margate in November 1955. Howe, *Anticolonialism*, 278–79.

excluded from the convention, arguing that they had not been informed of his presence. The Congress finally accepted this requirement and Pivert and his friends, who had made the simultaneous presence of the FLN and the MNA a condition for their participation, protested and left the conference. Brockway and his comrades, although they also condemned the exclusion of the MNA, decided to stay. This disagreement, however, did not damage the general concord between the two men in the long run. Indeed, it became an opportunity to reaffirm the need for better coordination between the British and French activists.[120]

During this period, the two men also increasingly relied upon their mutual respect and standing to strengthen their positions within their national organisations and political fields. For each of them, the purpose was to show that their respective positions were not marginal but were encouraged by other prominent socialists in Europe. Pivert counted on Brockway to support, with the resources he had, his opposition to the die-hard policy in Algeria led by the SFIO and Guy Mollet's government, which was a policy that mostly aimed at a French victory by military force. To this end, Pivert regularly sent his views to Brockway,[121] who was also very active in England on the Algerian question.[122] Until his death, Pivert was constantly writing to Britain to rally the British to his views. It is worth noting that Pivert's maintenance of these connections was motivated by factors beyond self-interest. Indeed, he also used his British correspondents to give more weight to the cause of other socialists fighting in France against the war in Algeria and against the SFIO leadership. For instance, he encouraged Edouard Depreux, another leader of the socialist opposition to Guy Mollet and his Algerian policies, to engage with Brockway. In this case, Pivert thought that his British friend could give great publicity to the oppositional action Depreux was carrying with his own comrades inside as well as outside the boundaries of the Socialist Party.[123]

Furthermore, for both Pivert and Brockway, the Suez crisis was another occasion to use each other as a resource of international legitimacy for their respective actions. During a demonstration in Trafalgar Square in 1956, organised to denounce the rising tensions around the Suez Canal, Brockway stood at the podium and read a message of solidarity that had been sent by Pivert. This message, Brockway asserted, 'made a deep impression'.[124] A few

[120] AN, 559AP29, Marceau Pivert to Fenner Brockway, 3 Dec. 1957; Fenner Brockway to Marceau Pivert, 9 Dec. 1957.

[121] AN, 559AP49, Fenner Brockway to Marceau Pivert, 29 Feb. 1956.

[122] Brockway, *Outside the Right*, 164.

[123] AN, 559AP73, Marceau Pivert to Edouard Depreux, 15 Oct. 1957.

[124] AN, 559AP29, Fenner Brockway to Marceau Pivert, 16 Oct. 1956.

months later, in November, Anthony Eden and Guy Mollet launched the invasion of the Suez canal zone together (Operation Musketeer), leading to a strong opposition by the Labour Party. Consequently, Pivert used the position adopted by the British to strengthen his own denunciation of Eden's French counterpart, depicting Mollet as a colonialist warmonger betraying socialism.

Besides using each other as an international symbolic backup for their individual actions, the two men also had the opportunity to work collectively. In the preparation of the Vienna Congress of the Socialist International (2–6 July 1957), they strove together to formulate denunciations of both Eden and Mollet that might be put forward to the Congress by their Scandinavian friends (i.e., from countries not involved in the events) who would attend in Austria.[125] Eventually, the Norwegian delegate Fin Mor, with the support of his Swedish counterpart and of Aneurin Bevan, delivered a vigorous speech against Mollet's action in Algeria. However, they did not succeed in bringing the International to their views: the final resolutions adopted by the Congress did not call for the independence of Algeria and did not condemn the Algerian policy of the SFIO. As for the Suez expedition, the Congress did not take any official position.[126]

Nevertheless, although they still worked together on some occasions, one must not be deluded: the closeness between the two men was no longer as productive as in the past. Pivert, whose health problems seriously increased after 1957 and who had been marginalised in the SFIO, saw his deteriorating physical state limit his capacity for action. Brockway remained very active, but mostly in his own British environment. It was, above all, the continued exchange of information that characterised the relationship between the two men in the months before Pivert's death rather than any real attempt to stand, shoulder to shoulder, against colonialism. Pivert was by then incapable of physical effort, although he did his best to attend the Anticolonial Congress in Athens. The little strength he had left in him before dying reflects a life committed to internationalism: one of the last letters he sent to his British friends dealt with an article on the Algerian question he had sent to Brockway for publication in *The Socialist Leader*.[127]

125 AN, 559AP29, Fenner Brockway to Marceau Pivert, 19 Dec. 1956; Marceau Pivert to Fenner Brockway, 4 June 1957.

126 'Le Congrès de l'Internationale Socialiste', *CSI*, July–Aug. 1957, 7–9.

127 AN, 559AP29, Marceau Pivert to John McNair, 9 Apr. 1958.

Conclusion

The study of the relationship between Fenner Brockway and Marceau Pivert reveals the specific aspects of the kind of anti-colonialism they both tried to embody. It also highlights their common commitment and unceasing endeavour, and the difficulties and constraints under which they worked both individually and together. In terms of an overall evaluation of their strengths and weaknesses and successes and failures, we must conclude that on a global scale their main objective – to establish a third international force based on their ideas – was not successful. They did not lead decolonisation movements on to the socialist path they believed in, nor did they succeed in working closely and in a sustained manner with the colonised. In addition, they did not manage to infuse the colonial liberation politics with the distinctive political and social features they so assiduously promoted. They were convinced that anti-colonialism was to be carried out jointly, under the folds of the flag of revolutionary and internationalist socialism, in Europe and in the colonial territories. However, at the end of the day, they could only support and encourage anti-colonialism within national movements of which they were not at the forefront and on which they exerted very limited influence. This is partly due to the fact that, in spite of all their work, they would remain under suspicious consideration by the struggling colonised peoples, by virtue of being Europeans.

Yet these key failures were tempered with some successes. For example, they both played a part within their respective national and labour-movement contexts of raising the profile of colonial matters. Despite the disappointments and distrust of colonial activists vis-à-vis metropolitan organisations, Brockway and Pivert were able, inside the Labour Party and the SFIO respectively, to keep alive the, albeit fluctuating, fortunes of anti-colonialism. Their impressive and enduring relationship and networks, rooted in shared and resolute commitments to radical internationalism and transnationalism, are worthy of special note. To be sure, Pivert probably benefited more from the relationship than did Brockway. This reflected the latter's more important place in their respective national political contexts. Lastly, this study has hopefully demonstrated that the employment of a comparative and transnational methodology can usefully complement a national approach to the question of anti-colonialism.

II

Labour, Decolonisation and Independence (1940s–1960s)

6

Decolonisation and Claim-Making in the Sudan, c.1945–1958

Gareth Curless

African labour history has experienced many twists and turns since its emergence as a discrete field of study.[1] At its height in the 1970s and early 1980s, historians were principally concerned with the development of capitalism under colonialism, the process of proletarianisation and the agency of African workers, with a particular emphasis on the emergence of organised labour activism.[2] The objective of these studies was to capture the revolutionary fervour of anti-colonial nationalism by demonstrating the relevance of class consciousness and class conflict to Africa.[3] However, with the collapse of socialist regimes across Africa during the late 1980s, historians began to question the relevance of universal conceptions of class and proletarianisation to the African context.[4] Instead, inspired by 'new social history', historians extended their focus to look beyond archetypal occupational groups – mineworkers, dockers and railwaymen – to a broader range

[1] For useful surveys of the field, see Bill Freund, 'Labor and Labor History in Africa: A Review of the Literature', *African Studies Review*, 27.2 (1984), 1–58; Frederick Cooper, 'African Labour History', in Jan Lucassen (ed.), *Global Labour History: A State of the Art* (Berne, 2008), 91–116; Andreas Eckert, 'Wage Labour', in Steffano Belluci and Andreas Eckert (eds), *General Labour History of Africa: Workers, Employers, and Governments, 20th to 21st Century* (Woodbridge, 2019), 17–44.

[2] Richard Sandbrook and Robin Cohen (eds), *The Development of an African Working Class: Studies in Class Formation and Action* (London, 1975); Jeff Crisp, *The Story of an African Working Class: Ghanaian Miners' Struggles, 1870–1980* (London, 1984); Bill Freund, *Capital and Labour in the Nigerian Tin Mines* (Harlow, 1981); Richard Jeffries, *Class, Power and Ideology in Ghana: The Railwaymen of Sekondi* (Cambridge, 1978). For a critique of this literature, which, nevertheless, acknowledges its relative strengths, see Frederick Cooper, 'Work, Class, Empire: An African Historian's Retrospective on E.P. Thompson', *Social History*, 20.2 (1995), 235–41.

[3] Cooper, 'Work, Class, Empire', 235–36.

[4] For a classic critique of structural approaches, see James Ferguson, *Expectations of Modernity: Myths and Meaning of Modern Life on the Zambian Copperbelt* (Berkeley, CA, 1999).

of social actors, such as women, peasants and other non-waged workers.[5] By this point, as Lyn Schler, Louise Bethlehem and Gaia Sabar argue, African labour history had 'not so much been abandoned as redefined'.[6]

For all its initial vibrancy, however, African labour history experienced a period of relative decline during the 1990s. One of the few historians to continue championing its cause was Frederick Cooper. Responding to the cultural and linguistic turns, Cooper argued for a conception of class as not just a 'contingent, changing set of relationships' but also an 'imaginative project'.[7] Cooper's work helped to reinvigorate the field, as historians sought to understand class formation in African contexts as a product of material conditions *and* discursive mediations between African labour, on the one hand, and capital, the state and other forms of identity and affiliation, such as gender, race, ethnicity and religion, on the other.[8] Such approaches drew praise from Cooper, who noted that 'fresh and thoughtful analysis … ha[d] emerged from confronting representation with the nitty-gritty [materialism] of labour'.[9]

The more recent 'global turn', with its emphasis on mobility and cosmopolitanism, promises to continue the revival of African labour history, although some historians have responded to this most recent scholarly turn with caution.[10] While accepting the benefits of methodo-

[5] See, for example, Elias C. Mandala, *Work and Control in a Peasant Economy: A History of the Lower Tchiri Valley in Malawi, 1859–1960* (Madison, WI, 1990) and Luise White, *The Comforts of Home: Prostitution in Colonial Nairobi* (Chicago, IL, 1990).

[6] Lynn Schler, Louise Bethlehem and Galia Sabar, 'Rethinking Labour in Africa, Past and Present', *African Identities*, 7.3 (2009), 287.

[7] Frederick Cooper, *Decolonization and African Society: The Labor Question in French and British Africa* (New York, 1996), 14.

[8] As Cooper puts it, 'power, on the shop floor as elsewhere, was rooted in particular cultural structures – from the racially based system of colonial authority to Africans' efforts to shape work patterns to their own needs. Labor movements were more than automatic responses to becoming proletarian, but were rooted in specific patterns of affiliation and strategies of mobilization and alliance building. Government interventions were of great importance precisely because the nature of work and of conflict were indeterminate'. *Decolonization and African Society*, 14. For works that take up these issues, see Carolyn Brown, *'We Were All Slaves': African Miners, Culture, and Resistance at the Engu Government Colliery* (Portsmouth, NH, 2003) and Lisa Lindsay, *Working with Gender: Wage Labor and Social Change in Southwestern Nigeria* (Portsmouth, NH, 2003). This chapter is indebted to the pioneering work of Brown, Cooper and Lindsay.

[9] Frederick Cooper, 'Back to Work: Categories, Boundaries and Connections in the Study of Labour', in Peter Alexander and Ralph Halpern (eds), *Racializing Class, Classifying Race* (London, 2000), 213. For a useful summary of how historians can combine materialist approaches that remain sensitive to local contexts and the need to dissect supposedly 'universal' categories and concepts, see Schler, Bethlehem and Sabar, 'Rethinking Labour in Africa'.

[10] For a cautionary review of the literature on these issues, see Ralph Callebert, 'African Mobility and Labor in Global History', *History Compass*, 14.3 (2016), 116–227. Callebert's

logical approaches informed by global history, this chapter is principally concerned with returning to the intersection between material conditions, colonial 'ways of seeing' and Africans' discursive representations of circumstances and subjectivity.[11] Taking Sudan as its case study, the chapter focuses on the experiences of Sudanese railwaymen, dockworkers and civil servants during the period of decolonisation, and in the process makes three interrelated arguments.[12] First, the chapter argues that despite Sudan's unusual 'Condominium' status, the Sudan Political Service (SPS) viewed the 'labour question' in much the same terms as other colonial administrations in British Africa.[13] That is to say, when confronted with the development of organised labour activism in the late 1940s, the Sudan government responded by introducing a series of labour reforms designed to 'modernise' industrial relations. In the introduction to this volume, the editors emphasised the importance of bringing metropolitan and imperial histories into a single frame of analysis. Nowhere is this need more apparent than in the study of the labour reforms that were introduced into colonial contexts over the course of the 1940s and 1950s.[14] Across the empire, employers and colonial officials sought to reshape colonial workers by

---

work is indicative of the pioneering role that Southern Africanists have played in steering the debate when it comes to labour history and the global turn. See, for example, Philip Bonner, Jonathan Hyslop and Lucien van der Walt, 'Rethinking Worlds of Labour: Southern African Labour History in International Context', *African Studies*, 66.2–3 (2007), 137–67. For a critical stance on the global turn and its methodological dangers, including arguments relating to the unevenness of capitalist development and waged-labour in Africa, see Franco Barchiesi, 'How Far from Africa's Shore? A Response to Marcel van der Linden's Map for Global Labor History', *International Labor and Working-Class History*, 82 (2012), 77–84 and Ralph Callebert, *On Durban's Docks: Zulu Workers, Rural Households, and Global Labor* (Rochester, NY, 2017).

[11] The idea of colonial 'ways of seeing' is taken from Miles Larmer, 'Permanent Precarity: Capital and Labour in the Central African Copperbelt', *Labor History*, 58.2 (2017), 171.

[12] It is important to note that these categories of worker are discussed separately for the most part in this chapter, albeit against the wider context of late colonial labour policy. Clearly, more could be done to bring the three categories of worker into dialogue with each other, with a particular emphasis on the intersectional relationship between race, ethnicity, religion and class in the Sudanese context. The two best accounts of Sudanese civil servants and railways workers remain: Heather Sharkey, *Living with Colonialism: Nationalism and Culture in the Anglo-Egyptian Sudan* (Berkeley, CA, 2003) and Ahmad Alawad Sikainga, *'City of Steel and Fire': A Social History of Atbara, Sudan's Railway Town, 1906–1984* (Portsmouth, NH, 2002).

[13] On Sudan's Condominium status, see Martin W. Daly, *Empire on the Nile: The Anglo-Egyptian Sudan, 1898–1934* (Cambridge, 1986). Justin Willis has made a comparable argument concerning indirect rule in his 'Violence, Authority and the State in the Nuba Mountains of Condominium Sudan', *Historical Journal*, 46.1 (2003), 89–114.

[14] For an article that traces this shift in colonial labour policy, see Frederick Cooper, 'From Free Labor to Family Allowances: Labor and African Society in Colonial Discourse',

drawing on metropolitan precedents when it came to the organisation of waged-labour, industrial relations and social welfare. In this endeavour, private business and colonial governments were aided by metropolitan experts, such as British Trades Union Congress (TUC) representatives, Ministry of Labour officials and social policy advisers, who sought to socialise colonial workers to the demands of urban life and industrial discipline by implementing policies first devised for use in Britain.[15] The Sudan was no exception. During the late 1940s and early 1950s, SPS officials briefly experimented with various metropolitan-inspired labour policies, as they 'reimagined' Sudanese workers, seeking to remodel them in the image of their idealised British counterparts.

The shift in colonial policy informs the chapter's second argument, namely that Sudanese workers and trade unionists responded to the language of industrial discipline by transforming it into a 'claim making' device.[16] The chapter investigates how Sudanese workers combined the colonial discourse of labour productivity and stability with local idioms and vernacular understandings of morality and modernity in order to advocate for improved labour rights, higher wages and greater social entitlements.[17] Finally, the chapter concludes by examining how the political space opened up by the new colonial discourse on labour closed down during the transition to independence as Sudanese political elites argued that the interests of Sudanese workers had to be subordinated to the immediate task of nation building.[18]

American Ethnologist, 16.4 (1989), 745–65. For a more detailed study of this shift in policy, see, of course, Cooper, *Decolonization and African Society*.

[15] For a general overview of the role played by the TUC in colonial labour policy, see Peter Weiler, 'Forming Responsible Trade Unions: The Colonial Office, Colonial Labour and the Trades Union Congress', *Radical History Review*, 28.30 (1984), 367–92.

[16] The transformation of post-1945 imperial labour policy into a claim making device lies at the heart of Cooper's work, especially, *Decolonization and African Society*.

[17] Cooper's work on French West Africa is particularly instructive. See Frederick Cooper, '"Our Strike": Equality, Anticolonial Politics and the 1947–48 Railway Strike in French West Africa', *Journal of African History*, 37.1 (1996), 81–118. Franco Barchiesi has explored the relevance of Cooper's arguments concerning claim-making to the South African context in his *Precarious Liberation: Workers, the State, and Contested Social Citizenship in Post-Apartheid South Africa* (Albany, NY, 2011). In keeping with this chapter's key arguments, modernity, following Cooper's work on the concept, is understood as a claim-making construct. For a discussion of this point, see Frederick Cooper, *Colonialism in Question: Theory, Knowledge, History* (Berkeley, CA, 2005), chapter five.

[18] Cooper, *Colonialism in Question*, 206. See also Miles Larmer, 'Historicising Activism in Late Colonial and Post-Colonial Sub-Saharan Africa', *Journal of Historical Sociology*, 28.1 (2015), 75–76.

The struggle over family wages

'Power in colonial societies', as Cooper famously remarked, 'was more arterial than capillary – concentrated spatially and socially, not very nourishing beyond such domains, and in need of a pump to push it from moment to moment and place to place'.[19] Nothing illustrates the limits of colonial power more clearly than colonial economic structure in Africa. Throughout the continent, colonial states were dependent upon the tax revenues generated by the export of primary commodities.[20] However, in many colonies the economic infrastructure – such as the railway network and port facilities, which were necessary for the export of raw materials – was often inadequate and underfinanced.[21] The situation was compounded by employers' and colonial states' preference for temporary male migrant labour over the creation of permanent workforces dependent upon wages alone. Since employers and the colonial state were unwilling to subsidise the social reproduction of labour, female-headed rural households and African entrepreneurs based in the rapidly expanding urban centres stepped in to fill the void.[22] This latter point is critical. As towns and cities in Africa expanded during the first half of the twentieth century, conditions deteriorated as ever-greater pressure was placed on limited urban infrastructure.[23] In the late 1930s and again in the late 1940s, these pressures exploded in the form of urban riots and industrial stoppages, as African workers and members of the wider community protested against deteriorating living conditions.[24]

19 Frederick Cooper, 'Conflict and Connection: Rethinking Colonial African History', *American Historical Review*, 99.5 (1994), 1533.

20 Timothy Oberst, 'Transport Workers, Strikes and the "Imperial Response": Africa and the Post World War II Conjuncture', *African Studies Review*, 31.1 (1988), 118.

21 In East Africa, for example, 'a single line of rail and a single port' connected the productive areas of Uganda and Kenya to the global economy, with the result that selective strike action by transport workers could cause severe disruption. Frederick Cooper, *On the African Waterfront: Urban Disorder and the Transformation of Work in Colonial Mombasa* (New Haven, CT, 1987), 115.

22 On the reproduction of migrant labour, see Lisa Lindsay, 'Domesticity and Difference: Male Breadwinners, Working Women, and Colonial Citizenship in the 1945 Nigerian General Strike', *American Historical Review*, 104.3 (1999), 784–85; Frederick Cooper, 'Introduction: Urban Space, Industrial Time, and Wage Labor in Africa', in Frederick Cooper (ed.), *Struggle for the City: Migrant Labor, Capital and the State in Urban Africa* (Beverley Hills, CA, 1983), 7–50, especially 29–32.

23 Andrew Burton, *African Underclass: Urbanisation, Crime and Colonial Order in Dar es Salaam* (Oxford, 2005), 17–42, especially 29.

24 Cooper, although he emphasises that each protest movement was rooted in locally specifically conditions, argues that the strikes that swept through Africa during the 1930s and the 1940s were related in so far as they were driven by shared grievances linked to socio-

The Sudan was no different. Sporadic strikes, limited to specific industries in the late 1930s and early 1940s, gave way to a sustained campaign of industrial unrest in 1947 and 1948, led by the Workers' Affairs Association (WAA), the representative body for Sudanese railway workers.[25] The WAA's emergence as the vanguard of the Sudanese labour movement was hardly surprising. By 1945, the government-run Sudan Railways employed 20,000 workers, the majority of whom lived and worked in Atbara – a town that owed its existence to the development of the colonial economy.[26] The concentration of railway workers in Atbara, combined with the highly stratified nature of the railway industry, gave rise to a strong sense of corporate identity amongst the town's residents.[27] In the post-war context, a time of deteriorating economic conditions and rising political ambitions, the WAA campaigned for recognition as a trade union and improved employment conditions for its members, commensurate with their perceived status as skilled workers.[28]

The unrest that swept through Africa during the late 1940s contributed to a growing appreciation of the need to 'stabilise' African workforces amongst colonial government and employers. Stabilisation typically involved setting a higher minimum wage, addressing malnutrition and poor health among workers, hiring only registered casual labourers and providing adequate housing and social services for urban workers and their families.[29] It was hoped that such measures would encourage African workers to form 'stable' nuclear families, which, in turn, would reduce the possibility of further industrial unrest, increase productivity and facilitate the social reproduction of labour.[30] The emergence of the stabilisation agenda, as Cooper has documented, was seized upon by African politicians and trade unionists,

---

economic conditions. *Decolonization and African Society*, 225–60, especially 225–27. See also Oberst, 'Transport Workers, Strikes and the "Imperial Response"', 118–19.

[25] On the development of the WAA, see Sikainga, *'City of Steel and Fire'*, 97–123.

[26] On the development of Atbara, see Sikainga, *'City of Steel and Fire'*, 43–64 and Daly, *Empire on the Nile*, 203.

[27] This is one of the key issues that is explored in Sikaigna's work. See, in particular, chapters 3 and 4.

[28] On the 1947–1948 strike campaign, see Gareth Curless, '"The Sudan is not yet ready for trade unions": The Railway Strikes of 1947–48', *Journal of Imperial and Commonwealth History*, 41.5 (2013), 804–22.

[29] The best account of the stabilisation policy remains Cooper, *Decolonization and African Society*, 324–60. For a useful discussion of the central tenets of the stabilisation policy and its objectives, see Cooper's case study work on Mombasa, *On the African Waterfront*, 124–36.

[30] As Frederick Cooper points out, stabilisation was not proletariaisation. The policy was designed to separate a select group of waged-workers from the wider population. See Frederick Cooper, *Africa since 1940: The Past of the Present* (Cambridge, 2002), 31 and 34.

who demanded that if employers and the colonial authorities expected African workers to commit to a life of waged-labour then they should be granted higher pay and improved workplace rights and entitlements.[31] Such a dynamic was apparent in the Sudan, where, the WAA claimed, as part of its submission to a Committee of Inquiry established to investigate the causes of the 1947–1948 unrest, a man with a wife and two children on a basic wage of 150 piastres (PT) a month and a cost of living allowance of 105 PT actually required a minimum of 360 PT a month just to meet the family's subsistence costs.[32] As Lisa Lindsay has argued in relation to similar demands issued by Nigerian trade unionists, by presenting wage claims on the basis of what workers required to support a family, the WAA framed its proposal in terms it hoped would appeal to the Sudan government: men's status as 'breadwinners' and the stabilisation of labour.[33]

The Committee of Inquiry agreed, in part, with the WAA's argument. It endorsed the family wage model, stating that the 'basic wage must be such as will suffice to keep a home together' but argued that substantial wage increases could not be introduced because of the financial costs involved and the inflationary effect that any pay rise for railway employees would have on the economy.[34] Rather than increasing the basic wage, the Commission proposed raising the cost of living allowance so that workers could afford an 'adequate diet'.[35] By retaining the basic wage, the Committee was in effect arguing that there were limits to the value of Sudanese labour.[36] The situation was similar in Nigeria, as Lindsay has documented. In the aftermath of the 1945 general strike the colonial authorities rejected the trade unions' demands for a 'breadwinner' wage. The authorities argued that Nigerian families were too different from their European counterparts: wives were economically independent, spouses' incomes were kept separate, polygyny was common and households were often large and extended.[37] In short, although the colonial authorities were receptive to arguments relating

[31] Cooper, *Africa since 1940*, 42–43. See also Frederick Cooper, 'Reconstructing Empire in British and French Africa', *Past and Present*, 210, supplement 6 (2011), 196–210.

[32] The National Archives (TNA), Foreign Office (FO) Papers, 371/69236, Sudan Railways' Employees, *Report of the Independent Committee of Enquiry* (Khartoum, 1948).

[33] On comparable demands made by Nigerian trade unionists, see Lindsay, 'Domesticity and Difference', 802–3. It is worth emphasising that the WAA's demand for higher wages is also discussed by Sikaigna, see *City of Steel and Fire*, 111–14.

[34] TNA, FO, 371/69236, Sudan Railways' Employees, *Report of the Independent Committee of Enquiry*.

[35] *Report of the Independent Committee of Enquiry*.

[36] As Cooper has argued, this conclusion was typical of many investigative commissions into industrial unrest in Africa. *Decolonization and African Society*, 129–30.

[37] Lindsay, 'Domesticity and Difference', 786–87.

to the stabilisation of labour, they were influenced by racial assumptions regarding the value of African labour and the nature of African societies, and continued to believe that the lives of African workers were simply too different 'to justify universalist claims to entitlements'.[38]

In the Sudanese public sector, as Ahmad Alawad Sikainga explains, employees were divided into two categories: 'classified' and 'unclassified' staff. 'Classified' referred to civil servants, while 'unclassified' referred to permanent employees on monthly salaries, such as the railway workers who led the WAA, and casual workers, such as labourers employed on a day-by-day basis.[39] Unclassified staff were paid according to the block grant system introduced in 1935. Under the terms of the system, heads of government departments were allocated a set budget and were then free to determine the scales of pay for unclassified staff.[40] This devolution of responsibility to heads of department resulted in the proliferation of job categories and wage scales.[41] The 1948 Committee of Enquiry reported that within the Sudan Railways alone there were 372 different job categories.[42] The complex job structure within many departments was a source of discontent for Sudanese workers because it meant that promotion was often an incremental and slow process.[43]

Northern Sudanese civil servants shared the unclassified employees' grievances regarding pay and working conditions. As Heather Sharkey has made plain, civil service employment was highly valued but Sudanese government employees resented the fact that they were routinely assigned menial tasks, were excluded from policymaking and had limited opportunity for promotion.[44] Mamoun Beheiry, an Oxford graduate who was appointed as the First Finance Officer in the Department of Finance in 1949, recalled that British officials regarded him as a 'junior' member of the department and he was therefore assigned 'practically every type of work'.[45] This corroborates the work of Sharkey, who has referred to the formality and politeness that masked what were often strained workplace relations between British and Sudanese officials.[46] For example, British officials addressed Sudanese

38 Lindsay, 'Domesticity and Difference', 806.

39 Sikainga, *City of Steel and Fire*, 59.

40 Sikainga, *City of Steel and Fire*, 59.

41 *Report of the Unclassified Staff Wages Commission* (Khartoum, 1951), 18.

42 *Report of the Independent Committee of Enquiry*. See also Ahmad Alawad Sikainga, *Slaves into Workers: Emancipation and Labor in Colonial Sudan* (Austin, 1996), 140–42.

43 *Report of the Unclassified Staff Wages Commission*, 25; Sikainga, *City of Steel and Fire*, 114.

44 On the recruitment, training and employment of Sudanese civil servants, see Sharkey, *Living with Colonialism*, especially chapters 3 and 4.

45 Mamoun Beheiry, *Glimpses from the Life of a Sudanese Public Servant* (Omdurman, 2003), 32.

46 Sharkey, *Living with Colonialism*, 99–101.

civil servants with the title *effendi*. An Ottoman-Arabic term, *effendi* is similar to 'Mr', but for British officials it became synonymous with ambition, pretension to European ideals and anti-colonialism.[47] Reflecting their junior status within the administrative hierarchy, adult Sudanese employees were referred to as 'boys', while British officials, who were often younger than their Sudanese subordinates, were referred to as 'men'.[48] As Carolyn Brown has documented, this was akin to the situation in Nigeria, where colonial officials infantilised African men. Brown argues that employment in the coal mines of Engu gave rise to the contradictory situation in which a miner could become a 'man' in the village and yet, owing to the discriminatory attitude of colonial officials, remain a 'boy' in the workplace.[49]

Not only were Sudanese civil servants belittled by British officials but expatriate employees were also granted a greater range of work-related benefits, including subsidised housing. Expatriate civil servants, railway administrators and commercial executives often lived in separate neighbourhoods close to their place of employment and away from the local population. In Atbara and Khartoum, for example, senior British officials lived in houses along the banks of the Nile, which offered protection against the heat and were close to the departmental offices of the Sudan government. By contrast, low-paid Sudanese employees lived in informal settlements around the edge of Atbara and in the Deims in Khartoum.[50] Expatriate officials also had exclusive access to sports and social clubs while, with the exception of the Omdurman Graduates' club, the Sudanese were denied permission to form their own official societies until the 1930s. One of these, the Graduates' General Congress, which was established in 1938, became a vehicle for expressing civil servants' grievances and mobilising government employees in support of the nationalist cause.[51]

Separate social clubs, combined with the highly stratified nature of government employment, meant that British and Sudanese officials had limited opportunities for social contact outside of the workplace.[52] Writing in 1946,

[47] Sharkey, *Living with Colonialism*, 99.

[48] Sharkey, *Living with Colonialism*, 99.

[49] Carolyn Brown, 'A "Man" in the Village is a "Boy" in the Workplace: Colonial Racism, Worker Militance and Igbo Notions of Masculinity in the Nigerian Coal Industry', in Lisa A. Lindsay and Stephen F. Miescher (eds), *Men and Masculinities in Modern Africa* (Portsmouth, NH, 2003), 156–74.

[50] Sikainga, *City of Steel and Fire*, 35. See also Sikainga, *Slaves into Workers*, chapter 6.

[51] On the formation of social clubs, see Martin W. Daly, *Imperial Sudan: The Anglo-Egyptian Condominium, 1934–1956* (Cambridge, 1986); Sikainga, *City of Steel and Fire*, 89–92. On the relationship between these clubs and anti-colonial resistance, see Sharkey, *Living with Colonialism*, 61–63, 76–80.

[52] Sharkey, *Living with Colonialism*, 100.

James W. Robertson, the Civil Secretary (1945–1953), complained that 'Many British seldom make any attempt to get into real contact with their Sudanese staff or to meet them socially and influence them in a friendly way'.[53] Informal contact between British and Sudanese officials increased during the post-war period but it was often strained and undermined by cultural misunderstandings. Jamal Muhammad Ahmad, a northern Sudanese contributor to Francis Deng and Martin Daly's *Bonds of Silk*, recalls joint Anglo-Sudanese social events as 'awkward affairs'. One British official reportedly instructed his Sudanese guests to wear shorts when coming for tea, to make them feel more comfortable, but Jamal and his colleagues resented this: 'we thought it was just a way to order us about … At one stage, one or two people used to go in pairs of trousers, just to establish their personalities!'.[54]

Aside from exclusive access to social clubs, expatriate officials were also granted higher cost of living allowances, special family allowances and other provisions such as subsidised housing and transport. During the Second World War, all government employees were allocated a bonus in 1942 and a cost of living allowance increase in 1943. However, since British officials were already granted higher awards, these pay increases only served to compound the inequalities between expatriate and Sudanese civil servants. During the first six months of 1943, the rate of inflation increased by 3 per cent for British officials compared with 16 per cent for Sudanese employees, and by the end of the year the cost of living index for Sudanese earning less than £E12 (12 Egyptian pounds) was 176 (1938=100) compared with 150 for British officials.[55] The gap between the incomes of Sudanese and expatriate officials widened in the post-war period as wartime price controls on basic commodities such as sorghum and cotton piece goods were lifted. In 1949 and 1950, the cost of living index for British officials stood at 223 and 231 compared with 287.9 and 292.5 for Sudanese workers.[56]

The Sudan government's failure to share the burden of austerity only served to highlight the hypocrisy of the wartime demand for equality of sacrifice. Consequently, aspirant northern Sudanese workers, sensitive to issues of racial discrimination and labour rights, demanded improved pay during the post-war period in order to obtain better housing, access to education for their children and consumer items.[57] According to Beheiry,

[53] The Sudan Archive, University of Durham (SAD), 521/5/30, J.W. Robertson Circular to All Governors, Civil Secretary's Office, Khartoum, 7 Aug. 1946.

[54] Martin Daly and Francis Deng, *Bonds of Silk: The Human Factor in the British Administration of the Sudan* (East Lancing, MI, 1990), 114, cited in Sharkey, *Living with Colonialism*, 101.

[55] On wartime inflationary pressures, see Daly, *Imperial Sudan*, 174.

[56] Sudan Government, *Report of the Terms of Service Commission* (London, 1951), 29.

[57] On these demands among Sudanese railway workers, see Sikainga, *City of Steel and Fire*, 108–9.

when he was appointed as the First Finance Officer the demand for equality of emoluments with British expatriate officials was a 'burning issue' among northern Sudanese civil servants, who argued that salaries should be determined not according to race but with regard to qualifications and experience.[58] This resentment was also evident among Sudanese railway artisans who, as skilled workers, regarded themselves as a labour elite. In its submission to the 1948 Committee of Enquiry, the WAA emphasised the high level of skill required to be an engineer or train driver.[59] This indicates that Sudanese workers' sense of entitlement was derived not only from the rhetoric of stabilisation but also from a desire to acquire the work and domestic benefits that reflected their perceived status within the job hierarchy.[60] This too had parallels elsewhere in colonial Africa. Jane Parpart has described how in the 1940s the creation of a 'respectable family based culture' in Northern Rhodesia became a key objective for the urban elite, who, like the Sudanese railway artisans, saw themselves as 'trendsetters'.[61] In short, as Luise White argues, Africans had their own clearly defined ideas about 'respectability, order, and rank in the home and work place'.[62]

Ideas relating to domestic respectability were closely tied to understandings of modernity among northern Sudanese civil servants and skilled workers. Sharkey, for example, has traced the development of national identity among young northern Sudanese government employees.[63] As Sharkey explains, the peripatetic nature of civil service employment, which often entailed the regular transfer of officials from one post to another, enabled educated northern Sudanese men to develop 'a sense of Sudan as a unitary whole', while access to Arabic and Western literature, such as specialist arts and science journals, provided officials with both the inspiration and the medium for political and cultural expression.[64] In the debates that followed, northern Sudanese officials sought to imagine a modern identity that combined imported ideas with values perceived to be specifically

[58] Beheiry, *Glimpses from the Life of a Sudanese Public Servant*, 31.

[59] *Report of the Independent Committee of Enquiry*.

[60] Sikainga, *City of Steel and Fire*, 103.

[61] Jane Parpart, '"Where Is Your Mother?": Gender, Urban Marriage and Colonial Discourse on the Zambian Copperbelt, 1924–1945', *International Journal of African Historical Studies*, 27.2 (1994), 267.

[62] Luise White, 'Separating the Men from the Boys: Constructions of Gender, Sexuality, and Terrorism in Central Kenya, 1939–1959', *International Journal of African Historical Studies*, 23.1 (1990), 4.

[63] Sharkey's arguments are thoughtfully discussed in Janice Boddy, *Civilising Women: British Crusades in Colonial Sudan* (Princeton, NJ, 2007), 282–84.

[64] Sharkey, *Living with Colonialism*, 10.

and authentically 'Sudanese'.[65] This attempt to 'indigenise modernity' found expression in debates over the relative merits of social reform and 'indigenous' values in relation to the role of women in areas such as marriage, family, education and employment.[66] One of the principal vehicles through which this debate over 'tradition' and 'modernity' was expressed was women's bodies, as Janice Boddy has documented.[67] In the Sudan, some practices, such as lip tattooing, which signified a woman's married status, and facial scarring, were denounced by male northern Sudanese graduates as 'un-Islamic'.[68] By contrast, Boddy argues that female circumcision was regarded as a cultural symbol that distinguished the northern Sudanese as a specific social group – this was despite the fact that the practice had previously been regarded as a symptom of 'backwardness'.[69]

Another means of expressing 'authentic' Sudanese culture was marriage and the gendered division of labour within the household. Among the riverain peoples of the northern Sudan, in accordance with local social values and Islamic practices, marriage was regarded as a key indicator of responsibility and respectability.[70] For men, marriage was understood as a symbol of maturity and senior masculinity. Marie Brown has recorded the centrality of the marriage ceremony to ideas of Sudanese masculinity: the groom was responsible for furnishing the home, in addition to contributing financially to the wedding preparations, which included paying for the bride's lip tattooing, food and dresses.[71] Beyond these immediate obligations relating to the wedding ceremony, men were expected to provide for the maintenance of their families, as well as sending remittances to relatives, contributing to

[65] Sharkey, *Living with Colonialism*, 10.

[66] Sharkey, *Living with Colonialism*, 10, 59, 129–30.

[67] Boddy, *Civilising Women*, 282–84.

[68] Boddy, *Civilising Women*, 283–84. See also Sharkey, *Living with Colonialism*, 10, 129–30.

[69] As Boddy points out, it is important to note that the debates surrounding female circumcision were contested. Brown, for example, has documented how northern Sudanese women debated the necessity of reforming practices that disproportionately affected female members of society. See respectively Boddy, *Civilising Women* and Carolyn Brown, *Khartoum at Night: Fashion and Body Politics in Imperial Sudan* (Stanford, CA, 2017), chapter 5, especially 146–52.

[70] On the importance of marriage to Northern Sudanese communities, see Ahmed al-Shahi, *Themes From Northern Sudan* (London, 1986), 69; Hayder Ibrahim, *The Shaiqiya: The Cultural and Social Change of a Northern Sudanese Riverain People* (Wiesbaden, 1979), 111–22; Sondra Hale, *Gender Politics in Sudan: Islamism, Socialism, and the State* (Boulder, CO, 1996), 78; Sudan M. Kenyon, *Five Women of Sennar: Culture and Change in Central Sudan* (Oxford, 1991), 225.

[71] Marie Grace Brown, 'Fashioning their Place: Dress and Global Imagination in Imperial Sudan', *Gender and History*, 26.3 (2014), 507–8.

social events and community projects and providing for the education and healthcare of their children.[72]

Marriage was also central to granting women the status of 'respectable' members of the community. As Boddy explains, it was expected that northern Sudanese women, particularly those from high-status families, would not contribute to household production but instead lead 'modest' and 'secluded' domestic lives within the confines of the *hosh* (courtyard).[73] As Brown puts it, for Sudanese women, marriage symbolised the transition 'from the house and protection of her father to that of her husband'.[74] One expression of this 'non-productive' role was the custom of abandoning the *râḥat* (skirt) once a woman was married in favour of the *tôb* (a decorative and expensive full-length wrap), which was a symbol of respectability as it was unsuitable for manual work.[75] However, as Brown argues, although a symbol of modesty and respectability, the wearing of a *tôb* enabled Sudanese women to leave the confines of the house and participate in public life, whether this was through performing routine everyday tasks or, as formal employment opportunities increased, as government employees. In the case of female public servants, the *tôb* came to represent not only ideas of respectability but also signified women's entry into the world of formal employment and the development of a new civic identity.[76]

This is a critical point. Not every Sudanese household reflected established social norms regarding gender and the division of labour. The expansion of female education during the 1920s and 1930s provided a greater range of professional and vocational opportunities for women, particularly in education and healthcare, as Sharkey has documented.[77] By the 1940s, women with a formal education, such as school teachers, were also playing an increasingly active role in the formation of social groups, charities and adult education programmes.[78] It was during this period that a number of women's organisations emerged. The most significant was the Women's Union (WU), which was formed in 1952 and had close ties with the Sudan Workers' Trade Union Federation (SWTUF) and the Sudanese Communist Party.[79] Although these developments were significant and

[72] Sikainga, *City of Steel and Fire*, 112–14.

[73] Boddy, *Civilising Women*, 162. On the relationship between gender and household roles more broadly, see al-Shahi, *Themes from Northern Sudan*, 133–36.

[74] Brown, 'Fashioning their Place', 507.

[75] Boddy, *Civilising Women*, 162; Kenyon, *Five Women of Sennar*, 47. The *tôb* is a key component in Brown's work. See *Khartoum at Night*, chapters 2 and 3.

[76] Brown, 'Fashioning their Place', 511.

[77] Heather Sharkey, 'Chronicles of Progress: Northern Sudanese Women in the Era of British Imperialism', *Journal of Imperial and Commonwealth History*, 31.1 (2003), 55–59.

[78] Sharkey, 'Chronicles of Progress', 72.

[79] On the WU, see Hale, *Gender Politics*, 151–83; Tim Niblock, *Class and Power: The*

had an impact on gender relations within the household, opportunities for women in the public sphere remained limited.[80] Broadly speaking, formal educational and employment opportunities were available only to a specific type of woman: 'urban, Muslim, Arabic-speaking, [and] from a relatively affluent background'.[81] Although it later expanded into a mass organisation, upon its formation WU members were drawn from wealthy families who campaigned for a range of social and political issues, such as independence from Britain, equal pay for women, greater employment opportunities for women and maternity leave rights.[82]

Among lower- and middle-income households, which would have included the railway artisans of the WAA, it was more common for women to engage in wage-earning activities such as petty trading, craftwork and domestic service.[83] Data relating to women's involvement in these sectors of the labour market is imprecise and fragmentary. The 1956 census provides some information, if only to suggest a general trend. In the capital, Khartoum, Omdurman and Khartoum North, of the 68,132 recorded adult women only 6,036 were listed as 'gainfully employed', in roles such as domestic servants (709) and shop assistants (1,326). By contrast, the primary occupation for 57,263 women was listed as 'household duties'.[84] Of course, this did not preclude the possibility that the women in this category were participating in the labour market or other forms of economic activity. Many of the income-generating activities that were available to women, such as petty trading and craftwork, took place within the household and were therefore integrated with women's other domestic activities. Not only did this mean that such economic activities were obscured from official observation but the close association between these activities and women's overall domestic responsibilities was indicative of a view that wives, even those who contributed to household income, were dependants of their husbands.[85]

Dynamics of Sudanese Politics, 1898–1985 (Basingstoke, 1987), 133–37.

[80] For a summary of the gender-related changes that took place in this period, see Sharkey, 'Chronicles of Progress', 73–74.

[81] Sharkey, 'Chronicles of Progress', 73.

[82] Sharkey, 'Chronicles of Progress', 72. See also Hale, *Gender Politics*, 167; Niblock, *Class and Power*, 136–37. For a broader overview of women's activism during this period, which highlights the relative agency of Sudanese women and the ways in socio-economic and cultural changes facilitated their participation in anti-colonial struggles, see Brown, *Khartoum at Night*, 160–63.

[83] Hale, *Gender Politics*, 162.

[84] Ministry for Social Affairs, *First Population Census of Sudan, 1955/56, Seventh Interim Report* (Khartoum, 1957), 5.

[85] On the economic dominance of Northern Sudanese men within households, see Sikainga, *City of Steel and Fire*, 109; al-Shahi, *Themes from Northern Sudan*, 135–36.

The Sudan government pointed to the gendered division of labour in order to justify lower wages, as it had in response to the WAA's demand for 'family' wages.[86] When attempting to explain why women were paid four-fifths of what men earned for the same category of job, the Wakefield Commission, which was established in 1950 to investigate the wages of non-classified staff, stated: 'We do not think that the time has yet come in this country to lay down definite rules of pay. The tradition of female employment has yet to be built up and the wage-rates have very little effect upon the relationship between supply and demand'.[87] The implicit assumption among British officials was that female employment was either vocational or supplementary and therefore not central to a household's income. This may well have been the case in many households, but during the 1947–1948 railway strikes the WAA's claims for higher wages on the basis of their status as 'breadwinners' in many households had been rejected in favour of technocratic wage increases based on cost-of-living indices and dietary requirements.[88] However, the Wakefield Commission was now citing the absence of 'the tradition of female employment' – an implied reference to men's status as the primary 'breadwinner' – in order to exclude the possibility of equal pay. As Lindsay has argued in relation to Nigeria, these contradictory arguments are indicative of how British officials misrepresented local domestic arrangements in order to justify racial and gender discrimination in relation to wages and other work-related pay issues.[89]

The Wakefield Commission's views on female employment reflected the widely held assumption among British officials that Sudanese men were 'masters of domestic life' and women 'subservient victims'.[90] By contrast, historians and ethnographers have argued that although there was a gendered hierarchy within northern Sudanese households, it was often more nuanced and ambiguous than colonial officials implied.[91] The demand for higher wages is a good example of this complexity, demonstrating how Sudanese men and women both reciprocally embraced local notions of domestic respectability.[92] During the 1947–1948 railway strike, workers' wives

[86] This was by no means specific to the Sudan. For a discussion of how gender and race impacted upon discussions relating to the desirability of paying so-called 'family wages' within the Colonial Office, see Cooper, *Decolonization and African Society*, 323–36.

[87] *Report of the Unclassified Staff Wages Commission*, 48.

[88] Sikainga, *City of Steel and Fire*, 109–14.

[89] Lindsay, 'Domesticity and Difference', specifically 787–88.

[90] Boddy, *Civilising Women*, 287.

[91] See Boddy, *Civilising Women*; Kenyon, *Five Women of Sennar*; Sharkey, 'Chronicles of Progress'; Brown, *Khartoum at Night*.

[92] Lindsay has identified a similar dynamic in the Nigerian case during the 1945 strike (see 'Domesticity and Difference').

engaged in economic activities – the income from which enabled striking workers to survive without pay.[93] Here was a 'crucial irony', as Lindsay has also observed of the 1945 Nigerian general strike. One of the WAA's key objectives was higher wages, but without the support of the workers' wives the campaign of industrial action could not have been sustained.[94] However, there was no sense of contradiction for Sudanese workers and their wives. As Sikainga explains, Sudanese workers struck for higher wages in order to provide for the maintenance of their families, and wives engaged in economic activities in order to facilitate the strike action.[95] Moreover, since the railway workers' wives were considered dependants of their husbands, the workers did not regard their wives' economic activities as incompatible with the demand for higher wages.[96] In short, as Carolyn Brown has argued in her study of Nigerian coal miners, the post-war call for family wages was not simply a response to an 'imported piece of top-down social engineering': a man's desire for healthcare, education and consumer items for his family was both an indicator of 'modernity' and a means of upholding local idealised notions of masculine responsibility and domestic respectability.[97]

Order and productivity on the docks

The WAA's strike action highlighted the vulnerability of the colonial economy to industrial unrest. During the course of the 1947–1948 strikes, for example, it was reported that the movement of goods had 'virtually ceased'.[98] As Sudan's principal import–export hub and the terminus for the Nile–Red Sea railway line, Port Sudan was vulnerable to strike action too.[99] The port infrastructure was publicly owned and managed by the Sudan Railways, but private contractors were responsible for port operations, including shore

[93] On this point, see Sikainga, *'City of Steel and Fire'*, 108–9.

[94] As Lindsay argues in relation to Nigeria, trade unionists' demands for family wages, although at odds with the realities of familial arrangements, served to consolidate men's status as the primary breadwinner ('Domesticity and Difference', 783). On the relative subordination of women within the trade union movement in Sudan, see Hale, *Gender Politics*, 161–62.

[95] Sikainga, *'City of Steel and Fire'*, 109.

[96] This point is based on interviews conducted by the author with Sudanese railway workers involved in the strike, including Ahmed al-Raies, Khartoum, 22 Oct. 2010; Abd al-Munim Abbas, Khartoum, 27 Oct. 2010; Minalla Abd al-Wahab, Khartoum, Oct. 2010.

[97] Brown, *We Were All Slaves*, 184, 236.

[98] *Sudan Monthly Record*, No. 210 (Feb.–Apr. 1948).

[99] On the development of Port Sudan, see Kenneth J. Perkins, *Port Sudan: The Evolution of a Colonial City* (Boulder, CO, 1993); Daly, *Empire on the Nile*, 203.

handling, stevedoring and lighterage.[100] In comparison with the railway industry, as Cooper has noted in relation to Mombasa, the skill differentials amongst dockworkers were much less significant.[101] In the case of Port Sudan, there was no class of worker equivalent to that of the skilled railway artisans who had emerged to lead the WAA during the 1947–1948 strike campaign. Of the port's 800-strong workforce, the majority of dockworkers were semi-skilled labourers responsible for moving the cargo on and off the ships.[102] The physicality of the work was compounded by long working hours, with the port operating three shifts over the course of a 24-hour period.[103] In a context where labour demands ebbed and flowed according to the volume of shipping, dockworkers were organised into gangs of twelve labourers, often linked by ties of ethnicity and kinship. The gangs were answerable to a *reis* (headman), who recruited the dockworkers on behalf of the port companies.[104] Such arrangements were common to many ports throughout East Africa, where complex social ties amongst dockworkers provided security in an otherwise precarious industry.[105]

Despite the arduous working conditions, Port Sudan was less militant than other East African ports, such as Mombasa or Dar es Salaam.[106] There were short strikes in 1937, 1939 and 1942 over pay.[107] The most serious incident occurred in March 1947, when 500 dockworkers issued a set of demands for improved working conditions. The strike lasted nine days, causing considerable disruption to shipping, and the dockworkers only returned to work following mediation by local merchants.[108] In the wake of the strike, the colonial authorities, blind to the social ties that bound the labour gangs, became increasingly critical of the casual labour regime in the port. One official later wrote:

100 B.A. Lewis, 'Deim El Arab and the Beja Stevedores of Port Sudan', *Sudan Notes and Records*, 43 (1962), 19.

101 Cooper, *On the African Waterfront*, 165.

102 On the occupational structure of the workforce, see Lewis, 'Deim El Arab', 21–25.

103 In his report, Lewis referred to himself as the 'government sociologist'. Lewis, 'Deim el Arab', 16, 21.

104 On the composition of the workforce in Port Sudan, see Perkins, *Port Sudan*, 123–38; Lewis, 'Deim el Arab', 23–25.

105 Cooper, *On the African Waterfront.*

106 On the prevalence of strike action in neighbouring East African ports, see Cooper, *On the African Waterfront*; John Iliffe, 'A History of the Dockworkers of Dar es Salaam', *Tanzania Notes and Records*, 71 (1970), 119–47.

107 *Sudan Monthly Record*, No. 120 (Apr.–May 1939); *Sudan Monthly Record*, No. 150 (Oct.–Nov. 1941).

108 On the 1947 strike, see TNA, FO, 371/63047, Sudan Political Intelligence Summary, Khartoum, Feb.–Mar. 1947; *Sudan Monthly Record*, No. 202 (Feb.–Mar. 1947); Perkins, *Port Sudan*, 217.

> The casual labourers referred to as 'mazuwaria' [mazwri] are extremely improvident and on days they earn good money go to bars or gamble in coffee shops or seek pleasure afforded by the unattached women in the deim. Their money soon goes on these pursuits. It is this semi-casual labour force which has earned the Beja dock labour force its reputation for irresponsible behaviour and wild living ... With their background of a free nomad's life in the hills they are bound to remain a problem for many years because they have never learned to work regularly.[109]

Such views were common throughout colonial Africa; it was presumed that Africans were incapable of adapting to the regular work rhythms of industrial capital and that where casual labour prevailed, social and political disorder usually followed.[110]

In response to the industrial strikes of the late 1930s and 1940s, colonial governments across British Africa commissioned social surveys, such as the one concerning Port Sudan's dockworkers, in order to better understand living conditions amongst the increasingly restive and dissatisfied urban populations.[111] Such surveys betrayed a wider confidence in technical and scientific expertise – many colonial administrators shared a belief that society was a 'complex machine' that had to be rendered legible in order to facilitate intervention.[112] Of course, in making society legible, surveys and commissions of inquiry produced new social kinds and categories.[113] As Ann Laura Stoler puts it, 'Ways of living were congealed into "problems", subject persons were condensed into ontological categories, innocuous practices were made into subjects of analysis and rendered political things'.[114] In the case of investigations into the working and living conditions experienced by African workers, social surveys collected data pertaining to a range of issues, such as the length of the working day, income levels, the size and structure of the workforce and its dietary

109 Lewis, 'Deim el Arab', 34.

110 This, of course, is one of the principal arguments that flows throughout Cooper's work. See, in particular, *From Slaves to Squatters: Plantation Labor and Agriculture in Zanzibar and Coastal Kenya, 1890–1925* (New Haven, CT, 1980) and *On the African Waterfront.*

111 See, for example, Kofi Abrefa Busia, *Report on a Social Survey of Sekondi-Takoradi* (London, 1950) and C.H. Northcott (ed.), *African Labour Efficiency Survey* (London, 1949).

112 Christophe Bonneuil, 'Development as Experiment: Science and State Building in Late Colonial and Postcolonial Africa, 1930–1970', *Osiris*, 15 (2000), 267.

113 The 'invention' or discovery of juvenile delinquency is a classic example. See Laurent Fouchard, 'Lagos and the Invention of Juvenile Delinquency in Nigeria, 1920–60', *Journal of African History*, 47.1 (2006), 115–37.

114 Ann Laura Stoler, *Along the Archival Grain: Epistemic Anxieties and Colonial Common Sense* (Princeton, NJ, 2009), 44.

requirements and housing needs.[115] The interpretation of such data was undermined, however, by the racial prejudices of colonial officials. Rather than recognising poverty as a structural problem stemming from years of neglect on the part of the colonial administration, statistics relating to disease, malnutrition and destitution were explained in highly racialised terms concerning the supposedly innate nature of African labour.[116] It was for this reason that Lewis referred to Port Sudan's dockworkers as 'improvident' and 'irresponsible'.

Colonial officials' faith in technical expertise was apparent elsewhere in the Sudan government's labour policy. In 1949, a Labour Board, which had been established after the war, evolved into a fully fledged Labour Department. Staffed by individuals with experience in industrial relations, such as T.M. Cowan, an official seconded from the British Ministry of Labour, members of the Labour Department were charged with administering labour legislation, mediating disputes, and conducting workplace inspections.[117] This was typical colonial thinking when it came to the post-1945 development agenda. As Joseph Hodge argues, development, whether understood in terms of agricultural production, welfare provision or the growth of civil society organisations, was conceived of as a technical problem requiring technocratic solutions. Of course, in a colonial context, which necessarily entailed the restriction of fundamental rights and the use of coercive state power, such development initiatives inevitably provoked resistance.[118]

The introduction of trade union legislation in the Sudan is a case in point. In the late 1940s, the Sudan government introduced a raft of industrial relations legislation under whose terms Sudanese trade unions were granted basic immunities and protections, including the right to strike and picket.[119] Commenting on the legislation, the Civil Secretary, J.W. Robertson, stated that 'Once these are all law and being properly run, we shall have a modern, democratic and reasonably liberal set

[115] Cooper, *Decolonization and African Society*, 370–71.

[116] For a discussion of social surveys, their findings and colonial analyses of the resulting data, see Cooper, *Decolonization and African Society*, 370–71.

[117] On the evolution and function of the Labour Department, see Peter Cross, 'British Attitudes to Sudanese Labour: The Foreign Office Records as Sources for Social History', *British Journal of Middle Eastern Studies*, 24.2 (1997), 248–52.

[118] Joseph Hodge, *Triumph of the Expert: Agrarian Doctrines of Development and the Legacies of British Colonialism* (Athens, OH, 2007), 263; Joseph Hodge, 'Colonial Experts, Developmental and Environmental Doctrines, and the Legacies of Late British Colonialism', in Christina F. Ax, Niels Brimnes, Niklas Jensen and Karen Oslund (eds), *Cultivating the Colonies: Colonial States and their Environmental Legacies* (Athens, OH, 2011), 209–31.

[119] On this legislation, see Cross, 'British Attitudes', 249.

of labour laws'.[120] However, although British officials recognised the necessity of labour laws for the purpose of creating a modern trade union movement, the legislation remained colonial in its design. In typically paternalistic style, officials expressed the fear that the 'majority of the workers are illiterate and are comparatively easy prey for the potential and real demagogue'.[121] As such, the legislation included a number of restrictions, including compulsory registration, thus raising the possibility that registration and, by extension, legal immunities might be withheld.[122] In other words, as Cooper writes, 'the fantasy of the modern and fear of the backward shaped each other'. On the one hand, officials believed that trade unions could be a channel for responsible politics, but, on the other, there was a concern that the nascent labour movements risked being led astray by irresponsible anti-colonial agitators.[123]

In response to the promulgation of the legislation, Sudanese trade unions organised a general strike on 15 March 1949 and issued a statement condemning the new labour laws, again drawing on the rhetoric of rights and responsibilities:

> this ordinance does not correspond with the good foundation of Unionism and will contradict with the wishes of the workers in establishing a free union which will work for the achievement of their demands and which will be far away from Government jurisdiction and administrative authority and police interference. We want unions which will have its rights in strikes and amalgamation and affiliation and which will have sufficient legal guarantees for the safeguarding of its members, its funds and properties.[124]

Although the protest drew some minor concessions, the authorities continued to monitor the activities of Sudanese trade unions. In 1950, C.M. Coutts, head of Special Branch, attributed ongoing labour unrest to communist agitation. As a consequence, Special Branch recruited informants to infiltrate the labour movement, the police compiled detailed reports of trade union activists and anti-communist legislation was passed.[125] Such measures

[120] SAD, 527/10/16, J.W. Robertson.

[121] TNA, Ministry of Labour (LAB) Papers, 13/480, D.H.J. Newman, 'Trade Unionism in the Sudan', 26 Apr. 1951, enclosed in C.G. Davies to D.J. Tomlinson, Sudan Agent in London to Overseas Department Ministry of Labour and National Service, 13 July 1951.

[122] Cross, 'British Attitudes', 249.

[123] Cooper, *Decolonization and African Society*, 329.

[124] TNA, FO, 371/73475, Petition from Representatives of Sudanese Workers to Governor-General, Khartoum, 3 Feb. 1949.

[125] TNA, FO, 371/80352, C.M. Coutts, Note on Communist Activity in the Sudan, 22 Oct. 1950; Cross, 'Attitudes to Sudanese Labour', 251; Daly, *Imperial Sudan*, 327–29.

were a typical response on the part of the colonial authorities during the era of decolonisation, when any trade union activist advocating enhanced labour rights, higher wages or strike action was automatically suspected of communist sympathies.[126] As Martin Thomas argues, such interpretations owed much to the process of 'othering' that was so central to the colonial authorities' construction of anti-colonial activists. As Thomas puts it, colonial security services 'recognised local variations, cultural differences, and complex social strata in the colonies under their charge, but in times of acute political crisis, security service personnel resorted to a simpler typology'.[127]

In the case of the Sudan, prominent trade union figures, such as Mohammed Sallam and al-Shafi Ahmad al-Shaykh, were labelled 'tub thumping' communists by the security forces.[128] Sallam and al-Shaykh did undoubtedly have links to Sudanese communists and networks of Egyptian leftists, whom the British suspected of providing material support to the Sudanese trade union movement.[129] However, as was the case in other colonial contexts, this alleged 'radicalism' stemmed not from a commitment to communist revolution but a desire to redress the social and economic inequities of colonial rule – an objective whose achievement appeared unlikely as long as the colonial authorities continued to work with Sudanese political elites drawn from conservative religious sects.[130] This is a critical point. Unlike Sudanese political elites, whose authority was largely derived from their leadership of religious sects tied to family lineages, Sudan's trade union leaders had emerged from the rank and file. Al-Shafi, for example, was a prominent student activist and from there he rose through the ranks of the railway union.[131] Labour leaders deployed these grass-roots connections to

[126] Cooper, *Decolonization and African Society*, 328–29.

[127] Martin Thomas, *Empires of Intelligence: Security Services and Colonial Disorder after 1914* (Berkeley, CA, 2008), 76.

[128] TNA, FO, 371/80352, J.W. Robertson to M.N.F. Stewart, Note on Communism, 3 Dec. 1950.

[129] These links are discussed in Mohammad Nuri El-Amin, 'The Sudanese Communist Movement: The First Five Years – II', *Middle Eastern Studies*, 32.4 (1996), 251–63, especially 255–56. See also Cross, 'British Attitudes', 242.

[130] Sayyid 'Abd al-Rahman, grandson of the Mahdi, led the Ansar sect and later the Umma Party. His great rival was Sayyid 'Ali al-Mirghani, leader of the Khatmiyyah order and later the National Unionist Party (NUP). The relationship between the Sudan's socio-economic order and the religious orders and political parties is best explained in Tim Niblock, *Class and Power in Sudan: The Dynamics of Sudanese Politics, 1898–1985* (Basingstoke, 1987). See especially chapters 3 and 4.

[131] The WFTU produced a biography of al-Shafi: *Shafie Ahmed El Sheikh: Son of the Sudanese People and International Trade Union Leader* (Prague, 1972).

good effect, often playing a highly visible role in protests.[132] Indeed, recent literature on African nationalism has emphasised its performative quality, highlighting the ways in which nationalist sentiment was generated through mediums such as ritual, dress and other forms of cultural expression.[133] The Sudanese labour movement was no different. Protest marches, labour nights at the Khartoum workers' club and songs all served as mobilising mechanisms. In this way, anti-colonial nationalism became part of people's everyday life, a lived and performed experience rather than an abstract ideological construct.[134]

Of course, such cultural repertoires were largely unintelligible to the colonial authorities. In the port industry, the system of casual labour – in which complex social ties bound the labour gangs and enabled dockworkers to combine paid employment with pastoralism – was reduced to a symptom of Africans' inability or refusal to work regularly.[135] To remedy this perceived problem, a system of decasualisation was proposed, akin to similar systems being implemented in other East African ports at this time.[136] Under the proposed decasualisation system, dockworkers would be recruited from a pool of registered stevedores under the management of a Dock Labour Committee.[137] Despite some initial opposition from the stevedoring companies, the Committee assumed responsibility for the supply of labour and by 1950 some 1,300 dockworkers had been interviewed. Of these, 750 were identified as 'regular' labourers and were issued with identification cards and formed into new gangs of twelve.[138] To administer the system, a Call Office was established in Deim al-Arab, the residential quarter where the majority of dockworkers lived. All the stevedoring companies were required to recruit dockworkers through the Call Office.[139]

The authorities framed the decasualisation scheme in terms of providing stable and regular work for Port Sudan's dockworkers. As J.W. Robertson,

[132] See, for example, Sikainga, *City of Steel and Fire*, 108–10.

[133] The classics remain Susan Geiger, *TANU Women: Gender and Culture in the Making of Tanganyikan Nationalism, 1955–1965* (Portsmouth, NH, 1997); Elizabeth Schmidt, *Mobilizing the Masses: Gender, Ethnicity and Class in the Nationalist Movement in Guinea, 1939–1958* (Portsmouth, NH, 2005). In the Sudanese context, the most standout recent example is Brown's *Khartoum at Night*.

[134] For an exemplary study on this precise point, one that highlights how nationalist ideology permeated everyday life and thereby produced a range of different responses amongst 'ordinary' people, see Jeffrey S. Ahlman, *Living with Nkrumahism: Nation, State, and Pan-Africanism in Ghana* (Athens, OH, 2017).

[135] Cooper, *On the African Waterfront*, chapter 2.

[136] Cooper, *On the African Waterfront*, chapter 4.

[137] Lewis, 'Deim el Arab', 19.

[138] *Sudan Monthly Record*, No. 243 (Feb.–Mar. 1951).

[139] Lewis, 'Deim el Arab', 19.

the Civil Secretary, explained: 'One of the main objectives of the scheme is to ensure a fair number of days' work in a month to enable the permanent labourer in the port to earn a fair minimum wage'.[140] However, as Cooper has argued in relation to decasualisation in Mombasa, the provision of regular work was also about reshaping African workers in order to promote social stability.[141] To do this, colonial officials reasoned, it was necessary to separate African workers from all that was presumed to be 'African'.[142] In the case of Port Sudan, it was proposed that 250 houses be constructed for dockworkers and their families on the East Bank, away from Deim al-Arab, which was described as an insanitary slum inhabited by a 'verminous' population.[143] Such language highlighted the colonial authorities' perception of the casual labourer, who was regarded not only as a threat to social order but also as a vector of disease who threatened to infect responsible workers with values that were antithetical to a disciplined work culture.[144]

It was not just casual labourers who were regarded as vectors of social disorder. One issue that received particular attention in Lewis's survey in connection with living conditions in Deim al Arab was prostitution. Reflecting assumptions that were apparent in other colonial urban settings, Lewis portrayed the incidence of prostitution in Port Sudan as a moral issue and a 'social problem', describing those involved in the trade as having departed from the 'path of virtue'.[145] Read against the grain, however, Lewis's survey reveals that the prostitution networks that had developed in Port Sudan were more complex than the discourse of vice allowed for. Some Beja women were involved in so-called 'companionate' marriages, known locally as *humajat*, while other women were procured by pimps for clients.[146] In other instances, female prostitutes operated independently but others appear to have lived and worked collectively.[147] What this suggests, albeit

140 SAD, 525/15/8, J.W. Robertson Circular to All Governors, Civil Secretary's Office, Khartoum, 4 Dec. 1952.

141 Cooper, *On the African Waterfront*, chapter 4.

142 Cooper, *Decolonization and African Society*; see, in particular, Part III, chapters 7–9.

143 Lewis, 'Deim al-Arab', 16.

144 For a discussion of colonial views regarding so-called casual labour, which draws explicitly on the work of Gareth Stedman-Jones, see Cooper, *On the African Waterfront*, chapter 2 and *From Slaves to Squatters*.

145 Lewis, 'Deim al-Arab', 47.

146 According to Lewis, there were 200 cases of companionate marriages in Deim Al Arab and twenty known brothels operated by 'procurers' (*kawat*) and procuresses (*kawadit*). Lewis, 'Deim al-Arab', 47.

147 An estimated fifty prostitutes operated from their own homes, while a further ninety worked in smaller groups. Lewis, 'Deim al-Arab', 47.

in very tentative terms given the limited source base, is that while colonial authorities associated the informal sector with immorality and criminality, for those Beja men and women involved in prostitution, the social, personal and economic relationships that developed in connection with the sex trade were more ambiguous.[148] Relationships – as was the case in other urban centres, mining towns and port cities throughout the continent – appear to have existed along a spectrum that ranged from the temporary and the transactional to more permanent and stable unions.[149]

What is not clear from the available evidence is the degree of coercion that was involved in Port Sudan's sex trade.[150] Lewis suggested that some husbands left their wives in Deim al Arab to 'augment the family budget' and other women were forced into prostitution as a result of food shortages.[151] However, although poverty was clearly an important push factor, women also became prostitutes because the trade offered opportunities for socio-economic advancement and autonomy that were unavailable in the rural countryside. Women could escape unhappy marriages, they could combine sex work with other income generating activities in the informal sector and they could earn sufficient money to purchase property – which provided the owner with greater economic security.[152] This too has similarities with other cases in colonial Africa. Prostitution was often regarded by colonial states and employers as necessary for the social reproduction of workforces composed of male migrant labourers. For those women engaged in the sex trade, however, Lewis's survey findings imply that prostitution in Port Sudan was about more than facilitating the reproduction of the city's labour force. Women moved to Port Sudan to escape the poverty and restrictions of rural life in the hope of improving their material status – motivating factors that historians have documented in other colonial urban contexts during this period.[153]

[148] Evidently, more research needs to be conducted in order to establish how communities in Port Sudan handled the issue of prostitution in cultural terms. Emmanuel Akyeampong's work is a good example of what such an approach might look like: 'Sexuality and Prostitution among the Akan of the Gold Coast, *c.*1650–1950', *Past and Present*, 156.1 (1997), 144–73.

[149] Luise White's work remains the exemplar here: *The Comforts of Home*.

[150] Carina Ray has highlighted the difficulty of establishing what role coercion played in prostitution networks in West Africa. See her 'Sex Trafficking, Prostitution, and the Law in Colonial British West Africa, 1911–1943', in Benjamin N. Lawrance and Richard L. Roberts (eds), *Trafficking in Slavery's Wake: Law and the Experience of Women and Children* (Athens, OH, 2012), 101–20.

[151] Lewis, 'Deim Al Arab', 47.

[152] Lewis, 'Deim Al Arab', 47.

[153] For studies that draw comparable conclusions in the context of West Africa, see Benedict B.B. Naanen, '"Itinerant Gold Mines": Prostitution in the Cross River Basin of Nigeria, 1930–1950', *African Studies Review*, 34.2 (1991), 57–79; Saheed Aderinto, 'Journey

Regardless of the lived experience of life in Port Sudan for ordinary Sudanese men and women, the identification of prostitution as a social problem that contributed to low productivity and irregular working habits among the city's dockworkers was indicative of how certain socio-economic activities associated with the informal sector became subject to increased surveillance and intervention as a result of the stabilisation agenda.[154] Indeed, the port industry was not the only sector to increase welfare provision during this period as part of efforts to reshape workers' lives and social relations beyond the workplace. The Sudan Railways established a welfare fund to provide services such as improved access to healthcare, education and housing. These initiatives were accompanied by a rhetoric that emphasised the relationship between health and productivity. One Sudan Railways' newsletter stated, for example, that 'Health is the Foundation of Wealth'.[155] In the cotton industry, the Marangan Ginneries, which employed 2,000 seasonal workers, cited poor timekeeping, high sickness rates and low productivity as common problems, and many labourers were reported to be 'physically incapable of a day's work'. To remedy this situation, every worker who arrived before the start of his shift was provided with a free cup of tea and a free meal. When justifying the scheme, the authorities stated that while 'no employer can be expected, nor can he afford, to pay wages which would allow every man to feed an unspecified number of relatives and dependents ... [he] has a direct interest in ensuring that his workers get enough to eat' – again evidence of how the colonial authorities drew on racial prejudices concerning local social structures and relations to justify a parsimonious approach to welfare.[156] More broadly, such provisions were typical of the post-war development strategy, as colonial governments and employers struggled to reconcile the competing aims of raising productivity and improving colonial living standards.[157]

In the case of the port industry, although the registration scheme was framed in modernising terms, with one official referring to 'progressive' reforms, discipline was central to the process of decasualisation. The registration of workers through the provision of identification cards transformed the anonymous mass of casual dockworkers into identifiable individuals, enabling the authorities to separate the 'regular' from the 'irregular' worker.[158] The

---

to Work: Transnational Prostitution in Colonial British West Africa', *Journal of the History of Sexuality*, 24.1 (2015), 99–124.

[154] On this point, see Cooper, 'Struggle for the City', 33.

[155] SAD, SudA PK1563, *Sudan Railways Bulletin*, No. 81 (Sept. 1945).

[156] *Sudan Monthly Record*, No. 243 (Feb.–Mar. 1951).

[157] Hodge, 'Colonial Experts, Developmental and Environmental Doctrines', 211.

[158] For a discussion of similar initiatives designed to separate the 'regular' worker from the 'irregular', see Cooper, *On the African Waterfront*, chapters 2 and 3.

implication is, of course, that dockworkers could see their identification cards withdrawn and, by extension, their right to work. The port authorities also established disciplinary committees which had the power to penalise dockworkers for a range of workplace infractions, such as poor timekeeping and disobedience. The penalties for such infractions ranged from fines to the ultimate sanction of deregistration.[159] Again, as Cooper argues, such initiatives were about transforming the nature of authority in the port. Where previously order and productivity would have been guaranteed by the *reis*, the shift to a formal system of workplace discipline was part of the colonial authorities' attempts to regulate the labour regime in the port, to determine when and how long dockworkers worked.[160] This emphasis on time discipline and its relationship to productivity can be seen in reports from 1950s, which began to record the average tonnage handled per hour by individual labour gangs.[161]

The first opportunity to evaluate the effectiveness of the scheme came in late August 1952. The number of ships calling at Port Sudan declined in the months of August, September and October, which resulted in insufficient work being available for the registered labour force. The Call Office was therefore able to allot work in rotation and to give priority to registered gangs. During this three-month period, registered gangs worked 23 days per month on average and unregistered gangs worked just 9 – a respective reduction of 5 and 8.5 days for each group.[162] Overall, a daily average of 832 stevedores were employed throughout 1952–1953, of whom 780 were registered workers. The latter averaged 24.6 days per month compared with 10 for unregistered workers – where during the previous six months the corresponding figures were 24 and 20, respectively.[163]

Officials pointed to the rotation of gangs during slack periods as evidence of the scheme's success. It was also argued that the Beja Dock Labourers' Union (BDLU), formed in 1952, was 'moribund' as a result of the 'progressive reforms' initiated by the Port Sudan Dock Labour Committee.[164] However, historians have documented that in many ports where the authorities sought to impose decasualisation schemes, dockworkers rarely welcomed the introduction of standardised working practices for fear it would lead to a loss of autonomy.[165] Rather, as Cooper argues regarding Mombasa,

159 Lewis, 'Deim el Arab', 32–33.

160 Cooper, *On the African Waterfront*, 144.

161 See Sudan Railways, *Sudan Railways Annual Report, 1954–55* (Atbara, 1956), 24.

162 SAD, 525/15/8, J.W. Robertson Circular to All Governors, Civil Secretary's Office, Khartoum, 4 Dec. 1952.

163 TNA, FO, 371/102930, Labour Department Report, 1952–53.

164 Lewis, 'Deim el Arab', 33.

165 See the relevant chapters in Sam Davies, Colin J. Davis, David de Vries et al. (eds), *Dock Workers: International Explorations in Comparative Labour History, 1790–1970* (Aldershot, 2000).

the principal objectives for many dockworkers were higher pay, the end of arbitrary discipline and flexible working routines, which would enable labourers to find alternative employment during slack periods.[166] This was reflected in the demands the BDLU submitted to the Commissioner of Labour, which included higher wages, a higher rate of pay for the unpopular night shift, improved cross-harbour transport and more opportunities for warehouse work.[167]

Reports dismissed the BDLU, claiming it was under the influence of 'professional agitators', thus drawing on established colonial tropes regarding the alleged radicalism of trade union activists.[168] Such allegations were without foundation. In comparison with the militant trade union leadership associated with the WAA's successor, the Sudan Railway Workers' Union (SRWU), Port Sudan's dockworkers rarely acted as a unified workforce. The segmented character of the port industry's workforce served to inhibit collective mobilisation. As a result, strike action tended to be limited to specific categories of worker. This did not make strike action any less effective, however. Between February 1951 and March 1952, five strikes prevented the transport of 21,600 tons of imports from Port Sudan, and further strikes in 1954 resulted in lockouts.[169] What was significant about the strikes in this period was the way in which the unions framed their demands, often requesting extended breaks and shorter working days. In other words, as the colonial authorities sought to regulate the dockworkers' day, to control when and how long stevedores worked, the union transformed this language of time discipline into a 'claim making construct', drawing an increasingly sharp distinction between the employers' time and the workers' 'own' time.[170]

[166] Cooper, *On the African Waterfront*, 144.

[167] Lewis, 'Deim el Arab', 33.

[168] TNA, FO, 371/96846, Sudan Political Intelligence Summary, Apr.–May 1952.

[169] *Sudan Monthly Record*, No. 255 (Feb.–Mar. 1952), No. 256 (Mar.–Apr. 1952).

[170] This is not to imply, however, that Beja dockworkers had been 'proletarianised'. Lewis's report reveals that many dockworkers maintained economic and social ties with Port Sudan's rural hinterlands. The report also refers to the relationship between employment in the port and vernacular understandings of gender and generation, particularly within the context of marriage, as well as the impact of waged-labour on patterns of consumption and bodily attire. More research on these issues needs to be carried out. Nonetheless, what can be inferred from Lewis's report is that work-related demands should be understood within a wider social order or moral framework, which had been imported and adapted to the context of Port Sudan. On these various points, see Lewis, 'Deim Al Arab', 24–40. On the instrumentalisation of the concept of time by dockworkers in Mombasa, see Frederick Cooper, 'Colonizing Time: Work Rhythms and Labor Conflict in Colonial Mombasa', in Nicholas Dirks (ed.), *Colonialism and Culture* (Ann Arbor, MI, 1992), 209–45.

Conclusion

The claim-making power of Sudanese trade unions and workers proved to be short-lived. In 1953, the Anglo-Egyptian agreement was signed, establishing a three-year transition period to self-government, after which the Sudan would become independent.[171] The SWTUF, the representative body for Sudanese trade unions, opposed the agreement, arguing that it would delay independence. As a consequence, during the transitional period of self-government the SWTUF continued its campaign for improved rights, highlighting the failure of the Sudanese political elites to deliver tangible social and economic dividends to ordinary workers.[172] In January 1955, for example, the SWTUF initiated a registration scheme for unemployed workers who, the Federation claimed, were 'facing the worst financial hardships'. Some 1,200 unemployed workers were registered and the SWTUF organised what it described as a 'hunger procession' through the streets of Khartoum.[173] The procession concluded with the submission of demands, including the abolition of temporary work in the public sector and the introduction of a social insurance scheme for the unemployed, and then in March 1955 the SWTUF staged a five-day strike in an effort to win concessions from the government.[174] Such actions underscore the validity of Miles Larmer's argument concerning the 'heterogeneity and ambiguity' of activism in late colonial Africa, where claims for improved socio-economic and political rights cannot be easily folded into a unified or linear narrative of triumphant anti-colonial nationalism.[175] In many cases, the disparate social groups that comprised the nationalist movements had different and competing visions for independence, which were often at odds with the views of African political elites.[176]

To counter such claims, African political elites often drew on the language of 'national development'.[177] In the Sudan, in response to the strike of March 1955, the government, which was led by the National Unionist Party (NUP), accused the SWTUF of 'breaking the industrial peace' and claimed that the

[171] For a discussion of the Anglo-Egyptian agreement and its implications for Sudan's transition to self-government and independence, see Daly, *Imperial Sudan*, 352–94.

[172] Tim Niblock provides a useful account of the tensions between the nationalist parties and the organised labour movement. See *Class and Power in Sudan*, 118–22.

[173] *Sudan Monthly Record*, No. 289 (Jan. 1955).

[174] *Sudan Monthly Record*, No. 289 (Jan. 1955).

[175] Larmer, 'Historicising Activism', 73.

[176] Geiger, *TANU women*; Schmidt, *Mobilizing the Masses*; Jean Allman, *The Quills of the Porcupine: Asante Nationalism in an Emergent Ghana* (Madison, WI, 1993); Ahlman, *Living with Nkrumahism*.

[177] Larmer, 'Historicising Activism', 72.

demands would be considered 'so as not to hamper the smooth functioning of the first national government during this historic phase'.[178] Beyond such discursive strategies, the Sudanese authorities also introduced anti-trade union legislation. In 1957, a year after independence, the government, now under the leadership of Umma Party's Abdallah Khalil, introduced a new trade union ordinance designed to neutralise the SWTUF.[179] The ordinance stipulated that only unions from the same industry could federate and that all federations would have to re-register. When the SWTUF staged a protest against the ordinance, Muhammed al-Sayyid al-Sallam and al-Shafi Ahmad al-Shaykh were arrested for their part in organising the demonstration. Subsequently, twenty unions were dissolved by the registrar of trade unions for failing to comply with the terms of the new ordinance.[180] These anti-trade union measures were commonplace across Africa during the era of decolonisation, as nationalist elites sought to curb the power of the organised labour movement, often by centralising trade unions under state control, introducing repressive legislation and co-opting labour leaders.[181] This underscores one of the paradoxes of decolonisation. During the struggle against colonial rule the discourse of rights had empowered trade unions, equipping labour leaders with the discursive power to claim greater social and economic rights. However, once independence was achieved, this language of rights was increasingly viewed as a threat by nationalist elites.[182] As a result, political leaders used the language of nation building and the primacy of state sovereignty in order to curb the power and influence of the organised labour movement.[183]

The Sudan is often treated as an outlier in African studies, due to its geographic position and status as a 'Condominium' of Britain and Egypt. This chapter has sought to challenge this exceptionalism by focusing on the Sudan government's response to the emergence of organised labour

[178] *Sudan Monthly Record*, No. 294 (June 1955).

[179] The NUP led Sudan to independence in January 1956, but al-Azhari, the first minister of Sudan, did not survive long in post. Political factionalism combined with economic uncertainty forced al-Azhari to resign, after which he was replaced by Abdallah Khalil, the leader of the Umma Party. These events are described by Niblock in *Class and Power in Sudan*, 204–10.

[180] Details concerning the trade union ordinance can be found in TNA, LAB, 13/1207, Extract of *Daily News Bulletin*, 22 Oct., enclosed in Chancery, British Embassy Khartoum to African Department Foreign Office, London, 31 Oct. 1957.

[181] The corporatist strategies adopted by postcolonial African states are detailed in Bill Freund, *The African Worker* (Cambridge, 1988), 91–109.

[182] This tension is thoroughly documented in Roland Burke, *Decolonization and the Evolution of Human Rights* (Philadelphia, 2010). In particular, see chapters two and three.

[183] The most insightful discussion of this paradox remains Cooper, *Decolonization and African Society*, 432–50.

activism after 1945. When confronted with strikes and labour unrest in the late 1940s, the Sudan government sought to 'stabilise' Sudanese workers through the introduction of regular work, improved industrial relations machinery and increased social welfare provision. In doing so, the colonial state sought to reshape Sudanese workers and their families in the image of their European counterparts. The limitations of these policies were quickly exposed. In response to British demands for order, productivity and stability, Sudanese trade unions combined the universalising implications of the stabilisation strategy with local understandings of morality and modernity in order to claim higher wages and improved labour rights.[184] However, while these 'expectations of modernity', to borrow James Ferguson's phrase, continued to inform Sudanese labour activism during the transitional period of self-government, Sudanese trade unions found that their rhetorical strategy was less effective once independence had been achieved.[185] Sudanese political elites, like their counterparts elsewhere in Africa, invoked the language of national cohesion and development, arguing that nation building took precedence over the claims of the organised labour movement. Simply put, in tracing these dynamics, this chapter adds the Sudanese case to an established body of labour history scholarship concerned with Africans' discursive representation of material conditions; local idioms relating to family, gender and community; and relations with capital, the colonial state and its postcolonial successor.

184 This is the principal argument in Cooper's *Decolonization and African Society*.

185 See Ferguson, *Expectations of Modernity*.

7

Class, Cold War and Colonialism

The Deportation of Albert Fava from Gibraltar to Britain, 1948

Tom Sibley

This chapter deals with the impact of the Cold War on the struggle for colonial freedom in the late 1940s. It examines the approach of the British labour movement and the British state including the role of the first majority Labour government (1945–1951) and explains how the anti-colonial currents existing in the British and international trade union movement were derailed to suit the interests of British and US foreign policy. In that period, the British Labour government was determined to protect the empire against what it saw as the subversive machinations of the Soviet Union and of the world Communist movement. The chapter presents a case study of that tendency: the story of the deportation of Albert Fava, Gibraltar's outstandingly successful but short-lived trade union leader. Fava was a Communist who had served in the Spanish Civil War (1936–1939) on the Republican side. In three short months in 1948, to the delight of Gibraltar's working class, he led the transformation of the Gibraltar Congress of Labour (GCL). He helped build a trade union with sound structures, democratic practices and progressive social policies. This was too much for the British-appointed Colonial Governor and his masters in London. Their first priority was to keep Franco's quasi-fascist regime in power as the best bulwark against the spread of socialism in the Mediterranean region. This required keeping Franco on their side by not giving encouragement to elements sympathetic to the ideals and traditions of Republican Spain. Secondly, the Governor wanted to protect his own privileged position against the challenges posed by the newly emerging nationalist movement for which Fava and the GCL provided a well-organised mass base. Fava was seen as a threat to both of the above objectives, so he had to go. In Fortress Gibraltar in 1948 the Governor had absolute, unchallengeable powers. He used the Strangers and Aliens Act to deport Albert Fava to Britain with his young family at three days' notice. Fava was neither an alien nor a stranger. Neither was he British. But, as this chapter will show, natural justice and due process were put aside in order to protect British imperialist interests.

British imperialism and the Attlee government

In 1945, at the end of the Second World War, the British Empire and Commonwealth still covered over a quarter of the globe. But Britain's position was quite different from the one occupied in 1939. The war effort had drained the country's reserves and put Britain in hock to the USA, the world's new military and economic superpower. In the colonies themselves, the national liberation movement was burgeoning. As one commentator put it: 'there are certain classes of natives who are proud of being African'.[1]

Against most expectations, the British people elected a Labour government with a large parliamentary majority on a programme promising reforms designed to improve working-class life opportunities without challenging the wealth and power of the rich. For the colonies, Labour's 1945 manifesto contained a vague commitment to progressive change reflecting the need to accommodate the lessons learnt in the late 1930s following episodes of violent labour unrest in Southern Africa and the Caribbean, when colonial workers had rebelled against poverty wages, insecure employment and terrible working conditions.[2]

But there were other, broader political issues at play. The United Nations adopted an anti-colonial charter. The spotlight was turned on the colonial powers although the UN had no machinery with which to enforce decolonisation. On the trade union side, the World Federation of Trade Unions (WFTU) was formed in Paris in 1945 with affiliates both in the metropolitan centres and in the colonies, where economic demands combined with aspirations to national independence.[3] In many parts of the world, notably in the colonial empires, boosted by the prestige of the USSR, Communist parties too were gaining new recruits. None of this was particularly encouraging for the British ruling class. For British capitalists, the Foreign Office and the Labour government, the need to maintain British power and influence in the world, including the wealth extracted from the colonies, took precedence over the rights of working people at home and abroad.

When the Second World War alliance between the USA, the British Empire and the USSR gave way to the Cold War, the newly elected

1 L.H. Gann, *A History of Northern Rhodesia: Early Days to 1953* (London, 1964), 348.

2 Rhiannon Vickers, *Manipulating Hegemony: State Power, Labour and the Marshall Plan in Britain* (Basingstoke, 2000).

3 Victor Silverman, *Imagining Internationalism in American and British Labor, 1939–1949* (Urbana, IL, 2000), 1–5, 184–85.

Labour government chose to side with the USA and its imperialist allies. One of their major aims was to resist decolonisation wherever this was possible.[4] With the precipitate rundown of sterling balances and overseas investment returns as a result of the costs involved in sustaining the war effort, by 1947 it had become clear that Britain could no longer retain its pre-war position as an economic and military superpower. Without aid from the USA (the Marshall Plan) or cuts to Labour's welfare state programme it would not have been possible to keep to the high levels of military expenditure thought necessary to police the Empire and contain the spread of Communism. Labour's choice was to continue with Britain's traditional foreign policy in order to remain a major imperialist power rather than to promote decolonisation and peaceful coexistence with the Soviet Union. This repositioned Britain as a junior partner to the USA in a broader imperialist alliance.[5]

At the top of the ministerial pyramid was Foreign Secretary Ernest Bevin, formerly the General Secretary of the Transport and General Workers Union (T&GWU) before becoming the Minister of Labour in the wartime coalition government. Bevin, a staunch patriot in the jingoist mould and a fierce anti-Communist, quickly became the favourite politician of the public school-educated Whitehall mandarins in the Foreign and Colonial Offices. Although, in class terms, they might have come from another planet, they shared Bevin's prejudices and, more importantly, his world view.[6] At the Colonial Office, Arthur Creech-Jones, also a former T&GWU official, was happy to follow Bevin's line and to work with the TUC General Council leadership to promote what he himself defined as responsible trade unions in the colonies. On the TUC General Council, Bevin's successor at the head of the T&GWU was Arthur Deakin, who shared his antipathy towards to the Soviet Union. For the crucial period of late 1946 to 1949, he was also President of the WFTU, which included in its membership the Soviet Union's trade unions and many Communist-influenced unions. Deakin

[4] Ralph Miliband, 'Reflections on Anti-Communism', *Socialist Register* (London, 1984).

[5] This subservience to dominant US interests has remained the default position of British foreign policy ever since, independent of the political colouring of the elected government.

[6] See Alan Bullock, *The Life and Times of Ernest Bevin* (London, 1960); John Saville, *The Politics of Continuity: British Foreign Policy and the Labour Government, 1945–46* (London, 1993); Silverman, *Imagining Internationalism*; Peter Weiler, *Ernest Bevin* (Manchester, 1993). For an unvarnished pro-Bevin account, see Denis MacShane, *International Labour and the Origins of the Cold War* (Oxford, 1992), which includes some useful insights but is often inaccurate and always reflexively anti-Communist. For several examples of this, see Tom Sibley, 'Anti-Communism: Studies of its Impact on the UK Labour Movement in the Early Years (1945–1948)', PhD thesis, University of Keele, 2008, chapter 3.

was, unsurprisingly, was one of the chief promoters of the 1949 split.[7] This T&GWU triumvirate was at the centre of the developments and events examined in this chapter.

The British TUC and trade unions in the colonies

The British TUC put great store on the establishment of branch and workplace structures in the colonies. Little credence was given to the demands made for political independence for the colonies. In essence, the TUC argued that if you could not organise a sound trade union structure you had no chance of playing an influential role in governing your country.[8] The TUC in the 1930s encouraged British state intervention in colonial trade union affairs and during the Second World War put itself at the head of the coalition government's labour-related development work. It was strongly represented in the tripartite Colonial Labour Advisory Committee (CLAC) set up in 1942. It provided experienced trade union officers to serve overseas as part of labour departments set up in all the colonies. The labour officers' tasks were to monitor developments, to identify potential 'trouble makers', particularly Communists, and to educate and train the 'natives' in the ways of trade union organisation and bargaining. Creech-Jones, active in CLAC work from the beginning, was also a Governor of Ruskin, the trade union college based in Oxford. He offered the college's facilities to develop specially designed courses for trade union officials from colonial countries, with the goal of inculcating the values and practices of 'responsible trade unionism'.

The British TUC leadership shared the Attlee government's values. To Citrine and Deakin the top priority was to support government policy, which often led to putting Britain's geopolitical interests before the rights and demands of colonial workers for trade union rights and improved living standards. In this period, in colony after colony, independent trade unions were supressed and activists were imprisoned and sometimes worse. In Malaya, the Communists led the struggle for national independence and developed a mass trade union movement. In this rubber-rich, dollar-earning colony, the Attlee government responded by banning the main trade union federation as part of a general policy of repression. In Kenya, the leader of the East African Trade Union Federation (EATUF), which campaigned for independence, was arrested and alternative unions were quickly established in the British mould. In Sierra Leone, the Pan-Africanist leader with

[7] V.L. Allen, *Trade Union Leadership: Based on a Study of Arthur Deakin* (London, 1957). See also D.I. Davies, 'The Politics of the TUC's Colonial Policy', *Political Quarterly*, 35 (1964), 23–34.

[8] Peter Weiler, *British Labour and the Cold War* (Stanford, CA, 1998), chapter 1.

Communist ties, Wallace-Johnson, helped to develop trade unions along militant lines. He was arrested and then interned under wartime defence regulations. The Colonial Office sent a labour adviser to Sierra-Leone to restructure the newly born trade union movement and isolate Wallace-Johnson's followers. In Cyprus, during the period of industrial unrest, the national trade union leaders were imprisoned under charges of sedition: any activist suspected of Communist sympathies was castigated as 'anti British'. All this was part of the Colonial Office's attempts, with the approval and involvement of the British TUC, to direct and control trade union developments in the colonies. By a mixture of patronage, persuasion, bribery, training and co-option of leaders, both the Labour government and the TUC hoped to direct the colonial unions along what they saw as 'responsible' lines. But where such blandishments failed, the British state – with British TUC support – was prepared to use coercion to deal with trade union developments they could not control by other means.

The TUC's attitude towards the WFTU reveals the same priorities. When the WFTU was formed in 1945 the leaders of the TUC and of the Congress of Industrial Organizations (CIO) took leading parts in the process. In the TUC's case it was from a sense of entitlement to occupy a leadership position, being the only large centre with extensive experience of international work. The CIO was more concerned to build its relationship with the US State department so as to replace the American Federation of Labor (AF of L) as the US administration's go-to trade union body. Both the TUC and CIO were subject to strong rank-and-file pressures from activists to build a new international centre incorporating the Soviet trade unions in order to advance working people's rights in the broadest sense across the globe. For its part, the Soviet All Union Central Council of Trade Unions (AUCCTU) was determined to keep the WFTU as a united body and to this end made several concessions to the TUC and the CIO, even where these contravened the world organisations' policies – for example, in Greece, Spain and Germany. With the heightening of the Cold War in late 1947–1948, and realising that the majority of WFTU affiliates opposed the Marshall Plan, the TUC and the CIO, aided by the powerful AF of L, which remained outside the WFTU on anti-Communist grounds, set out to sabotage the WFTU with the assistance of US and UK government departments. By 1948, the Cold War had weakened the position of the WFTU. The TUC and the American unions engineered divisions which led to the breakaway of January 1949 and the formation of the International Confederation of Free Trade Unions (ICFTU) in December that year.[9] The reasons for the split had been hotly debated by

[9] Anthony Carew, 'Schism within the WFTU', *International Review of Social History*, 29 (1984), 297–335.

academics. Carew puts the breakaway down to fundamental differences about the aims and methods of trade unionism. More convincingly, in summing up the debates, Victor Silverman argues: 'The split has more to do with the unions' loyalty to the demands of their nations' foreign policies than it had to do with any disagreements about fundamental union practices. The Cold War in labour was imposed from the top'.[10] The Fava case presented below is a telling illustration of that phenomenon, particularly as the TUC cited Fava's campaign to affiliate the Gibraltar Congress of Labour (GCL) to the WFTU as proof positive that he was a threat to British interests and used this as a pretext to back his deportation.

Albert Fava: a Gibraltarian and transnational working-class leader

In October 1948, Gibraltar's British-appointed Governor, with the full support of Labour government ministers, deported Albert Fava, the General Secretary of the colony's first mass trade union, the Gibraltar Congress of Labour (GCL). At seventy-two hours' notice he was sent with his wife and four children from his homeland to Britain, where he was to spend the rest of his life. The deportation of a trade union leader who had committed no crime and had neither taken nor encouraged any actions which imperilled Gibraltar's security is one of the many egregious measures taken by the British authorities against labour movement and national independence activists in the period under review. It happened under the tutelage of the first majority Labour government, led by Clement Attlee (1945–1951), which had come to power making noises in support of decolonisation and of the development of independent trade unions in the British Empire.

Albert Fava was born in October 1912 in the Spanish border town of La Linea in Andalusia. His early history is not well documented but we know from Colonial Office files that he was issued with a British passport in Gibraltar in 1940 and that his father was Gibraltarian.[11] The same files show that Fava was economically active in Gibraltar during the mid-1930s and that in 1936 he was engaged in arms procurement work for the Spanish Republican government then under attack by the rebel Franco forces. According to his nephew Pepe Nuza, Fava went to Spain during the Civil War to advance the Republican cause. Apparently he served as a political

[10] Silverman, *Imagining Internationalism*. See also Anthony Carew, 'The Trade Union Congress in the International Labour Movements', in Alan Campbell, Nina Fishman and John McIlroy (eds), *British Trade Unions and Industrial Politics*, vol.1, *The Post War Compromise, 1954–1964* (Ashgate, 1999), 145–67; Sibley, 'Anti-Communism'.

[11] 'MI5 letter to Colonial Office', 28 Sept. 1948, The National Archives (TNA), Public Record Office (PRO), CO, 537/4060.

educator, i.e., a non-combatant.[12] In the same letter, Nuza tells us how Fava arrived in Britain via a French refugee camp. He had initially gone to Seville to study, and while there he ended up in Madrid working for the Republican government. With the advance of the Francoists in 1939, he managed to escape from Malaga on a fishing boat and was taken to a French refugee camp. However, he was able to return to Gibraltar in a British warship after his father made repeated requests for assistance to the Governor. During the Second World War, Fava was evacuated to Britain along with many other Gibraltarian families.[13]

According to MI5 records, Fava led an active political life in Britain during the war. He moved to Swansea in 1940 and by 1942 had served as both Secretary and Chair of the Swansea branch of the CPGB. Early in 1943, Fava moved to Stirling and quickly became a member of the party's Scottish Committee. During this period, he worked at the Keirfield Aircraft Factory at Bannockburn and was active in the Amalgamated Engineering Union (AEU). In April 1945, he was a delegate to the Scottish Congress of the party. His record was clearly one of continuing activity, leadership and responsibility. In the January 1946 issue of the Scottish District of the CPGB's *Bulletin*, there is an announcement that Albert Fava had been 'newly appointed organiser for Stirlingshire' and this was almost certainly a full-time position at that time. The *Bulletin* notes that Fava was already hard at work and amongst other initiatives was sending out weekly notes on branch organisation. There follows an example of Fava's notes relating to the Bannockburn branch, a small branch in a mining village. Here Fava sets out in some detail advice for branch organisation and work.[14]

The contents of these notes are evidence that Albert Fava was a serious politician and a meticulous organiser, traits that were to stand him in good stead with the Gibraltarian work. But these same strengths also panicked the Governor and the local employers into taking draconian action against Fava and his young family. It appears that Fava did keep links with Gibraltar during his period of evacuation. His main contact was Joe Balloqui, an active trade unionist who became a leading lay figure within the GCL. Once it became clear that the newly formed GCL required an experienced organiser if it were to prosper, and that such an individual was not available within Gibraltar, Balloqui put Fava's name forward for consideration. Fava took up his position as General Secretary of the GCL in July 1948. He was deported three months later.

[12] Jonathan Jeffries, 'The Politics of Colonialism: The Case of Albert Fava', *Socialist History*, 29 (2006).

[13] Jeffries, 'Politics of Colonialism'.

[14] 'MI5 letter to Colonial Office', 28 Sept. 1948.

The story unfolds during the early post-war years when in Gibraltar the Governor had wide and unchallengeable powers and was accountable to the British government, not to the Gibraltarian people. This coincided with a worldwide wave of struggles against colonial oppression during which the British Labour government worked with the British TUC to undermine attempts by the working people in British colonies to organise independent radical unions campaigning for economic, social and political change, including demands for measures to promote self-government. There were, however, also factors at play specific to Gibraltar. To understand these factors, we need to know something of the history of Gibraltar's labour movement and the impact of British trade union intervention on the way racial and national divisions were exploited by the colonial authorities.

The early history of trade union organisation in Gibraltar (1890s–1945)

In many British colonies trade unions have been recognised as not only leading workers' movements but also undertaking a crucial role in independence movements. In Gibraltar, this pattern of development was never fully followed through. The control exerted by both the colonial authorities and employers ensured that this would not happen. Importantly, it was the sowing of divisions of the working class into nationalities and languages that would assist them in this endeavour. As Béliard notes, the term 'Gibraltarian' applied to workers who were British immigrants or descendants of British immigrants and also to Spanish workers having settled in Gibraltar.[15] The rest of the workforce was not only Spanish in origin but also from other parts of the Mediterranean including Maltese, Italian and Portuguese.

The fact that many workers in Gibraltar were immigrants enabled the colonial authorities to exploit divisions on racial and nationality grounds. The intervention by British trade unions may have also played its role in encouraging the strengthening of the links to the metropolitan power, even though there might have been pragmatic overtones to this move. This reinforces Weiler's argument that the involvement of British trade unions in organised labour in the colonies, with its emphasis on maintaining industrial and eschewing political involvement, was strongly preferred by the colonial authorities.[16]

[15] Yann Béliard, 'Labour and Empire in the Edwardian Age: The Gibraltar Dockers' Strike of 1902', unpublished paper given at the Transnational and Comparative Labour Movement Conference, University of Huddersfield, 21 July 2014.

[16] Weiler, *British Labour*.

Early trade union activism in Gibraltar from the 1890s until the 1920s was marked by strikes by the coal heavers.[17] This resulted in violent and usually brutal responses from the authorities. During these years, strikes were organised by Gibraltarian and Spanish workers. It would be the Spanish workers who would bear the brunt of the worst victimisation by the colonial authorities. One key strategy would be to have their work permits removed, which meant not being able to travel into Gibraltar to work or worse still be arrested and eventually imprisoned. The coal-heaving companies also had the assistance of the colonial authorities with work permits issued for non-unionised labour from Spain, and the use of the army to strike-break.

As a senior colonial official remarked in a confidential report on trade unionism in Gibraltar, 'The Spanish employees in the Dockyard have never been particularly sympathetic to the Gibraltarians. Their outlook and standard of living are very different and in consequence their interests are not likely to be along parallel lines with those of the Gibraltarians'.[18] As observed by Béliard, steps were taken by the colonial authorities to destroy the bonds existing between Gibraltarian and Spanish workers.[19] This ensured effective control over the workforce. This was also its Achilles heel since the Spanish workforce was the most numerous and they were needed to keep the military base and coal heaving functioning. The British colonial authorities in Gibraltar clearly demonstrated also that they strongly opposed any radical – anarchist, socialist or communist – tendencies among the workers.

The earliest developments of trade unionism were organised by the Circulo Obrero (Workers' Circle) during 1893. However, Gibraltar had previously observed strikes. For example, in 1890, the Riot Act was invoked and soldiers with fixed bayonets were deployed to break a strike by the coal heavers. The Circulo Obrero, founded by a Gibraltarian, B. Corralles, came into being during the strike as did the Centro de Resistencia de Panaderos de Gibraltar (Gibraltar Bakers' Centre of Resistance). The Circulo Obrero had also created the Asociación de Trabajadores en Carbón Denominada Primero de Mayo (the First of May Coal Heavers' Association). It was assisted by the Spanish Socialist Party, with workmen's associations linked to the nearby towns in La Linea, Algeciras and San Roque. In its

[17] Chris Grocott, Gareth Stockey and Jo Grady, 'Anarchy in the UK('s Most Famous Fortress): Comradeship and Cupidity in Gibraltar and Neighbouring Spain, 1890–1902', *Labor History*, 56.4 (2015) and Chris Grocott, Gareth Stockey and Jo Grady, 'Reformers and Revolutionaries: The Battle for the Working Classes in Gibraltar and its Hinterland, 1902–1921', *Labor History*, 59.6 (2018), 692–719.

[18] TNA, PRO, CO, T217/4.

[19] Béliard, 'Labour and Empire'.

later development, in 1896, it affiliated to the British Social Democratic Federation (SDF).

The 1902 strike of coal heavers was significant in that it was one of the biggest that Gibraltar had witnessed. The initial affiliation to the SDF allowed for a delegation to be sent to Britain. This strike showed that the SDF had been able to work with the Circulo Obrero, which *The Times* described as follows: 'prime movers were a group of Spanish socialists of the extreme, some of whom carried on the machinery on Spanish soil while others who had been forced to leave Spain for political reason lived in Gibraltar'. This strike by the coal heavers was to protect their closed shop practice. It related to a notice posted by the coal heavers' employers' group, stating that the employers would employ who they liked whether in a union or not. The employers wanted to bring in non-unionised labour from Spain and Morocco. It was reported a month later, on 14 July, that at Trafalgar Square in London a delegation from Gibraltar spoke of the lock-out and the use by the Governor of soldiers and bluejackets to upload private vessels.

Trade union solidarity combining Spanish and British trade unionists was to change with the arrival of the Workers' Union in 1919. The colonial authorities said that before this date 'Spanish and Gibraltarian workmen in fact looked upon themselves as united in a common bond namely the upholding of the interests of labour against those of the capitalists and took the field as natural allies against a common foe'.[20] An official report to the Governor of Gibraltar stated that a split within the labour movement occurred early on during the establishment of a Workers' Union branch. Comments from the colonial authorities asserted that Matt Giles, organiser from the Workers' Union, viewed the Spanish unions as 'syndicalist, bolshevist and anarchist and that he had no ground in common with their view'.[21] It is true that at the time the Confederación Nacional del Trabajo (CNT), the anarchist-led trade union, had the largest representation in Andalusia. If we are to believe the Colonial Office reports, Matt Giles's view was that all workers should join the Workers' Union and leave the Spanish-led trade unions. The Workers' Union policy once a branch was set up overseas was that of strengthening its links with the head office in Britain. This was only strengthened once the Workers' Union merged with the T&GWU in 1928.

With the Spanish Civil War in 1936 followed by Franco's dictatorship from 1939, the T&GWU in Gibraltar focused on supporting the refugees

[20] TNA, PRO, CO, T217/4.

[21] Ironically, an official secret file was kept in Malta on Matt Giles, detailing where he lived before moving on to Gibraltar, his political history and activism. A comment from the Maltese-based Colonial Secretary in Gibraltar saw him as a 'very sound man'. TNA, PRO, CO, T217/4.

that had arrived as a result of the conflict. The concerns of the colonial authorities were still rooted in the fears over Spanish left-wing influences. The Colonial Office did not wish to upset the new authorities established in Spain and were afraid of the political meetings the refugees might hold. This was reflected in comments from the Colonial Office: 'to have Gibraltarian and Spanish unions would divide the good working relationships, so important to the smooth running of this military fortress'.[22] Yet the military fortress relied so strongly on the Spanish and Gibraltarian labour coming from nearby towns that it could not close its doors altogether. The Second World War was a quiet period for trade unions in Gibraltar. By this stage, the concerns of the British authorities had focused on ensuring that the incipient Cold War and Communist politics did not influence workers on the Rock. In fact, this attitude went so far as appeasing the Franco government in Spain to ensure the continued supply of workers across the border to maintain the military base.

The post-war situation (1945–1948)

In November 1945, the Association for the Advancement of Civil Rights (AACR) sent a deputation to the British Colonial Secretary. Its objective was to press the British government to introduce democratic reforms in Gibraltar which would give the people rights to self-government. At this time, the British-appointed Governor, traditionally a military figure, was omnipotent, at the head of a non-elected executive council, which he had picked. A report prepared by the National Council of Civil Liberties' (NCCL) national organiser put it like this:

> The Governor is all-powerful and he is surrounded by a small clique of people who are the selected members for the Executive Council and who are always appointed from the same families. This clique is pro-fascist and very reactionary and does not conceal its admiration for General Franco. There is a workers' Trade Union but many of its members have lapsed and no longer support it in protest against the Organiser of the Union who is thought to be in the pay of the Governing clique.[23]

The trade union referred to above was the British-based T&GWU, whose organiser at the time was Augustine Huart, a fierce opponent of the AACR and who had a close working relationship with the colonial authorities, including the secret services, both in Gibraltar and Britain.

[22] Sept. 1946. TNA, PRO, CO, T217/4.

[23] 'Report by H.E. Bell, National Organiser', 28 Jan. 1945, Hull University Archives, Hull History Centre, National Council of Civil Liberties (NCCL) Archive.

Another issue raised by the delegation was freedom of the press. The Colonial Secretary had the authority to withdraw a newspaper's right to publish without explanation or possibility of appeal. On a day-to-day basis, the Governor and Colonial Service personnel had the right to censor publications. In the case of the Colony's main newspaper, the *Gibraltar Chronicle*, the Governor of the day acted very much like a director in chief of the publications. Editors were kept on a tight rein. One such example was that of T.H. Theobald, a civilian contracted as *Chronicle* editor for a brief period in 1947, and later removed by the military authorities because he wanted the newspaper to have an independent line and freedom to criticise official decisions. Not only was he expected to take orders from the President of the Garrison Library Committee but also to obey every member of that committee, which consisted of military and colonial service personnel. In effect, what this meant was that any lackey in a uniform could give instructions to the editor on what could or could not be published.

But things were on the move. In 1947, universal suffrage was won and the governing Executive Council for the first time included elected members although these remained in a minority. Very importantly for the emerging GCL, the right to strike became law. For the first time organised trade disputes were protected by law, paralleling the position in Britain. Before this Ordinance was introduced it was unlawful to strike and striking workers faced arrest and imprisonment. In an interview with the *Gibraltar Chronicle*, commenting on the trade union situation in 1947, Jose Netto, a retired and respected trade union leader, said: 'At the end of the war the atmosphere here at the time was one of people waking up and realising there was something extremely important that had to be done'.[24] Netto went on to state that the post-war climate, well into the 1950s, was marked by fervent British patriotism and rabid anti-Communism, which influenced the T&GWU to the extent that it sold out to the UK Intelligence Service.

The Fava effect and Britain's response (1948)

In 1947, the GCL was set up as the trade union wing of the AACR, the nationalist movement formed in 1942. It is not clear what part, if any, Fava played in this from his Scottish base. But he kept contact with a number of active trade unionists, some of whom took up leadership positions in the newly formed federation. It is very probable that he used his British trade union experience, which was extensive, at workplace, union branch and regional level to proffer advice and encouragement. Thus, when the GCL

[24] Interview with Jose Netto in the *Gibraltar Chronicle Bicentenary Special Edition* (2001).

found it necessary to appoint a new General Secretary, Fava's reputation went before him.

Fava proved to be an outstandingly successful trade union organiser. He quickly set up branch and trade group structures, organised new and effective union dues collection systems, focused active members on the need to recruit new members and encouraged all of the unions' new sections to play a part in the AACR to raise demands for full political rights and a social wage for Gibraltarians based on the welfare state reforms enacted by the Labour government in Britain. Almost overnight the GCL had replaced the T&GWU as the main union for Gibraltarian workers and Fava promoted broader links spearheading the campaign to form a Trades Council open to all unions as well as strengthening the GCL's work in the AACR. A number of British unions as well as the T&GWU had small memberships in the civil service and the dockyards. Their memberships consisted mainly of non-manual workers of British origin working as administrators, managers and technicians. These unions included the civil service union (the CSCA) and the draughtsmen's union (the AESD).

None of these activities pleased either the Governor or the big employers in Gibraltar, which included the British government, but they did please Gibraltarian workers. In just over three months, Fava built a collective leadership which had transformed the trade union situation for the better, much to the chagrin of the T&GWU hierarchy in Transport House (Deakin) and Whitehall (Bevin and Creech-Jones). The problem for the British establishment, which at this time included the labour movement's top leaders, was that the Fava-inspired trade unionism did not conform to the model of responsible trade unionism that they promoted throughout the British Empire. In essence, the establishment model was apolitical and non-combative, based on collaboration with the colonial authorities with guidance, verging on interference, from TUC-recommended labour officers. So the British authorities decided that Fava had to go quickly before, in the Governor's words, 'he did more damage'.[25]

Fava faced a perfect storm of interrelated factors and powerful forces that were impossible to resist. In 1948, he was a British Communist abroad in the early days of the Cold War. The British Labour government, blindly supported by the overwhelming majority of trade union leaders, was determined to maintain the empire wherever this was possible and was prepared to use anti-Communism and anti-Sovietism as one of the pretexts to support its anti-union actions. Fava found many friends in Gibraltar and a few powerful enemies, including the local employers. His main enemy was the British-appointed Governor, a military man full of pompous self-esteem

[25] TNA, PRO, CO, 537/4059.

who had a patronising contempt for Gibraltar's working class. Anderson was also pro-Franco and had excellent relations with the Spanish authorities, including the secret service. He had strongly advised the leadership of the GCL not to appoint Fava and was offended when the 'poor mutts' – Anderson's stated appraisal of the GCL leadership – rejected his advice and went ahead with the appointment. From day one of Fava's taking up post, Anderson strove to undermine him and working closely with the secret services looked for evidence to justify Fava's deportation under the Aliens and Strangers Order. Fava's MI5 and police files show that when he was in Britain during the war he listened to Radio Moscow and wrote to the legendary Spanish revolutionary and Civil War leader Dolores Ibarruri, then exiled in the Soviet Union. When in Gibraltar he had received a letter from the CPGB national organiser wishing him well in his new job, and had corresponded with John Horner, the General Secretary of the Fire Brigades Union (FBU) and a member of the CPGB's Colonial Committee, about fire safety regulations in the Docks. This, according to the Secret Service files available at the Public Records Office, was the extent of Fava's interaction with individuals and organisations with some connection to the Communist Party.[26]

Albert Fava, trade union organiser and anti-fascist

Fava's trade union practice was modelled on his British experience. For him trade unions best served their members by concerning themselves with broad political and social issues impacting on the lives of the working class as a whole as well as wages and conditions at the workplace. In Gibraltar's case, this approach could not but raise the Spanish question and the nature of Franco's regime. Nor, in this period in particular, could it ignore the position of the United Nations relating to decolonisation. This raised the question of affiliation to the WFTU, to which the British TUC in 1948 was also affiliated. The WFTU was represented in some of the UN specialised agencies and had some influence on policies concerning rights for colonial workers.[27]

Both the above issues were raised at the GCL's 1948 Annual General Meeting (AGM), the Union's policy making body.[28] Motions condemning the Franco regime, while declaring solidarity with Spanish workers and supporting affiliation to the WFTU, were both tabled for debate, no doubt

[26] TNA, PRO, CO, 537/4060.

[27] Hugh Williamson, *Coping with the Miracle: Japan's Unions Explore International Relations* (London, 1994), 10.

[28] Sibley, 'Anti-Communism', chapter 4.

as a result of Fava's influence. But as a result of Fava's deportation neither issue was pursued by the GCL. Thanks to the efforts of the TUC, the Colonial Office and the Governor, the WFTU affiliation issue was quietly buried some months before the TUC General Council took the decision to suspend its own membership of the WFTU to set up with the US unions a breakaway anti-Communist world organisation, the International Confederation of Free Trade Unions (ICFTU), in December 1949.[29] Enormous pressure, including a threat to cancel the booking for the AGM's venue, was placed on the GCL to withdraw the anti-fascist motion and the matter was subsequently referred back to its branch sponsors to pursue. Shortly after the AGM, Fava was summarily deported without right of appeal.

In 2001, Jose Netto recalled the events: Fava gave a speech to the GCL in the Inces Hall where he hit out at fascism, and in forty-eight hours the military had moved to have him deported. 'Police repression followed and many Gibraltarians who were simply honest workers were branded as dangerous elements. They were to suffer persecution and humiliation at the hands of the military authorities because the enemy was no longer fascism but communism'.[30] In retrospect, Netto did not doubt that 'Fava was expelled from Gibraltar because he was a Communist and was considered dangerous by the military authorities'.[31] An important element in Britain's attitude, at both Colonial Office and TUC levels, was indeed the possibility of the GCL affiliating to the WFTU, a body in which Communist-led or Communist-influenced unions from every Continent played a significant role.

Nowhere was the symbiotic relationship between the trade union leadership, through the TUC General Council, and the imperialist state more starkly illustrated than in Fava's deportation. Not surprisingly the GCL's Executive Council was bitterly opposed to the deportation, seeing it as a draconian attack on their organisation and the rights of working people.[32] Under Fava's direction the organisation had made great strides in under four months. Now all this and future prospects for further positive development were to be put in jeopardy as a result of the seemingly arbitrary actions of an unelected Governor. When a GCL deputation went to see the Governor they were told a pack of lies and offered help in the patronising way the Governor always treated Gibraltarian working people.[33] Anderson told the GCL delegation that the deportation was not an attack on the union, which he held in high regard, but was necessary to protect Gibraltar

[29] Weiler, *British Labour*, 121–23.

[30] Netto, *Gibraltar Chronicle Bicentenary*.

[31] Netto, *Gibraltar Chronicle Bicentenary*.

[32] TNA, PRO, Foreign Office (FO) Papers, 371/67613.

[33] Sibley, 'Anti-Communism', chapter 4.

from the Communist threat.[34] He had evidence, he assured them, that Fava was engaged in subversive activities compromising the very security of Fortress Gibraltar. When challenged to provide that evidence, of which there was none, he informed the delegation that for security reasons he could not disclose information to support the charges or its sources.

Shortly after this unfruitful meeting the GCL wrote to a number of British unions asking them to intercede on Fava's behalf in the interests of trade union rights and the needs of Gibraltar's workers. Inter alia, the letter said:

> This deportation is a clear case of direct interference with the right of trade union organisation. By this undemocratic order our Confederation and the bulk of the workers in Gibraltar are forcibly deprived of the services of their democratically elected General Secretary – a man with personality, a wide experience of trade union matters, and an intimate knowledge of local conditions.[35]

As was usual in that period, the minority of British unions which took some interest in international affairs referred the matter to the TUC General Secretary, Vincent Tewson. He promptly asked the Colonial Office, the very body which had sanctioned the deportation, to draft a suitable letter in reply to the enquiries received from TUC affiliated unions. If this was not shameful enough, Tewson proceeded to send out the Colonial Office Minister's draft letter, barely changed, under his signature as General Secretary of the TUC. He finished his reply by stating, without a hint of irony: 'It is not proposed to pursue this matter with the Colonial Office'.[36]

The Colonial Office letter makes it clear that Fava's biggest sin in the eyes of the Colonial Office and the TUC was 'to induce the GCL to affiliate to the Communist-dominated WFTU', something which in the event did not transpire and, if it had, had no bearing on the security of Fortress Gibraltar, except in the fevered imaginations of the 'Colonel Blimps' at the Foreign and Colonial Offices. The key section of the letter signed by Lord Listowel states:

> It was soon clear that Mr Fava was engaged in reinvigorating the small and hitherto quiescent Communist element in Gibraltar and that under the cloak of genuine trade union activity he was preparing communist infiltration into local labour organisations. There was also reason to believe that he was in touch with Communist organisations outside of Gibraltar. It was not long before the Governor came to the conclusion that Mr Fava should be ordered to leave the Colony before further harm was done, a

34 Sibley, 'Anti-Communism', chapter 4.

35 Letter from GCL Executive Committee to British unions reported in *Gibraltar Chronicle*, 26 Oct. 1948.

36 Sibley, 'Anti-Communism', chapter 4.

> step which the Governor has full power to take under the provisions of the Gibraltar law.[37]

No evidence is adduced for any of the alleged subversive activities for the good reason that none existed.

It is significant that Listowel did not pursue the Franco connection. It is doubtful that the Governor knew or cared about the WFTU issue. But he knew about Franco and was sympathetic to the regime. He often visited Spain, joining hunting parties with Franco's Foreign Office and secret service officials.[38] It is arguable that what really tipped the balance on Fava was the motion attacking Franco's regime and offering solidarity to the Spanish workers. This is certainly Netto's view.[39] But Listowel knew better than to make this known, although it represented a much greater short-term threat to British imperialist interests than the non-existent one represented by WFTU affiliation. Both British foreign policy and Gibraltar's manpower needs required the British authorities to stay on the right side of Franco while keeping quiet about it. Certainly, this disclosure would have persuaded some British unions to pursue the matter further and possibly prepare to support Fava's return to Gibraltar.

On the political front, the Communist MP Willie Gallacher, who would have known Fava from his days in Scotland, took up the case. Writing to Creech-Jones, Gallacher commented that the response to the GCL's case against Fava's deportation was 'to say the least, very unsatisfactory'. Gallacher, probably briefed by Fava, wrote:

> It is obvious that there is nothing whatever against the character or conduct of this man. It is deliberate discrimination and victimisation of an honest Trade unionist whose political views do not happen to be in accord with those of the Military Governor, or presumably of your own. ... I am enclosing one or two facts about the case which show that you were a party to his return to this country from Gibraltar. You had all the information about him at that time and you had no objection to his returning, even although you knew the Military Governor was prejudiced against him because of his political views. That requires some explanation. I would like to know what you have to say about it.[40]

When further pressed by Gallacher in Parliament, a Colonial Office minister is quoted as saying: 'Nobody has ever suggested to Mr Fava that he should refrain from lawful political activities. Communists must, unfortunately, be

[37] Modern Records Centre (MRC), TUC, Correspondence file, MS 9329/1.

[38] Jonathan Jeffries, 'Governor Wanted Good Relations with Francoist Spain to Play Polo', *Gibraltar Chronicle*, 21 Mar. 2003.

[39] Netto, *Gibraltar Chronicle Bicentenary*.

[40] *Daily Worker*, 28 Oct. 1948.

expected to be treated in this way'.[41] This exposes the arbitrary nature of the action taken against Fava. Communist Party activity was not unlawful and no evidence was produced at the time, or has been since, to indicate that Fava was engaged in Communist activities or in unlawful actions threatening the security of Gibraltar.

The campaign to rescind the deportation order was a disappointing one. Fava was advised by lawyers, both in Gibraltar and London, to take the legal road to challenge the order. Although the Governor's action offended all notions of natural justice and proper legal process, the Governor's powers in Fortress Gibraltar proved to be unchallengeable. He could deport whom he pleased on the grounds of a threat to national security without the need to provide evidence, provided he had the backing of the relevant government minister. In hindsight it is clear that only a campaign of mass industrial action and civil disobedience by Gibraltarian working people, supported by a significant number of British unions, could have forced the British authorities to back down and to insist that the deportation order be rescinded. Such as path, for a union with less than two years' experience and deprived of its charismatic leader, was several steps too far.

Conclusion

Following the failure of his legal challenge Fava continued to correspond with members of the GCL leadership. He proffered advice, offered encouragement and, at least until the mid-1950s, entertained hopes that he would be able to return to Gibraltar as GCL General Secretary. But as time went by it was probably inevitable that Fava became increasingly out of touch and discouraged. He was disappointed both by the GCL's leadership failure to campaign effectively for his return and by his relationship with the CPGB. Although his party membership had lapsed when he went to Gibraltar in 1948, he still considered himself to be a Communist. But he felt let down by the failure of the legal process and the advice he received from CPGB lawyers. He drifted away from the CP and joined his local Labour Party sometime in the late 1950s.

All his adult life Fava campaigned for self-determination for Gibraltar's people, free from British colonialism and Franco's dictatorship. To this end he wrote the occasional article for the British left-wing weekly *Tribune* and gave an interview to the Gibraltarian progressive journal *Vox*.[42] In *Tribune*,

[41] *Daily Worker*, 4 Oct. 1948. See also 10 Oct. 1948 Parliamentary proceedings; correspondence between Lord Listowel (Colonial Office Minister) and Willie Gallacher (Communist Party Member of Parliament), MRC, TUC, Correspondence file, MS 9329/1.

[42] *Vox*, 14 Aug. 1964.

Fava wrote: 'Above all the Gibraltarians must come forward with a clear anti-colonialist policy including the demand for immediate independence'.[43] His last job before retirement was as a senior administrative officer for the AEU working under Jim Conway, the fiercely anti-Communist General Secretary.

Fava left a rich legacy and his memory has sustained generations of Gibraltarian trade unionists and civil rights activists in their struggle for social, political and economic advance. Thus, on the fiftieth anniversary of Fava's deportation, the Unite union branch, the dependency's major union organisation, published a pamphlet entitled *The Shameful Deportation of a Trade Union Leader: The Story of Albert Fava*, which was launched at a packed public meeting and widely reported by both the written and broadcasting press.[44] This legacy is encapsulated in a plaque in the entrance hall of a council housing development named after him. The plaque reads:

ALBERTO FAVA (1912–1993)
Anti-fascist and anti-colonialist.

> Fought in support of the democratically elected Government of Spain in 1936. In 1948, held the position of secretary general of the Gibraltar Confederation of Labour, the largest Gibraltar trade union at the time. Despite his British nationality the governor expelled him From Gibraltar as a subversive under the Aliens and Strangers Order. During his term as secretary general, his union proposed, for the first time in Gibraltar's history, a social insurance system, old age pension, family allowance, sickness and accident benefit, redundancy compensation, public health service, health and safety legislation, unemployment benefit, and civilian participation in the legislative process. And the self-determination group, which campaigns for Gibraltar's independence, made their first 'Gibraltar Award' to Albert Fava's relatives in recognition of his contribution to the political and economic development of Gibraltar.

As E.J. Hobsbawm recognised, colonial occupation and democratic culture cannot coexist: 'great powers … may do things that suit the champions of human rights … but this is quite incidental to their purposes, which, if they think it necessary, are today pursued with the ruthless barbarism that is the heritage of the twentieth century'.[45] Fava was the victim of such barbarism and as a result trade union organisation and activity in Gibraltar was set back by some twenty years.

[43] *Tribune*, July 1966.

[44] Jonathan Jeffries and Tom Sibley, *The Shameful Deportation of a Trade Union Leader: The Story of Albert Fava* (Gibraltar, 2008).

[45] E.J. Hobsbawm, *Globalisation, Democracy and Terrorism* (London, 2007), preface.

8

Decolonisation and 'Development Untoward'

Crisis and Conflict on Kenya's Tea Plantations, 1959–1960

Dave Hyde

Kenya's Labour Department acknowledged that 1960 'was remarkable for its unprecedented number of trade disputes'.[1] These engulfed the plantation economy and involved more strikes and strikers than the previous two decades combined. They occurred in successive strike waves that touched almost all sectors of Kenya's economy and its public services as it transitioned the decolonisation process during 1959–1965.[2] These struggles collided with preparations for African majority government and challenged the imperial variant of decolonisation that involved the handover of power to a bourgeois nationalist elite. The aim here is to examine the initial strike waves that triggered this short but critical era of struggle that has hitherto been overlooked. They were part of a pendulum of struggle between the shifting and mutually reinforcing epicentres of the Kericho Valley's tea estates and the coffee plantations of Thika and Kiambu in Central province where Limuru's tea estates also served as an articulating joint. In all cases the strike waves drew in processing factories, pockets of industry and local townships. What follows draws upon select case studies that illustrate the essential issues raised by plantation strikes in the Kericho Valley. It also attempts to bring out the interconnectedness of the strike movement that nonetheless veered between unity and fragmentation. Overall, this is part of a continuing examination of the unresolved issues about the role and influence of organised labour within Kenya's independence struggle.

[1] The National Archives (TNA), Public Record Office (PRO), CO, 544/98: Labour Department Annual Reports (LDAR), 1960. Throughout Kenya, there were 232 officially reported strikes during the year, involving 72,545 workers and incurring a loss of nearly 758,000 man-days.

[2] See table on next page for the numbers of industrial disputes and strikers involved for these years in Kenya as a whole.

Stoppages of work caused by industrial disputes in Kenya, 1951–1974

Year	No. of stoppages	No. of workers involved	No. of man-days lost
1951	57	6,610	10,708
1952	84	5,957	5,718
1953	39	3,221	2,674
1954	33	1,518	2,026
1955	35	17,852	81,870
1956	38	5,173	28,230
1957	67	21,809	23,657
1958	96	21,395	59,096
1959	67	42,214	431,973
1960	232	72, 545	757,860
1961	167	26,677	120,454
1962	285	132,433	745, 799
1963	230	54,576	235,349
1964	221	67,155	167,767
1965	200	105,602	345,855
1966	155	39,123	114,254
1967	138	29,985	109,128
1968	93	20,508	47,979
1969	124	37,641	87,516
1970	84	18,945	60,761
1971	72	17,300	162,108
1972	110	26,000	141,000
1973	72	15,834	449,053
1974	132	23,157	101,241

Sources: 1951–1965 figures compiled from Labour Department Annual Reports throughout the period; 1966–1974 Ministry of Labour statistics cited in R. Kombo, 'The Role of Unions and Employers' Organisations in Economic Development and Promotion in Kenya', East African Research Symposium, Zambia, January 1976, 47.

Decolonisation and 'development untoward'

Prior to the unplanned arrival of a rural proletariat, the urban working class appeared unexpectedly in Mombasa in the 1930s and in Nairobi in the 1940s as part of a post-war strike wave throughout colonial Africa.[3] The problem that then faced the colonial administration was how to mould an orderly and respectable working class while taming its unruly and revolutionary side, and the threat that it posed to capital accumulation and to the state.[4] For the Labour Department, the key issue was managing grievances by transforming them into negotiable issues that involved grooming moderate trade unions and steering them into an architecture of conflict resolution and wage-fixing. For those trade unions able to survive the dictatorship and repression of the Emergency, this took place under tenuous conditions of semi-legality.

The eruption of plantation struggles occurred just as the Emergency was lifted and the transition to African majority government was announced in January 1960. Arresting control mechanisms in the form of industrial relations machinery and plantation trade unions had yet to be put into place to institutionalise these conflicts. These appeared by way of a belated panic response in the heat of events, an untested course fraught with serious risks to decolonisation. The role of the international trade union bureaucracies in forming fledgling plantation unions was crucial to managing and derailing the upsurge in order to protect the bourgeois nationalist transition to a truncated independence.[5]

[3] See David Hyde, 'Plantation Struggles in Kenya: Trade Unionism on the Land, 1947–63', PhD thesis, School of Oriental and African Studies, University of London, 2000; Frederick Cooper, *On the African Waterfront: Urban Disorder and the Transformation of Work in Colonial Mombasa* (New Haven, CT, 1987); David Hyde, 'The Nairobi General Strike (1950): From Protest to Insurgency', in Andrew Burton (ed.), special issue on 'The Urban Experience in Eastern Africa *c.*1750–2000', *Azania. Journal of the British Institute in Eastern Africa*, 37 (2002). General strikes also erupted in Uganda and Nigeria (1945), Tanganyika (1947) and Zanzibar (1948) together with 'city-wide' labour actions that engulfed Dakar and Dar-es-Salaam. Other important struggles were the watershed Rand gold miner's strike (1946) and strikes by miners and railway men in the Gold Coast (1947–1948) and on the docks and plantations of Laurenco Marques (1947).

[4] Cooper, *On the African Waterfront.* See also Frederick Cooper, *Decolonization and African Society: The Labor Question in French and British Africa* (New York, 1996).

[5] The main bureaucracies involved were: The British Trades Union Congress (TUC), the American Federation of Labor–Congress of Industrial Organizations (AFL–CIO) and the International Confederation of Free Trade Unions (ICFTU). From the early 1930s, the TUC had mentored the development of British-modelled trade unions in the colonies. The TUC worked essentially as a handmaiden of the Colonial Office, often through the articulating joint of the Colonial Labour Advisory Committee. Many of those who worked as labour advisors at the Colonial Office formerly came from a trade union background.

Their mentoring of Tom Mboya, the colony's foremost labour leader, was essential to achieving these goals.[6] What united those steering Kenya to independence was the need to minimise unpredictability and to prevent a revolutionary movement from emerging. The nervousness and unease aroused by the potential force of this conflict revealed itself in the shadow puppeting of factional rivalries within and between the major African bourgeois nationalist parties, the Kenya African National Union (KANU) and the Kenya African Democratic Union (KADU).[7] Alongside the withdrawing imperial power, they were preoccupied with the continued development of the African working class: in their eyes, if it could not be averted but only postponed, then the brakes had to be applied to consolidate the basis of the elite transition.[8] This was made possible due not least to Kenya's trade union leaders who mostly looked to Tom Mboya and were thus guided to surrender union autonomy to the state.

The erstwhile focus of the social history of Kenya's Emergency (1952–1960) has mostly overlooked the development of the colony's working class or discounted its social weight and struggles in determining the outcome of Kenya's decolonisation. The dictatorship and repression of the Emergency was primarily the state's response to the emergence of an urban working class whose advanced layers had become quickly organised into a political trade union movement, the East African Trade Union Congress (EATUC), which expressed an advanced form of class awareness. Throughout its short

[6] Tom Mboya had been identified as a promising union leader from his early days as a sanitary inspector in Nakuru. He played an important part in the founding of the Kenya Local Government Workers Union (KLGWU) from the early 1950s. He became a rising star in the trade union movement and was mentored by the Labour Department, which was looking to groom moderate officials it could work with. A scholarship at Ruskin College, Oxford followed, where Mboya was taken under the wing of Marjorie Perham, a leading light in the Fabian Colonial Bureau. He later became the general secretary of the Kenya Federation of Labour (KFL).

[7] Gary Wasserman, *The Politics of Decolonization: Kenya Europeans and the Land Issue, 1960–1965* (Cambridge, 1976), chapter 4; see also Cherry Gertzel, *The Politics of Independent Kenya* (London, 1970), chapter 1.

[8] See Karl Marx, *The Class Struggles in France, 1848–50* (London, 1942); Leon Trotsky, *History of the Russian Revolution* (London, 1932); Leon Trotsky, *The Permanent Revolution* (London, 1962); Leon Trotsky, *Trade Unions in the Epoch of Imperialist Decay* (London, 1990). Marx and Trotsky advance key theoretical principles for testing and the analysis attempted here. The theory of the Permanent Revolution argues that the local bourgeoisie in countries of belated capitalist development is too weak to play an independent role in the face of the dominance of foreign capital and the development of the proletariat. It is incapable of finding any democratic solution to their internal conflicts, let alone securing lasting independence from imperialism. Only the proletariat can play an independent and consistently revolutionary role through leading all of the oppressed sections of society against both the native bourgeoisie and imperialism.

life (1945–1952), the EATUC was at the very forefront of the campaign for the early withdrawal of Britain from the East African territories and adopted a threatening posture towards the colonial state. Following Mombasa's general strike in 1947, this movement came to its highest point in the Nairobi General Strike (1950) led by the EATUC whose influence resonated far beyond the trade unions. For a while, it became the leading force within African nationalism at a time when the fortunes of the Kenya African Union (KAU), the moderate elite-based party, were seriously waning.[9]

Thereafter, the state reacted with extreme violence in its attempt to atomise the urban working-class movement and forcibly displace its remnants from Nairobi into detention or into the forests and highlands. With Operations 'Jock Scott' (21 October 1952) and 'Anvil' (24 April 1954), tens of thousands of workers were rounded up, tortured and incarcerated as the trade unions were driven into a fragile, barely legal existence.[10] It has previously been argued that Mau Mau was the form taken by the embryonic working class that quickly developed a political consciousness after the Second World War amidst Nairobi's urban cauldron.[11] The idiosyncrasies of Mau Mau were mostly to do with the disorientation and unprocessed customary baggage of those that took up the fight against British forces from the rural areas. Mau Mau took distinctive form as it resurfaced in the Aberdares and the foothills of Mount Kenya where it clothed itself in a garb that had been on the way to being discarded in the forms of oathing, ceremony and ritual, the glue that lay to hand to weld its heterogeneity together. It is in this sense that we can define Mau Mau as the expression of a movement that was rolled backwards.

However, this setback facilitated the subsequent emergence of a rural proletariat. The system of so-called rehabilitation in detention was in essence intended as a brutal reconditioning of a compliant and predictable proletariat within the colony's many concentration camps.[12] After often long spells of confinement, many detainees were released and entered the labour market and the plantation workforce in Kenya's Central Province and further afield upcountry on the tea estates of the Kericho Valley. Despite the government's efforts to pre-empt the resurgence of the labour

[9] The KAU renamed itself KANU (for Kenya African National Union) in 1960.

[10] Makhan Singh, *Kenya's Trade Unions: The Crucial Years, 1952–56* (Nairobi, 1980).

[11] See Hyde, 'The Nairobi General Strike'. There is a wide literature on Mau Mau, though amongst the best accounts are David Anderson, *Histories of the Hanged: Britain's Dirty War in Kenya and the End of Empire* (London, 2005) and David W. Throup, *Economic and Social Origins of Mau Mau* (London, 1990).

[12] Caroline Elkins, 'Detention, Rehabilitation and Destruction of Kikuyu Society', in J. Lonsdale and E.S. Atieno Odhiambo (eds), *Mau Mau and Nationhood* (Oxford, 2003).

movement, it resurfaced no less threateningly as independence approached. While energies and resources had been committed to violently breaking up the protoplasm of the urban proletariat, it was a predominantly rural proletariat that emerged as a consequence.[13] While displacing the essential contradictions of capitalism from key urban locations and pivots of the colony, they stood to resurface elsewhere, especially in the rural presence of monopoly capital such as Brooke Bond and James Finlay in the Kericho Valley.[14] This notwithstanding, there was a Herculean attempt to avoid this outcome by taking the heat out of the widespread and deep-seated rural unrest that accompanied the run-up to independence, through the establishment of land resettlement schemes.

Diverting development for decolonisation: 'proletarianisation' or 'peasantisation'?

By engineering class formation in the form of individual, family-based peasant households, it was envisaged that absolute landlessness would be delayed and urban-led proletarianisation slowed down.[15] The government's Million Acre Scheme, facilitated in the wake of the Swynnerton Plan and subsequent resettlement social engineering schemes, was essentially a strategy to restructure the rural economy around already prospering

[13] In terms of the organised working class, the Kenya Plantation and Agricultural Workers Union (KPAWU) was by far the largest. It was founded on 4 August 1963 as an amalgamation of trade unions representing sisal, coffee, tea and general agricultural workers. See Hyde, 'Plantation Struggles in Kenya', chapter 10, 'The KPAWU and the Course Towards Corporatism'.

[14] This was what welfare colonialism attempted to do, following metropolitan welfare capitalism, designed and heavily influenced by the ideology of Fabian social democracy. The protagonist wanted a capitalism without its contradictions or at least their mitigation within the boundaries of the social order. For work that approaches this issue, see Cooper's *Decolonization and African Society* and *On the African Waterfront*; Michael Cowen and Robert Shenton's 'The Origins and Course of Fabian Colonialism in Africa', *Journal of Historical Sociology*, 4 (1991) and *Doctrines of Development* (London, 1996); and Nicola Swainson's *The Development of Corporate Capitalism in Kenya, 1918–77* (London, 1980).

[15] For a seminal analysis of anticipatory and pre-emptive development as the political being of the capitalist state, see Cowen and Shenton, *Doctrines of Development*. The work here on tea plantation workers maintains that the development of a working class was an objective necessity of capitalist development and in this sense 'immanent', a key term deployed by Cowen and Shenton, see Hyde, 'The Nairobi General Strike'. The role of Kenya's colonial state and its function of 'trusteeship' under these circumstances was to control and manage the emergence of the proletariat through the dual strategy of industrial relations and 'peasantisation'. The latter took on various guises, from the Swynnerton Plan, imposed under the protective canopy of the Emergency, to the Million Acre Scheme and subsequent land resettlement programmes. This was, to borrow Cowen and Shenton's phrase, the 'intention of development' in Kenya.

Africans.[16] It combined with a mutually reinforcing attempt to fragment and individualise an emergent agricultural working class.[17] The overarching aim was to canalise landless farmers away from waged employment by tethering them down as individuals on to subsistence plots. These were established to relieve the pent-up demand for more land in order to avert the risks of peasant war and renewed insurgency.

Correlatively, plantation labourers with weakening rural ties demanded more stability and security in their widespread claim for residency rights on the estates.[18] The demand for permanent residence, which surfaced in the plantation strikes both in the Kericho Valley and in Central province, signified the struggle to resolve the tortuous pendulum of circulatory migrant labour that had hitherto sustained the colonial economy.[19] Workers were struggling to achieve the break-up of this system on their own terms. To derail this process of proletarianisation, the state attempted to engineer the growth of small-scale farmers and a landed gentry, in what Leys termed 'peasantisation'.[20] This was prompted by seething discontent and the ongoing dangers of land seizures, and was intended to pre-empt any generalised movement of workers and small-scale farmers together with the unemployed and the landless, especially in Kikuyuland, in a wider movement of resistance to land hunger, which was already widespread and had by the end of 1963 reached 'dangerous proportions'.[21]

[16] Ministry of Land Settlement, 'A Project to Settle 50,000 to 70,000 African Farmers in the Scheduled Areas', July 1962.

[17] Planners calculated that creating an indigenous gentry would consolidate the rural populace around a moderate government and stabilise the potentially disruptive rural society by giving important elements in it a vested interest in property rights and economic growth. See Wasserman, *Politics of Decolonization*, 151. See also Anne Thurston, *Smallholder Agriculture in Colonial Kenya: The Official Mind and the Swynnerton Plan* (Cambridge, 1987).

[18] J.M. Osoro, 'African Labourers in Kericho Tea Estates, 1920–1970', MA thesis, University of Nairobi, 1979.

[19] As Wasserman explained, the 'advantages of the temporary labour system were to inhibit the development of an urban proletariat, lower the costs to the administrator and employer of social services and wages, and prevent the complete disruption of the traditional social and political order'. *Politics of Decolonization*, 24.

[20] Colin Leys, 'Politics in Kenya: The Development of a Peasant Society', *British Journal of Political Science*, 1.3 (1971), 307–37. Leys was sceptical about the transition to capitalism and argued that the most striking feature of the development of the forces of production in Kenya was not proletarianisation but peasantisation. Small-scale agriculture based on family labour, far from being displaced, was expanded by the Million Acre Scheme and the other resettlement schemes that accompanied independence.

[21] Christopher Leo, *Land and Class in Kenya* (Toronto, 1984), 161. Government officials expected a land grab in the first six months after independence. The Central Land Board in its final report explained that 'an explosive situation existed and would have detonated if this demand had not been at least partly satisfied' (report quoted by Wasserman in *Politics of*

This was especially marked by a new Mau Mau resurgence in the form of the Land and Freedom Army. Throughout this period, the various governments charged with navigating the process of decolonisation were engaged with defusing rural unrest, especially amongst the Kikuyu peasantry, which had previously fuelled Mau Mau. Ultimately, peasantisation, given the poor quality and insufficient land on the high-density settlement schemes, was a dead end for the vast majority, who were unable to progress much beyond subsistence production. For those able to find jobs during this period of high unemployment, wage labour had more potential earning power. So, while an essential contradiction of class formation was displaced, this lent more force to the inevitability of its appearance elsewhere in the form of plantation struggles.[22] This course rhymed with but did not repeat the years preceding the Emergency when large numbers of squatters with tenuous cultivation rights had been reduced to landlessness, with few alternatives but to enter the labour market and make themselves wage dependent.[23]

The land schemes were the government's major method of 'letting steam out of the boiling kettle' and Central Province was on the hottest burner.[24] Amongst the reasons for this pressure, besides population increase, were the land consolidation programmes which displaced many people (including many of the recently released 60,000 Mau Mau detainees), the economic downturn which had caused widespread unemployment, and the nearness of independence which brought on a heightened political awareness. Rural resettlement was also designed to divert migration away from Nairobi and Kenya's townships. As one high-ranking European in an agricultural agency put it, 'the masses were to be diverted from the cities to the fields'.[25] These combined to form an embedded and then a pronounced tendency subsequently investigated and designated in the context of the Kericho tea

Decolonization, 146). The economic deprivation and land hunger felt by the mass of the rural poor by the end of the colonial period dominated their expectations that they would receive or seize land freely at independence.

22 R.J.M. Swynnerton, the then Director of Agriculture, summarised this contradiction whereby 'able, energetic or rich Africans will be able to acquire more land and bad or poor farmers less, creating a landed and a landless class. This is a normal step in the evolution of a country'. Swynnerton, *A Plan to Intensify the Development of African Agriculture in Kenya* (Nairobi, 1954), 10. See also Gavin Kitching, *Class and Economic Change in Kenya: The Making of an African Petite-Bourgeoisie* (New Haven, CT, 1980).

23 Throup, *Origins of Mau Mau*, 91–119. See also Tabitha Kanogo, *Squatters and the Roots of Mau Mau* (London, 1987).

24 According to Nottidge and Goldsack, the two coauthors of the Million Acre Scheme, the Kikuyu areas in Central province were at 'boiling point' (cited in Wasserman, *Politics of Decolonization*, 145).

25 Cited in Wasserman, *Politics of Decolonization*, 146.

estates as 'rural to rural migration' by John Oyaro Oucho.[26] This strategy was intended both to dislocate and to disorientate the threat to the state, just as the Emergency had been. The principal fear at this later stage, however, was not that urban class formation and politicisation would spread far and wide into the countryside but that the agrarian problem would fuel political agitation that would engulf the cities.

The settlement programmes were thus determined by the necessity to obstruct rural–urban migration and re-route development backwards.[27] This was a litmus test for modernisation theory with its prescribed stages of national development, which, in Kenya at least, were to be turned in on themselves.[28] Management of land hunger and the agrarian problem in Kenya was driven by a concerted attempt to displace the threatening and 'untoward' contradictions that accompanied decolonisation and enable a soft landing for the neo-colony, thus stabilising the bourgeois configuration of independence. Like the colonial government's Emergency response to Mau Mau, this involved demobilising, defusing, fragmenting and disaggregating the emerging unity of the working class by deflecting and disorientating this movement back into the rural areas where it was to be managed into peasantisation. Overall, the colonial government wanted a handpicked working class, midwifed and groomed under controlled conditions by the state.

The resettlement schemes aimed to facilitate an embryonic African landed bourgeoisie and buy time for their consolidation by appeasing the land hunger of large numbers of expectant Africans, especially Kikuyu, on 'high density' schemes, which were barely able to sustain subsistence. This was calculated to fragment the protoplasm of the incipient working class by recreating small-scale farmers out of the already landless and dispossessed, or those on the verge of being so. Once again, this was in almost every respect an attempt to reel the film of development backwards. However, the land earmarked for mass resettlement avoided the plantation estates many of which were owned by foreign companies. Tea, coffee and pyrethrum estates extended to some two million acres, providing the

[26] John Oyaro Oucho, 'Rural–Rural Migration and Population Change: A Study of the Kericho Tea Estates Complex in Kenya', PhD thesis, University of Nairobi, 1981 and John Oyaro Oucho, 'Rural–Rural Migration Field in Kenya: The Case of Kericho Tea Estates Complex in a Regional Setting', *Human Geography*, 66.2 (1984), 123–34.

[27] David Hyde, 'Paying for the Emergency by Displacing the Settlers: Global Coffee and Rural Restructuring in Late Colonial Kenya', *Journal of Global History*, 4.1 (2009), 81–103. This work discusses the problems incurred by the economic straitjacket of late nation-state development in neo-colonial states in the context of Kenya.

[28] Walt W. Rostow, *The Stages of Economic Growth: A Non-Communist Manifesto* (Cambridge, 1990). See also Colin Leys, *The Rise and Fall of Development Theory* (London, 1996).

country's main export wealth, were to be left alone. And so it was here that a concentrated rural working class was inadvertently given space to develop on the estates of the most concentrated and rurally sited monopoly capital.[29] Land-transfer schemes did not touch them, allowing a plantation proletariat to emerge unlike other sections of the rural economy where a socially differentiated peasantry was recreated. Let us turn to the conditions under which the former emerged.

Kenya's tea industry in brief

The total tea acreage in Kenya by 1960 stood at 30,000 acres and the yields at up to 800 lb. per acre were consistently the highest in the region. There were nonetheless considerable fluctuations in the range of yields from individual estates. While the older gardens could produce 500–600 lb. per acre, later plantings of basically Indian varieties could produce 800–900 lb. and if well managed over 1,000 lb. About 80 per cent of Kenya's tea was exported, about half of to Britain and the remainder spread among other African countries, the USA and Canada. There were 69 estates in the Kericho district returning statistics to the Labour Department, of which 60 were producing tea. The average size of these estates was about 450 acres, which was small by Indian standards.[30] However, the control of the industry was much more concentrated than these figures suggest.

Kenya's tea industry was dominated by British capital: companies with either former or present plantation interests in India and Ceylon. The most important firms were Brooke Bond, James Finlay and Company and George Williamson. However, it was Brooke Bond that became the industry's most powerful actor. Initially specialising in tea marketing rather than production, it established monopoly over tea distribution in East Africa before the Second World War. By 1945, Brooke Bond and other large foreign firms had moved to dominate the conditions of tea production in Kenya. Alongside James Finlay and Company, Brooke Bond undertook large-scale growing programmes that thrust forward on the back of the rising prices of the post-war primary commodities boom. This was assisted by low production costs and lower company taxation. By 1954, the Kenya Tea Company, part of the Brooke Bond group, and James Finlay directly controlled over a third of all tea acreage in East Africa. Along with two smaller companies, they

[29] While Leo, Wasserman, Leys, Kaplinsky and Langdon gave much attention to class formation and speculated about neo-colonial development and the potential role of the African bourgeoisie and petite-bourgeoisie, the working class was not attended to.

[30] UNL/TUC Collection/International Federation of Plantation and Agricultural Workers (IFPAW), Tea Survey No. 1 (1960), 10.

controlled the 34 largest estates in Kenya, employing 26,000 of a total work force of 30,000.[31] By 1960, Brooke Bond had over 3,000 hectares under tea and produced almost 5 million kilogrammes of made tea.

While estate tea production expanded rapidly after 1945, there was a parallel development of the African smallholder tea cultivation scheme which was given a push forward under the Swynnerton Plan (1954). Following the buyout of European settlers, the implementation of land transfer schemes to alleviate the land hunger of rural Africans after 1960 gave a further push forward to small-scale farmers, although many struggled to scratch a living on the high-density schemes often on the least suitable land. Both Brooke Bond and James Finlay became closely involved with the government, and subsequently the Kenya Tea Development Authority (KTDA), which coordinated the scheme in ensuring quality control over smallholder tea with the firms lending their expertise to growers. The tea firms insisted on higher plucking standards, enabling them to buy up smallholder tea and blend it with their own lower-quality tea.[32] For the smallholder, this involved individual farmers being responsible for their own self-exploitation although without dispossession.[33] Along this course, the plan was to avoid the formation of a rural proletariat as it was intently disaggregated into petty bourgeois individualism.

However, the plantation sector, so crucial to the export economy, evaded the government buyout of swathes of European agriculture. And so it was here that a planation proletariat was unavoidable. While the tea companies 'quality-controlled' small-scale farmers and bought up their tea for a song, the employers levelled repeated allegations against their workers of a low standard of fieldwork and 'greedy plucking' on the plantations.[34] In order to

[31] UNL/TUC Collection/ICFTU, Kenya Plantation Research Report, J.H. Gaya, Brussels, 1955, 3.

[32] Swainson, *Corporate Capitalism in Kenya*, 258.

[33] Sara Berry, *No Condition is Permanent: The Social Dynamics of Agrarian Change in Sub-Saharan Africa* (Madison, WI, 1993).

[34] 'Tea harvesting theoretically consists in plucking from the bush the unopened leaf bud from a growing shoot and the two young leaves below it. One reason for this selectivity is that the quality falls very rapidly as the leaves mature, since the polyphenols and the fermenting enzymes – the chemical associated with quality – are concentrated in the growing shoots. The other reason is that the tree must be left with sufficient foliage to continue growing. Complete defoliation would kill the tree, greedy plucking will seriously weaken it; a careful balance has to be struck between plant vitality and commercial profit. So only hand plucking has been able to command the necessary skill. Where machine plucking has been extensively employed, as in Georgia (Russia) and Japan, the product is for an undiscriminating market. In East Africa the standard of skill is so low that there is probably little difference between hand and machine plucked tea in many cases, but the cost advantage is in favour of labour so far'. Michael McWilliam, 'The East African Tea

achieve quality control, workers were instructed to pluck tea leaf more finely and avoid random picking.[35] This related to the low-waged semi-proletarian character of the workforce, which worked for only a few months at a time before returning to their family plots. Wages were notoriously low even by East African standards and for resident labourers there was an accentuated tendency among their employers to gradually withdraw marginal plots on plantations, thus undermining their subsistence and depriving them of a wage subsidy. As to the gender composition of the workforce, figures for 1956 revealed that 66 per cent were men, 10 per cent women and 24 per cent juveniles. Around 75 per cent of labourers were engaged on a thirty-day ticket system and wage rates would increase after a specified number of tickets had been completed. Wage rates were fixed by company-controlled production committees and settler-dominated district associations with the involvement of local chiefs.[36]

A 'ticket system' prevailed on the tea estates whereby workers were paid not by the month but after the completion of thirty working days, according to a daily rate. Legally, a ticket had to be completed within seven weeks but in practice many workers took longer. The employers' oft refrain was that the labour force 'comes and goes when it likes' but the system brought great benefits to the tea companies in keeping wages low, supported by the 'rural subsidy' of domestic plots. Most workers in Kericho worked six-hour days, often finishing at noon and then returning to their neighbouring villages and attending to food production on their own plots. There were obvious mutual benefits in making local people part of a pool of labour available for plantation work, especially at the most critical time of the year. However, it was also a somewhat wasteful system, with absenteeism running at between 30 per cent and 40 per cent and the number appearing for work each morning unknown in advance. Planters therefore felt obliged to sign on to their labour rolls a far greater number of workers than they actually needed. Many estate workers had established a routine in their economic lives, shifting their time between jobs that gave them cash and small-scale farms that provided food and long-term security. For many though, the dwindling reliance on their plots en route to proletarianisation became an impetus to their struggle as wage labourers for better pay and conditions.

The plantation strikes that accompanied the transition to independence began as initiatives by workers themselves already bonded together by less visible ties of association. At least in Limuru, the plantation unions

Industry, 1920–1956: A Case Study in the Development of a Plantation Industry', B.Litt. thesis, University of Oxford, 1957, 6.

[35] Swainson, *Corporate Capitalism in Kenya*, 253.

[36] UNL/TUC Collection/IFPAW, Tea Survey No. 1 (1960), 70.

were especially dominated by unrestricted Kikuyu who had been convicted of oathing and other Emergency offences and brought this very recent experience into the workplace with them. Dictatorship, repression and dispossession were embedded in the social being of the vast majority who entered plantation employment. The employers wanted their labour power because of its quality and skill in tea and coffee growing and assumed that the experience of detention and rehabilitation had taught these workers a lesson and reconditioned them into embracing their subordinate status. They could not have been more wrong.

Cumulative conflicts and the qualitative leap forward

During 1957–1959, as the colony's masses began to show visible signs of recovery from the Emergency, a rising number of strikes occurred on the tea estates around the Kericho Valley in Western Kenya.[37] These were mostly reactions to increased tasks stemming from a generalised productivity offensive in which resistance to dismissals, poor housing, tightened discipline and failure to pay wages also surfaced. A major presence in what became an escalating strike movement were tens of thousands of unrestricted Kikuyu who had been forcibly moved out of Kiambu's overcrowded reserves in Central province: 18,000 during 1957 alone. Many were transported upcountry to the Rift Valley, with the Kericho Valley's tea estates then a principal destination for those seeking employment.[38] Although a region less touched than other areas by the years of repression, as Emergency restrictions were lifted demands for higher wages became widespread – fuelled by expectations of independence in the wake of the announcement of transition to African majority government. This lit the touchpaper for a firestorm of strikes that engulfed the coffee plantation districts of Central Province, triggering a succession of strike waves that escalated in the run-up to independence on 12 December 1963, with their embers glowing well into the 1960s.

The strike at the Kenya Tea Company's Kaimugu Estate demonstrates within a single dispute the main characteristics and problems of plantation workers' struggles taking place during this period. It was here that the Tea Plantation Workers Union (TPWU) made its inaugural appearance in October 1959. From the outset, the union's officials moved to bargain down far short of workers' demands and to broker a deal that cost many their jobs. The strikers, processing factory workers and field labourers, were mostly

[37] In the coffee plantation districts of Central province, which had been at the centre of a ferocious state violence, labour actions were still relatively subliminal.

[38] Leo, *Land and Class*, 62.

Luos from Nyanza province bordering Lake Victoria. They set out their demands in 'a badly written anonymous letter' for an immediate wage rise and conversion to a monthly rate of pay, and cash in lieu of rations, demands that subsequently became widespread. After several arrests, the strikers 'thereupon formed up into a crocodile' and marched on Kericho township.[39]

The company insisted that wages in the industry were decided by the Kenya Tea Growers Association (KTGA) and that the TPWU was not recognised as a negotiating partner.[40] This preoccupied the union's officials who became party to a deal that involved the summary dismissal of factory workers who were paid up and transported home. The field labourers then returned unconditionally following intervention by the Kenya Federation of Labour (KFL) that manoeuvred a conclusion to the dispute in an effort to reassure the company, and other employers looking on, of the union's reliability.[41] This course was predictably affirmed by the Labour Department.[42] It observed that the TPWU 'was not responsible for the strike action taken by the men concerned, but on the contrary was embarrassed by it in relation to its attempts to secure recognition by the KTGA'.[43]

39 Kenya National Archives (KNA)/ABK 8/207 LD 98 Reports, 1959: Acting Labour Commissioner to the Labour Commissioner, 3 Oct. 1959.

40 KNA/ABK 8/207 LD 98 Reports, 1959, Enclosure 61.

41 From the mid-1950s, the KFL became the organising centre of the colony's trade unions. Repression-related grievances as well as demands for better wages and conditions became increasingly inseparable from nationalist politics, which transformed the KFL into a principal vehicle for the anti-colonial struggle, a role reinforced by the ban on African political parties. This trend stirred immense alarm, real and imagined, that the movement was already recovering itself and venturing into politics. This fed government anxieties that the KFL was overstepping the demarcation line laid by the Societies Ordinance (1952), prohibiting it from becoming involved in colony-wide political questions other than those connected to trade or craft issues. Fearing a resurgence of the strike movement that dominated the late 1940s, the Labour Department urged the KFL to confine itself to industrial problems, while the Registrar threatened deregistration to disable its political involvement. The federation was brought to heel after the intervention of Sir Vincent Tewson, when the TUC general secretary secured an understanding with KFL leaders on a visit to Kenya in 1956 about the limits of their political involvement, beyond which they could not go without chancing the threat of deregistration.

42 Specialist labour departments had been established in over thirty colonies by 1941 to supervise labour legislation, regulate labour conditions, limit trade union action to bargaining over wages and hours and generally to oversee the relationship between employers and workers. The most important work of these departments was to diagnose the incipient causes of unrest and then deal with them before they got out of hand and led to widespread disturbances. In Kenya, the labour department worked to nurture a compliant layer of union officials whose training was to work for accommodation during the delicate period of decolonisation.

43 KNA/ABK 8/207/ LD 98 Reports, 1959: R.A.J. Damerell/Industrial Relations Officer to Labour Commissioner, 8 Oct. 1959.

Nonetheless, even though the TPWU did not appear on the scene until near the dispute's end, the strikers embraced the union as their own, although with little comprehension of its role as a managing agent of discontent. Although this outcome was to reveal itself time and again throughout the coming period as Kenya came to independence, these were fraught and fragile resolutions in face of a persistent and increasingly conscious strike movement.

This movement soon showed itself again in the first ever recorded region-wide strike within Western Kenya.[44] Apparently, news had reached factory operatives and field labourers on the cotton estates around Kibos in Central Nyanza that 'a general strike had been arranged' in support of the railwaymen, who engaged in region-wide action in November 1959 that continued intermittently until April 1960.[45] Workers 'struck out in the belief that they were supporting a general strike' and wasted no time to add wage demands of their own. This extended to estates and farms in Central Nyanza, around Kericho and Nakuru, where labourers came out on strike simultaneously 'in the belief that a general strike had been called'.[46] Even when the rail strike had been paused, estate managers were unable to convince their workers that the railmen had gone back and that they should follow.

The Labour Department were stunned by the speed and intensity of events, and by the absence of trade union involvement. How could such a movement surface concurrently over such a wide area without any obvious organisation? What is clear is that workers initiated the strike action and then looked around for the tools to take them forward. It was along this course that they met the ready-made forms of trade unionism.[47] The upsurge

[44] Kibos was the centre of the colony's cotton growing industry and the site of the government's cotton research station.

[45] The inter-territorial East African Railway strike had an immense impact throughout the region, far surpassing all previous levels of militancy, and triggered an avalanche of strikes throughout the plantation economy. Kenya's railwaymen disseminated news, catalysed and articulated grievance, and conducted resistance along their routes. For a full account, see David Hyde, 'East African Railways and Harbours, 1945–60: From "Crisis of Accumulation" to Labour Resistance', in Sandip Hazareesingh and Harro Matt (eds), *Local Subversions of Colonial Cultures: Commodities and Anti-Commodities in Global History* (Basingstoke, 2015), 147–69. See also David Hyde, 'The East African Railway Strike, 1959–60: Labour's Challenge of Inter-Territorialism', in Gareth Curless (ed.), special issue on 'Trade Unions in the Global South', *Labor History*, 57.1 (2016), 71–91.

[46] *East African Standard*, 14 Dec. 1959. This newspaper is referred to hereafter as *EAS*.

[47] Initiated by the Labour Department, the move to form plantation unions was taken on the joint initiative of the Federation of Kenya Employers (FKE), the Rural Employers Committee (REC) and the KFL. While these employers were often at odds with each other in their scramble for labour power from the African reserves, they came together to arrest the spread of agricultural trade unionism by establishing 'unions' under their wing from

propelled the KFL into a campaign to organise plantation labourers around Nakuru district.[48] There, it attempted to tame the contagion by putting the resolution of struggles into the hands of Jesse Gachago, the federation's plantation organiser. There had been speculation during November about the KFL calling a general strike in support of the railmen but the union confederation stopped short of translating this into organised action. With this already materialising from below, Mboya and the KFL were anxious for restraint and hoped that the threat of such action would be enough to force East African Railways and Harbours to back down.

Taken as a whole, the strike became the most important precursor to the historic avalanche of plantation disputes that ran through 1960 and reverberated thereafter until the mid-1960s. This was characterised by a pendulum of labour action alternating between Thika and Kiambu in Central Province, and the Kericho Valley in Western Kenya.[49] To a significant extent, the strike action had been nourished by networks that had been formed as workers moved backwards and forwards between plot and plantation. The concreteness of such connections involving the process of molecular interpenetration of thousands of labourers undergoing proletarianisation can only be hypothesised here and advanced as a possible explanation for the cohesion of such action. What we can be sure of is that hurricanes of wild rumour could not have been responsible for such a level of synchrony. The maturity of such a strike seems to reveal that in the Kericho Valley as in the coffee- and sisal-producing districts of Central Province, there had been an irresistible crystallisation of hitherto formless labouring masses that had been synthesised by the rail strike and then took form as an organised movement.

The general tea strike presaged

Almost from the start, both the KFL and the TPWU leadership were embarrassed and overwhelmed in the face of an unexpected explosion of spontaneous energy that collided with their efforts to assemble agencies of accommodation with the employers. The drag of a conservative leadership was just able to prevent the coalescence of Kericho's plantation strikes with

the start. A decision was reached to form individual plantation unions for the tea, coffee and sisal sectors. Three organising secretaries were appointed and financed by the IFPAW, and a British TUC official, David Barrett, was seconded to assist the fledglings. The three plantation unions emerged almost simultaneously, all with identical constitutions. The KFL was closely involved from the outset and assigned Jesse Gachago, a former local government workers' union official, as its plantation organiser to shepherd them.

48 *EAS*, 14 Dec. 1959.

49 Hyde, 'Plantation Struggles in Kenya', chapter 5, 'The Qualitative Leap Forward'.

an upsurge on the coffee plantations around Thika in Central Province in the early part of 1960 that resurged in April and May as it expanded into Kiambu.[50] Nonetheless, the incipient movement in Kericho was far from invisible during this phase. Throughout the period, from January leading up to the fourteen-day general strike in September, weeders, pluckers, factory hands, even headmen and clerical grades participated in a series of concomitant strikes. As on Thika's coffee plantations, most of these centred on productivity and discipline.[51]

In early January 1960, the TPWU had notified the Labour Department of its intention 'to cause a strike' in response to the KTGA's refusal to recognise or allow its officials access to estates for recruitment. The Labour Department were anxious to impress upon the KTGA that a showdown was 'very likely' and that it 'would be wiser' to draw up an agreement with the union providing for negotiation on terms of service and procedures for handling disputes. They drew attention to the agreement concluded with the Tanganyika Tea Growers Association that had 'considerably increased' wage rates in return for a union agreement to a 33 per cent increase in tasks and a forty-five-hour week.[52] The Labour Department's concerns to manage a similar outcome in Kenya were strongly influenced by the Thika strikes and the KFL's apparent determination 'to show all plantation employers that the new plantation unions are forces to be reckoned with'. As things stood, until the employers resolved the issue of recognition the department was unable to intervene under the Trade Disputes (Arbitration and Inquiry) Ordinance to use its powers to formalise a dispute.[53]

The Provincial Commissioner in Nakuru noted 'considerable activity' by the TPWU around the Rift Valley in the months prior to the region-wide strike of September 1960.[54] This may have persuaded the KTGA, on behalf of its Kericho branch, to sign a recognition agreement with the union on 12 July providing for the establishment of joint consultation and negotiating machinery, although at the core of the agreement were strict rules of access to the Kericho estates.[55] Formal recognition was immediately followed by

[50] David Hyde, 'Undercurrents to Independence: Plantation Struggles in Kenya's Central Province, 1959–60', *Journal of Eastern African Studies*, 4.3 (2010), 467–89.

[51] Hyde, 'Qualitative Leap Forward'.

[52] KNA/VK 2/42/ TWU: Overseas Employers Federation News Letter, No. 6011 (9 June 1960), Enclosure 2a.

[53] KNA/VK 2/42/ TWU: J.I. Husband, Labour Commissioner to Senior Labour Officer, Nyanza Province in Kisumu, 14 Jan. 1960, Enclosure 11.

[54] KNA/PC/NKU/2/1/23: Intelligence Reports, 1951–1962, Quarterly Report for Kericho District, July–Sept. 1960.

[55] KNA/TPWU. Recognition Agreement between the KTGA and the TPWU on behalf of its Kericho branch, 12 July 1960. This provided for the establishment of joint consultation

negotiations on wage levels for the district where the adult wage inclusive of rations had been 2 shillings 40 cents (2/40) a day. The union demanded that the adult minimum wage be raised to 120 shillings a month, but the KTGA refused to go beyond a consolidated cash wage of 2/80 a day, an increase of about 17 per cent. Here the seeds of the September strike were sown as union officials dared not negotiate below 120 shillings since the pattern of wage demands in disputes of previous months had been considerably higher. No sooner was the ink dry on the recognition agreement than the KTGA unilaterally imposed a wage rise to 2/80 a day from 1 August.[56] To the chagrin of the union and Labour Department, the facade of union recognition and joint consultation they had worked so hard to erect now seemed in tatters. The exposure of this short-lived veil stood to hasten the developing confrontation.

While the TPWU had acceded to an agreement that gave the employers complete control over the conditions under which the union could operate, the KTGA was still far from committed to recognition, and was playing for time in assenting to an 'agreement' that was made to be broken. The Labour Department's anxiety that the Thika–Kiambu strikes would spread to other parts of Kenya, especially into the tea-growing areas, informed its advice to the employers to accede under duress to what passed as a recognition agreement. The department's objective was to anticipate and arrest further strikes that they saw as very likely given the precarious state of the plantation economy and the heightened awareness and expectation of plantation labourers with the approach of independence. However, the KTGA's action of imposing a wage settlement considerably below the hopes of estate workers now put the department's strategy at serious risk.

---

and negotiating machinery and formulated the rules of access to the estates. It agreed to recommend that union meetings, defined as a gathering of ten or more members, be allowed under strictly controlled conditions. The place and time of meetings was to be set out on a written permit to be applied for in writing from the management at least fourteen days in advance. In all events, meetings were to be restricted to one per month on each estate and be held within the hours of daylight, though outside of labour time, lessening, in the employers' mind, the potential for 'conspiracy'. Discussions over union affairs and working-class politics generally were easily aroused and most likely to occur during the course of a collection, which was always a barometer of feeling amongst the membership. To allay management apprehensions, union leaders conceded that their representatives could attend all union meetings to ensure 'that only trade union matters were discussed' and write a report 'giving a full and accurate description of the manner in which the meeting was conducted and the speeches made at the meeting'. In the transition to the nationhood under way, rival conceptions of independence were being absorbed and argued over, and labourers were reaching out for and defining their own independence in a struggle that had the potential to go well beyond the prescribed boundaries of 'trade unionism'. Both the employers and union leaders were attempting to limit this trajectory.

[56] 'Holiday Mood among Strikers', *EAS*, 14 Sept. 1960.

General strike in the Kericho Valley

Following the East African Railway strike, the tea strike of September 1960 was the largest industry-wide strike to take place in colonial Kenya. It involved 35,134 workers over 19 days and caused the loss of 348,558 man-days.[57] The strike had been building up for some time, erupting into a bitter dispute that threatened to spin out of control. It was virtually 100 per cent successful throughout Western Kenya, the Rift Valley and Limuru in Central province. The Rift Valley Provincial Commissioner later observed that the strike was 'regarded by the workers as a major victory by the union, and the prestige of the latter has been considerably enhanced as a result'. He conceded that the strike had been 'extremely successful' and that even after two weeks 'the vast majority' of workers were still out.[58] Although the employers had 'for a considerable time' refused to go to arbitration, the outcome of the dispute was eventually settled by an arbitration award.[59] While the TPWU 'firmly established' itself as a force to be reckoned with as a result of this struggle, it became embroiled in an internal conflict, torn between the powerful spontaneity of plantation labourers and the pressures for accommodation introduced by union functionaries.[60]

There was deep and widespread dissatisfaction with the imposed pay settlement of 1 August and a simultaneous confrontation shortly erupted on 13 September 1960. The TPWU announced the strike in support of a minimum wage of 120 shillings a month and the establishment of a monthly wage to replace the ticket system of payment based on a daily rate of pay for days completed.[61] Conjoined with this, estate labourers advanced a wide variety of demands, including cash instead of rations, sick pay and bonuses, housing, cultivation rights, medical facilities and the removal of abusive supervisors. Union recognition featured very highly as did the defence of those victimised for union activity. Workers also vocalised their grievances about police raids on estate labour lines, excessive hours and tasks, and allegations levelled against them of poor and insufficient work. On the eve of the strike, the union was a force to be reckoned with of 20,000 members, although almost twice this number would join the action. The strike was 'fully observed' throughout the plantation districts of Kericho, Sotik and

[57] Only the Nairobi general strike (1950) and the East African Railway strike (1959–1960) had evidenced greater colony-wide and regional impacts.

[58] KNA/PC/NKU/2/1/23: Intelligence Reports, 1951–1962, Quarterly Report for Kericho District, July–Sept. 1960.

[59] TNA, PRO, LDAR, 1960.

[60] TNA, PRO, LDAR, 1960.

[61] 'Tea Workers to Strike for Higher Wages', *EAS*, 13 Sept. 1960.

Nandi Hills, and a 'holiday atmosphere' characterised the entrance to many estates. While there were no official pickets, 'there were enough strikers to discourage any workers who might want to continue working'.

The strike in Kericho

At Brooke Bond's tea-processing factory, two miles from Kericho township, a group of Kipsigis workers, one of the region's main ethnicities, was prevented from going into work by 'about 200' Luo labourers. The crowd 'seemed happy and would occasionally break into song' and when a press photographer went to take their picture 'there were shouts of "kwenda" and "Uhuru"'.[62] From the outset, workers linked the strike and their wage demands to the looming national independence that they expected would both secure their gains and deliver new ones. Thenceforth, though, the holiday atmosphere reportedly 'evaporated in several centres' as pickets clashed with strike breakers and the police.[63]

As police confrontations with strikers intensified, the Electrical Power Operators Union (EPOU) and the KLGWU were compelled to issue a joint statement in which they gave their 'full support' to the strike, criticising the police for 'flagrant interference' with the tea strikers and recalled an early KFL conference resolution 'that police interference be a sufficient reason to generate a general strike'. The Kericho branch of the Transport and Allied Workers Union (TAWU) also weighed in, responding to a TPWU call on 21 September to join the strike with 'many' drivers subsequently staying away from work.[64] Meanwhile, the TPWU appealed to strikers to 'behave in an orderly manner', although union officials were not strong enough to achieve a return to work as a precondition for talks with the employers as insisted on by the KTGA. While the employers bemoaned 'inexperienced trade unionists', they retaliated by withdrawing rights of access to estates to union officials to visit their members.[65] The employers condemned the TPWU's wage demands as 'completely unrealistic' and accused other unions of exploiting the situation 'with a view of raising the general wage levels in the country'.[66] This was compounded by fears of sympathy strikes in other plantation industries.[67] Ephraim Oduno, TPWU general secretary, had

[62] 'Holiday Mood among Strikers'. 'Uhuru' is a Swahili term meaning freedom.

[63] 'Extra Police moved into Tea Strike District', *EAS*, 16 Sept. 1960.

[64] 'Storm Sweeps Strike Bound Tea Estate', *EAS*, 21 Sept. 1960; 'Tea Strike Tension Eases', *EAS*, 22 Sept. 1960.

[65] 'Inexperience of Tea Union Makes Strike Talks Harder', *EAS*, 19 Sept. 1960.

[66] 'Inexperience of Tea Union Makes Strike Talks Harder', *EAS*, 19 Sept. 1960.

[67] 'Arrests as Tea Strike Enters its Fifth Day', *EAS*, 17 Sept. 1928.

warned that the strike 'might last for three months and possibly continue until next March' and pledged the union would provide food for the strikers 'when the need arose'. Financial support had been requested from the International Federation of Plantation and Agricultural Workers (IFPAW) and a joint meeting of the plantation unions 'to discuss a support strike by all plantation workers' was proposed.[68]

As the employers began to buckle, there was an increase in the marked tendency by the Labour Department to underplay the extent of, and support given to, the strike. This was aided and abetted by official reports and the media, which were all eager to portray a crumbling resistance. All were gambling on hopes that the dispute would run its course as they moved to pre-empt and arrest the growing struggle. As the strike entered its second week, an additional pressure was brought to bear on the employers as nature intervened with heavy storms that struck the Kericho Valley causing 'considerable damage' around the estates, so bad that on 'some estates there will be no tea to pluck'. Elsewhere, estate dams had overflowed and drainage schemes had broken down.[69] Even as the official minds worked hard to portray a dissipating strike, the movement resurged as 770 plantation and factory workers came out at Kaimosi tea estate in Nandi district on 24 September. The strikers were drawn from all the major tribal groupings in Western Kenya and from the recently resident Kikuyu. However, on 26 September, at a critical juncture when the employers were at their weakest and most threatened, the TPWU capitulated and agreed a return to work as a precondition for arbitration.[70] This did not prevent 1,365 labourers at Kipkebe, Kapkimolwa and Moniere estates from striking again on 2 October in anger at the 'attitude' of estate managers to the union's wage claim, although the TPWU insisted that it 'was not aware' of these stoppages and that workers 'had come out on their own'.[71]

The strike in Nandi Hills

On 13 September, 'every estate' throughout Nandi Hills had reported that 'all' employees were on strike.[72] A large procession 'some hundreds strong danced and sang' along the main Nandi Hills to Lessos Road. On the majority of estates, milkers, sweepers, watchmen, pump men and

[68] 'Inexperience of Tea Union Makes Strike Talks Harder', *EAS*, 19 Sept. 1960.

[69] 'Storm Sweeps Strike Bound Tea Estate', *EAS*, 21 Sept. 1960.

[70] 'Kericho Tea Strike Ends', *EAS*, 26 Sept. 1960.

[71] KNA/ABK 8/205: L.D.98, Reports for 1960.

[72] Nandi Hills is an urban town settlement and farming hinterland that was situated during this period within Nandi provincial district.

dispensers were nowhere to be seen, defying the agreement between the KTGA and the union that essential service employees would remain on the job in the event of a dispute. Many house staff had also joined the strike. By 17 September, 'it was evident by the number of people on the roads that a large number of employees were returning to their homes', a sign that workers were preparing themselves for a long dispute in seeking succour from their extended families.[73] As the strike continued to spread beyond the tea plantations, women casual workers on the coffee berry disease experimental scheme at Savani Estate came out on 19 September, and 'were adamant' that they too would not return without a pay increase. Fearful that a year's experimental work would be lost, the agricultural officer's attempt to concede was trounced by the Labour Department who thought it a bad precedent for a government department 'to be held at ransom in such a way'.[74]

The contradictory reports arriving at the labour office reflected swift transformations in mood amongst the strikers. So that while on 20 September 'it was apparent that the life of the district was returning to a more normal tense', by the following day 'a crowd' estimated at three to four thousand had converged on the Nandi Hills football stadium for a meeting called by the union. Oduno passed on the unacknowledged concerns of the Labour Department, warning his listeners 'against intimidation and any other act constituting a breach of the peace'. He urged the assembled to stay on strike until their demands were met and promised that the union would supply food to its members and that other unions would 'probably shortly' be joining them in sympathy strikes. The assembled strikers, who had been 'very orderly', dispersed quickly 'in sombre and thoughtful mood', in marked contrast to their arrival that had featured 'marching and singing squads'. The district became 'very quiet' and estates reported the absence of erstwhile thronging crowds around their entrances. More strikers, estimated at between 50 per cent and 75 per cent, anticipating the long haul, had left or were leaving the area to stay with their families.[75] Shortly, though, a rumour was abroad that the TPWU and the employers had agreed to arbitration and some workers in Nandi Hills returned on 27 September with the Kericho branch. After visiting TPWU headquarters in Kericho, local branch secretary Silas toured the district accompanied by a labour officer to dispatch the return to work instruction although the strikers 'were very disgruntled at the news'.[76]

[73] KNA/ABK 8/205: Nandi Hills Labour Officers Report, Enclosure 103A.

[74] KNA/VK 2/42/ TPWU: H.T. Pryor, Registrar of Trade Unions to General Secretary, TPWU, 16 Sept. 1960.

[75] KNA/ABK 8/205: Nandi Hills Labour Officers Report, Enclosure 103A.

[76] Nandi Hills Labour Officers Report, Enclosure 103A.

Overall, according to Labour Department returns, 7,984 workers had participated in the action including 1,342 workers at Nandi tea estate and 1,173 workers at Chemomi estate.[77] While the district labour officer acknowledged that 'the strike was the heartfelt wish of the vast majority of employees and accounts for the 100% refusal to work', he lamented the labourers' refusal to appreciate that the strike 'was in sympathy' with the Kericho dispute and that union officials had 'made little or no attempt to enlighten them further'. This overlooked the strong indications from the start that the strikers in Nandi Hills, and in Limuru, had adopted the Kericho wage demands as their own and had thus nationalised the dispute. The Labour Department focused its frustration on the breakdown of its designated role of the union bureaucracy, grounded upon separatism and containment, on the 'appalling communications' between Nandi Hills and other centres that made the situation 'at times, difficult to handle', as other parties were often 'out of the picture'.[78] As elsewhere, the Labour Department, in order to fulfil its role, was dependent upon the willingness and effectiveness of union officials to be used as a proxies to bring the strike under control.

The strike in Limuru

In Limuru, Mr J. Fowler, Limuru branch chairman of the KTGA, had met TPWU branch secretary Francis Muniu Muchai on 13 September. He argued that 'there was no dispute in the Limuru area but only at Kericho' but failed to persuade him to call off the strike. The following day, around 2,500 workers joined their counterparts upcountry with strikes at twenty-two estates in Limuru that 'seemed to be 90% effective on all estates'.[79] Following Kericho's lead, Kiambu's labour office pressured the TPWU into ordering essential workers such as sweepers, watchmen, milkers and dressers to return the following day, a decision that was 'not entirely popular'.[80]

As a sympathy strike called by the union leadership in Kericho it was defined as a secondary action under the terms of the Trade Union Ordinance, making this a direct challenge to the law. However, Limuru branch officials insisted that the strike was called for the Kericho demands to be implemented in Limuru and that this was their strike. This was too much for the Oduno leadership, which feared it was losing control. No sooner had

[77] Nandi Hills Labour Officers Report, Enclosure 103A.

[78] Nandi Hills Labour Officers Report, Enclosure 103A.

[79] '2000 Tea Workers Strike at Limuru', *EAS*, 15 Sept. 1960.

[80] KNA/VK 1/50: Central Province Senior Labour Officer's Quarterly Report for October 1960.

Kericho branch officials called out Limuru than instructions were issued by Oduno for workers to go back the next day. The Limuru branch leadership, which also demanded a formal recognition agreement, refused to beckon to this retreat and instructed workers to stay out in opposition to the separatist plans of the employers until the KTGA accepted that any arbitration settlement on the Kericho dispute should also apply to Limuru.

The Oduno leadership had manipulated the Limuru branch to pressure the employers into brokering a deal that would be exclusive to Kericho, thus leaving the Limuru strikers out in the cold. This played directly into the hands of the employers who had worked to play off tea workers in Limuru and Kericho against each other. Francis Muchai 'refused' to carry out the instructions of the Oduno leadership that had been anxious for 'a complete resumption' of work on 27 September.[81] So Limuru stayed out when most Kericho strikers had gone back to work. It was only after the intervention of the KFL that the local branch leadership was pressured into organising a return on 30 September. This was followed by a meeting in early October between Limuru branch officials and the employers to discuss recognition, although on the condition that the branch's demand for the Kericho terms be dropped.

Arbitration

The Labour Department, mindful of the conflict flaring up again, speedily facilitated the arbitration tribunal that went into session in Kericho during 11–14 October 'to inquire into and make an award' to end the dispute.[82] The tribunal was appointed under section 5 of the Trades Disputes (Arbitration and Inquiry) Ordinance and dealt with the contractual basis of employment, working hours, wages, plucking, overtime, juvenile workers, sick leave, annual holidays and provident fund benefits. Slight concessions were made in most of these categories. The TPWU was represented by Tom Mboya, confirming a trend whereby the seasoned and wily labour leader represented fledgling unions, with inexperienced officials still cutting their teeth in the 'arts' of class collaboration.

The evidence before the tribunal revealed that currently all labourers 'in the lower tier', both in the factories and in the field, were employed either on a ticket contract or on a so-called daily-rated contract. The tribunal was confronted with changed circumstances, increasingly apparent since the mid-1950s, whereby changes in land ownership, the pressures of capitalisation on small-scale farmers and the insufficient productivity on high-density

[81] Central Province Senior Labour Officer's Quarterly Report for October, 1960.

[82] 'Tribunal Starts Tea Inquiry', *EAS*, 12 Oct. 1960.

settlement schemes were pushing more members of the extended family on to the labour market to earn 'off farm' income for extended periods. The monthly ticket system that had given workers a limited flexibility and choice of non-attendance was giving way to wage dependence. Workers were breaking from the migrant labour cycle of the past under these new conditions of increased wage dependency.[83] This was especially the case in Limuru where large numbers of Kikuyu labourers had either lost their farms or found themselves on smaller and less fertile plots following the Swynnerton Plan's draconian land consolidation carried out throughout Central Province under the repressive conditions of the Emergency.[84]

Furthermore, the implementation of contractual waged employment created a potential place for trade unions at the negotiating table. The TPWU wanted the introduction of a monthly contract to replace the ticket system for all workers, contending that 'only by such means' could the casual worker, 'who comes and goes to suit his own convenience, be eliminated'. The latter was a tiresome refrain of the employers who, while set upon maintaining a convenient reservoir of cheap and vulnerable labour supplies, were unwilling to embrace the costs of monthly contracts to create a more permanent and settled workforce.[85] The tribunal recognised that the shift from ticket to monthly contracts would help 'create a stable and contented workforce' but upheld the employers' feigned reservation that there were still many workers unprepared to give continuous service. With this in mind, the tribunal recommended that any male who had completed two years' consecutive service on the same estate should be given the option of converting to a monthly contract, whereas ineligible workers would remain as they were.

The issue of the working day, though, was 'a bit sticky'. The tribunal recommended a six-hour working day, 7 a.m. to 1 p.m., for field workers, while others would remain on eight hours. This left things as they were, since field labourers throughout the Kericho valley 'had made it a practice' to work for no more than six hours a day. This was largely determined by the specific climatic and environmental conditions of the area, characterised by torrential rains in most months and a short dry season that impacted on patterns of working and the tasks that could be carried out at various times.[86]

[83] Hyde, 'Plantation Struggles in Kenya', chapter 3, 'Production Relations at a Turning Point', 53–72.

[84] Hyde, 'Paying for the Emergency', 84. For a full account, see Thurston, *Smallholder Agriculture.*

[85] 'Ministers' Statement of Labour Policy in East Africa', *EAS*, 23 Aug. 1962.

[86] KNA/VK/2/17/Labour and Trade Unions (General): O.J. Mason/Senior Labour Officer/Central Province to John Watts/Labour Officer/Thika, 21 Oct. 1960. 'As you know torrential rain frequently starts in the Kericho area at about noon during most months of the year, and I wonder if this is not the reason why workers there are disinclined to do more than

The union doubted whether an extension of working hours accompanied by increased tasks would be acceptable to workers even if accompanied by a substantial wage rise. The employers on the other hand did not believe that a longer working day in itself, without measured tasks, would lead to increased productivity. While the tribunal reluctantly agreed to a six-hour working day for field workers, it made its award leaving it to both parties to agree to a longer working day on the basis of an increased wage with a proportionate increase in tasks.[87] Both parties agreed to the principle of equal pay for equal work with an increase in women's wages to the male equivalent subject to the sameness of task.[88]

There were evidently problems in persuading the TPWU to sign the ensuing agreement, with the KTGA and the Labour Department jointly asking Tom Mboya, then KFL General Secretary, 'to use his influence to persuade' the union to consent to a wage settlement that applied to the tea estates in Western Kenya. The union relayed that its members were 'extremely angry' at this twist to the negotiations and while the Kericho and Nandi Hills branches consented to the agreement a 'deadlock' had ensued about its application to Limuru. These problems were aggravated when TPWU national officials, who had 'been asked by the employers to intervene', nonetheless went ahead and signed the 18 October agreement without a mandate from the Limuru branch.[89] What followed was a fraught attempt by the informal triumvirate of the KTGA, the government and the

six hours work per day, and why the tea companies do not try to extract a longer working day from them'.

[87] KNA/AF I/9/Thika/Labour Officer's Monthly Report/*Hours of Work*, Oct. 1960. 'The recommendation of a six hour day for field labourers led to a marked apprehension amongst coffee growers …'. Estate employers were anticipating a potential conflict with their labourers with likely demands for a reduction of the working day. KNA/VK/2/17/Labour and Trade Unions (General): O.J. Mason/Senior Labour Officer/Central Province to John Watts/ Labour Officer/Thika, 21 Oct. 1960. Mason impressed upon Watts the need to advise coffee growers to resist such demands and emphasise the specific conditions in the Kericho valley 'if representations are made to them to reduce working hours on coffee estates in Thika District'. The fear that the demands of the tea strikers would spread to other plantation sectors was undoubtedly a consideration in the arbitration award. 'A certain amount of apprehension is felt by Coffee Growers in this district over the fact that a six hour working-day for field labourers was awarded by the recent Tea Dispute Arbitration Tribunal. It is felt that this award will have its repercussions in other plantation industries. At the present time the Coffee Board Wage Scale is officially tied up to an eight hour working day, although many estates in practice do not achieve more than six hours of work'.

[88] TNA, PRO, CO, 822/2871 'Labour Unrest in Kenya': Tea Dispute Arbitration Tribunal, convened within the terms of the Trade Disputes (Arbitration and Inquiry) Ordinance, 18 Oct. 1960.

[89] KNA/VK 2/42/ TWU: WMP Heath-Saunders/L.O. Kiambu to S.L.O. Central Province, 15 Oct. 1960.

TPWU leadership to manoeuvre the Limuru branch into signing a discrete agreement in which they would be significantly worse off, with separate and inferior pay scales, terms and conditions to their Kericho counterparts. It was an agreement calculated to split the union after tea labourers had demonstrated such a powerful and unprecedented unity. As to the future prospect of unified terms and conditions for the industry, there was to be none.

This was the source of the anger and upheaval in Limuru where workers had come out, not in support of differentiation with the other branches but in expectation of the union agreeing uniform gains for all its members. Immediately after the signing, the Limuru branch of the union resubmitted the strike's demand for a minimum wage of 120 shillings a month together with the abolition of the ticket system, effectively the Kericho terms as applied to Limuru. By 2 November, however, this challenge to the national union had dissipated as branch officials gave in under pressure and capitulated to a differential set of terms and conditions that fell far short of those now obtaining in the Kericho Valley. This effectively divided the membership and set back the cohesion of the union.

The KTGA justified the separate agreements, which were 'incorporated' and passed off as one, by the lower yields in Limuru that averaged 81.4 per cent per acre of those in Kericho. The new plucking rate in Limuru was set at 7 cents a lb, approximately 87 per cent of that in Kericho. The Limuru agreement not only set wages lower but the standard working day was to be set at eight as compared with six hours in Kericho. Taking these factors into account, the Limuru wage was in fact just 61 per cent of that in Kericho.[90] The separate agreements were rationalised by the tribunal repeating the spurious and tiresome refrain of the employers that it would 'not be easy' to establish stable and uniform conditions across the tea industry so long as a large section of its labour force preferred spasmodic employment to continuous service. It affirmed that the Kericho Valley and Limuru, because of the varying climatic and environmental conditions in which tea was grown, should be treated as separate bargaining units for wage negotiations.

To enforce the differential terms and conditions, the tribunal became preoccupied with the consultative and conciliation machinery required to uphold the imposed divisions within the industry. Sir Barclay Nihill, the chief arbitrator, rationalised that the dispute, occurring 'so soon' after the signing of the July recognition agreement in Kericho, was proof that both sides 'were inexperienced in dealing with each other'. He did not trust that

[90] KNA/VK 2/42/TWU: W.M. Heath-Saunders/L.O. Kiambu to O.J. Mason, S.L.O. C., 16 Nov. 1960.

'matters in dispute' could be dealt with directly between officers of the KTGA and the union, and that their relationships were in need of institutionalisation so as to minimise and contain the potential of conflicts to spread. Nihill wanted a 'successful partnership' of workers and employers, but under the guardianship of the neo-colonial corporate state that was emerging. He envisioned a tripartite structure of relationships whereby the Ministry of Labour would effectively become overseer, facilitator and arbiter to keep all parties within the boundaries of an imposed order.

To this end, an architecture of conciliation was proposed consisting of a lower tier of elected estate committees, above them four regional councils and at the apex a central council, with official union representatives on each tier above the estate level. Where settlement could not be reached, cases could be raised to the next tier. If these tiers failed to resolve outstanding differences, then either side could refer the case to the Standing Joint Committee for the tea industry, consisting of nominated representatives from each side. Failing all tiers of conciliation, the disagreements would be referred to the Labour Commissioner for arbitration under the Trade Disputes (Arbitration and Inquiry) Ordinance. During conciliation at any tier, both the KTGA and the union agreed to a period of fourteen days' notice of any lockout or strike action.

While this apparatus was cloaked in the appearances of neutrality and collective consultation, it was a controlled consensus whereby potential conflicts and disputes were absorbed through a process of dilution and exhaustive procedure to effect cooling-off periods. The significance of the tea tribunal was that it attempted to design and take over a role that the employers had been unable to perform for themselves. The success of its proposals was dependent on the ability of the unions to police their members into resignation and acceptance, a role imperilled by the upsurge on the plantations. These arrangements anticipated the Industrial Court, erected into place just prior to independence, which functioned to castrate the independence of the trade unions by binding them into the strait-jacket of the corporate state. Amongst its principal architects was the KFL General Secretary, soon to become Minster of Labour, Tom Mboya. These arrangements ensured decades of relative 'class peace' creating the essential stability for the consolidation of the neo-colonial state founded upon a truncated independence.

Conclusion: the making of a plantation proletariat

Just as employers were anxious to measure the variable costs of the factors of production, so labourers were also demanding a wage contract to meet the full reproduction costs of their labour power and their families residing with them, or elsewhere.[91] This meant earning an income sufficiently above the 'bachelor minimum', as defined by the Carpenter Commission (1954).[92] Hence, workers were struggling to shed their migrant skin to become a permanent workforce on the estates where they spent most of their working lives. Alongside them, the relative conditions of a seasonal pool of labourers also stood to improve. This involved the struggle to replace the ticket system with a monthly wage enabling labourers to be fully committed to wage dependency. Hence, the family wage, at least as defined by the Carpenter Commission, was a baseline departure for any bargaining between the TPWU and the employers. While removing the option of non-attendance and part-time work that defined the ticket system, this was a diminished option given that workers were less able to sustain their homesteads and rely on them as a rural subsidy.

Full-blown wage dependency, which estate labourers in Kenya were struggling to establish on their own terms, took place in a context of rural–rural migration defined by the insufficient resources and fragile capital accumulation of small-scale farmers.[93] The mass labour actions of the past had been urban affairs 'fuelled by the problems and contradictions of rural Kenya' as migrants flocked into urban spaces to find themselves flung into a struggle to find their place in the burgeoning informal economy.[94] In Kericho, though, rural migrants were mostly bound for the rural destinations of monopoly capital that had provided some outlet for the rural excess population given that the urban vents for the latter were closing off. Migrant labourers experiencing various degrees of dispossession would no doubt have opted to go back to their rural homesteads if sufficient and fertile arable land and cheap credit had been available to sustain them. Unless locally resident, labourers needed to stay working away for longer in order to save and remit their earnings, rendering the links to rural homesteads increasingly tenuous. Semi-proletarian migrant labour, with its characteristic oscillating motion, reflected the incompleteness of a process.[95] And the strikes examined here were part of a surge by labourers to achieve a permanent family wage contract to conclude this unstable phase.[96]

[91] Karl Marx, *Capital*, vol. 1 (Moscow, 1959), chapter 6, 'The Buying and Selling of Labour-Power'; chapter 7: 'The Labour-Process and the Process of Producing Surplus-Value'.

[92] Colony and Protectorate of Kenya, *Report of the Committee on African Wages* (Nairobi, 1954).

[93] Oyaro Oucho, 'Rural–Rural Migration'.

[94] Hyde, 'The Nairobi General Strike'.

[95] Sharon Stichter, *Migrant Labour in Kenya: Capitalism and African Response, 1895–1975* (Harlow, 1982).

[96] Hyde, 'Plantation Struggles in Kenya', chapter 3: 'Production Relations at the Turning Point', 53–72.

The classic pattern of rural–urban migration as evidenced in the first capitalist countries had been completed relatively early. In Kenya, solutions to the problems of the rural excess population, which were evidenced in England in the early Industrial Revolution, were found wanting. In Britain, the urban population eventually exceeded the rural population by 1850, whereas in Kenya the outflow of people of working age from Kericho's rural economy could find few outlets apart from oases of capital within the rural economy itself.[97] Small-scale farming was relatively saturated, overblown and unable to absorb this population excess whereas urban opportunities beckoned but under conditions where they had yet to materialise on the scale required. This fuelled fears within the government and the media about rising levels of unemployment during the transition to independence and was expressed in a concern to keep unemployment rates stable in order to lend political stability to the transition.[98] The expansion of the urban informal economy was a symptom of these problems that reflected the incompleteness of larger processes.

To make sense of the dynamic of what was taking place, it is important to consider Marx's theory of the relative surplus population. Capitalism's tendency to generate a relative surplus population is one of the most important points of discussion in *Capital* in relation to the dissolution of the traditional rural economy: 'As soon as capitalist production takes possession of agriculture, and in proportion to the extent that it does do so, the demand for a rural working population falls absolutely … Part of the agricultural population is therefore constantly on the point of passing over into an urban or manufacturing proletariat'.[99] That course of development in Kenya was fraught with problems. Even though there had been a significant shift from the late 1950s, there was a persistently chronic shortage of employment outlets in industry and manufacturing due to the colonial legacy of underdevelopment. To a certain extent, Kenya's labour-intensive plantation economy was able to soak up the rural excess population and alleviate some of the unemployment that surged in the years 1960 to 1965. A significant part of the rural excess population was therefore destined to make itself as a proletariat within the rural areas themselves, especially in those areas where large-scale capital had penetrated and concentrated itself. The latter's demand for low-waged labour established associated patterns of migration

[97] E.J. Hobsbawm, *Industry and Empire: An Economic History of Britain since 1750* (London, 1968).

[98] KNA/AAL/10/12: 'Work Found for 35,000 Unemployed', E.N. Mwendwa, *EAS*, 12 Dec. 1964.

[99] Karl Marx, *Capital*, vol. 1, chapter 25: 'The General Law of Capitalist Accumulation', section 4: 'Different Forms of the Relative Surplus Population'.

within Western Kenya that were defined by John Oyaro Oucho as 'rural to rural'.[100] Thus, the erosion of pre-capitalist social formations in Western Kenya occurred on the frontiers of collision where monopoly capital in the form of large-scale tea companies had entered the rural economy.[101]

The forcible incorporation of subsistence peasantries, uprooting vast numbers from their traditional tenures, picked up a pace in Europe in the second half of the nineteenth century. While there are many similarities in this regard between European states and their colonies, there are also principal differences. In Europe, the build-up of the rural excess population followed the industrialisation of agriculture and was soaked up by rural to urban migration. Even in Europe, though, industrialisation fell far short of providing enough jobs to absorb the growth of work seekers, pushing millions to migrate and secure their permanence elsewhere such as in the Americas and the white dominions. However, in the colonies this migration was mostly internal with few external outlets.[102]

During the Emergency, the relative dissolution of traditional economies and weakening ties to the land created many obstacles and physical boundaries to absorbing into wage labour those made destitute by this process. The freedom of movement by workers across district and provincial boundaries was severely constrained and mobility was thus slowed significantly by bureaucratic obstacles erected to weed out those supposedly sympathetic or active within Mau Mau, and thus to fragment and head off any colony-wide resistance to the state. Almost the entire active adult workforce, especially the Kikuyu, had at various times been in detention or severely restricted in their movements thus blocking and slowing the pace and tempo of interactions within the labour market. This labour regime was extended to other sections of the economically active population, dragging the sifting and selection processes within the labour market to unacceptable levels given the new course and orientation towards international firms and

100 Oyaro Oucho, 'Rural–Rural Migration'.

101 Swainson, *Corporate Capitalism in Kenya*, 78–92.

102 Between 1850 and 1920, the era of mass migration from Europe to the Americas and the white dominions was a time when, according to ILO economist Deepak Nayyar, 'there were no restrictions on the mobility of people across national boundaries – passports were seldom needed and immigrants were granted citizenship with ease'. Deepak Nayyar, 'Globalization and Development', in Ha-Joon Chang (ed.), *Rethinking Development Economics* (London, 2003), 70. This movement mitigated the growth of pauperism and the reserve army of labour in Europe. According to Ajit Ghose, another ILO economist, 'For several European countries, emigration was large and sustained enough to make growth rates of population and labour force insignificant or negative for years'. Ajit K. Ghose, *Jobs and Incomes in a Globalizing World* (New Delhi, 2005), 17. There were no such outlets in Kenya and other British colonies in Africa.

overseas investors to which the colonial government was intent on opening its doors.[103] This included the merchant houses and plantation companies already well established in Kenya's export economy who could tolerate no obstacle to the tempo of capital accumulation. The colonial economy had to change and the labour market unchained to create the enabling conditions for foreign capital that had precedence over all else. Inherent within these transformations was the emergence of the working class as a class actor that challenged the imperial power and the African political parties involved in the handover. These were amongst the most important issues at stake in Kenya as it decolonised and traversed the course towards independence.

[103] Alice Amsden, *International Firms and Labour in Kenya, 1945–70* (London, 1971).

9

For Socialist Revolution or National Liberation?

Anti-Colonialism and the Communist Parties of Great Britain, Australia and South Africa in the Era of Decolonisation

Evan Smith

In 1950, the discussion journal of the Communist Party of Great Britain (CPGB), *Communist Review*, published a statement by the Communist Party of India (CPI) on the changing world situation.[1] Adapted from an editorial of the Communist Information Bureau's (Cominform) *For A Lasting Peace, For A People's Democracy*, the CPI statement outlined the five factors that seemed to present new opportunities for the international Communist movement (viewed through the lens of high Stalinism), now tied up in the Cold War and the decolonisation process:

1. The Great October Socialist Revolution, the victory of Socialism in the U.S.S.R. and the Lenin–Stalin national policy which turned the former oppressed peoples into equal Socialist nations.
2. Victorious people's liberation war led by the U.S.S.R. against fascism, the defeat of German and Japanese imperialism, and the weakening of such colonial powers as Britain, France, Italy, Holland and Belgium.
3. The establishment of People's Democratic power in the countries of Central and South-Eastern Europe.
4. The resolute struggle of the democratic camp head by the U.S.S.R. against Britain and American imperialism – the main oppressors of the freedom of the colonial peoples.

The author would like to thank Jon Piccini, Lawrence Parker and Gavin Brown for their comments on previous versions of this chapter.

1 'The Situation in India', *Communist Review*, June 1950, 175–76.

5. The world-historic victory of the Chinese people over the combined forces of the reactionary Koumintang and American imperialism.[2]

Overlooking the role that the Soviets had in creating puppet governments in Eastern Europe and imposing their foreign policy in countries like Finland and Austria, the period after the Second World War looked to present the international Communist and anti-colonial movements with an 'interlude of hope' as the forces of socialism and national liberation seemed to gather pace.[3] Based on Lenin's theory of imperialism, Communists saw the collapse of the European colonial systems in Africa, Asia and the Americas as the catalyst for worldwide socialist revolution.[4] Critics, however, have argued that this was not actually the intention of the Soviet Union under Stalin, who sought to create a network of 'buffer states' to protect the USSR and foster anti-American sentiment in the decolonising countries in the carving up of spheres of influence during the Cold War.[5]

As the Party at the centre of the largest empire at the time, the CPGB became a conduit between anti-colonialists across the empire and Moscow. While a number of scholars have focused on the role of Communists in national liberation movements in the colonies, such as Malaya, India and Cyprus, this chapter will focus on how links with these movements and broader anti-colonial rhetoric was developed by the Communist Parties in the settler colonies, particularly South Africa and Australia. These Communist Parties acted as local representatives of the international Communist movement within their spheres of influence, assisting in the anti-colonial struggle in surrounding areas – the CPSA helping to organise activists in South-West Africa, Southern and Northern Rhodesia and the CPA helping organise activists in Indonesia and Malaya. These parties looked to the Soviet Union and until the Sino-Soviet split in 1959–1960, China, but were also, in some way or another, connected to the British party. From the late 1940s until the 1960s, the CPGB, alongside the CPSA and the CPA, were greatly involved in building solidarity with anti-colonial movements across the British Empire. This chapter seeks to uncover the transnational links created by these parties in the era of decolonisation and the ways in which the Communist Parties in the Dominions worked with fraternal organisations in the colonial sphere.

[2] Cominform, 'Mighty Advance of the National Liberation Movement in the Colonial and Dependent Countries', *For A Lasting Peace, For A People's Democracy*, 27 Jan. 1950.

[3] Robin Gollan, *Revolutionaries and Reformists: Communism and the Australian Labour Movement, 1920–1950* (Sydney, 1985), 143.

[4] V.I. Lenin, *Imperialism, the Highest Stage of Capitalism* (Peking, 1975).

[5] See Anne Applebaum, *Iron Curtain: The Crushing of Eastern Europe* (London, 2013), 233–37 and Odd Arne Westad, *The Global Cold War: Third World Interventions and the Making of Our Times* (Cambridge, 2007).

Two camps: the Cold War and decolonisation

In the early Cold War period, the absence of the Comintern as a directing hub for the international Communist movement meant that competing metropoles opened up for the movement, particularly within the British Commonwealth, with the Soviet Union allowing the CPGB to act as an organising hub for the Anglophone Communist movement. While Moscow was the main determinant of policy and strategy for the international Communist movement (although this was much more informal after the dissolution of the Comintern in 1943), the delegation of responsibilities to the British Party meant that Communist Parties in the colonies, ex-colonies and dominions could look to Moscow or London, sometimes with conflicting advice.

There has been a long historiographical debate about the level of 'control' that the Soviet Union had on the national Communist Parties.[6] It is certainly the case that there was a high level of pressure placed upon these parties by Moscow, with each party developing its own version of internalised Stalinism. In the colonial sphere, the changing needs of the Soviet Union's foreign policy had affected its support, and the support of the international Communist movement, for anti-colonial movements across the world.[7] But there was a revived push to support anti-colonial movements in the late 1940s and early 1950s, for both ideological and geopolitical reasons.

As the Cold War began in 1947, Britain as well as the USA was less likely to allow colonies to become independent if there was a chance of a Communist or pro-Soviet takeover, such as in Malaya or Ghana. Thus decolonisation was a haphazard and sometimes violent affair in the British Commonwealth – an attempt to procure decolonisation on British terms that led to disastrous interventions in Kenya, Aden and Cyprus.[8] At the same

[6] For example, see Andrew Thorpe, 'Comintern "Control" of the Communist Party of Great Britain, 1920–43', *English Historical Review*, 113.452 (1998), 637–62; Matthew Worley, 'Courting Disaster? The Communist International in the Third Period', in Matthew Worley (ed.), *In Search of Revolution: International Communist Parties in the Third Period* (London, 2004), 1–17; Oleksa Drachewych, 'The Communist Transnational? Transnational Studies and the History of the Comintern', *History Compass*, 17.2 (2019); John McIlroy and Alan Campbell, 'Bolshevism, Stalinism and the Comintern: A Historical Controversy Revisited', *Labor History*, 60.3 (2019), 165–92; Bryan D. Palmer, 'How Can We Write Better Histories of Communism?', *Labour/Le Travail*, 83 (2019), 199–232.

[7] Robert P. Halger, '"The Laughing Third Man in a Fight": Stalin's Use of a Wedge Strategy', *Communist and Post-Communist Studies*, 50 (2017), 16–17; Fredrik Petersson, 'Imperialism and the Communist International', *Journal of Labor and Society*, 20.1 (2017), 39.

[8] See Benjamin Grob-Fitzgibbon, *Imperial Endgame: Britain's Dirty Wars and the End of Empire* (Basingstoke, 2011), 1–3.

time, the Soviet Union, under the auspices of the short-lived Cominform, promoted the idea that the world was being divided into two camps: the fascist/imperialist camp and the anti-fascist/anti-imperialist camp. The Soviet Union was, theoretically, to support all anti-colonial struggles and, where possible, the local Communist Party was to help lead the rebellion. As the Cominform only incorporated the countries of the Eastern Bloc, plus the Communist Parties in France and Italy, the CPGB was given the task of being a liaison between Moscow and the anti-colonial movements in the Commonwealth.

The CPGB attempted to co-ordinate and promote anti-colonialism and solidarity with national liberation movements throughout the British Empire. Without the Comintern providing a direct link to the independence struggles, the CPGB became an influential leader for various anti-colonial organisations across Asia, Africa and the Middle East. These organisations 'acquired the habit of looking to London for guidance' and 'in the absence of direct links with Moscow, the CPGB remained the nearest authoritative resource'.[9] In early 1947, the CPGB hosted the Conference of the Communist Parties of the British Empire in London, with twenty-eight delegates from eleven countries attending. The conference demonstrated an optimism in the Communist Party and in the international Communist movement in the late 1940s that the present system was unstable and progressive and democratic forces were growing stronger across the globe. Rajani Palme Dutt, one of the CPGB's leading anti-colonial activists, in addressing the conference, pointed with confidence that the imperial system had been greatly weakened by the Second World War and the Soviet Union, increasing its world influence at the end of the war, was extending its leading role in the promotion of colonial liberation.[10] For Dutt, this signalled that the capitalist and imperialist system was on the verge of transformation towards a socialist and post-colonial system. At the 1947 conference, he stated:

> We meet at a moment when great changes are developing in all countries of the Empire and when the Communist Parties all over the Empire are playing an ever more leading part in the advance of their peoples. Today we approach the colonial question in a new context – in the world after the victory over fascism, with the enormous advance of liberation and democracy arising from that victory, with the rising consciousness of the colonial peoples and the weakening of the power of imperialist reaction. On all sides there is increasing recognition that the old basis of Empire

[9] John Callaghan, *Rajani Palme Dutt: A Study in British Stalinism* (London, 1993), 256.

[10] Rajani Palme Dutt, 'Political Report to the Conference of the Communist Parties of the British Empire', in CPGB, *We Speak for Freedom* (London, 1947), 8–9.

must come to an end and must be replaced by a new relationship of free peoples.[11]

Amongst the Communist Parties represented at this conference were the Communist Party of South Africa (CPSA) and the Communist Party of Australia (CPA). Despite being proscribed during the early stages of the Second World War, the CPA had, like the CPGB, emerged from the war with an increased membership, but was more militant in its outlook than the British party. This included a greater interest in the anti-colonial struggles happening on Australia's doorstep, in Malaya, Indonesia and Indo-China. The CPSA had almost been decimated by infighting during the 1930s.[12] But it was revived by the Popular Front era and the anti-fascism of the Second World War, with the CPSA one of the organisations that linked fighting fascism abroad with fighting racial oppression in South Africa. In the post-war period, the CPSA sought to capitalise on their wartime popularity and in 1946, supported a strike by African mine workers, led by the African Mine Workers' Union. The President of this union was J.B. Marks, who was a high-ranking official in both the CPSA and the African National Congress (ANC). The strike was brutally put down by the police, killing nine striking workers; several of the strike leaders and other CPSA members were put on trial for sedition; and the office of the unofficial newspaper of the CPSA, *The Guardian*, was raided.[13] The strike and the trial were used by the incoming Nationalist Party in 1948 as one of the reasons for banning the Communist Party in South Africa, which occurred in 1950. It was in this context of increased militancy amongst the CPA and the CPSA, as well as the hysteria of the early Cold War and the uncertainty of the decolonisation process, that the three Communist Parties became involved in anti-imperial and anti-colonial struggles across Africa and Asia.

[11] CPGB, *We Speak for Freedom*, 5.

[12] Irina Filatova and Apollon Davidson, *The Hidden Thread: Russia and South Africa in the Soviet Era* (Johannesburg, 2013), 102.

[13] Alan Wieder, *Ruth First and Joe Slovo in the War against Apartheid* (Auckland Park, SA, 2013), 55–56; James Zug, *The Guardian: The History of South Africa's Extraordinary Anti-Apartheid Newspaper* (East Lansing, MI, 2007), 72–73. Regarding the relationship between the CPSA and *The Guardian*, Christopher Webb has explained: 'While the newspaper was never the formal mouthpiece of the CPSA, its journalism reflected the viewpoint of the party and it was widely seen as the party's unofficial mouthpiece'. Christopher Webb, 'Fighting Talk: Ruth First's Early Journalism, 1947–1950', *Review of African Political Economy*, 42.143 (2015), 7–21.

The Malayan Emergency

The relationship between the CPA, the CPGB and Moscow was very different from that of the CPSA, which was much more reverent to the CPGB and Moscow.[14] In the era of decolonisation that started after the Second World War, the CPA increasingly looked towards Asia and the revolutionary precedent established by the Communist Party of China. As the dual processes of the Cold War and decolonisation got under way, there was a clear division of labour between Moscow and Beijing, with the Soviet Union's sphere of influence concentrating on Europe, while it was accepted that the colonial countries of Asia would follow the 'Chinese path' of national liberation and guerrilla warfare led by a vanguard party.[15] As Lin Chun has written, 'The Chinese revolution with its far-reaching global impacts was never a *mere* Chinese event'.[16]

The CPA was to provide support to the anti-colonial movements in Asia and formed particularly close links with the Communist Parties of Malaya, Indonesia and India, as well as the Chinese Party. A 1949 report on Communism in Australia compiled by the CIA noted the support that the CPA had given to Communists in Indonesia, Malaya and India, and stated:

> It is one of the strongest Communist parties of the region and has extended assistance to various independence movements ... The relationship between the Communist Parties of Australia and of Indonesia appears to be particularly close. The Malayan Communist Party was invited to send a delegate to the National Congress in 1948.[17]

The same report claimed, via 'unverified reports', that the CPA has set up an amateur radio station in Queensland to communicate with sister parties in South-East Asia, and also used 'smugglers and seamen' to communicate with the armed rebellions in Malaya and Indonesia.[18] A map of Communist

[14] Evan Smith, 'Policing Communism across the "White Man's World": The Co-ordination of Anti-Communism within the British Commonwealth in the Early Cold War', *Britain and the World*, 10.2 (2017), 170–96.

[15] David Lockwood, *The Communist Party of India and the Indian Emergency* (New Delhi, 2016), 10–11. For further information on the influence of the Chinese Communist Party in South-east Asia and the exportation of the 'Chinese path', see Boon Kheng Cheah, *Red Star Over Malaya: Resistance and Social Conflict during and after the Japanese Occupation of Malaya, 1941–1946* (Singapore, 2003); Hong Liu, *China and the Shaping of Indonesia* (Singapore, 2011).

[16] Lin Chun, 'The Lost International in the Transformation of Chinese Socialism', in Vjiay Prashad (ed.), *Communist Histories* (New Delhi, 2017), 284.

[17] CIA, *The Communist Influence in Australia*, 11 Apr. 1949, 3 (www.cia.gov/library/readingroom/docs/CIA-RDP78-01617A003400070002-5.pdf), accessed 2 Sept. 2019.

[18] CIA, *Communist Influence*, 3.

networks by the Dutch authorities also emphasised the links between the CPA and Communists in Indonesia.[19]

In his autobiography, Chin Peng, the leader of the Malayan Communist Party (MCP), claimed that CPA President L.L. Sharkey inspired the MCP to take a more militant approach in their fight against the British. According to Peng, at a meeting of the MCP's Central Committee in Singapore in 1948, Sharkey was asked how Australian Communists dealt with strike-breakers, to which Sharkey allegedly said: 'We get rid of them'.[20] Seeking to clarify whether this meant that strike-breakers were killed, Sharkey, according to Peng, said: 'But not in the cities. Only in the outlying areas. The rural areas. The mining areas'.[21] Retrospectively Peng maintained:

> at no point during his address to the Central Committee did Sharkey urge us specifically to take up arms against the British. What he said, however, was pivotal in its overall effect ... Laurence Sharkey's words has inspired us to the point that, as the meeting progressed to its final stages, there emerged total commitment among those present for a toughening of our policy line towards strikebreakers.[22]

Sharkey denied his role in inciting the MCP towards political violence and wrote in *Tribune* that all he had said in his meeting in Singapore was that 'a struggle for national independence ... was justified' and 'such a struggle would be supported by the whole of progressive mankind'.[23] He continued: 'Such questions as when they should start an armed insurrection, or whether they should start one at all and how they should carry it on, is a matter for the Malayans themselves'.[24]

Phillip Deery has shown that some anti-Communists at the time believed Sharkey had delivered instructions from Moscow, given to him in Calcutta, to the Central Committee of the MCP instructing them to begin their armed insurrection.[25] But Deery dismisses this conspiracy theory and argues

[19] 'Organisational Chart of Comintern Branches in South-East Asia', n.d., 40 Dossiermap 70-II LI, Dutch National Archives, The Hague. Thanks to Kankan Xie for this document.

[20] Chin Peng (with Ian Ford and Norma Miraflor), *Alias Chin Peng: My Side of History* (Singapore, 2003), 202–4.

[21] Peng, *My Side of History*, 204. In recent years, conservative historian Hal G.P. Colebatch has also suggested that Australian trade unionists might have killed dissenters during the Second World War, writing 'fatal accidents would have been very easy to arrange in practically every one of the trades and occupations affected'. Hal G.P. Colebatch, *Australia's Secret War* (Sydney, 2013), 286.

[22] Peng, *My Side of History*, 204–5.

[23] L.L. Sharkey, 'No "Orders" for Malayan Uprising', *Tribune*, 14 Aug. 1948, 1.

[24] Sharkey, 'No "Orders"'.

[25] Phillip Deery, 'Malaya, 1948: Britain's Asian Cold War?', *Journal of Cold War Studies*, 9.1 (2007), 34–35.

that, at most, 'Sharkey gave advice, clarification, and his imprimatur but left the question of a Malayan uprising to local decision'.[26] It is unlikely that Sharkey passed along orders to the MCP, but the episode does demonstrate the close ties between Australian and Malayan Communists during this period.

The British party also played a significant role in campaigning against British imperialism in Malaya. In April 1952, the *Daily Worker* ran a story on the decapitation of two Malayan 'bandits' by British soldiers, which caused widespread controversy for the Tory government and highlighted to many the brutal nature of the British counter-insurgency. This led to questions in parliament, with Labour MP Stan Awbery declaring that 'nearly all' Labour MPs 'desire[d] to see Malaya achieve nationhood as quickly as possible', as well as criticism of the Colonial Secretary Oliver Lyttelton for the Conservative government's continued fighting against the insurgents.[27] Several months later, the *Daily Worker*, using material first publicised in the Eastern Bloc press, highlighted similar atrocities perpetrated by the British in Kenya against the Mau Mau rebellion.[28]

Alongside its coverage in the *Daily Worker*, other publications by the CPGB also featured regular material on the Malayan Emergency. Lim Hong Bee, a representative of the Malayan Democratic Union (MDU) in Britain, contributed a number of articles to the CPGB weekly journal *World News* and to *Labour Monthly*.[29] Both Hong and his sister Gladys eventually joined the Movement for Colonial Freedom (MCF), which became the Communist Party's preferred vehicle for anti-colonial campaigning from the mid-1950s onwards.

The rift between the CPGB and the CPA

On the eve of the Malayan Emergency in mid-1948, the CPA's leadership used the situation in Malaya to attack the CPGB for its reformist tendencies. The CPA saw the CPGB's support for Labour as 'Browderist' and substituting the struggle for socialism with the acceptance of bourgeois democracy, even though the CPA had supported the Popular Front era during the late 1930s and throughout most of the Second World War.[30] The CPA believed

[26] Deery, 'Malaya, 1948', 49.

[27] Hansard, House of Commons, vol. 500, col. 388 (7 May 1952).

[28] Lawrence James, *Empires in the Sun: The Struggle for the Mastery of Africa* (London, 2016), 263.

[29] The MDU was a broad front organisation involving the MCP.

[30] 'Browderism' was coined after CPUSA leader Earl Browder, who argued during the Popular Front era of the Second World War that the Communist Party no longer needed to exist as a vanguard party, as it had been established in the 1920s, as capitalism and socialism

that the CPGB had lost its way. In particular, the Australian Communist Party accused the British Communist Party of reformism, 'of Browderism' and of not fully committing to the struggle against colonialism.[31] This began in 1947 with Sharkey's heavy criticisms in the newspaper *Tribune* of the new pamphlet by CPGB General Secretary Harry Pollitt, *Looking Ahead*, for 'mislead[ing] the British working-class' and evading the logic of Marxism–Leninism.[32]

Part of the CPA's critique of the CPGB was that, as the British party supported the Labour government under Clement Attlee, they were unwilling fully to support anti-colonial rebellions in the British Commonwealth as this would upset any prospective 'Labour–Communist' alliance. With its enthusiasm for the Malayan Communist Party, the CPA could highlight the contrast between its agenda and the 'reformism' of the CPGB and also depict itself as a supporter of the emerging anti-colonial movements in Asia.

A letter from the Central Committee of the CPGB to Sharkey in July 1948 accused him of 'uncomradely and un-Communist' behaviour for using the theoretical journal of the Malayan Communist Party to attack the CPGB.[33] The CPGB described Sharkey's article, entitled 'The International

could live in 'peaceful coexistence'. Communists were encouraged to work with the Democratic Party in elections and act as a pressure group rather than a separate political organisation. In 1945, French Communist Jacques Duclos, on prompting from Moscow, denounced Browder, leading to a shift in the CPUSA and across the international Communist movement against 'Browderism'. See Edward P. Johanningsmeier, *Forging American Communism: The Life of William Z. Foster* (Princeton, NJ, 1994), 293–313; James G. Ryan, '"Communism is Twentieth-Century Americanism": The Communist Party's Americanization Campaign', in J.B. Bennington, Zenia Sacks Da Silva and Michael D'Innocenzo (eds), *The 1930s: The Reality and the Promise* (Newcastle upon Tyne, 2016), 111–21; Socialist Labor Party, *Workers of the World Unite: Declaration on the Dissolution of the Communist International* (New York, 1943), 25–26; Jacques Duclos, 'On the Dissolution of the Communist Party of the United States', April 1945 (www.marxists.org/history/usa/parties/cpusa/1945/04/0400-duclos-ondissolution.pdf), accessed 22 Oct. 2017.

31 See 'Exchange of Letters between the Australian and the British Communist Parties', *World News and Views*, 31 July 1948, 332–39.

32 L.L. Sharkey, 'Critical Comment on Harry Pollitt's Book', *Tribune*, 25 Oct. 1947, 7. This opposition to 'British Browderism' was not just limited to the Australian Communist Party, with a vocal minority inside the CPGB also opposing the British party's direction in the Party press, mainly around the concept of the 'people's government' and the Party's relationship with Labour, as well as its 'nationalist' turn. Neil Redfern, 'Winning the Peace: British Communists, the Soviet Union and the General Election of 1945', *Contemporary British History*, 16.1 (2002), 29–50; Lawrence Parker, *The Kick Inside: Revolutionary Opposition in the CPGB, 1945–1991* (London, 2012), 32–43.

33 Letter from CPGB to L.L. Sharkey, 16 July 1948, CP/CENT/INT/34/02, CPGB Archive, Labour History Archive and Study Centre (LHASC), Manchester.

Situation and Opportunism', as 'an entirely false presentation of the policy of our Party' and pronounced: 'Such methods as you have seen fit to adopt have nothing in common with international practice among Communist Parties and between Communist Party leaders'.[34]

This is somewhat ironic given the divisions within the international Communist movement since the late 1920s, often driven by competing notions of loyalty to the movement and the Soviet Union. In another exchange of letters between the two parties, published in the CPGB's *World News and Views*, Sharkey further criticised the British party over its anti-colonial work, accusing it of 'insufficient struggle on behalf of the independence of the colonies; and worse still, the example of the British comrades which led to opportunism and confusion in a number of the colonial Communist Parties'.[35] Although Sharkey did not elaborate on this accusation, it is true that some national liberation movements and Communist Parties in the colonial sphere, such as those in India, believed that the resolve of the CPGB on anti-colonial issues had waned in the 1940s, with some scholars, such as Neil Redfern, arguing that the CPGB had abandoned such issues altogether.[36] The CPGB believed that the Australian party was possibly 'pro-Tito', and thus willing to criticise the British party, because Sharkey had spent time in Calcutta with a Yugoslav delegate in 1948 as the only two non-Asian Communist representatives at the congress of the Communist Party of India.[37]

However the CPGB maintained that anti-colonial politics was central to its programme and that 'as the Party in the ruling centre of the Empire', it held 'the greatest responsibility ... to combat the vicious and harmful policies of imperialism'.[38] And despite these fractures the CPA still sent delegates to the CPGB's Communist Parties of the British Empire conferences in 1947, 1954 and 1958, while several leading CPGB members, such as Harry Pollitt and Willie Gallacher, toured Australia in the 1950s.

[34] Letter from CPGB to L.L. Sharkey, 16 July 1948.

[35] 'Exchange of Letters between the Australian and the British Communist Parties', 334. In further private correspondence between Sharkey and Pollitt, the Australian Communist leader wrote: 'you have an incorrect understanding of the present day maneuvers of British imperialism in relation to the colonial revolutions'. Copy of letter from L.L. Sharkey to Harry Pollitt, 22 Oct. 1948, CP/CENT/INT/34/02, LHASC.

[36] Evan Smith, 'National Liberation for Whom? The Postcolonial Question, the Communist Party of Great Britain, and the Party's African and Caribbean Membership', *International Review of Social History*, 61.2 (2016), 289. See also Neil Redfern, *Class or Nation: Communists, Imperialism and Two World Wars* (London, 2005).

[37] Letter from Brian Pearce to CPGB Executive Committee, 7 Aug. 1948, CP/CENT/INT/34/02, LHASC.

[38] Dutt, 'Political Report', 24.

The CPGB as the co-ordinating centre of anti-colonialism

At the practical level, the British Party was heavily involved in anti-colonial activism in the Caribbean, West Africa, Southern/Eastern Africa and South Asia, linking with national liberation and Communist movements in these regions. For example, in 1952, the newly reformed South African Communist Party requested discussion for the 'establishment of contacts and rendering of support' from the Soviet Union through the CPGB and the Soviet Embassy in London.[39] Tom Lodge has noted that the South African exiles in London formed a special branch of the CPGB, with a number of members retaining dual membership of the British and South African parties.[40] A London branch of SACP was eventually formed.[41]

In the Caribbean, strong links were formed with the Guyanan People's Progressive Party (PPP), and when there was a coup in 1953 against the PPP several of its leading members came to London.[42] These PPP exiles made connections with the CPGB but also with other Caribbean people who fled to the USA and had joined the CPUSA,[43] such as Frank Bailey, Ranji Chandrisingh, Cleston Taylor and, most famously, Claudia Jones. Jones was a West Indian-American member of the CPUSA, who had been expelled from the USA to Britain in 1955 and had several confrontations with the British Party leadership, particularly over whether the concerns of the CPGB's black membership were taken seriously by the Party leadership.[44] For the rest of the Caribbean, the Communist Party primarily supported the work of the Caribbean Labour Congress (CLC), which pushed for a West Indian Federation and Dominion status in the British Commonwealth,[45] a broad left position rather than an explicitly Communist one – a general position evidenced by the CPGB's alignment with the agenda of Labour MP Fenner Brockway's Movement for Colonial Freedom. Many of the CPGB's West Indian members also joined the London Branch of the CLC,

[39] Vladimir Shubin, *ANC: A View from Moscow* (Bellville, 1999), 34–35.

[40] Tom Lodge, 'Secret Party: South African Communists between 1950 and 1960', *South African Historical Journal*, 67.4 (2015), 443.

[41] Lodge, 'Secret Party', 443.

[42] Kevin Morgan, Gidon Cohen and Andrew Flinn, *Communists and British Society, 1920–1991* (London, 2007), 203–4.

[43] Morgen, Cohen and Flinn, *Communists*, 203–4.

[44] See Marika Sherwood, *Claudia Jones: A Life in Exile* (London, 1999); Bill Schwarz, 'Claudia Jones and the *West Indian Gazette*: Reflections on the Emergence of Post-Colonial Britain', *Twentieth Century British History*, 14.3 (2003), 264–85; Carole Boyce Davies, *Left of Karl Marx: The Political Life of Black Communist Claudia Jones* (Durham, NC, 2008), 167–89.

[45] 'Caribbean Federation: Draft Statement', Jan. 1956, 7, Billy Strachan Papers, Institute of Commonwealth Studies, London, ICS 158/14/1.

with Billy Strachan serving as secretary for both the CPGB's West Indian Committee and the CLC's London Branch, as well as Ranji Chandisingh, who was a CPGB member and President of the branch.[46]

In the West African region, the CPGB was also important for training potential Communist movement leaders in a region where no Communist Parties previously existed. As Hakim Adi has shown, the Communist Party's International Department worked closely with members of the West African Students Union in London and started to build a cadre of West Africans, primarily Nigerians, who were supposed to take their Marxist teachings back to their homelands to help build national liberation movements there.[47] However, Adi shows that despite fostering these links 'British members took little interest in West African affairs, and West Africans little interest in British political life'.[48] Even as the process of decolonisation got under way and the Party promoted greater anti-colonial awareness in its publications, in the 1950s and 1960s, much of its activism in this area was limited to its International Department, with many rank-and-file CPGB members inattentive to issues surrounding anti-colonialism.[49] Douglas Jordan has identified a similar contradiction in the CPA. Although the majority of the Party were internationalist in their outlook and stressed the need for unity between workers of different races and ethnicities, the Party was also not immune from the prejudices that were harboured by the wider Australian working class.[50] This meant that the 'importance that the leadership of the Party placed on the issue of combating working class racism' did not filter down to the rank-and-file membership.[51] This was demonstrated by the CPA's 'long and conflicted' approach to migrant workers and their equivocal campaign against the 'White Australia Policy' between the 1920s and 1960s.[52]

While most of the West Africans that came into contact with the CPGB were from Nigeria, Kwame Nkrumah, Prime Minister of independent Ghana (formerly the Gold Coast), was also in close contact with the

[46] Letterhead of the CLC London Branch, n.d., Billy Strachan Papers, ICS 158/28/1.

[47] Hakim Adi, 'West Africans and the Communist Party in the 1950s', in Geoff Andrews, Nina Fishman and Kevin Morgan (eds), *Opening the Books: Essays on the Social and Cultural History of British Communism* (London, 1995), 175–94.

[48] Andrews, Fishman and Morgan, *Opening the Books*, 191.

[49] Evan Smith, *British Communism and the Politics of Race* (Leiden, 2018), 3.

[50] Douglas Jordan, *Conflict in the Unions: The Communist Party of Australia, Politics and the Trade Union Movement, 1945–1960* (Ultimo, NSW, 2013), 160–62.

[51] Jordan, *Conflict in the Unions*, 167.

[52] Jon Piccini and Evan Smith, '"The 'White Australia' Policy Must Go": The Communist Party of Australia and Immigration Restriction', in Jon Piccini, Evan Smith and Matthew Worley (eds), *The Far Left in Australian since 1945* (London, 2018), 77–96.

Party. Occasionally meeting with anti-Stalinists C.L.R. James and George Padmore in the late 1940s during his stays in London, he remained in contact with some Party members, such as Emile Burns, once in power.[53] In East Africa, the Party made significant links with the liberation movement in Kenya and the Kenya African Union, showing a strong interest in land reform and highlighting the terror undertaken by the British in the name of counter-insurgency during the 1950s.[54] From these networks of solidarity formed between the CPGB and national liberation movements across the Empire/Commonwealth, it is important to highlight that the International Department, in many cases, tried not to segregate activists from different regions from cross-collaborating but attempted to emphasise a sense of internationalism amongst those it came into contact with. An example of this was a statement of solidarity from the CLC's London Branch, signed by Billy Strachan, that declared:

> When we West Indians raise our voices in defence of the KENYA Africans, we are only defending a common front that faces the supreme enemy, IMPERIALISM. The people of KENYA need our support and every single action against the open aggressors is another nail in the coffin of a corrupt decadent system that is dying, and the death-throes are dangerous … The British workers will only save their country, IF they UNITE with the colonial liberation movements, and DEMAND independence for KENYA, all British colonies & the WEST INDIES.[55]

Practically, the MCF became the focus of the Party's anti-colonial efforts in the 1960s because of the Movement's strong influence in the British labour movement. Despite the different intellectual origins of the CPGB's Marxist–Leninist and the MCF's liberal anti-colonialism, in practical terms, there was little divergence between the aims of the MCF and the CPGB. The objects of the MCF, as defined in the MCF Constitution that was published in April 1961, were:

(a) The right of all peoples to full independence (including self-determination and freedom from external political, economic and military domination).

(b) The principle of international mutual aid by the extension to under-developed territories of economic aid free from exploitation or external ownership, technical assistance in the economic, social and

[53] Marika Sherwood, 'Kwame Nkrumah; The London Years, 1945–47', in David Killingray (ed.), *Africans in Britain* (London, 2012), 164–94.

[54] John Callaghan, *Cold War, Crisis and Conflict: The CPGB 1951–68* (London, 2003), 135.

[55] Billy Strachan, 'Statement on Current Events in Kenya, 1952', 27 Oct. 1952, 4, Billy Strachan Papers, ICS 158/28/1.

political fields, and assistance in the development of trade unions and co-operative organisations.

(c) The application of the Four Freedoms and the Declaration of Human Rights to all peoples, including Freedom from Contempt by the abolition of the Colour Bar.

(d) The substitution of internationalism for imperialism in all political and economic relations.[56]

These objects were very similar to the demands of the CPGB made at the Party's 27th National Congress, also held in April 1961:

1. Immediate political independence for all the remaining colonies.
2. The withdrawal of military occupying forces and the cancellation of military treaties or strategic rights.
3. The release of all national and trade union leaders imprisoned in British-dominated territories.
4. The restoration of economic assets now held by overseas monopolies.
5. Genuine economic aid to the colonies and the newly independent states.[57]

The statements by the MCF and the CPGB seem very similar, with both organisations stressing the right to political and economic self-determination by the colonies. The long-term socialistic aspects of the Communist Party's anti-colonial programme seemed to be limited, with emphasis placed upon the immediate measures of decolonisation. The Communist Party asserted that there was general consensus, 'at least on all the immediate issues', between the CPGB, the left of the Labour Party and many trade union organisations on the issue of colonial freedom, meaning that there was 'an agreed programme on which wide sections [could] co-operate'.[58] This consensus on the immediate issues of decolonisation amongst sections of the labour movement was at the basis of the MCF, indicating a possible dilution of anti-colonial rhetoric in the post-war period, promoting national liberation rather than socialist revolution.[59] As Stephen Howe observed, there was little

[56] Movement for Colonial Freedom, *Objects and Constitution* (London, 1961), CP/IND/KAY/01/01, LHASC.

[57] CPGB, *27th Communist Party Congress Report* (London, 1961), 46.

[58] Kay Beauchamp, 'The Common Struggle of the British and Colonial Peoples', *Marxism Today*, Mar. 1960, 77.

[59] In some ways, this was similar to the 'two-stage' revolution outlined by the South African Communist Party and the African National Congress, with the support of the Soviet Union, in the 1960s. Thomas Stanley Kolasa, *The South African Communist Party: Adapting to Thrive in a Post-Communist Age* (Jefferson, NC, 2016), 8.

practical difference between the anti-colonial positions of the CPGB and of the Labour Party or the trade unions in the 1950s and 1960s.[60] One possible exception was the support for the Anti-Apartheid Movement, which was much more robust amongst the CPGB than the trade unions.[61]

The emergence of Apartheid and the CPSA in exile

During the interwar period, the fortunes of the CPSA waxed and waned as the Party navigated the problems of class and race in the settler colony, particularly concerning the 'native' question. The Comintern had long encouraged the CPSA to undertake activist work in neighbouring countries, particularly the other British colonies in southern and eastern Africa. In 1923, the Comintern directed the CPSA to 'reach the Negroes of southern Africa', including 'Mozambique, German East and British West Africa, and Rhodesia'; the directive said: '[o]ur delegates informed us that you would be able to penetrate these parts and possibly obtain representatives of the natives to attend the [International Negro] conference'.[62]

Throughout the 1920s and 1930s, the CPSA wrestled with the directives of the Comintern, primarily regarding the implementation of the 'native republic' thesis, which saw the Communist Party call for independent black republics within southern Africa, co-existing alongside European communities. Occurring at the same time as the international Communist movement underwent the process of 'Bolshevisation' and the shift in the Comintern's line to 'Class Against Class', the CPSA's membership fractured between 1928 and 1935. Once the Popular Front period began, the CPSA was seen as less militant and much more willing to accommodate British imperialism and Afrikaner settler colonialism in the region. In late 1938, or early 1939, Wallie Kalk, a leading figure in the CPSA in the late 1930s, criticised the Party for its 'neglect in developing the National Liberation struggle' and 'failure to carry out anti-fascist propaganda amongst the native and coloured masses', before adding:

> comrades will realise that we have not as yet succeeded in (e)ven building an effective anti-Imperialist movement amongst the Africans nor has the

[60] Stephen Howe, *Anticolonialism in British Politics: The Left and the End of Empire, 1918–1964* (Oxford, 1993), 263.

[61] Christabel Gurney, 'The 1970s: The Anti-Apartheid Movement's Difficult Decade', *Journal of Southern African Studies*, 35.2 (2009), 477.

[62] 'Letter from Provisional Secretary for Calling the Negro Conference to Executive Committee, CPSA', 23 July 1923, in Apollon Davidson, Irina Filatova, Valentin Gorodnov and Sheridan Johns (eds), *South Africa and the Communist International: A Documentary History*, vol. 1, *Socialist Pilgrims to Bolshevik Footsoldiers, 1919–1930* (London, 2003), 131.

class struggle and national struggle reached the stage that would make this slogan a rallying cry for acting and capture political power.[63]

Many have argued that the Comintern's shift to the Popular Front dampened enthusiasm for the anti-colonial struggle across the world, or indeed completely reversed the rhetoric of the early 1930s.[64] But Kalk stated otherwise, proposing:

> At no time was it the policy of the C.I. to tone down the colonial struggle, this can clearly be seen [in] the struggles of the colonial and semi-colonial peoples in China, India, Palestine and South American Republics ... To blame the C.I. for our weaknesses is going a bit too far and clearly shows the ideological trend of some comrades.[65]

In the early 1930s, the Comintern further encouraged the CPSA in distributing its material in its neighbouring countries, instructing that its journal *Umsebenzi* be sold in South West Africa, Northern and Southern Rhodesia and in the Belgian Congo.[66] Lucien van der Walt has shown that the CPSA reached small circles of skilled manual workers and white-collar professionals in South West Africa and in Southern Rhodesia in the 1930s and 1940s.[67] The author Doris Lessing was part of a covert Left Book Club that operated within the Southern Rhodesian Labour Party and also distributed to the CPSA-aligned newspaper *The Guardian* during the 1940s.[68]

This activism across borders continued in the early post-war period. In December 1947, the CPSA publication *Inkululeko* reported that the Industrial and Commercial Workers' Union in Southern Rhodesia had held its annual conference with input from the CPSA and the CPGB, including a

[63] Willie Kalk, 'Annexure 1: Minutes of a Meeting of the CPSA, held in Johannesburg, Dec. 29th 1938 to Jan. 1st, 1939', 3, Jack and Ray Simons Papers, University of Cape Town Special Collections, O13.1.

[64] Neil Redfern, 'British Communists, the British Empire and the Second World War', *International Labor and Working-Class History*, 65 (2004), 117–35.

[65] Kalk, 'Annexure 1', 3–4.

[66] 'Letter from Negro Bureau to Eastern Secretariat', 1 Mar. 1931, in Apollon Davidson, Irina Filatova, Valentin Gorodnov and Sheridan Johns (eds), *South Africa and the Communist International: A Documentary History*, vol. 2, *Bolshevik Footsoldiers to Victims of Bolshevization, 1919–1930* (London, 2003), 3.

[67] Lucien van der Walt, 'The First Globalisation and Transnational Labour Activism in Southern Africa: White Labourism, the IWW, and the ICU, 1904–1934', *African Studies*, 66.2–3 (2007), 243.

[68] Letter from Sir David Petrie to Major H.W. Clemow, 21 Oct. 1944, The National Archives (TNA), KV2/4054; Letter from Security Liaison Officer (Central Africa) to Director-General of the Security Service (London), 21 Apr. 1949, TNA, KV2/4054.

message of solidarity from General Secretary Harry Pollitt.[69] Industrial and Commercial Union (ICU) and Southern Rhodesian Labour Party activist Charles Mzingeli wrote to the same publication in May 1949 with May Day greetings, describing *Inkululeko* as 'widely read'.[70]

The victory of the Nationalist Party led by D.F. Malan in 1948 saw the installation of the apartheid regime and the banning of the CPSA under the Suppression of Communism Act in 1950. The threat of Communism to the racial hierarchy that had existed since the creation of the Union of South Africa in 1910 was felt intensely by the Nationalist Party. While the Nationalist Party had a long-running hatred of Communism, it was the appeal to the 'natives' of South Africa that led to the banning of the CPSA in 1950, as it was assumed that without this Communist agitation the 'native problem' would be much more manageable. In a parliamentary debate just prior to the Malan government's win in May 1948, one Nationalist Party MP stated that the 'communist ideal' was to extend 'the franchise for all adults, Black or White or Yellow, or whatever the colour of their skin'.[71]

Although the CPSA 'initially refused to emphasize anti-imperialism in its country', Oleksa Drachewych has written, the Communist party 'eventually played a significant role in the destruction of arguably the longest-lasting colonial regime'.[72] Throughout the 1950s, former members of the CPSA gathered around organisations such as the Springbok Legion and the journal *New Age* and continued to meet clandestinely in Johannesburg and Cape Town. Alongside the ANC, which remained a legal party until 1960, these Communists started to organise resistance to the 'fascist' apartheid regime. As the Nationalist Party cracked down on dissent in South Africa, a number of leading activists started to leave the country, first to neighbouring countries, such as Bechuanaland (after 1966, Botswana), and then to London, Moscow, East Berlin and Peking/Beijing. From the mid-1950s onwards, the CPGB lent the remnants of the CPSA, now exiled in London, practical support on the administrative side.[73] The new South African Communist

69 'S. Rhodesian ICU', *Inkululeko*, Dec. 1947, 4.

70 'Greetings from Rhodesia', *Inkululeko*, 7 May 1949, 4.

71 Union of South Africa, House of Assembly Debates, 15 Mar. 1948, col. 3249.

72 Oleksa Drachewych, *The Communist International, Anti-Imperialism and Racial Equality in British Dominions* (London, 2018), 157.

73 For example, Yusuf Dadoo was provided assistance by CPGB member Bridget Tunnard, who was also involved in the Commonwealth of India League, while Pauline Podbrey and H.A. Naidoo were assisted by CPGB representative Bob Stewart. Arianna Lissoni, 'Yusuf Dadoo, India and South Africa's Liberation Struggle', in Anna Konieczna and Rob Skinner (eds), *A Global History of Anti-Apartheid: 'Forward to Freedom' in South Africa* (Basingstoke, 2019), 212; Tal Zalmanovich, 'From Apartheid South Africa to Socialist Budapest and

Party (established in 1960) and the ANC, on the other hand, looked to Moscow (and, to a lesser extent, Peking) for military support, starting in the early to mid-1960s.[74]

1956 and the Sino-Soviet split

Between 1949 and the Sino-Soviet split in 1960, the CPA looked increasingly to the Chinese Communist Party for direction and, as Mark Aarons has written, '[t]he CPA was the first Australian political party to understand that Australia is geographically located in Asia'.[75] This was part of a wider distinction inside the international Communist movement, with David Lockwood stating that after 1949 'an informal "division of labour" within the world movement seems to have been agreed upon between the Soviet and Chinese parties in which Communists in the colonies, "semi-colonies" and ex-colonies would receive their advice from Beijing'.[76] Although Australia was a settler colonial power, rather than a colony, it seemed to make sense, geographically, for the CPA to build closer ties with China, rather than simply looking to the Kremlin and the CPGB in London, with whom ties had been loosened throughout the late 1940s, as demonstrated above.

After the denunciation of the 'crimes' of the Stalin era by Khrushchev in 1956 and the Soviet invasion of Hungary in October 1956, Communist Parties across the world went into shock, with many suffering significant membership loss and debate spilling over into the public sphere. Inside the British Communist Party, dissidents, such as E.P. Thompson, John Saville, Brian Pearce, Peter Fryer and Malcolm MacEwen (amongst others), sought channels outside the Party to denounce the actions of the Soviet Union, as well as the lack of internal debate within the Party. Trevor Carter wrote that the events of 1956 affected the CPGB's black membership, who saw themselves much more as part of the international Communist movement than specifically the *British* Communist Party.[77] Sympathy for China was prevalent amongst the CPGB's black membership and there was some criticism, from figures such as Pakistani migrant Albert Manchanda (who

---

Back: Communism, Race and Cold War Journeys', *Wiener Zeitschrift für Afrikastudien*, 34/18 (2018), 123–24.

[74] See Vladimir Shubin, *The Hot 'Cold War': The USSR in Southern Africa* (London, 2008).

[75] Mark Aarons, *The Family File* (Melbourne, 2010), 172.

[76] Lockwood, *Communist Party of India*, 10–11. For further discussion of this division of labour, see John Herouvim, 'Australian Communists and Peking: New Light on an Elusive Source', *Politics*, 20.1 (1985), 127–29.

[77] Trevor Carter, *Shattering Illusions: West Indians in British Politics* (London, 1986), 59.

was eventually expelled in 1965), for the CPGB's alleged acceptance of Khrushchevite 'revisionism'.[78] Similar discontent existed amongst the Indian Communists in the UK, with the eventual Sino-Soviet split heralding a similar split between some involved in the Indian Workers' Associations in Britain and the CPGB.[79]

Phillip Deery and Rachel Calkin have shown that similar scenes occurred in the CPA.[80] Although the leadership of both the CPGB and CPA supported the invasion of Hungary in October 1956, the backlash in these Parties fostered a much deeper debate about the role of the Soviet Union in the international Communist movement. In Britain, the Communist Party lost over 8,000 members between February 1956 and February 1958.[81] This led to the creation of the first New Left that attempted to negotiate a path between Western capitalism and Stalinism.[82] In Australia, Communist Party membership 'slumped from about 8,000 to less than 6,000', which was followed by further divisions inside the CPA over the Sino-Soviet split in the early 1960s.[83]

On the other hand, the SACP had not undergone this public bloodletting in 1956 and remained quite loyal to the Soviet Union. Unlike other Communist Parties in the West, the fact that the CPSA had disbanded and gone underground meant similar open debates that occurred in the British, French and Italian parties could not happen. In general, amongst South African progressives, the events in Hungary were seen as justified in comparison with the Anglo-French-Israeli actions in Egypt during the Suez Crisis, which happened almost concurrently with the Hungarian invasion. In the *New Age*, it was pronounced that comparison between the two interventions was a 'false analogy', stating:

[78] Tom Buchanan, *East Wind: China and the British Left, 1925–1976* (Oxford, 2012), 203.

[79] John DeWitt, *Indian Workers' Associations in Britain* (London, 1969), 66–81; Sasha Josephides, 'Organisational Splits and Political Ideology in the Indian Workers Associations', in Pnina Werbner and Muhammad Anwar (eds), *Black and Ethnic Leaderships in Britain: The Cultural Turn of Political Action* (London, 1991), 253–76.

[80] Phillip Deery and Rachel Calkin, '"We All Make Mistakes": The Communist Party of Australia and Khrushchev's Secret Speech, 1956', *Australia Journal of Politics and History*, 54.1 (2008), 69–84.

[81] Willie Thompson, *The Good Old Cause: British Communism, 1920–1991* (London, 1992), 218.

[82] Michael Kenny, *The First New Left: British Intellectuals after Stalin* (London, 1995); Wade Matthews, *The New Left, National Identity and the Break-Up of Britain* (Leiden, 2013), 1–26.

[83] Tom O'Lincoln, *Into the Mainstream: The Decline of Australian Communism* (Sydney, 1985), 98.

- The Anglo-French aggression was directed against the Egyptian government; the Soviet (gave) assistance on the invitation of the Hungarian government.
- The Anglo-French forces invaded Egypt. The Soviet forces were stationed in Hungary with the recognised responsibility of protecting Hungary's independence and preventing her return to fascism.
- Britain and France had no shred of legal right to invade; the Soviet armed forces were legally in Hungary in terms of the Warsaw pact.
- Most important of all – the issue of Egypt is between imperialism and national liberation; the issue in Hungary is between socialism and reaction ...[84]

In the editorial of *Liberation*, the ANC made a similar case for the differences between Suez and Hungary:

> we should not forget that the Soviet Union has not suddenly 'invaded' Hungary, as the British and French have invaded Egypt. Soviet troops have been in Hungary ever since the end of the second world war, and as a result of that war.[85]

From these statements, it is evident that the progressive forces in South Africa were particularly concerned about other national liberation movements in Africa and across the rest of the world in their fight against imperialism and colonialism. Experiencing a severe racialist reaction against the decolonisation process in the form of apartheid, South African progressives expressed solidarity with the Egyptian people and viewed the Anglo-French-Israeli invasion as part of a wider reaction by the global West against decolonisation. In the following years, southern Africa would be viewed by many of the left as an anomaly where the imperialist powers had not relinquished their stranglehold on these settler colonies in the face of a generally decolonised African continent. The CPGB published an article in 1964 stating: 'Imperialism sees Southern Rhodesia as the central bastion in the line of colonialist strongholds stretching across the southern part of the African continent, linking the Portuguese colonies of Angola in the west and Mozambique in the East'.[86] The SACP and the ANC would form ties with many of the other national liberation movements across Africa in the 1960s, including in the National Liberation Front in Algeria, FRELIMO in Mozambique and the Zimbabwean African People's Union.

[84] 'Victory in Egypt Not Yet Won', *New Age*, 22 Nov. 1956, 4.
[85] 'Editorial: The International Scene', *Liberation*, 22 Nov. 1956, 5.
[86] 'Salazar – Smith – Verwoerd', *Comment*, 5 Sept. 1964, 562.

On the other hand, those progressives that were part of the SACP and ANC looked to the Soviet Union, as well as the Non-Aligned Movement, which had first met the previous year in Bandung, as guiding forces in the anti-colonial struggle. The ANC called the USSR 'a great power openly and irrevocably hostile to imperialism' that had 'enabled the former colonies triumphantly to proclaim and consolidate their independence'.[87] Criticism of the Soviets would come later on, but in 1956 there was little dissent amongst what the ANC and the underground SACP expressed towards the Soviet Union, and not a particularly strong commitment to China.

Between 1956 and 1960, the Soviet Union and the People's Republic of China seemed to be heading towards a major split in the international Communist movement, divided predominantly by geopolitical interests.[88] And it was up to each individual country or Communist Party to decide where their support lay. Right up until 1960, the CPA seemed to take the side of the Chinese in the dispute, with Nick Knight claiming that during the late 1950s 'virtually the entire National Secretariat of the CPA was ideologically and psychologically in favour of the Chinese position'.[89] However, Sharkey, despite visiting China in 1959 and 1961, pulled back at the last moment and shifted its support back to Moscow when attending the 81 Communist and Workers Parties conference in Moscow in November 1961.[90] The Australian Security Intelligence Organisation (ASIO) noted that the Sino-Soviet split also had a major impact upon the CPA's relationship with the Communist Party of New Zealand (CPNZ) – the only Western Communist Party to side with China in the split.[91] While Mark Aarons suggests that Sharkey was partially swayed by some large cash payments by Moscow, Tom O'Lincoln submits that the rank-and-file membership had little appetite for the extreme rhetoric of the Chinese Communist Party at this time, while Knight argues that it was Sharkey's probable realisation that the CPA 'would become isolated from the fraternity of the international Communist parties should its support for the Chinese position continue'.[92]

87 'Editorial: The International Scene', *Liberation*, 22 Nov. 1956, 5.

88 Jeremy Friedman, *The Shadow Cold War: The Sino-Soviet Competition for the Third World* (Chapel Hill, NC, 2015).

89 Nick Knight, 'The Theory and Tactics of the Communist Party of Australia (M–L)', *Journal of Contemporary Asia*, 28.2 (1998), 236.

90 Knight, 'Theory and Tactics', 236. See also Mark Aarons, *The Family File* (Melbourne, 2010) 172–85.

91 ASIO, 'Oceania: Communism's Last Target', A 12388, 81 PART 2, NAA.

92 O'Lincoln, *Into the Mainstream*, 102; Knight, 'Theory and Tactics', 236; Aarons, *Family File*, 192.

After the realignment of the CPA towards Moscow, a pro-Chinese faction broke away and formed the Communist Party of Australia (Marxist–Leninist) in 1964, led by Ted Hill.[93] In Britain, the CPGB experienced similar breakaways from anti-revisionists. In the same year that the CPA (M–L) was formed, Michael McCreery formed the Committee to Defeat Revisionism for Communist Unity and led a small number of party members disgruntled with the 'revisionism' of *The British Road to Socialism*.[94] A larger group left in early 1968 when AEU leader Reg Birch formed the Communist Party of Britain (Marxist–Leninist).[95]

As mentioned above, the armed struggle being undertaken by the SACP and the ANC, and the military support granted by the Soviet Union, meant that flirtation with China was brief and left to other organisations, primarily the Pan-Africanist Congress.[96] Despite some military training and assistance in the early 1960s, the SACP leadership felt that the peasant-based guerrilla struggle of the Chinese could not translate to the South African situation.[97] Both the SACP and ANC started to develop international links with other national liberation movements across Europe, the Middle East, Africa and Asia, as well as with Cuba and the other Eastern European states, particularly East Germany. Soviet foreign policy with regards to these national liberation movements seemed to be creating sympathetic decolonised nations rather than formulating socialist revolution in the post-colonial sphere.

Conclusion

By the 1960s, the international Communist movement had fractured, partly because of the events of 1956, partly because of the Sino-Soviet split and partly because of the Non-Aligned Movement, which presented an alternative to both Stalinism or Maoism for the new decolonised nations across the global South. This was very different from the situation in 1945 when Communists the world over looked to the newly triumphant Soviet Union, the People's Democracies in Eastern Europe and the Chinese Communist Party on the verge of winning a decades-long civil war. As the Cold War got under way, coinciding with the era of decolonisation, Communist Parties in the

[93] Drew Cottle and Angela Keys, 'The Current of Maoism in the Australian Far Left', in Piccini, Smith and Worley (eds), *The Far Left in Australia since 1945*, 41–44.

[94] Parker, *The Kick Inside*, 45–50.

[95] Will Podmore, *Reg Birch: Engineer, Trade Unionist, Communist* (London, 2004).

[96] Ian Taylor, 'The Ambiguous Commitment: The People's Republic of China and the Anti-Apartheid Struggle in South Africa', *Journal of Contemporary African Studies*, 18.1 (2000), 91–106.

[97] Lodge, 'Secret Party', 457.

West shifted to the left and embraced this enthusiasm for socialism and anti-imperialism, including the Communist Parties in Britain, Australia and South Africa. The CPGB, although taking a more conciliatory approach to domestic politics, was charged by Moscow with assisting anti-colonial struggles within the British Empire/Commonwealth.

As well as making links with Communists and anti-colonial activists in the colonies, the British party also made connections with its sister parties in the settler colonies of Australia and South Africa, who had their own spheres of influence in Africa and South-East Asia/Oceania. The CPSA developed significant links with the CPGB, particularly after the South African party was banned in 1950 and a number of exiled party members relocated to London in the early 1960s. On the other hand, the CPA quarrelled with the CPGB over its reformism and alleged that this political shift had left the CPGB unable to assist its comrades in the colonial sphere. This tumultuous relationship was not repaired until the 1950s, when important figures such as Harry Pollitt visited Australia, and grew closer after L.L. Sharkey was replaced as Party leader in the mid-1960s.

This chapter has explored the horizontal, as well as vertical, relationships that coexisted in the international Communist movement and within the British Commonwealth in the first two decades of the Cold War. It has revealed that these relationships were complex and often overlapped but were also strained as domestic and internationalist concerns sometimes conflicted. Furthermore, these relationships, which seemed quite straightforward at the end of the Second World War, became much more fraught by the 1960s, as the international Communist movement drifted further apart. This was reflected in the relationship between the CPGB, the CPSA and the CPA.

Conclusion

Eight Points on Labour and the End of the British Empire

Neville Kirk

I wish to argue in the concluding chapter that despite their diverse and distinct characteristics and the wide range of topics they cover, the essays in this edited collection share important common assumptions, guiding principles, approaches, claims and conclusions. To be sure, these are made more explicitly in some of the essays than others. I do not, furthermore, want to artificially impose a common uniformity on the essays whether methodologically, conceptually or substantively. Yet it is important in a book that lays claim to an integrated approach to the closely related areas of empire, imperialism, labour and anti-colonialism to tease out and make explicit, where necessary, and explicate these areas of commonality and similarity, while at the same time being duly attentive to diversity and distinctness. I will also signpost, on the basis of the material presented in the essays, areas of potentially fruitful future research.

1

The first conclusion to be drawn from the essays is that they make an attempt not only to fill an important gap in, but also to make a new and useful contribution to, the historical literature on empire, imperialism, colonialism and anti-colonialism with special reference to the British experience. As observed by Yann Béliard in the Introduction to this book, this gap resides in the neglect of the labour dimension in the traditional body of work mainly concerned with the official, establishment mindset. I may add that Béliard's observation holds true not only for the British case but also, to varying degrees, for studies of imperialism and colonialism in general. The essays in this collection seek to make an original attempt to correct this imbalance and in so doing to contribute to the wider development among scholars of a more complete and balanced picture of imperial history.

In contrast to top-down and core-periphery traditionalism, the essays in this volume both introduce the reader to a bottom-up approach and attempt to integrate the top-down and bottom-up studies of metropole and/or colony into their frameworks of analysis. Relations between metropole and colony, furthermore, are seen to be based not only on the outward flow of ideas, institutions, movements and people from the core to the periphery but also on reverse flows, complex circuits and reciprocal exchanges and influences. (The same conclusion may be drawn for other imperial systems.)

In terms of these methodological considerations, the essays by Gareth Curless and Dave Hyde explore relations between, on the one hand, rural and urban workers, their labour movements and their struggles and, on the other hand, employers, local elites and anti-colonial bourgeois nationalists in respectively Sudan and Kenya during the post-Second World War era of decolonisation. Both of these authors also explore the British colonial connection, in terms of employer and state structures and influences. Curless and Hyde agree that these local and British elite forces were united in both their hostility to militant and left-wing labour movements and their desire to tame these movements, institutionalise conflict and mould local workers and their movements in the image of their moderate and 'responsible' British counterparts. In these ways the transition to independence in Sudan and Kenya would be divested of militant, left-wing associations. Bourgeois nationalism would triumph at the expense of radical class consciousness.

The operation of complex exchanges and reciprocal influences between metropole and colony, combined with the interplay between top-down and bottom-up approaches, are clearly brought out in the essays on Britain and India by Marie Terrier, Nicholas Owen and Matt Perry. Terrier and Perry explore the ways in which British Labour's Annie Besant, British-born but mainly resident in India, and British resident, the Labour Party's Ellen Wilkinson, who visited India in 1932, were both influenced by and attempted to influence elite nationalist and popular-radical movements and class-, gender-, caste- and racially based social forces and issues in India. Besant and Wilkinson sought to forge links between progressive socio-political movements and social groups in India and Britain. Owen shows how the Communist Party of Great Britain (CPGB) attempted both to influence the course of events in India and to build a base for anti-imperialism at home in interwar Britain. The CPGB made 'what was probably the most significant attempt to organise a popular anti-imperialism in interwar Britain' with India constituting 'the dominant imperial question' of the period, according to Owen. In turn, Evan Smith explores the tactics and strategies employed by the Communist Parties of Great Britain, South Africa (CPSA) and Australia (CPA) during the post-Second World War era of decolonisation towards colonial bourgeois-nationalist and popular-radical movements. Finally, Tom Sibley pays tribute to the remarkable life and career of Albert Fava. Fava, a Gibraltarian, communist and trade union activist and leader who had fought on the Republican side during the Spanish Civil War, was evacuated to Britain during the Second World War. While in Britain he was very active in trade union and communist circles, particularly in Scotland. Upon his return to Gibraltar Fava was loud in his demand for self-determination for Gibraltar's people. He played a key role in building up the Gibraltar Congress of Labour into a well-organised and progressive base not only for trade unionism but also the anti-Franco and anti-British nationalist movement. Seen as a dangerous socialist subversive, Fava met with the opposition of not only the British-appointed Colonial Governor but the Labour government in Britain, keen to demonstrate its anti-communist credentials to the USA during the early Cold War, and Britain's 'responsible' nationalist and imperialist mainstream trade union leaders. With the backing of Attlee's government, Fava was deported by the Governor to Britain in 1948. Thereafter he remained active in left-wing political and trade union movements in his enforced country of residence.

2

Second: in terms of their focus on labour, most of the essays concentrate primarily upon the anti-imperialism and anti-colonialism of minority-based left-wing activists, leaders and organisations. Terrier's essay on the more moderate, and in many ways mainstream, Labour perspective of Annie Besant constitutes the exception to this general rule. As a corollary, the views of the majority, mass-based labour movement, the wider working class, and labour and related struggles receive far less attention than activists and leaders. Although the essays by Béliard, Curless, Owen, Perry, Sibley, Smith and Terrier variously contain material on labour movements and working-class social structure in the empire, including the dimensions of caste, gender and race, in overall terms these are of secondary concern. At the same time, it is important to note that Hyde centrally concerns himself with the structure of the urban and rural labouring and producing classes in Kenya and the post-Mau Mau Emergency avalanche of strikes. While these strikes hit almost all sectors of the Kenyan economy during the transition to independence from the late 1950s to the mid-1960s, they operated with particular force on the extensive, British-owned tea plantations. As such they contributed powerfully to the creation of a radical rural proletariat.

The activists and leaders selected by our contributors were mainly British male and female members of communist and socialist parties and groups.

Many of them experienced varied and changing allegiances and careers and moved relatively easily from one left group to another. For example, as demonstrated by Quentin Gasteuil, Fenner Brockway, a stalwart of the interwar Independent Labour Party (ILP), disaffiliated, along with the rest of the ILP, from the Labour Party in 1932, but returned to it in the post-war years and served as a Labour MP from 1950 until 1964. Ellen Wilkinson, best known as the leader of the 1936 Jarrow March and a pioneering and longstanding Labour MP, had also been a member of the ILP, a national union organiser, a suffrage campaigner, an admirer of the October 1917 Bolshevik Revolution, a member of the CPGB for a short period of time and a visitor to India in 1932.[1] Sylvia Pankhurst, the subject of Béliard's essay, had similarly been enthused by the Bolsheviks and likewise joined the CPGB. She soon broke with it but remained an independent Marxian socialist concerned to overthrow global capitalism and imperialism. Our selected group also included a revolutionary French socialist, Marceau Pivert, who, as shown in the comparative and transnational essay by Gasteuil, worked within or on the margins of the Socialist Party in France and collaborated in anti-imperialist and socialist activities with Brockway for almost thirty years, and, as noted above, the Gibraltarian communist transnational, Albert Fava. During the late 1950s, Fava moved from the CPGB to the Labour Party. In the same comparative and transnational vein, Smith's contribution highlights the anti-colonial and revolutionary socialist activities and links between the Communist Parties of Britain, South Africa and Australia during the 1960s. Owen also concentrates on a Communist Party, in this instance the CPGB during the 1920s and 1930s. While the subjects of the essays were mainly British they were internationalist rather than 'Little Englander' or 'Little Britisher' in spirit and outlook.

Annie Besant, the subject of Terrier's essay, constitutes the exception to the dominant focus on left-wingers. Involved in the socialist revival during the 1880s, Besant, nevertheless soon renounced socialism in favour of individual and societal spiritual and moral reform. In 1889, she adopted theosophy complete with its key commitment to the 'universal brotherhood of humanity without distinction of race, creed, sex, caste or colour'. In 1895, Besant moved to India. She believed that India and its ancient civilisation rooted in faith, duty and fraternity was superior to the individualism and materialism of the West. In opposition to the mainstream Labour Party leaders, Besant believed that India already possessed the requisite capacities, most crucially the political maturity, to merit immediate self-government.

[1] Matt Perry, *'Red Ellen' Wilkinson: Her Ideas, Movements and World* (Manchester: Manchester University Press, 2014), Introduction.

She accordingly supported the nationalist movement and was elected president of the Indian National Congress in 1917. This was a remarkable achievement for a Western woman. Thereafter, however, Besant's criticism of the non-cooperation movement launched by Gandhi and her belief in legal means of agitation and constitutional reform as the true paths to self-government lost her the support of the younger generation of Indian nationalists. Besant continued to hold that British rule in India was economically, politically and morally exploitative and oppressive. She condemned the 'degradation of the lower castes' and the inferior conditions of women. She brought her feminism indirectly to bear upon her attempts to achieve reform and improvement in women's lot in India. Yet at the same time Besant believed in a 'reformed' kind of imperialism based upon 'righteousness, justice, love and of truth'. Besant wanted India to enjoy dominion status within a reformed empire of self-governing nations rather than the complete independence from Britain demanded by the Congress. In 1919, Besant joined the British Labour Party and continued for the most part to support the mainstream labour movement's gradualism, constitutionalism and 'enlightened' attitude towards the colonies and movements for colonial independence. Finally, Besant saw the political reform movement in India as the key means to achieve independence and liberation. By contrast, declares Terrier, Besant 'considered the labour movements as only auxiliaries in the fight for Home Rule' and 'would not promote the British model of socialism and trade unionism in India'. In the opinion of Besant, Indian workers and peasants lacked the 'maturity' to make political decisions. They needed advice and guidance from their more-educated and affluent Indian nationalists. Although she supported some strikes and other forms of labour-movement activity in India, Besant's overriding priority lay with nationalism and persuading Congress to adopt her preferred course of action.

3

Third: while the majority of our subjects did not constitute a united ideological and party-political group; nevertheless, they did, with the obvious exception of Besant, express a broadly shared, systemic and revolutionary kind of anti-imperialism and anti-colonialism. This stood in marked contrasted to the far more pragmatic, conditional, cautious and reformist view expressed by the mainstream British labour movement. The pre-Second World War leaders of the British Labour Party sought to divest British imperialism of what they considered to be its minority 'coercive' aspects and further develop what they saw as its majority 'enlightened' features. They routinely drew a marked contrast between the mainly 'civilised' and 'liberty-loving' character of Britain and British imperialism and the alleged autocratic, insensitive, cruel and bellicose German, Belgian and Russian variants. During the interwar period and beyond, the party maintained that, while it would put the national interest first – certainly above colonial demands for self-determination – it would fight hard to implement Ramsay MacDonald's 'imperial standard' or 'enlightened' imperial and Commonwealth rule. While firmly committed to the view that the 'capacities' of 'whites' – for self- and collective advancement, material progress, educational and other forms of improvement and self-government – were generally historically superior to those of 'coloureds', the party would do its utmost to extend self-government beyond the 'white dominions' to the 'coloured' dependencies. This, however, would be a gradual and uneven process, conditional upon the attainment of higher capacities by the 'coloured' colonies. They would be helped by the Labour Party to aim and reach higher. Through such activities and its growing presence and influence in British society the Labour Party would thus 'rid the British Empire of any lingering connotations of coercion and repression'. By the 1950s, the Labour Party trumpeted the development of the empire into 'the first inter-racial Commonwealth of free nations' as the 'supreme achievement of the 1945 Labour government'.[2] As observed by Sibley and other contributors, however, post-war mainstream Labour Party and trade union leaders, most prominently Ernest Bevin, were quick to denounce and strike hard against 'Communist subversion' in the colonies and to preach the supreme virtue of 'responsible' trade unionism along British lines.

The Labour Party's commitment to enlightened imperialism was a contradictory mixture of self-interest and generosity, conservatism and progressivism. Yet most scholars would agree that at its core it was paternalistic and patronising in character. Above all, it greatly underestimated both the historically coercive character of British imperialism and the capacity of non-white colonial peoples for self-rule and self-determination. For example, while the Labour Party expressed sympathy for the nationalist cause in India and condemned government repression during the post-First World War years, it did not believe that the Indians were yet 'ready' for independence. This would be a staged process as the Indians further developed their capacities helped by the sympathetic but paternalistic socialists and Labourites abroad. Despite his undoubtedly sincere wish to see

[2] Neville Kirk, *Labour and the Politics of Empire: Britain and Australia, 1900 to the Present* (Manchester, 2014), 141; Neville Kirk, *Comrades and Cousins: Globalization, Workers and Labour Movements in Britain, the USA and Australia from the 1880s to 1914* (London, 2003), chapter 3, 'The Rule of Class and the Power of Race', especially 166–74 (enlightened imperialism) and 189–99 (capacities).

'the social emancipation of the downtrodden masses of India' and self-rule, Keir Hardie, a strong critic of coercive imperialism, had also maintained before his death in 1915 that the time was not yet right for complete independence in India.[3]

4

In contrast to the mainstream Labour Party, most of our subjects expressed unequivocal attitudes towards imperialism, colonialism and the right to self-determination on the part of colonial peoples. Socialists Brockway, Pivert and Wilkinson were at one with the independent Marxist Pankhurst, the British, Australian and South African Communist Parties, and the communist Fava in denouncing imperialism as a *system* of exploitation, oppression, power and control. This system, moreover, included not only socio-economic class-based oppression, but also the racist oppression of the mainly non-white subjects of empire by the largely white Western imperial powers. Perry and Béliard demonstrate that, as socialist-feminists, Wilkinson and Pankhurst, furthermore, saw imperialism as yet another means to exploit women, especially working-class women. These included women in households, in social production, in the fields and in the factories and workshops. On her visit to India in 1932, Wilkinson was appalled not only by the terrible material conditions suffered by the Indian people and the high levels of government repression and cruelty, but also the dire plight and exploitation of its poor women. Both Wilkinson and Pankhurst made strenuous efforts to overcome the cultural, national and class-, gender- and racially based differences between often privileged Western socialists and poor Indians by supporting their struggles, making them better known to Western radicals, and promoting British-Indian and wider international labour, women's, feminist, racial and socialist solidarity. Their goals were to unite 'subalterns' in both the Western and non-Western worlds against capitalism, imperialism, colonialism, racism and sexism and in favour of national liberation, racial and sexual equality *and* class-based socialism. The goals of international solidarity, anti-racism, socialism and colonial independence were shared by most of our subjects.

To be sure, some were more outspoken and militant than others, while, as noted above, Besant's position was generally more moderate and cautious. The passage of time, furthermore, saw changes in the outlooks of some of our subjects. By the later 1940s, Wilkinson was to be found championing the interests of Britain over those of India, while Pankhurst had moved to support bourgeois nationalism and pan-Africanism rather than attaching

[3] Perry, *'Red Ellen'*, 155–56 and 165; Kirk, *Comrades and Cousins*, 197.

primary importance to independent popular revolutionary anti-colonial movements. From its birth in 1920 until 1924, the CPGB, as Owen informs us, adopted a critique of imperialism and colonialism based upon morality and humanitarianism. Pragmatism was also a key ingredient. A key question for many British communists was whether British workers gained or lost from empire. From the mid-1920s onwards, however, continues Owen, the CPGB's critique became scientific and structural in character. By the 1960s, furthermore, some Communist Parties were practising more reformist tactics and strategies than others. For example, Smith shows that the CPA was loud in its criticism of the CPGB's post-war support for the British Labour Party's reformism in colonial matters. In contrast to its South African counterpart, the Australian Communist Party, mindful of the racist views of some of its actual and potential supporters, also adopted a cautious and equivocal stance towards the immediate abolition of the White Australia policy. The latter had been a key feature of the new Commonwealth of Australia since 1901. It was formally abolished only in the 1970s. The Sino-Soviet split of 1960, moreover, brought about a fundamental divide in the international communist movement between pro-Soviet and pro-Chinese forces and parties. On balance, however, we cannot escape the overall conclusion that our subjects constituted important oppositional voices to the dominant pragmatic and reformist 'common-sense' of the mainstream British labour movement.

These oppositional voices, moreover, have been unduly neglected in most of the relevant labour history literature. The latter has both concerned itself with the mainstream movement and argued that immediate, nationally based 'bread-and butter' issues, revolving around wages and living and working conditions, have been of paramount importance to British labour and British workers in general. In turn, international, including imperial and colonial, and transnational matters have been claimed to have been of little or no concern to insular and pragmatic British workers and their labour movements. As a result, the dominant concerns of British labour historiography have traditionally rested with the nation-state and its sub-national components of localities and regions. These, along with workers' and organised labour's bread-and-butter concerns, have constituted the 'natural' framework of investigation.[4] Without denying the importance of these subject areas, I wish to argue that, when placed alongside other relevant past and present studies, the essays in this collection demonstrate that the issues of empire, imperialism and colonialism and anti-colonialism mattered more to British labour, or at least parts of it, than traditionally claimed. The

[4] Kirk, *Labour and Politics of Empire*, 5, 7–8; Neville Kirk, *Transnational Radicalism and the Connected Lives of Tom Mann and Robert Samuel Ross* (Liverpool, 2017), 4–6, 40–1.

views of our subjects cannot rationally or reasonably be reduced to a mere footnote in the history of labour in Britain. At the very least they reached a wider audience than often thought and, although their influence on the mainstream movement was undoubtedly limited, they greatly enriched and added to the wide range and diversity of views within British (and other) labour movements concerning empire and colonialism. In sum, these minority radical voices constitute an important area of past, present and future study. My fourth conclusion, therefore, is that the essays make a contribution towards the important tasks of rescuing minority and oppositional labour voices to imperialism and colonialism from historical neglect and invisibility, assessing their nature and significance and integrating them more fully into the relevant parts of British labour historiography.

5

Fifth: the essays, albeit more implicitly than explicitly, help us to identify the complex, different, conflicting and contradictory locations and patterns of consciousness of labour within the British Empire and Commonwealth. For example, despite their subordinate position and generally radical stance in Britain and other parts of the empire, labour movements and their constituents have also been part of the ruling nation, a part of the consciousness and 'motive force' of the British Empire. As such, and despite their support for labour and subaltern movements abroad, they have by no means been totally immune to the dominant conservative top-down values, ideas and practices of imperialism and colonialism. These have resided, for example, in notions of British superiority, Britain's right to 'rule the world' and its 'duty' to 'civilise' colonials, especially non-white colonials and citizens of the Empire and Commonwealth. Attitudes of superiority and racism have thus at times accompanied the anti-socialism and anti-Communism of sections of the British labour movement and the (particularly white) working class at home and overseas.[5] On a broader canvas, relatively privileged white workers in the colonies and dominions, including white 'settlers' and their descendants from Britain, have expressed their superiority and at times hostility, cruelty and violence towards 'inferior coloureds', including both indigenous 'coloureds' and non-white immigrants to their societies. In Australia, for example, the Janus-faced labour movement sought to preserve the 'Australian standard' and create a 'Workers' Paradise' in part by excluding non-white immigrants and the aboriginal people from citizenship. Although at times contested by some of its left-wing elements, the mainstream Australian labour movement's

[5] Kirk, *Labour and Politics of Empire*, 7, 11–12.

commitment to White Australia lasted for seventy years. Despite its current multiculturalism and official celebration of difference, Australia remains to this day an extremely racist society. In South Africa, the white-dominated labour movement, of course, was unashamedly racist for a long period of time. Racism in South Africa and, we might add, the USA and many other parts of the colonial and ex-colonial world, has served to protect the material and cultural 'wages of whiteness'.[6]

6

Sixth: as briefly noted earlier in this Conclusion, the experiences of some of our subjects highlight the importance of bringing, where appropriate, comparative and transnational perspectives to bear upon the study of empire and colonialism. As Sibley demonstrates, Albert Fava became an important, if historiographically neglected, international and transnational activist and labour leader with contacts in Gibraltar, Spain and Britain. In his study of Brockway and Pivert, Gasteuil highlights the cross-national collaborative nature of their work, their profound internationalism, their extensive international and transnational contacts, their attempts to spread the socialist critique of empire, colonialism and war in Britain, France and many other places, and the commonalities, similarities and differences of context they faced in writing as British and French socialists. Terrier, Perry and Béliard, furthermore, provide us with insights into the ways in which Besant, Wilkinson and Pankhurst sought to overcome the question of cultural and political difference and attempt to forge bonds of solidarity among socialists, Labourites, anti-racists and feminists in Britain, India and other places across the globe. Terrier also shows us how Besant developed many contacts in Britain and India and, in her comings and goings both between and within the two countries, gained insights into and shed light upon their political, cultural and social differences and similarities. Smith not only draws out important commonalities, similarities and differences among the Communist Parties of Britain, South Africa and Australia in terms of revolutionary and reformist tactics and strategies at home and towards nationalist liberation movements and the achievement of socialism abroad, but also their attitudes to race. In terms of attitudes to race, Smith's findings, including both outright opposition to and equivocation with

[6] Marilyn Lake and Henry Reynolds, *Drawing the Global Colour Line: White Men's Countries and the Question of Racial Equality* (Carlton, Victoria, 2008); Kirk, *Comrades and Cousins*, 198–205; Satnam Virdee, *Racism, Class and the Racialized Outsider* (Basingstoke, 2014); David Roediger, *The Wages of Whiteness: Race and the Making of the American Working Class* (London, 2007).

racism, may usefully be fed into wider debates about the national, international, transnational and global character and influence of 'whiteness'.[7]

7

Seventh: the essays commonly reveal that the successes and influence of our subjects' anti-imperialism and anti-colonialism were varied and limited. On the one hand, for example, Smith observes that the CPSA and the CPA helped to organise activists, respectively, in south-west Africa and northern Rhodesia and Indonesia and Malaya. On the other hand, elsewhere in the colonial and decolonising world communists had far more varied and generally limited successes. For example, Owen convincingly argues that the interwar CPGB's aims – to forge links and synchronise actions with the revolutionary popular movement in India, to recruit British workers to the anti-imperialist movement and so build an effective challenge to imperialists at home – had disappointing results. Divisions among communists, changes in the official party line and the strong sense that most communists were seen to be elitist outsiders seeking to impose their world view on India rather than basing their politics upon and truly engaging with situations and developments within the Indian colony itself, all contributed to a sense of frustration and often failure. In addition, and despite their intrinsic interest and wider reach than often supposed, the revolutionary socialist anti-imperialism of Brockway, Wilkinson and Pankhurst were similarly found wanting. Above all, they, along with the CPGB, failed to connect sufficiently with the organic experiences of workers and wider labour-movement people either at home or in the colonies. As a result, they failed to pose a serious challenge to the dominant labourism of the British movement and the kind of elite anti-colonial nationalism prevailing in many British colonies or ex-colonies. Despite her attachment to the mainstream British movement, Besant lost much of her erstwhile support in India when she defended the British Labour Party's constitutionalism and cooperation in the face of the non-cooperation policy of the Indian Congress and rising Indian labour militancy.

As Curless, Hyde and Terrier indicate respectively for Sudan, Kenya and India, political elites often enjoyed success in their attempts to control workers and their militant, class-based based mobilisations and movements for their own bourgeois-nationalist ends. Curless concludes that this, furthermore, was a dynamic that was 'observable across Africa during the period of decolonisation'. In India, the mainstream nationalist movement of the early 1920s, moreover, was reluctant to regard the labour movement

[7] See chapter 6, 'Race and Whiteness', in Kirk, *Transnational Radicalism*.

as anything more than an auxiliary force in the struggle for national independence.[8] At the same time, however, there were a few exceptions to this rule. For example, Albert Fava and his comrades were highly successful in mobilising labour in Gibraltar as a 'well-organised mass base' of the newly developing radical nationalist movement. These important issues of nationalism, class, the mobilisation of labour and the relationship between anti-colonial nationalism and labour, socialism and communism merit extended future study.

8

Eighth: it naturally follows from observations made in the previous two paragraphs that our subjects were forced to confront numerous obstacles in attempting successfully to achieve their objectives. In terms of the overriding goal of most of them – to achieve dominance for their anti-imperialism, anti-colonialism and socialism both in Britain and in the colonies – these obstacles would prove to be impossible to overcome. Obstacles and difficulties also presented themselves in the attainment of more modest goals. The former included differences in the structure, experiences and outlooks of subalterns in metropole and colony, racism, the opposition of mainstream labour and some workers to the ideology and practices of the left, divisions and conflicts within the latter and the hostility of the dominant classes and groups in both metropole and colony. In overall terms it will be evident to the reader that the successes and failures of our subjects depended heavily upon the overall balance of social and political forces and the precise nature of the historical context in which they operated. The ability of socialists and communists, furthermore, to transcend all manner of differences and divisions and, by means of their language and actions, successfully to relate to the actual experiences and perceptions of their intended supporters and allies, was of crucial importance.

They also had to tackle major tactical and strategic issues. For example, as Owen observes, a key question for communist (and many socialist) anti-colonialists and anti-imperialists in relation to interwar India was whether they should offer immediate support to the ascendant and newly militant Gandhian Congress with a view to undermining it later and promoting revolutionary socialism, either by means of insurgency from below or from above by winning over some of the nationalist leaders. Or should total opposition be registered to the nationalists at the very outset and support given to an independent and potentially revolutionary movement of

[8] Anthony Cox, *Empire, Industry and Class: The Imperial Nexus of Jute, 1840–1940* (London, 2013), 125.

workers and peasants? In answer to these questions, Owen shows us how the policies of the CPGB changed over time, largely in response to the controlling influence and direction of the Soviet Union. For example, as a result of the Comintern's adoption of the 'class against class' policy in 1928 communists jettisoned their previous, albeit fluctuating and inconsistent, efforts to make closer contact with the Congress in favour of an attempt to 'swamp the Congress from below and carry it towards revolution'. The agents of this revolution would be peasants and workers organised under the leadership of 'an unveiled Communist Party'. Yet the results of his change of policy were very disappointing. Smith, furthermore, shows how the 1960s communist movement was also compelled, with very mixed results, to address the bourgeois-nationalist and potentially revolutionary popular-movement dichotomy. More recently, of course, socialists, albeit in the formally non-colonial contexts of Scotland and the Basque and Catalan parts of Spain, have had to decide whether to throw their support behind nationalist movements. While the ruling Scottish National Party (SNP) maintains that it is predominantly social-democratic, contemporary nationalism in Spain has been more varied in its political orientation and complexion. Yet the key question which exercised the minds of communists and socialists from the 1920s to the 1960s has continued to inform recent and current socialist political debate in Scotland and Spain. Does nationalism, in its many and varied forms, advance or retard the attainment of the ultimate goal of socialist transformation?[9]

* * *

In conclusion, the essays in this collection hopefully will act as a stimulus to further research. Some of this research doubtless will continue to focus upon a single case study within the wide range of imperial, colonial and Commonwealth systems. As a comparative and transnational labour historian, however, I hope that other parts of it will consider several case studies across these systems and bring to bear upon them appropriate comparative, transnational and even global approaches and perspectives.[10]

[9] Wade Matthews, 'Class, Nation and Capitalist Globalization: Eric Hobsbawm and the National Question', *International Review of Social History*, 53.1 (2008), 63–99; Tom Nairn, *The Break-up of Britain: Crisis and Neo-Nationalism* (Champaign, IL, 2015); J.H. Elliott, *Scots and Catalans: Union and Disunion* (New Haven, CT, 2018).

[10] I am grateful to Matt Perry for his helpful comments on the Conclusion.

Afterword

Towards a People's History of British Decolonisation

Yann Béliard

Our intention in convening the November 2013 conference in Paris was to make a double contribution, to imperial studies and to labour history, possibly to break down sub-disciplinary boundaries and help those fields of research cross-fertilise each other. We were also hoping to overcome some of the weaknesses in the usual treatment of labour's role in British decolonisation: the artificial separation between the metropole and the colonies; the narrow focus on Labour Party headquarters on the one hand, and on nationalist elites on the other. In short, we were determined to highlight the initiatives of transnational actors and the role of the workers themselves, both in Britain and in its imperial domain. We were fully aware that we were not the first to ask, as Bernard Porter had in 2004: 'What about the workers?'.[1] But whereas most studies have tended to scrutinise times of imperial expansion and consolidation, what we were seeking to do was analyse the role of workers and their organisations in a time of disruption and destabilisation. Besides, whereas British decolonisation had been so often presented as a relatively smooth transfer of power from London to new nation-states, we felt that top-down approach was not satisfactory, that the intervention of anti-colonial left-wing activists and of the labouring masses themselves in the process needed to be examined more seriously.

The need to push the efforts of our predecessors a little further stemmed partly from the frustration towards interpretations that painted too rosy a picture of British decolonisation, of the British Left and also of its relationship with anti-imperial fighters in the colonies – misgivings apparent, for example, in Tony Benn's foreword to Frank, Horner and Stewart's *The British Labour Movement and Imperialism*. Benn's piece unduly transformed what was so often a story of missed encounters between metropolitan

[1] Bernard Porter, 'What about the Workers?', chapter 9 in his *The Absent-Minded Imperialists: Empire, Society and Culture in Britain* (Oxford, 2004).

and colonial anti-imperialists into a barely credible success story in which 'Democracy dissolved the British Empire'.[2] The claim that 'a relatively peaceful end to British imperialism' was made possible by 'the good will of influential socialists in the post-war government of Britain' was also problematic.[3]

The vision of Britain as a 'smooth decoloniser' has been torn apart by so much recent research that there is no need to go into much detail here. To summarise, in their very different narratives of the end of empire, Darwin, Hyam and Cain and Hopkins have all highlighted the messy character of Britain's retreat: the fact that it was imposed on all British governments, including the Labour governments, rather than planned; and that it resulted above all from changes in the international balance of forces and revolts in the colonies, but only marginally from the concerted action of British anti-colonialists and colonial freedom fighters.[4] Such observations have only been confirmed by the growing literature on the policing of the Empire and on the British art of counter-insurgency. Studies of the partition of the Indian Empire as well as histories of British disengagement from Palestine point in the same direction, that of a process that was no less bloody than in the French or the Portuguese Empires, and that left a possibly greater number of time bombs behind. Of course, for labour historians, those ongoing revisions are welcome, in so far as they are invitations to ditch a number of established 'truths' and question the part played by working-class actors in those untidy transitions.

As for the role of the Left, it is true that, until Howe's pioneering *Anticolonialism in British Politics*, it had been grossly underestimated. But the risk is to overestimate the influence of the leftists inside the Labour Party, when the shift in Labour Party policy on colonial questions in the late 1950s had probably less to do with the left wing convincing the centre and the right wing than to the shift away from direct colonial rule inside the Establishment itself.[5] Here again, in the eyes of labour historians, one of the values in re-evaluating the impact of the metropolitan Left on colonial policies is that

[2] Tony Benn, foreword to Billy Frank, Craig Horner and David Stewart (eds), *The British Labour Movement and Imperialism* (Newcastle upon Tyne, 2010), xi.

[3] Benn, foreword to Frank, Horner and Stewart, *British Labour*, ix–x.

[4] John Darwin, *The End of the British Empire: The Historical Debate* (Oxford, 1991); Ronald Hyam, *Britain's Declining Empire: The Road to Decolonisation, 1918–1968* (Cambridge, 2006); P.J. Cain and A.G. Hopkins, *British Imperialism*, 2 vols (London, 1993).

[5] Stephen Howe, *Anticolonialism in British Politics: The Left and the End of Empire, 1918–1964* (Oxford, 1993). Several reviewers of Howe's book called for a qualification of the MCF's direct impact on the dismemberment of the Empire. See reviews by John Darwin (*English Historical Review*, 110 (1995), 429–32) and Andrew Porter (*History Workshop Journal*, 40 (1995), 261–63).

it could lead to a useful shift towards a so far neglected object of study: the working-class mobilisations in the colonies, which owed little to metropolitan influences and were probably more disturbing for the managers of the Empire than Stafford Cripps' or Aneurin Bevan's manoeuvres behind the curtains.[6]

On top of this, the thesis that the links established by the metropolitan Left with colonial liberation movements were essential in making the liquidation of Empire smooth is also debatable. Such ties did exist – a point worth underlining, as Marie Terrier does in her chapter on Annie Besant, since it goes against those post-colonial readings that reify or essentialise cultural barriers. But those convergences and alliances were in general fragile and temporary. Indeed, although the British Left could in theory have collaborated with colonised people on their road to independence around the common objective of a socialist reorganisation of the world, several factors – clearly identified by Howe and explored in more depth by Owen and others after him – made that bonding of forces impossible.[7] All in all, neither the bourgeois nationalists nor the labouring classes in the colonies had reason to feel particularly confident in the metropolitan Left – which helps understand why, in the aftermath of the Second World War, colonial rebellions against the British Empire were led along nationalist lines and not under the flag of labour internationalism.

Diverse approaches and common assumptions

Many accepted views of labour's part in British decolonisation therefore need to be discussed and qualified. The chapters collected here were produced by writers with distinct methodological and political outlooks. Yet they are united by a common refusal to hide any of the dark sides of British imperial rule and retreat; and a parallel refusal to obliterate any of the ambiguities or contradictions of the British Left in its proclaimed attempts to connect with anti-colonial forces around the Empire. To put it in a nutshell, the essays we have gathered here seek neither to celebrate nor to deplore but to understand.

To take steps towards a more balanced and more complex understanding of the question, we were also driven by a number of common assumptions, which were probably implicit at the start but are worth summing up in a

[6] This was notable in Trinidad and Tobago. See Jerome Teelucksingh, *Labour and the Decolonization Struggle in Trinidad and Tobago* (Basingstoke, 2014).

[7] In the case of the British Labour Party, trade unions and cooperatives, many studies have shown that they were too integrated in the domestic institutions, too afraid of rocking the boat, to behave as consistent internationalists. In the case of the much smaller communist movement, especially once it was Stalinised, its policy seems to have been determined more by the interests of the Kremlin bureaucracy than by those of colonial peoples and workers.

more explicit way in this concluding essay. For those preconceptions, seen from another angle, were also hypotheses that needed to be tested. One of those assumptions was that the building of bridges between anti-colonialists in the metropole and around the Empire, between left-wing opponents of imperialism in Britain and working-class rebels in the colonies, was not doomed from the start. Obstacles on that road were numerous, as our chapters confirm in different and complementary ways. Labour movement leaders were in general more loyal to the Empire than to their class sisters and brothers in the colonies. Workers in Britain and their cousins in the white dominions were often imbued with the dominant ideology, and not immune to the official and media discourses on the Britons' superiority and civilising mission. Under particular circumstances, those vague and mostly dormant conceptions were actually formulated in the clear-cut, unashamed language of white labourism and racial socialism.[8] But the picture was always more mixed. Even in Australia and South Africa there were militants attached to the values of internationalism and antiracism, minorities who preserved at least in principle the possibility of a connection with the non-white oppressed and exploited.[9] The range of possible positions on the racial question inside the labour movement is well illustrated by Neville Kirk's study of the life-long relationship between Britain's Tom Mann and Australia's Bob Ross, two socialist labour leaders and friends who adopted contrasting, indeed contradictory, stances on the matter. While Mann was a consistent anti-racist, Ross was a staunch defender of the White Australia policy.[10] As for the sentiments of the rank and file, they were not homogeneous either, combining prejudice or even rejection with sympathy for the non-white poor, and at times, although more rarely, the sense of a common destiny. Most of our chapters testify therefore both to the existence of a solid colour bar and to the possibility for some activists on the left to cross it, and not always in vain.[11]

Another one of those assumptions was the idea that labour mobilisations in the colonies could not be reduced to a subset of nationalist and anti-colonial resistance, that they deserved to be studied in their own right, that the working-class rebellions that accompanied the fights for national

[8] Jonathan Hyslop, 'The Imperial Working Class Makes Itself "White": White Labourism in Britain, Australia and South Africa before the First World War', *Journal of Historical Sociology*, 12.4 (1999), 398–421.

[9] Neville Kirk, *Comrades and Cousins: Globalization, Workers and Labour Movements in Britain, the USA and Australia from the 1880s to 1914* (London, 2003).

[10] Neville Kirk, *Transnational Radicalism and the Connected Lives of Tom Mann and Robert Samuel Ross* (Liverpool, 2017).

[11] See Kirk's conclusion in this volume and his reflections on the 'global colour line' explored by Lake and Reynolds.

liberation had a logic and potentialities of their own, even though most of them ended up being subsumed within a nationalist framework. This is the fruitful option embraced by Sumithra Janaka Biyanwila in his recent history of trade unions in Sri Lanka: to consider trade unions not as 'accessories of political parties' or 'small footnotes in larger political tapestries', not just as supporting actors but as main players.[12] Biyanwila observes that the passage from colonial rule to independence saw not only the emergence of combative trade unions on the tea plantations and in the garment industry, but also their incorporation into the Sinhala Buddhist state, reproducing in another setting the model of integration into the state apparatus theorised by Sidney Webb. This explains why the unions are so often seen as playing second fiddle. Comparable evolutions took place during the decolonisation process in the West Indies and Africa too, where trade union struggles became subordinated to 'national liberation' and, in exchange for their association with the new dominant parties and the co-optation of their leaders, lost much of their subversive and oppositional power. In spite of that, and because writing history is precisely about not taking the end of the story for granted, the chapters gathered here, in particular in Part II, make a point of not assuming that this subordination was a foregone conclusion.

What emerges here is a common determination to recapture the sense of uncertainty that accompanied the final decades of the British Empire. With hindsight, it is easy to forget the array of possible futures that emerged from anti-colonial resistance, in particular when it took the shape of massive working-class movements, before such initiatives from below were constrained by the framework of the new nation-states.[13] It is easy to forget the dreams and practical attempts of the radical minorities who believed that coordinated efforts across borders might lead not only to the destruction of the British Empire but to that of capitalism and imperialism in general, and to its replacement by some form of universal socialism. So, while our edited volume helps understand why the 1945–1965 anti-colonial revolts were eventually not led under the flag of socialist internationalism but under that of national liberation, it also emphasises the roads not taken, to retrieve, in a gesture inspired by E.P. Thompson's philosophy, the sheer sense of openness and opportunity so prevalent in the phase when the foundations of the British Empire started to shake.[14]

[12] Sumithra Janaka Biyanwila, *The Labour Movement in the Global South: Trade Unions in Sri Lanka* (London, 2010).

[13] On counter-factual history, see Quentin Deluermoz and Pierre Singaravélou's stimulating *Pour une histoire des possibles: analyses contrefactuelles et futurs non advenus* (Paris, 2016).

[14] On crossroads and paths not taken, see also Michael Collins, 'Decolonisation and the "Federal Moment"', *Diplomacy and Statecraft*, 24.1 (2013), 21–40.

Where do we go from here?

The list of the themes and locations that we have left untouched or have only been able to tackle superficially is too long to be presented here. But, developing some of Neville Kirk's concluding remarks, I wish to outline in this final part several dimensions that may deserve more attention in future research.[15]

Organisations

Some branches of the British labour movement which do not appear in these pages should undoubtedly be rescued from oblivion. This is particularly necessary because, in spite of the remarkable expansion of the social and cultural history of the British Empire since the 1980s (which came as a very useful corrective to narrow, top-down traditionalism), it has for the most part concerned itself with the attitudes of sections of the wider 'people' rather than specifically with the labouring classes and their labour movements.[16] The cooperative movement's investment in the imperial field and the way the promoters of cooperation navigated the decolonisation process are areas where more inquiries are surely needed, if only to test how the intentions of the MacDonald and Attlee governments to use cooperation as a vehicle for enlightened imperialism translated on the ground. Beyond cooperators, none of the social, cultural and educational networks through which workers tried to organise voluntary individual and collective self-help should be neglected by historians of decolonisation. If we turn to political groups, the Trotskyists' approach to anti-colonialism would also be worthy of further inquiry, in the wake of important publications on their general history.[17] Here the focus would once again be on minute groupings with limited impact on the bulk of the working class. But as a tendency whose opposition to British imperialism rarely wavered, Trotskyism deserves more than a footnote.

International relations

On a different level, future historians might also be tempted to relate labour and decolonisation issues more firmly to the context of Cold War tensions, as illustrated by Tom Sibley's chapter in this volume. The rivalry between the

[15] See Kirk's concluding chapter in this volume.

[16] Neville Kirk, *Labour and the Politics of Empire: Britain and Australia, 1900 to the Present* (Manchester, 2014), 7 (nn. 8, 9, 11), 25 and 26 for references to the work of Porter, MacKenzie and related scholars.

[17] Evan Smith and Matthew Worley (eds), *Against the Grain: The British Far Left from 1956* (Manchester, 2014); John Kelly, *Contemporary Trotskyism: Parties, Sects and Social Movements in Britain* (London, 2018).

World Federation of Trade Unions (WFTU) and the International Confederation of Free Trade Unions (ICFTU) from the moment of the split in 1949 was played out on a global scale that included British territories, and many aspects of that competition for influence affected colonial workers in their relation to their employers as well as in their political engagements. From the sending of African American activists as emissaries to West Africa to the fomenting of strikes so as to upset anti-imperialist regimes, the American Federation of Labor (AFL)'s manoeuvres merit closer examination, as does the relationship between Soviet foreign policy and the trade unions attracted to the WFTU.

Rank-and-file workers in the metropole

Looking beyond the workers who at one point or another in their lives were members of national and international organisations, it is the workers that did not belong to trade unions or political parties who in many ways remain a terra incognita for the labour historian. Although the contributors to this volume share a common determination not to write a history of 'big men' or 'big women' and a common desire to shed light on the material conditions and mental preoccupations of the labouring majority, the reconstruction of rank-and-file attitudes towards imperialism and decolonisation is not so easy – certainly more complex than the study of the positions of activists for whom political expression was as essential as breathing. Common people do not leave as many written traces behind as the 'uncommon' militant, hence our difficulties in imagining their mentalities. One of the rare blind spots in Stephen Howe's study of anti-colonialism was precisely that: a focus on the politics of organised Labour that left the social question of working-class attitudes somehow in the background. The dominant attitude in high places – in ministries, in TUC and Labour Party headquarters, on Fleet Street – was to discard the demands of colonial workers as immature, or as the work of agitators. But to what extent did British workers adhere to such visions? Our collection revisits – without providing any definite or unilateral answer – the usual paradox: being subordinate, the British worker could feel solidarity with other subordinates around the world; but belonging to the richest nation in the world, he or she could share the paternalistic ideology of the ruling class.[18] Further attention should be given to the variety of labour responses to the imperial system, especially as individuals and groups could and did change their attitudes to empire and colony

[18] On metropolitan attitudes towards colonial workers, Laura Tabili's work is essential reading. See *'We Ask for British Justice': Workers and Racial Difference in Late Imperial Britain* (Ithaca, NY, 1994) and *Global Migrants, Local Culture: Native and Newcomers in Provincial England, 1841–1939* (Basingstoke, 2011).

over time. Besides, working-class attitudes in the metropole should not be artificially homogenised. If decolonisation and the break-up of the United Kingdom can be seen as interrelated processes, maybe there is reason to wonder whether labour perceptions of decolonisation differed significantly in England, Wales, Scotland and Northern Ireland.

Rank-and-file workers in the colonies

Another question worth examining more profoundly than our collection does is the relation of white workers in the Dominions to the decolonisation process. Above all, the area where the greatest strides forward should be taken concerns the colonial labourers themselves. Both Gareth Curless's work on the Sudan and Dave Hyde's work on Kenya have allowed our knowledge of that proletarian experience to expand, but every territory that was ever coloured in red on the world map would deserve such scrutiny. We need to know much more about the unpaid women and children employed in the imperial economy, even once the International Labour Organisation (ILO) started to elaborate international norms against coerced labour and British governments pretended to combat unfree labour.[19] As for the distinction between purely industrial and purely political strikes in the colonies, it should be teased out in every context, as economic and anti-colonial considerations were rarely confined to separate areas in the striking workers' brains. In this respect the exploration of a 'new' source may prove fruitful: since the revelation in 2011 that the Foreign Office had hidden more than one million papers that should have been declassified, those documents have slowly been made accessible to researchers. However, major obstacles remain. One is the fact that British authorities destroyed a significant proportion of their archives while retreating from the colonies; another is that the archives that were saved reveal the contours of the 'official mind' more directly than the masses' psychology.

Varieties of anti-colonialism

In terms of its spatial scope, this collection could not, given its limited size, cover the British Empire as a whole. Appropriately contextualised continuities and changes in the nature and meanings of imperialism and colonialism, but also of anti-colonial nationalism, thus merit further investigation. Some omissions the editors regret more than others. One is that of Arab and Jewish workers and activists, especially at a moment when the labour movement in Britain stands accused of antisemitism. Studying how anti-colonialists of the socialist kind, whatever their ethnic origin and

[19] See Beverly Grier, *Invisible Hands: Child Labor and the State in Colonial Zimbabwe* (Portsmouth, NH, 2006).

whether living in the metropole or in the Mediterranean world, discussed the future of Palestine after the departure of the British or imagined a solution to the persecution of the Jews, would have been immensely rewarding. Just as frustrating is the absence of a chapter on anti-colonialism and decolonisation in the West Indies. That absence is maybe even more regrettable when we recall that the role of working-class rebellions in the anti-colonial process was probably more visible and essential there than in any of Britain's colonies. Whether in Guiana, Tobago or Trinidad, it was the wave of labour unrest of the 1930s that opened the way to the fight for independence. Many of the men who came to power in the 1950s and 1960s – from Grantley Adams and Clement Payne in Barbados to Alexander Bustamante and Norman Manley in Jamaica – were popular leaders, although not always trade unionists, who had shaped and been shaped by those fiery years.[20] Analysing the link between industrial disputes and anti-colonial nationalism in the West Indies would have been relevant to our collection, especially as those disputes were never just Caribbean affairs: a significant number of the strikes' leaders had lived in the British Isles and could rely both on a rich metropolitan experience and on their transnational connections.[21] Those men had their foibles and shortcomings, and as the leaders of newly emancipated countries they did not succeed any more than their African counterparts in putting an end to worker exploitation or to the domination of Anglo-American capital. But, should this volume on labour and decolonisation have a sequel, it should pay due attention to their story, and to that of the labouring women and men who mobilised with them. This would shed light more generally on the important and much neglected area of relations between, on the one hand, elite nationalist movements and, on the other hand, the mobilisation of labour and other popular movements – an area which requires much wider and deeper examination and explication.

Race and gender

Individuals and groups could hold complex and contradictory attitudes, combining, for example, commitments, on the one hand, to national liberation and social transformation, with, on the other hand, racialised and gendered boundaries and exclusions. Some, such as Wilkinson and Pankhurst, made genuine 'universalising' attempts to overcome differences between the West

[20] See Colin A. Palmer's trilogy: *Eric Williams and the Making of the Modern Caribbean* (Chapel Hill, NC, 2006); *The Politics of Power: Cheddi Jagan and the Struggle for British Guiana's Independence* (Chapel Hill, NC, 2010); *The 1938 Labor Rebellion and the Birth of Modern Jamaica* (Chapel Hill, NC, 2014).

[21] Christian Høgsbjerg, *Mariner, Renegade and Castaway: Chris Braithwaite, Seamen's Organiser, Socialist and Militant Pan-Africanist* (London, 2014).

and the East. Their attempts embraced anti-racism, support for women and feminism and class-based solidarity and internationalism. As such, as highlighted by Perry in relation to Wilkinson, these attempts constitute an important challenge to the key tenet of post-colonial and Subaltern Studies that cultural difference and the assumptions, values and practices of Orientalism formed an insuperable barrier to the development of genuinely equal bonds of solidarity between radicals in the West and the East. There is nonetheless room for further studies of how principled anti-colonialism or internationalism did not necessarily exclude racist or sexist prejudice. Labour historians of imperialism and colonialism would be well advised to follow the example of feminist historians in more thoroughly examining the issue of women's agency and conditioning in metropole and colony, including enslaved and free women.[22] Future studies should address, where appropriate, both issues and relations of gender and race more extensively and intensively than has often been the case in the past. They could also contribute to new and exciting developments at the intersection of political economy and environmental and labour history as applied to empire and imperialism.[23]

Comparative perspectives

Finally, an approach that our chapters do not adopt systematically but which is promising indeed is the method which compares the British imperial experience with other imperial experiences, and also considers our historical objects from a trans-imperial perspective. The interest in the comparative angle is evident when one thinks about labour and British decolonisation in comparison with the French case, especially at a moment when French historians embracing transnational and 'from below' perspectives seem to be reaching a wider readership.[24] The balance of forces inside the Left in the post-war years was completely different in Britain and in France, with an overwhelming Labour Party facing a smallish CPGB on the one hand and a massive PCF (Parti communiste français) facing a declining SFIO (Section française de l'Internationale ouvrière) on the other. Yet that discrepancy did not significantly affect the attitude of the Left towards anti-imperial revolts in the colonies. In May 1945, the bloody repression of the nationalist

[22] Diana Paton, *No Bond but the Law: Punishment, Race, and Gender in Jamaican State Formation, 1780–1870* (Durham, NC, 2004) and Philippa Levine (ed.), *Gender and Empire* (Oxford, 2017).

[23] Mike Davis, *Late Victorian Holocausts: El Nino Famines and the Making of the Third World* (London, 2000).

[24] Patrick Boucheron (ed.), *Histoire mondiale de la France* (Paris, 2017); Gérard Noiriel, *Une histoire populaire de la France, de la guerre de Cent Ans à nos jours* (Marseilles, 2018); and Michelle Zancarini-Fournel, *Les luttes et les rêves: une histoire populaire de la France de 1685 à nos jours* (Paris, 2016).

troubles in Algeria took place under the auspices of a coalition government comprising both SFIO and PCF ministers. As for the war against Algerian independence, it was launched by Guy Mollet, an SFIO prime minister who was given full powers in 1954 by a majority in the National Assembly that included PCF representatives, representatives who during most of the war called for 'peace in Algeria', not independence.[25] As in the British case, colonial workers fought for the independence of their countries with little support from metropolitan French socialists. This does not mean that the French proletariat was as supportive of the state's military interventions as the parties speaking in its name, as testified by the numerous spontaneous protests against conscription and the often humane behaviour of working men wearing the uniform.[26] In contrast to SFIO and PCF positions, the political and material support brought by anarchists and Trotskyists to the Algerian independence fighters has recently been studied more closely.[27] But it was not without its paradoxes, one of them being that the two biggest Trotskyist groups in France, the PCI and the OCI, disagreed as to which tendency of the nationalist movement should be helped, with the former siding with the FLN (Front de libération nationale) and the latter with the MNA (Mouvement national algérien). Such dilemmas were not a French preserve and historians would benefit immensely from comparing the choices made by the radical Left across imperial metropoles.

Trans-imperial perspectives

This would naturally lead, beyond comparisons, to a study of the circulation of ideas and activists across imperial borders. That trans-imperial angle has already helped enhance our understanding of decolonisation, in particular in the works which consider the military support that Britain brought to the French Empire in Indochina, to the Dutch one in Indonesia or to the 'American Empire' during the Korean War. The study of anti-colonialism and of labour responses to imperialism would also gain from such an approach, as shown by Quentin Gasteuil's chapter and its emphasis on

[25] Alain Ruscio, *Les communistes et l'Algérie: des origines à la guerre d'indépendance, 1920–1962* (Paris, 2019); Jacques Le Gall, *La question coloniale dans le mouvement ouvrier en France, 1830–1962* (Pantin, 2013).

[26] Many of those initiatives were taken by PCF sympathisers who at that moment did not follow the party line or were not aware that their actions contradicted it. Comparable individual trajectories were observed during the war in Indochina, where dozens of French soldiers with communist sympathies deserted to join the ranks of Ho Chi Minh's army and became his 'white soldiers'. See Jacques Doyon, *Les soldats blancs de Ho Chi Minh* (Paris, 1973).

[27] Sylvain Pattieu, *Les camarades des frères: trotskistes et libertaires dans la guerre d'Algérie* (Paris, 2002).

cross-imperial networks.[28] Mélanie Torrent, for example, has highlighted the contrast between the Labour Party's moderation in dealing with British imperial interests and its whole-hearted support, at the very same moment and mostly via MCF initiatives, to the FLN in its war against France.[29] There is certainly much to learn from case studies that, likewise, include several imperial zones in their scope and explore the crossing of imperial borders, allowing intriguing parallels to be made.[30]

* * *

Since our 2013 conference in Paris, news from around the world has confirmed how timely the gathering was. In recent years, the deaths of important nationalist figures who, in their youth, had been fellow travellers of the British Left, have reminded us of the long-neglected connection between Empire and Labour. Michael 'King Cobra' Sata, who died on 28 October 2014, had been a platform sweeper, a baggage porter and a trade unionist at Victoria Station long before joining the fight for independence and becoming Zambia's fifth president in 2011. Calling himself a social-democrat until the very end, he was known to use fiery language to denounce the foreign capitalists' hold over the country's copper mines. Lee Kuan Yew, the founding father of independent Singapore, who died on 23 March 2015, had campaigned for the Labour Party in the late 1930s and his People's Action Party (PAP), founded in 1954, gave allegiance to the Socialist International for about two decades. His proclaimed progressivism did not stop him from accepting honours such as the Knight Grand Cross of the Order of St Michael and St George in 1972, the Freedom of the City of London ten years later and a place at the top of Rockefeller's International Council and of the Forbes' Brain Trust – an indication that a socialist past did not necessarily exclude access to the upper echelons of the global capitalist class. With the passing of Tony Benn on 14 March 2014, one of the pioneers of the MCF disappeared, granting historians one more motive to start looking back more seriously at the part played by the labour movement in the British experiences of decolonisation.

Over the past decade, labour issues from Britain's ex-colonies have been unusually prominent in the headlines, from the Marikana massacre in South

[28] Michael Goebel explores similar networks in his *Anti-Imperial Metropolis: Interwar Paris and the Seeds of Third World Nationalism* (Cambridge, 2015).

[29] Mélanie Torrent, *British Decolonisation (1919–1984): The Politics of Power, Liberation and Influence* (Paris, 2012).

[30] On the need for historians of the British Empire to become less strictly British and more global in their outlook, see Simon J. Potter and Jonathan Saha, 'Global History, Imperial History and Connected Histories of Empire', *Journal of Colonialism and Colonial History*, 16.1 (2015).

Africa (16 August 2012) to the Rana Plaza collapse in Bangladesh (24 April 2013), raising questions about the reality of emancipation for the labouring masses in the post-colonial world and revealing to large audiences the perpetuation of a form of neo-imperial world order. The workers exploited at the Rana Plaza produced clothes to be sold on Britain's high streets by household brands such as Primark and Store 21. As for the Lonmin company, who refused to pay the platinum miners in Marikana a living wage and asked for police and army intervention to put an end to the strike, it is listed on the London Stock Exchange and belongs to the FTSE 250. The way the capitalist market connects workers with each other across borders and oceans, within a structure that is fundamentally unequal, is still striking – another reason why the timing for this collection seems appropriate.

In 2019, many centenary commemorations also resonated with the questions raised at our 2013 conference. The year 1919 was indeed a year of global unrest in which issues of class, empire and race were addressed in violent and often contradictory ways. It was the year when British ports saw white sailors physically attack colonial sailors in most British ports.[31] But 1919 was also the year of the foundation of the Communist International, an International whose anti-colonial and antiracist positions were much sharper than its predecessors'. Contemporary reasons to think of labour and empire in connected ways are therefore plentiful, as two major conferences convened in 2019 have confirmed: the first, 'Imperial Legacies of 1919', at the University of North Texas, on 18–20 April; the second, 'The Global Challenge of Peace: 1919 as a Contested Threshold to a New World Order', at Newcastle University, on 17–18 May. It is be hoped that the coming months and years will see the present momentum confirmed and stimulating new studies flourish and circulate, as ideas should, across frontiers and continents.

Whatever the point of focus, there is ample scope to widen and deepen our knowledge and understanding of labour, imperialism, colonialism and decolonisation. It will be a demanding but rewarding task successfully to meet this wide-ranging research agenda.[32]

[31] Jacqueline Jenkinson, *Black 1919: Riots, Racism and Resistance in Imperial Britain* (Liverpool, 2009).

[32] Since the 2013 conference at the Sorbonne Nouvelle, Gareth Curless and I have set up a 'Labour and Empire' working group that meets every two years at the European Labour History Network (ELHN) conferences, and occasionally in between. For making those events possible, for constant financial and technical support, I wish to thank my research team, CREW (Centre for Research on the English-Speaking World), and everyone at the Maison de la Recherche de la Sorbonne Nouvelle, especially Patrick Belmonte. For inspiring many of the reflections summed up in these final pages, I am grateful to all the colleagues and friends who, over the years, have taken part in the adventure, and to those who, in the future, will make sure it goes on.

Bibliography

NB: This general bibliography does not include references to academic articles and book chapters, which can be found in the footnotes of each chapter of this book.

Primary Sources

Books and pamphlets by individuals

Aarons, Mark, *The Family File* (Melbourne: Black Inc, 2010).

Bandaranaike, S.W.R.D., *Speeches and Writings* (Colombo: Department of Broadcasting and Information, 1963).

Beheiry, Mamoun, *Glimpses from the Life of a Sudanese Public Servant* (Omdurman: M.O. Besheer Centre for Sudanese Studies, 2003).

Besant, Annie, *Annie Besant: An Autobiography* (London: T. Fisher Unwin, 1893).

——, *The Birth of New India: A Collection of Writings and Speeches on Indian Affairs* (Adyar: Theosophical Publishing House, 1917).

——, *The Case for India* (London: At the Office of The Herald, 1917).

——, *England, India, and Afghanistan* (London: Freethought Publishing, 1879).

——, *Essays and Addresses*, vol. 4, *India* (London: Theosophical Publishing Society, 1913).

——, *From Within the Iron Ring: Being an Appeal to British Labour* (London: Home Rule for India League, 1918).

——, *The Guild System as a Substitute for Trade Unionism* (Madras: National Home Rule League, 1921).

——, *India, Bond or Free? A World Problem* (London and New York: G.P. Putnam's Sons, 1926).

——, *Presidential Address of the First Reform Conference under the Auspices of the National Home Rule League* (Madras: Besant Power Press, 1921).

——, *Wake up, India: A Plea for Social Reform* (Adyar: Theosophical Publishing House, 1913).

——, *War Articles and Notes* (London: Theosophical Publishing Society, 1915).

——, *Winning Home Rule: The Presidential Address at the Second Reform Conference* (Madras: National Home Rule League, 1921).
Brockway, Fenner, *Inside the Left: Thirty Years of Platform, Press, Prison and Parliament* (London: Allen & Unwin, 1942).
——, *Outside the Right: A Sequel to 'Inside the Left'* (London: Allen & Unwin, 1963).
——, *Towards Tomorrow: The Autobiography of Fenner Brockway* (London: Hart-Davis MacGibbon, 1977).
Busia, Kofi Abrefa, *Report on a Social Survey of Sekondi-Takoradi* (London: Crown Agents for the Colonies on behalf of the Govt. of the Gold Coast, 1950).
Chettur, G.K., *The Last Enchantment: Recollections of Oxford* (Mangalore: B.M. Bookshop, 1934).
Dilke, Charles, *Greater Britain: A Record of Travel in English-speaking Countries during 1866 and 1867* (London: Macmillan, 1869).
Froude, Anthony, *Oceana or England and her Colonies* (London: Longmans, 1886).
Gandhi, M.K., *Collected Works*, 100 vols (New Delhi: Government of India, 1960–1994).
Hardie, James Keir, *India: Impressions and Suggestions* (London: Independent Labour Party, 1909).
Kaye, (Sir) Cecil, *Communism in India* (Delhi: Government of India, 1926; repr. Calcutta: Editions Indian, 1971).
Lajpat Rai, Lala, *Young India: An Interpretation and a History of the Nationalist Movement from Within* (London: Home Rule for India League, British Auxiliary, 1917).
Lenin, V.I., *Collected Works*, 47 vols (Moscow and London: Progress Publishers/Lawrence & Wishart, 1960–1986).
——, *Imperialism, the Highest Stage of Capitalism* (Peking, 1975; 1st ed. 1917).
——, *'Left Wing' Communism: An Infantile Disorder* (London: Communist Party of Great Britain, 1920).
MacEwen, Malcolm, *The Greening of a Red* (London: Pluto, 1991).
Menon, K.P.S., *Many Worlds: An Autobiography* (London: Oxford University Press, 1965).
Northcott, C.H., *African Labour Efficiency Survey* (London: HMSO, 1949).
Pankhurst, Sylvia, *The Home Front: A Mirror to Life in England during the First World War* (London: Hutchinson, 1932).
——, *India and the Earthly Paradise* (Bombay: Sunshine Publishing House, 1926).
——, *Soviet Russia as I Saw It* (London: Workers' Dreadnought Publishers, 1921).
——, *The Suffragette Movement: An Intimate Account of Persons and Ideals* (London: Longmans, 1931).

Pannikar, K.M., *An Autobiography* (Madras: Oxford University Press, 1977).
Peng, Chin (with Ian Ford and Norma Miraflor), *Alias Chin Peng: My Side of History* (Singapore: Media Masters, 2003).
Petrie, (Sir) David, *Communism in India, 1924–27* (Calcutta: Government of India Press; 1927; repr. Calcutta: Editions Indian, 1972).
Roy, M.N., *Selected Works*, 4 vols, ed. Sibnarayan Ray (Oxford: Oxford University Press, 1987).
Salter, James Arthur, *Slave of the Lamp: A Public Servant's Notebook* (London: Weidenfeld & Nicolson, 1967).
Seeley, John Robert, *The Expansion of England: Two Courses of Lectures* (London: Macmillan, 1883).
Spratt, Philip, *Blowing Up India: Reminiscences and Reflections of a Former Comintern Emissary* (Calcutta: Prachi Prakashan, 1955).
Swynnerton, R.J.M., *A Plan to Intensify the Development of African Agriculture in Kenya* (Nairobi: Department of Agriculture, 1954).
Trotsky, Leon, *History of the Russian Revolution* (London: Victor Gollancz, 1932; 1st ed. in Russian, 1930).
——, *The Permanent Revolution* (London: New Park, 1962; 1st ed. in Russian, 1931)
——, *Trade Unions in the Epoch of Imperialist Decay* (London: Pathfinder, 1990; 1st ed. 1940).
Wadia, B.P., *Aims of the Labour Movement in India* (Madras: Vasanta Press, 1920).
——, *Labour in Madras* (Madras: Gameson, 1921).
——, *A Memorandum on Labor Problems in India* (London: Victoria House, 1919).
Wedgwood, Josiah C., *The Future of the Indo-British Commonwealth* (Adyar: Theosophical Publishing House, 1921).
Whately, Monica, Ellen Wilkinson, Leonard W. Matters and V.K. Krishna Menon, *Condition of India: Being the Report of the Delegation Sent to India by the India League in 1932* (London: Essential News, 1933).
Williamson, (Sir) Horace, *India and Communism* (Calcutta: Indian Intelligence Department, Home Bureau, 1933).

Books and pamphlets by organisations

Home Rule for India League (HRIL), British Auxiliary, *The Waste of Loyalty* (London: HRIL, 1916).
——, *What India Wants* (London: HRIL, 1916).
Labour Party, Advisory Committee on Imperial Questions, *The Colonies: The Labour Party's Post-War Policy for the African and Pacific Colonies* (London: Labour Party, 1943).
Movement for Colonial Freedom (MCF), *Objects and Constitution* (London: MCF, 1961).

Socialist Labor Party (SLP), *Workers of the World Unite: Declaration on the Dissolution of the Communist International* (New York: New York Labor News Company, 1943).

World Federation of Trade Unions (WFTU), *Shafie Ahmed El Sheikh: Son of the Sudanese People and International Trade Union Leader* (Prague: WFTU, 1972).

Conference and congress reports

Comintern, *Workers of the World and Oppressed Peoples, Unite! Proceedings and Documents of the Second Congress, 1920*, ed. John Riddell (London: Pathfinder, 1991).

Communist Party of Great Britain (CPGB), 27th Congress Report (London: CPGB, 1961).

——, *We Speak for Freedom: Proceedings of the Conference of Communist Parties of the British Empire, Beaver Hall, London, February 26–March 2, 1947* (London: CPGB, 1947).

Conference of the Peoples of Europe–Asia–Africa Against Imperialism (CPEAA) (Report of the First International) (London: CPEAA, 1948).

International Bureau for Revolutionary Socialist Unity (IBRSU), *A Lead to World Socialism: Report of Revolutionary Socialist Congress, Brussels, October 31st–November 2nd 1936* (London: IBRSU, 1936).

——, *A New Hope for World Socialism: The Resolutions Adopted at the Revolutionary Socialist Congress, Paris, February 19th–25th 1938, together with the Introductory Speeches* (London: IBRSU, 1938).

National Conference of Labour Women, Brighton, 14–16 June 1932, Report.

Trades Union Congress (TUC), Annual Conference Reports.

Collections of documents

Adhikari, Gangadhar (ed.), *Documents of the History of the Communist Party of India*, 8 vols (New Delhi: People's Publishing House, 1971–1982).

Davidson, Apollon, Irina Filatova, Valentin Gorodnov and Sheridan Johns (eds), *South Africa and the Communist International: A Documentary History*, vol. 1, *Socialist Pilgrims to Bolshevik Footsoldiers, 1919–1930* (London: Cass, 2003).

—— (eds), *South Africa and the Communist International: A Documentary History*, vol. 2, *Bolshevik Footsoldiers to Victims of Bolshevization, 1919–1930* (London: Cass, 2003).

Degras, Jane (ed.), *The Communist International, 1919–1943: Documents*, 3 vols (London: Oxford University Press, 1956–1965).

Hall, Catherine (ed.), *Cultures of Empire. A Reader: Colonisers in Britain and the Empire in the Nineteenth and Twentieth Centuries* (Manchester: Manchester University Press, 2000).

Roy, Purabi, Sobhanlal Datta Gupta and Hari Vasudevan (eds), *Indo-Russian Relations, 1917–1947: Select Documents from the Archives of the Russian Federation*, 2 vols (Calcutta: Asiatic Society, 1999).

Archival funds (a selection)

All-India Congress Committee (AICC) Papers, Jawaharlal Nehru Memorial Library, New Delhi.

Billy Strachan Papers, Institute of Commonwealth Studies, London.

Cabinet (CAB) Papers, The National Archives (TNA), Kew.

Communist Party of Great Britain (CPGB) Archive, National Museum of Labour History (NMLH)/People's History Museum (PHM), Manchester.

Fabian Society Archives, London School of Economics.

Foreign Office (FO) Papers, The National Archives (TNA), Kew.

Home Office (HO) Papers, The National Archives (TNA), Kew.

Home-Political Proceedings, National Archives of India (NAI), New Delhi.

Indian Political Intelligence (IPI) Records, British Library – Oriental and India Office Collections (OIOC), London.

Jack and Ray Simons Papers, University of Cape Town Special Collections.

Kenya National Archives (KNA), Nairobi.

Labour Party Archive, National Museum of Labour History (NMLH)/People's History Museum (PHM), Manchester.

Marceau Pivert Papers, Archives nationales (AN), Pierrefitte-sur-Seine, France.

Metropolitan Police (MEPO) Papers, The National Archives (TNA), Kew.

Ministry of Labour (LAB) Papers, The National Archives (TNA), Kew.

National Council of Civil Liberties (NCCL) Archive, Hull University Archives, Hull History Centre.

Russian State Archive of Socio-Political History (RGASPI), Moscow.

Saklatvala Papers, British Library – Oriental and India Office Collections (OIOC), London.

Security Service Records (KV), The National Archives (TNA), Kew.

Trades Union Congress (TUC) Archive, Modern Records Centre (MRC), University of Warwick.

Dailies and periodicals (a selection)

The place of publication is specified only when situated outside of the British Isles.

Bulletin d'information du Congrès des peuples contre l'impérialisme [Paris]

Bulletin d'informations du Comité d'initiative pour un Mouvement pour la Justice et la Liberté Outre-Mer [Paris]

Bulletin du Mouvement pour les Etats-Unis socialistes d'Europe [Paris]

The Call

The Clarion

Comment

Commonweal

The Communist

Communist Review

Daily Herald

Daily Mail
Daily Worker
East African Standard [Nairobi]
The Englishman [Calcutta]
For A Lasting Peace, For A People's Democracy! [Belgrade]
Gibraltar Chronicle [Gibraltar]
Hindustan Times [New Delhi]
India Bulletin
Indus. The Journal of the Indian Students' Union
Informations internationales [Paris]
Inkululeko
Juin 36 [Paris]
La Gauche révolutionnaire [Paris]
La Révolution prolétarienne [Paris]
Labour Leader
Liberation [Johannesburg]
Madras Weekly Mail [Madras]
Manchester Guardian
Marxism Today
Masses
New Age [Cape Town]
New Clarion
New Dawn
The New Leader
The New Statesman
Plebs
Socialisme et Liberté [Paris]
The Socialist [Melbourne]
The Socialist Leader
The Statesman
Sudan Monthly Record [Khartoum]
Sudan Railways Bulletin [Atbara]
The Theosophist
Time and Tide
The Times
Times of India [Bombay]
Tribune
Vox [Gibraltar]
Workers' Dreadnought
Workers' Weekly
World News and Views

Secondary Sources

Books

Monographs

Ahlman, Jeffrey S., *Living with Nkrumahism: Nation, State, and Pan-Africanism in Ghana* (Athens: Ohio University Press, 2017).
Ahmad, Aijaz, *In Theory: Classes, Nations, Literatures* (London: Verso, 1992).
Ahmed, Mesbahuddin, *The British Labour Party and the Indian Independence Movement, 1917–1939* (London: Oriental University Press, 1987).
Allen, V.L., *Trade Union Leadership: Based on a Study of Arthur Deakin* (London: Longmans, 1957).
Allman, Jean, *The Quills of the Porcupine: Asante Nationalism in an Emergent Ghana* (Madison: University of Wisconsin Press, 1993).
al-Shahi, Ahmed, *Themes From Northern Sudan* (London: Ithaca Press, 1986).
Amsden, Alice, *International Firms and Labour in Kenya, 1945–70* (London: Psychology Press, 1971).
Anderson, David, *Histories of the Hanged: Britain's Dirty War in Kenya and the End of Empire* (London: Weidenfeld & Nicolson, 2005).
Applebaum, Anne, *Iron Curtain: The Crushing of Eastern Europe* (London: Anchor, 2013).
Arora, K.C., *Indian Nationalist Movement in Britain, 1930–1949* (New Delhi: Inter-India Publications, 1992).
Bakshi, S.R., *Annie Besant: Founder of Home Rule Movement* (New Delhi: Anmol, 1990).
Balachandran, Gopalan, *Globalizing Labour? Indian Seafarers and World Shipping, c.1870–1945* (New Delhi: Oxford University Press, 2012).
Banerjee, Mukulika, *The Pathan Unarmed: Opposition and Memory in the North West Frontier* (Oxford: Oxford University Press, 2000).
Barchiesi, Franco, *Precarious Liberation: Workers, the State, and Contested Social Citizenship in Post-Apartheid South Africa* (Albany: State University of New York Press, 2011).
Barooah, Nirode K., *Chatto: The Life and Times of an Indian Anti-Imperialist in Europe* (New Delhi: Oxford University Press, 2004).
Bartley, Paula, *Ellen Wilkinson: From Suffragist and Communist to Government* (London: Pluto, 2014).
Bayly, Christopher, *The Birth of the Modern World, 1780–1914: Global Connections and Comparisons* (Oxford: Blackwell, 2004).
Beers, Laura, *Red Ellen: The Life of Ellen Wilkinson, Socialist, Feminist, Internationalist* (Boston, MA: Harvard University Press, 2016).
Benjamin, Walter, *Illuminations* (New York: Schocken, 1969).
Berry, Sara, *No Condition is Permanent: The Social Dynamics of Agrarian Change in Sub-Saharan Africa* (Madison: University of Wisconsin Press, 1993).

Bertrand, Romain, *L'histoire à parts égales: récits d'une rencontre Orient–Occident, XVIe–XVIIe siècle* (Paris: Seuil, 2011).

Bhabha, Homi K., *The Location of Culture* (New York: Routledge, 1994).

Biondi, Jean-Pierre and Gilles Morin, *Les anticolonialistes (1881–1962)* (Paris: Robert Laffont, 1992).

Biyanwila, Sumithra Janaka, *The Labour Movement in the Global South: Trade Unions in Sri Lanka* (London: Routledge, 2010).

Body, Janice, *Civilising Women: British Crusades in Colonial Sudan* (Princeton, NJ: Princeton University Press, 2007).

Booker, Keith, *The Modern British Novel of the Left* (Westport, CT: Greenwood Press, 1998).

Boon Kheng Cheah, *Red Star Over Malaya: Resistance and Social Conflict during and after the Japanese Occupation of Malaya, 1941–1946* (Singapore: Singapore University Press, 2003).

Boyce Davies, Carole, *Left of Karl Marx: The Political Life of Black Communist Claudia Jones* (Durham, NC: Duke University Press, 2008).

Brown, Carolyn, *Khartoum at Night: Fashion and Body Politics in Imperial Sudan* (Stanford, CA: Stanford University Press, 2017).

——, *'We Were All Slaves': African Miners, Culture, and Resistance at the Engu Government Colliery* (Portsmouth, NH: Heinemann, 2003).

Buchanan, Tom, *East Wind: China and the British Left, 1925–1976* (Oxford: Oxford University Press, 2012).

Bullock, Alan, *The Life and Times of Ernest Bevin* (London: Heinemann, 1960).

Burke, Roland, *Decolonization and the Evolution of Human Rights* (Philadelphia: University of Pennsylvania Press, 2010).

Burton, Andrew, *African Underclass: Urbanisation, Crime and Colonial Order in Dar es Salaam* (Oxford: Currey, 2005).

Burton, Antoinette, *The Trouble with Empire: Challenges to Modern British Imperialism* (Oxford: Oxford University Press, 2015).

Bush, Barbara, *Imperialism, Race and Resistance: Africa and Britain, 1919–1945* (London: Routledge, 1999).

Cain, P.J. and A.G. Hopkins, *British Imperialism: Crisis and Deconstruction, 1914–1990* (London: Longmans, 1993).

——, *British Imperialism: Innovation and Expansion, 1688–1914* (London: Longmans, 1993).

Callaci, Emily, *Street Archives and City Life: Popular Intellectuals in Postcolonial Tanzania* (Durham, NC: Duke University Press, 2017).

Callaghan, John, *Cold War, Crisis and Conflict: The CPGB, 1951–68* (London: Lawrence & Wishart, 2003).

——, *The Labour Party and Foreign Policy: A History* (London: Routledge, 2007).

——, *Rajani Palme Dutt: A Study in British Stalinism* (London: Lawrence & Wishart, 1993).

Callebert, Ralph, *On Durban's Docks: Zulu Workers, Rural Households, and Global Labor* (Rochester, NY: University of Rochester Press, 2017).

Carter, Trevor, *Shattering Illusions: West Indians in British Politics* (London: Lawrence & Wishart, 1986).

Castle, Barbara, *Sylvia and Christabel Pankhurst* (Harmondsworth: Penguin, 1987).

Chakrabarty, Dipesh, *Provincialising Europe: Postcolonial Thought and Historical Difference* (Princeton, NJ: Princeton University Press, 2000).

Challinor, Raymond, *The Origins of British Bolshevism* (London: Croom Helm, 1977).

Chandra, Jyoti, *Annie Besant: From Theosophy to Nationalism* (New Delhi: K.K., 2001).

Charle, Christophe, *La Crise des sociétés impériales, Allemagne, France, Grande-Bretagne (1900–1940): essai d'histoire sociale comparée* (Paris: Seuil, 2001).

Chatterjee, Partha, *The Nation and Its Fragments: Colonial and Postcolonial Histories* (Princeton, NJ: Princeton University Press, 1993).

Chibber, Vivek, *Postcolonial Theory and the Specter of Capital* (London: Verso, 2013).

Claeys, Gregory, *Imperial Sceptics: British Critics of Empire, 1850–1920* (Cambridge: Cambridge University Press, 2010).

Colebatch, Hal G.P., *Australia's Secret War* (Sydney: Quadrant, 2013).

Connelly, Katherine, *Sylvia Pankhurst: Suffragette, Socialist and Scourge of the Empire* (London: Pluto, 2013).

Cooper, Frederick, *Africa since 1940: The Past of the Present* (Cambridge: Cambridge University Press, 2002).

——, *Colonialism in Question: Theory, Knowledge, History* (Berkeley, CA: University of California Press, 2005).

——, *Decolonization and African Society: The Labor Question in French and British Africa* (New York: Cambridge University Press, 1996).

——, *From Slaves to Squatters: Plantation Labor and Agriculture in Zanzibar and Coastal Kenya, 1890–1925* (New Haven, CT: Yale University Press, 1980).

——, *On the African Waterfront: Urban Disorder and the Transformation of Work in Colonial Mombasa* (New Haven, CT: Yale University Press, 1987).

Cox, Anthony, *Empire, Industry and Class: The Imperial Nexus of Jute, 1840–1940* (London: Routledge, 2013).

Crisp, Jeff, *The Story of an African Working Class: Ghanaian Miners' Struggles, 1870–1980* (London: Zed Books, 1984).

Daly, Martin W., *Empire on the Nile: The Anglo-Egyptian Sudan, 1898–1934* (Cambridge: Cambridge University Press, 1986).

——, *Imperial Sudan: The Anglo-Egyptian Condominium, 1934–1956* (Cambridge: Cambridge University Press, 1986).

Daly, Martin W. and Francis Mading Deng, *Bonds of Silk: The Human Factor in the British Administration of the Sudan* (East Lancing: Michigan State University Press, 1990).

Damousi, Joy, *Women Come Rally: Socialism, Communism and Gender in Australia, 1890–1955* (Melbourne: Oxford University Press, 1994).

Darwin, John, *The End of the British Empire: The Historical Debate* (Oxford: Basil Blackwell, 1991).

Davis, Mary, *Sylvia Pankhurst: A Life in Radical Politics* (London: Pluto, 1999).

Davis, Mike, *Late Victorian Holocausts: El Nino Famines and the Making of the Third World* (London: Verso, 2000).

Davis, Richard, Trevor Harris and Philippe Vervaecke, *La Décolonisation britannique: perspectives sur la fin d'un empire, 1919–1984* (Paris: Fahrenheit, 2012).

Deluermoz, Quentin and Pierre Singaravélou, *Pour une histoire des possibles: analyses contrefactuelles et futurs non advenus* (Paris: Seuil, 2016).

Dewar, Hugo, *Communist Politics in Britain: The CPGB from its Origins to the Second World War* (London: Pluto, 1976).

DeWitt, John, *Indian Workers' Associations in Britain* (London: Oxford University Press, 1969).

Dixon, Joy, *Divine Feminine: Theosophy and Feminism in England* (Baltimore, MD: Johns Hopkins University Press, 2001).

Douglas, Ray M., *The Labour Party, Nationalism and Internationalism, 1939–1951* (New York: Routledge, 2004).

Doyon, Jacques, *Les Soldats blancs de Ho Chi Minh* (Paris: Fayard, 1973).

Drachewych, Oleksa, *The Communist International, Anti-Imperialism and Racial Equality in British Dominions* (London: Routledge, 2018).

Eaden, James and David Renton, *The Communist Party of Great Britain since 1920* (Basingstoke: Palgrave Macmillan, 2002).

Elkins, Caroline, *Imperial Reckoning: The Untold Story of Britain's Gulag in Kenya* (New York: Henry Holt, 2005).

Elliott, J.H., *Scots and Catalans: Union and Disunion* (New Haven, CT: Yale University Press, 2018).

Ferguson, James, *Expectations of Modernity: Myths and Meaning of Modern Life on the Zambian Copperbelt* (Berkeley: University of California Press, 1999).

Ferguson, Niall, *Empire: How Britain Made the Modern World* (London: Allen Lane, 2003).

Filatova, Irina and Apollon Davidson, *The Hidden Thread: Russia and South Africa in the Soviet Era* (Johannesburg: Jonathan Ball, 2013).

Fischer, Georges, *Le Parti travailliste et la décolonisation de l'Inde* (Paris: Maspero, 1966).

Forbes, Geraldine, *Women in Modern India* (Cambridge: Cambridge University Press, 1999).

Fraser, Hamish, *A History of British Trade Unionism, 1700–1998* (Basingstoke: Palgrave Macmillan, 1999).
Freund, Bill, *The African Worker* (Cambridge: Cambridge University Press, 1988).
——, *Capital and Labour in the Nigerian Tin Mines* (Harlow: Longman, 1981).
Friedman, Jeremy, *The Shadow Cold War: The Sino-Soviet Competition for the Third World* (Chapel Hill: University of North Carolina Press, 2015).
Gann, Lewis Henry, *A History of Northern Rhodesia: Early Days to 1953* (London: Chatto & Windus, 1964).
Geiger, Susan, *TANU Women: Gender and Culture in the Making of Tanganyikan Nationalism, 1955–1965* (Portsmouth, NH: Heinemann, 1997).
Gertzel, Cherry, *The Politics of Independent Kenya* (London: Heinemann, 1970).
Ghose, Ajit K., *Jobs and Incomes in a Globalizing World* (New Delhi: Bookwell, 2005).
Goebel, Michael, *Anti-Imperial Metropolis: Interwar Paris and the Seeds of Third World Nationalism* (Cambridge: Cambridge University Press, 2015).
Goldsworthy, David, *Colonial Issues in British Politics, 1945–1961: From 'Colonial Development' to 'Wind of Change'* (Oxford: Clarendon Press, 1971).
Gollan, Robin, *Revolutionaries and Reformists: Communism and the Australian Labour Movement, 1920–1950* (Sydney: Allen & Unwin, 1985).
Goody, Jack, *The Theft of History* (Cambridge: Cambridge University Press, 2006).
Gopal, Priyamvada, *Insurgent Empire: Anticolonial Resistance and British Dissent* (London: Verso, 2019).
Grier, Beverly, *Invisible Hands: Child Labor and the State in Colonial Zimbabwe* (Portsmouth, NH: Heinemann, 2006).
Grob-Fitzgibbon, Benjamin, *Imperial Endgame: Britain's Dirty Wars and the End of Empire* (Basingstoke: Palgrave Macmillan, 2011).
Guérin, Daniel, *Front populaire, révolution manquée* (Paris: Julliard, 1963).
Gupta, Partha S., *Imperialism and the British Labour Movement, 1914–1964* (London: Sage, 2002; 1st ed. 1975).
Haithcox, John P., *Communism and Nationalism in India: M.N. Roy and Comintern Policy, 1920–1939* (Princeton, NJ: Princeton University Press, 1971).
Hale, Sondra, *Gender Politics in Sudan: Islamism, Socialism, and the State* (Boulder, CO: Westview, 1996).
Halévy, Elie, *Histoire du peuple anglais au dix-neuvième siècle*, 6 vols (Paris: Hachette, 1926–1947).
——, *A History of the English People in the Nineteenth Century*, 6 vols (London: Benn, 1949–1952).
Harrison, Shirley, *Sylvia Pankhurst: Citizen of the World* (London: Hornbeam, 2009).

——, *Sylvia Pankhurst: The Rebellious Suffragette* (Newhaven: Golden Guides, 2012).

Hobsbawm, Eric John, *The Age of Empire, 1875–1914* (London: Weidenfeld & Nicolson, 1987).

——, *Globalisation, Democracy and Terrorism* (London: Abacus, 2007).

——, *Industry and Empire: An Economic History of Britain since 1750* (London: Weidenfeld & Nicolson, 1968).

——, *Primitive Rebels: Studies in Archaic Forms of Social Movement in the 19th and 20th Centuries* (Manchester: Manchester University Press, 1959).

Hodge, Joseph, *Triumph of the Expert: Agrarian Doctrines of Development and the Legacies of British Colonialism* (Athens: Ohio University Press, 2007).

Høgsbjerg, Christian, *C.L.R. James in Imperial Britain* (Durham, NC: Duke University Press, 2014).

——, *Mariner, Renegade and Castaway: Chris Braithwaite, Seamen's Organiser, Socialist and Militant Pan-Africanist* (London: Bookmarks, 2014).

Holmes, Rachel, *Sylvia Pankhurst: Natural Born Rebel* (London: Bloomsbury, 2020).

Howe, Stephen, *Anticolonialism in British Politics: The Left and the End of Empire, 1918–1964* (Oxford: Clarendon Press, 1993).

Hyam, Ronald, *Britain's Declining Empire: The Road to Decolonisation, 1918–1968* (Cambridge: Cambridge University Press, 2006).

Ibrahim, Hayder, *The Shaiqiya: The Cultural and Social Change of a Northern Sudanese Riverain People* (Wiesbaden: Steiner, 1979).

Ivaska, Andrew, *Cultured States: Youth, Gender and Modern Style in 1960s Dar es Salaam* (Durham, NC: Duke University Press, 2011).

Jaffrelot, Christophe, *Dr Ambedkar and Untouchability: Analysing and Fighting Caste* (London: Hurst, 2005).

James, Lawrence, *Empires in the Sun: The Struggle for the Mastery of Africa* (London: Weidenfeld & Nicolson, 2016).

Jayawardena, Kumari, *The White Woman's Other Burden: Western Women and South Asia during Colonial Rule* (London: Routledge, 1995).

Jeffery, Keith, *Ireland, India and Empire: Indo-Irish Radical Connections, 1919–1964* (Manchester: Manchester University Press, 2008).

Jeffries, Jonathan and Tom Sibley, *The Shameful Deportation of a Trade Union Leader: The Story of Albert Fava* (Gibraltar: TGWU Section of Unite Gibraltar, 2008).

Jeffries, Richard, *Class, Power and Ideology in Ghana: The Railwaymen of Sekondi* (Cambridge: Cambridge University Press, 1978).

Jenkinson, Jacqueline, *Black 1919: Riots, Racism and Resistance in Imperial Britain* (Liverpool: Liverpool University Press, 2009).

Johanningsmeier, Edward P., *Forging American Communism: The Life of William Z. Foster* (Princeton, NJ: Princeton University Press, 1994).

Jones, Jean, *The League Against Imperialism* (London: Socialist History Society, 1996).

Jordan, Douglas, *Conflict in the Unions: The Communist Party of Australia, Politics and the Trade Union Movement, 1945–1960* (Ultimo, NSW: Resistance Books, 2013).

Kaiwar, Vasant, *The Postcolonial Orient: The Politics of Difference and the Project of Provincialising Europe* (Leiden: Brill, 2014).

Kanogo, Tabitha, *Squatters and the Roots of Mau Mau* (London: Currey, 1987).

Kaul, Chandrika, *Communications, Media and the Imperial Experience: Britain and India in the Twentieth Century* (Basingstoke: Palgrave Macmillan, 2014).

Kelly, John, *Contemporary Trotskyism: Parties, Sects and Social Movements in Britain* (London: Routledge, 2018).

Kendall, Walter, *The Revolutionary Movement in Britain, 1900–21* (London: Weidenfeld & Nicolson, 1969).

Kenny, Michael, *The First New Left: British Intellectuals after Stalin* (London: Lawrence & Wishart, 1995).

Kenyon, Sudan M., *Five Women of Sennar: Culture and Change in Central Sudan* (Oxford: Clarendon Press, 1991).

Kergoat, Jacques, *Marceau Pivert, 'socialiste de gauche'* (Paris: L'Atelier, 1994).

Kiernan, Victor, *The Lords of Human Kind: European Attitudes to Other Cultures in the Imperial Age* (Chicago: University of Chicago Press, 2015; 1st ed. 1969).

Kirk, Neville, *Comrades and Cousins: Globalization, Workers and Labour Movements in Britain, the USA and Australia from the 1880s to 1914* (London: Merlin, 2003).

——, *Labour and the Politics of Empire: Britain and Australia, 1900 to the Present* (Manchester: Manchester University Press, 2014; 1st ed. 2011).

——, *Transnational Radicalism and the Connected Lives of Tom Mann and Robert Samuel Ross* (Liverpool: Liverpool University Press, 2017).

Kitching, Gavin, *Class and Economic Change in Kenya: The Making of an African Petite-Bourgeoisie* (New Haven, CT: Yale University Press, 1980).

Klugman, James, *History of the Communist Party of Great Britain*, vol. 1, *Formation and Early Years, 1919–1924* (London: Lawrence & Wishart, 1968).

Kolasa, Thomas Stanley, *The South African Communist Party: Adapting to Thrive in a Post-Communist Age* (Jefferson, NC: McFarland, 2016).

Krikler, Jeremy, *White Rising: The 1922 Insurrection and Racial Killing in South Africa* (Manchester: Manchester University Press, 2005).

Lahiri, Shompa, *Indians in Britain: Anglo-Indian Encounters, Race and Identity, 1880–1930* (London: Cass, 2000).

Lake, Marilyn and Henry Reynolds, *Drawing the Global Colour Line: White Men's Countries and the Question of Racial Equality* (Carlton, VIC: Melbourne University Publishing, 2008).

Le Gall, Jacques, *La Question coloniale dans le mouvement ouvrier en France, 1830–1962* (Pantin: Les Bons caractères, 2013).
Leo, Christopher, *Land and Class in Kenya* (Toronto: University of Toronto Press, 1984).
Leys, Colin, *The Rise and Fall of Development Theory* (London: Currey, 1996).
Lindsay, Lisa, *Working with Gender: Wage Labor and Social Change in Southwestern Nigeria* (Portsmouth, NH: Heinemann, 2003).
Linebaugh, Peter and Marcus Rediker, *The Many-Headed Hydra: The Hidden History of the Revolutionary Atlantic* (London: Verso, 2000).
Liu, Hong, *China and the Shaping of Indonesia* (Singapore: National University of Singapore Press, 2011).
Lockwood, David, *The Communist Party of India and the Indian Emergency* (New Delhi: Sage, 2016).
Lutyens, Mary, *Krishnamurti: The Years of Awakening* (London: Murray, 1975).
MacIntyre, Stuart, *Imperialism and the Labour Movement in the 1920s* (London: Journeyman, 1975).
MacKenzie, John, *Propaganda and Empire: The Manipulation of British Public Opinion, 1880–1960* (Manchester: Manchester University Press, 1984).
MacShane, Denis, *International Labour and the Origins of the Cold War* (Oxford: Clarendon Press, 1992).
Mandala, Elias C., *Work and Control in a Peasant Economy: A History of the Lower Tchiri Valley in Malawi, 1859–1960* (Madison: University of Wisconsin Press, 1990).
Marx, Karl, *Capital*, vol. 1 (Moscow: Progress, 1959; 1st ed., in German, 1867).
——, *The Class Struggles in France 1848–50* (London: Lawrence & Wishart, 1942; 1st ed., in German, 1850).
Matthews, Wade, *The New Left: National Identity and the Break-Up of Britain* (Leiden: Brill, 2013).
Mawby, Spencer, *The Transformation and Decline of the British Empire: Decolonisation after the First World War* (London: Palgrave Macmillan, 2015).
Metcalf, Thomas R., *Ideologies of the Raj* (Cambridge: Cambridge University Press, 1998).
Morgan, Kevin, Gidon Cohen and Andrew Flinn, *Communists and British Society, 1920–1991* (London: Rivers Oram, 2007).
Mukherjee, Sumita, *Nationalism, Education and Migrant Identities: The England-Returned* (London: Routledge, 2010).
Murray, Colin, *Families Divided: The Impact of Migrant Labour in Lesotho* (Johannesburg: Ravan, 1981).
Nairn, Tom, *The Break-up of Britain: Crisis and Neo-Nationalism* (Champaign, IL: Common Ground, 2015).
Naumann, Michel, *La Décolonisation britannique, 1919–1984* (Paris: Ellipses, 2012).

Nethercot, Arthur Hobart, *The Last Four Lives of Annie Besant* (London: Hart-Davis, 1963).

Newsinger, John, *The Blood Never Dried: A People's History of the British Empire* (London: Bookmarks, 2006).

Niblock, Tim, *Class and Power: The Dynamics of Sudanese Politics, 1898–1985* (Basingstoke: Macmillan, 1987).

Noiriel, Gérard, *Une histoire populaire de la France, de la guerre de Cent Ans à nos jours* (Marseilles: Agone, 2018).

O'Lincoln, Tom, *Into the Mainstream: The Decline of Australian Communism* (Sydney: Stained Wattle, 1985).

Overstreet, Gene D. and Marshall Windmiller, *Communism in India* (Berkeley: University of California Press, 1959).

Owen, Nicholas, *The British Left and India: Metropolitan Anti-Imperialism, 1885–1947* (Oxford: Oxford University Press, 2007).

Palmer, Colin A., *Eric Williams and the Making of the Modern Caribbean* (Chapel Hill: University of North Carolina Press, 2006).

——, *The 1938 Labor Rebellion and the Birth of Modern Jamaica* (Chapel Hill: University of North Carolina Press, 2014).

——, *The Politics of Power: Cheddi Jagan and the Struggle for British Guiana's Independence* (Chapel Hill: University of North Carolina Press, 2010).

Parker, Lawrence, *The Kick Inside: Revolutionary Opposition in the CPGB, 1945–1991* (London: November Publications, 2012).

Paton, Diana, *No Bond but the Law: Punishment Race and Gender in Jamaican State Formation, 1780–1870* (Durham, NC: Duke University Press, 2004).

Pattieu, Sylvain, *Les camarades des frères: trotskistes et libertaires dans la guerre d'Algérie* (Paris: Syllepse, 2002).

Paxman, Jeremy, *Empire: What Ruling the World Did to the British* (London: Viking, 2011).

Pécastaing-Boissière, Muriel, *Annie Besant (1847–1933): Struggles and Quest* (London: Theosophical Publishing House, 2017).

Pelling, Henry, *A History of British Trade Unionism* (Harmondsworth: Penguin, 1963).

Pennybacker, Susan D., *From Scottsboro to Munich: Race and Political Culture in 1930s Britain* (Princeton, NJ: Princeton University Press, 2009).

Perkins, Kenneth J., *Port Sudan: The Evolution of a Colonial City* (Boulder, CO: Westview, 1993).

Perry, Matt, *'Red Ellen' Wilkinson: Her Ideas, Movements and World* (Manchester: Manchester University Press, 2014).

Pervillé, Guy, *La Guerre d'Algérie* (Paris: Presses universitaires de France, 2012).

Podmore, Will, *Reg Birch: Engineer, Trade Unionist, Communist* (London: Bellman Books, 2004).

Popplewell, Richard, *Intelligence and Imperial Defence: British Intelligence and the Defence of the Indian Empire, 1904–1924* (London: Routledge, 1995).

Porter, Bernard, *The Absent-Minded Imperialists: Empire, Society and Culture in Britain* (Oxford: Oxford University Press, 2004).
——, *Critics of Empire: British Radical Attitudes to Colonialism in Africa, 1895–1914* (London: Macmillan, 1968).
Raw, Louise, *Striking a Light: The Bryant and May Matchwomen and their Place in Labour History* (London: Continuum, 2009).
Redfern, Neil, *Class or Nation: Communists, Imperialism and Two World Wars* (London: I.B. Tauris, 2005).
Reid, Alastair, *United We Stand: A History of Britain's Trade Unions* (London: Allen Lane, 2004).
Robertson, Emma, *Chocolate, Women and Empire: A Social and Cultural History* (Manchester: Manchester University Press, 2009).
Roediger, David, *The Wages of Whiteness: Race and the Making of the American Working Class* (London: Verso, 2007; 1st ed. 1991).
Romero, Patricia, *E. Sylvia Pankhurst: Portrait of a Radical* (New Haven, CT: Yale University Press, 1987).
Rostow, Walt W., *The Stages of Economic Growth: A Non-Communist Manifesto* (Cambridge: Cambridge University Press, 1990).
Ruscio, Alain, *Les Communistes et l'Algérie: des origines à la guerre d'indépendance, 1920–1962* (Paris: La Découverte, 2019).
Said, Edward W., *Orientalism* (New York: Pantheon, 1978).
Saunier, Pierre-Yves, *Transnational History* (Basingstoke: Palgrave Macmillan, 2013).
Saville, John, *The Politics of Continuity: British Foreign Policy and the Labour Government, 1945–46* (London: Verso, 1993).
Schmidt, Elizabeth, *Mobilizing the Masses: Gender, Ethnicity and Class in the Nationalist Movement in Guinea, 1939–1958* (Portsmouth, NH: Heinemann, 2005).
Sen, Samita, *Women and Labour in Late Colonial India: The Bengal Jute Industry* (Cambridge: Cambridge University Press, 1999).
Sharkey, Heather, *Living with Colonialism: Nationalism and Culture in the Anglo-Egyptian Sudan* (Berkeley, CA: University of California Press, 2003).
Sherwood, Marika, *Claudia Jones: A Life in Exile* (London: Lawrence & Wishart, 1999).
Shubin, Vladimir, *ANC: A View from Moscow* (Bellville: Mayibuye, 1999).
——, *The Hot 'Cold War': The USSR in Southern Africa* (London: Pluto, 2008).
Sikainga, Ahmad Alawad, *'City of Steel and Fire': A Social History of Atbara, Sudan's Railway Town, 1906–1984* (Portsmouth, NH: Heinemann, 2002).
——, *Slaves into Workers: Emancipation and Labor in Colonial Sudan* (Austin: University of Texas Press, 1996).
Silverman, Victor, *Imagining Internationalism in American and British Labor, 1939–1949* (Urbana: University of Illinois Press, 2000).

Singh, Makhan, *Kenya's Trade Unions: The Crucial Years, 1952–56* (Nairobi: Uzima Press, 1980).
Smith, Evan, *British Communism and the Politics of Race* (Leiden: Brill, 2018).
Stichter, Sharon, *Migrant Labour in Kenya: Capitalism and African Response, 1895–1975* (Harlow: Longman, 1982).
Stoler, Ann Laura, *Along the Archival Grain: Epistemic Anxieties and Colonial Common Sense* (Princeton, NJ: Princeton University Press, 2009).
Subrahmanyam, Sanjay, *Mughals and Franks: Explorations in Connected History* (Oxford: Oxford University Press, 2005).
Swainson, Nicola, *The Development of Corporate Capitalism in Kenya, 1918–77* (London: Heinemann, 1980).
Tabili, Laura, *Global Migrants, Local Culture: Native and Newcomers in Provincial England, 1841–1939* (Basingstoke: Palgrave Macmillan, 2011).
——, *'We Ask for British Justice': Workers and Racial Difference in Late Imperial Britain* (Ithaca, NY: Cornell University Press, 1994)
Teelucksingh, Jerome, *Labour and the Decolonization Struggle in Trinidad and Tobago* (Basingstoke: Palgrave Macmillan, 2014).
Thomas, Martin, *Empires of Intelligence: Security Services and Colonial Disorder after 1914* (Berkeley, CA: University of California Press, 2008).
——, *Violence and Colonial Order: Police, Workers and Protest in the European Colonial Empires, 1918–1940* (Cambridge: Cambridge University Press, 2012).
Thompson, Andrew, *The Empire Strikes Back? The Impact of Imperialism on Britain from the Mid-Nineteenth Century* (Harlow: Pearson, 2004).
——, *Imperial Britain: The Empire in British Politics,* c.*1880–1932* (Harlow: Longman, 2000).
Thompson, Willie, *The Good Old Cause: British Communism, 1920–1991* (London: Pluto, 1992).
Thorpe, Andrew, *The British Communist Party and Moscow, 1920–43* (Manchester: Manchester University Press, 2000).
Throup, David W., *Economic and Social Origins of Mau Mau* (London: Currey, 1990; 1st ed., 1987).
Thurston, Anne, *Smallholder Agriculture in Colonial Kenya: The Official Mind and the Swynnerton Plan* (Cambridge: African Studies Centre, 1987).
Tomlinson, Jim, *Dundee and the Empire: 'Juteopolis', 1850–1939* (Edinburgh: Edinburgh University Press, 2014).
Torrent, Mélanie, *British Decolonisation (1919–1984): The Politics of Power, Liberation and Influence* (Paris: Presses universitaires de France, 2012).
van der Linden, Marcel, *Transnational Labour History: Explorations* (Aldershot: Ashgate, 2003).
——, *Workers of the World: Essays toward a Global Labor History* (Leiden: Brill, 2008).

Vickers, Rhiannon, *The Labour Party and the World*, vol. 1, *The Evolution of Labour's Foreign Policy, 1900–51* (Manchester: Manchester University Press, 2003).
——, *Manipulating Hegemony: State Power, Labour and the Marshall Plan in Britain* (Basingstoke: Macmillan, 2000).
Virdee, Satnam, *Racism, Class and the Racialized Outsider* (Basingstoke: Palgrave Macmillan, 2014).
Ward, Paul, *Red Flag and Union Jack: Englishness, Patriotism and the British Left, 1881–1924* (Woodbridge: Boydell & Brewer, 1998).
Wasserman, Gary, *The Politics of Decolonization: Kenya Europeans and the Land Issue, 1960–1965* (Cambridge: Cambridge University Press, 1976).
Webb, Beatrice and Sidney Webb, *The History of Trade Unionism* (London: Longmans Green, 1920; 1st ed., 1894).
Weiler, Peter, *British Labour and the Cold War* (Stanford, CA: Stanford University Press, 1998).
——, *Ernest Bevin* (Manchester: Manchester University Press, 1993).
Westad, Odd Arne, *The Global Cold War: Third World Interventions and the Making of Our Times* (Cambridge: Cambridge University Press, 2007).
White, Luise, *The Comforts of Home: Prostitution in Colonial Nairobi* (Chicago, IL: University of Chicago Press, 1990).
White, Nicholas, *Decolonisation: The British Experience since 1945* (London: Routledge, 2014; 1st ed., 1999).
Wieder, Alan, *Ruth First and Joe Slovo in the War against Apartheid* (Auckland Park, SA: Jacana, 2013).
Williamson, Hugh, *Coping with the Miracle: Japan's Unions Explore International Relations* (London: Pluto, 1994).
Young, Robert, *Postcolonialism: An Historical Introduction* (Oxford: Blackwell, 2001).
Zancarini-Fournel, Michelle, *Les Luttes et les rêves: une histoire populaire de la France de 1685 à nos jours* (Paris: La Découverte, 2016).
Zug, James, *The Guardian: The History of South Africa's Extraordinary Anti-Apartheid Newspaper* (East Lansing: Michigan State University Press, 2007).

Edited books and journals

Amin, Shahid and Dipesh Chakrabarty (eds), *Subaltern Studies: Writings on South Asian History and Society*, vol. 9 (New Delhi: Oxford University Press, 1996).
Anderson, David and David Killingray (eds), *Policing and Decolonization: Politics, Nationalism and the Police, 1917–65* (Manchester: Manchester University Press, 1992).
Behal, Rana P. and Marcel van der Linden (eds), *Coolies, Capital and Colonialism: Studies in Indian Labour History* (Cambridge: Cambridge University Press, 2006).

Belluci, Steffano and Eckert, Andreas (eds), *General Labour History of Africa: Workers, Employers, and Governments, 20th to 21st Century* (Woodbridge, 2019).

Boucheron, Patrick (ed.), *Histoire mondiale de la France* (Paris: Seuil, 2017).

Chatterjee, Partha and Pradeep Jeganathan (eds), *Subaltern Studies: Writings on South Asian History and Society*, vol. 11 (New York: Columbia University Press, 2000).

Corthorn, Paul and Jonathan Davis (eds), *The British Labour Party and the Wider World* (London: I.B. Tauris, 2008).

Davies, Sam, Colin J. Davis, David de Vries, Lex Heerma van Voss, Lidewij Hesselink and Klaus Weinhauer (eds), *Dock Workers: International Explorations in Comparative Labour History, 1790–1970* (Aldershot: Ashgate, 2000).

Douki, Caroline and Philippe Minard (eds), 'Histoire globale, histoires connectées: un changement d'échelle historiographique?', special issue of *Revue d'histoire moderne et contemporaine*, 54.4 (2007).

Frank, Billy, Craig Horner and David Stewart (eds), *The British Labour Movement and Imperialism* (Newcastle upon Tyne: Cambridge Scholars, 2010).

Guha, Ranajit (ed.), *Subaltern Studies: Writings on South Asian History and Society*, vols 1–6 (Oxford: Oxford University Press, 1982–1989).

—— (ed.), *A Subaltern Studies Reader, 1986–1995* (Minneapolis: University of Minnesota Press, 1997).

Hirsch, Steven and Lucien van der Walt (eds), *Anarchism and Syndicalism in the Colonial and Postcolonial World, 1870–1940: The Praxis of National Liberation, Internationalism, and Social Revolution* (Leiden: Brill, 2010).

Holland Rose, J., A.P. Newton and E.A. Benians (eds), *The Cambridge History of the British Empire*, 8 vols (Cambridge: Cambridge University Press, 1929–1959).

Kirk, Neville, Don MacRaild and Melanie Nolan (eds), 'Transnational Ideas, Activities, and Organizations in Labour History, 1860s to 1920s', special issue of *Labour History Review*, 74.3 (2009).

—— (eds), 'Transnational Labour in the Age of Globalization', special issue of *Labour History Review*, 75.1 (2010).

Levine, Philippa (ed.), *Gender and Empire* (Oxford: Oxford University Press, 2017).

Lucassen, Jan (ed.), *Global Labour History: A State of the Art* (Berne: Peter Lang, 2006).

Mohapatra, Prabhu and Marcel van der Linden (eds), *Labour Matters: Towards Global Histories, Studies in Honour of Sabyasachi Bhattacharya* (New Delhi: Tulika, 2009).

Ness, Immanuel and Zak Cope (eds), *The Palgrave Encyclopedia of Imperialism and Anti-Imperialism* (Basingstoke: Palgrave Macmillan, 2016).

Raj, Kumar, Devi Rameshwari and Romila Pruthi (eds), *Annie Besant: Founder of the Home Rule Movement* (Jaipur: Pointer, 2003).

Sandbrook, Richard and Robin Cohen (eds), *The Development of an African Working Class: Studies in Class Formation and Action* (London: Longman, 1975).
Smith, Evan and Matthew Morley (eds), *Against the Grain: The British Far Left from 1956* (Manchester: Manchester University Press, 2014).
Thompson, Andrew (ed.), *Britain's Experience of Empire in the Twentieth Century* (Oxford: Oxford University Press, 2012).
van der Linden, Marcel (ed.), 'Travail et mondialisation', special issue of *Le Mouvement social*, 241 (2012).
van der Velden, Sjaak, Heiner Dribbusch, Dave Lyddon and Kurt Vandaele (eds), *Strikes around the World, 1968–2005: Case Studies of 15 Countries* (Amsterdam: Aksant, 2007).

Theses

Chevalier, Pierre, 'Jean Rous (1908–1985): une vie pour le socialisme et la décolonisation', PhD thesis, University of Perpignan, 1999.
David, Bruno, 'Récurrences et figures de l'autonomie ouvrière: histoire sociale du "pivertisme" (1935–1940)', PhD thesis, EHESS, 1996.
Dreyfus, Michel, 'Bureau de Londres ou IVe Internationale: socialistes de gauche et trotskystes en Europe de 1933–1940', PhD thesis, EHESS and Paris Nanterre University, 1977.
Hyde, David, 'Plantation Struggles in Kenya: Trade Unionism on the Land, 1947–63', PhD thesis, School of Oriental and African Studies, University of London, 2000.
McWilliam, Michael, 'The East African Tea Industry, 1920–1956: A Case Study in the Development of a Plantation Industry', B.Litt. thesis, University of Oxford, 1957.
Morin, Gilles, 'De l'opposition socialiste à la guerre d'Algérie au Parti socialiste autonome (1954–1960): histoire d'un courant socialiste', PhD thesis, Paris 1-Panthéon Sorbonne University, 1991.
Osoro, J.M., 'African Labourers in Kericho Tea Estates, 1920–1970', MA thesis, University of Nairobi, 1979.
Oyaro Oucho, John, 'Rural–Rural Migration and Population Change: A Study of the Kericho Tea Estates Complex in Kenya', PhD thesis, University of Nairobi, 1981.
Sibley, Tom, 'Anti-Communism: Studies of its Impact on the UK Labour Movement in the Early Years (1945–1948)', PhD thesis, University of Keele, 2008.
Tsiang, Tingfu F., 'Labor and Empire: A Study of the Reaction of British Labor, Mainly as Represented in Parliament, to British Imperialism since 1880', PhD thesis, Columbia University, 1923.

Index